Jim Morrison & Michael Hutchence

A TALE OF TWO BROTHERS:

Jim Morrison

and

Michael Hutchence

Volume One and Two

By

Jacqueline Murray

Jim Morrison & Michael Hutchence

© 2012 *Jacqueline Murray and Francine Milano*

No part of this book may be reproduced, stored in a retrieval system, or transmitted by any means without the written permission.

First edition published by AuthorHouse 2008
Second edition published 2012

Contributing editor, Doreen Fenn

Printed in the United States of America

ISBN: 978-1468053562

I dedicate this book to my true eternal soul mate, the woman I never got to meet on Earth but I will wait for as long as it takes — this is for Rebecca, my Rebecca who completes me as no other woman ever could.

—Jim Morrison

Jim Morrison & Michael Hutchence

A TALE OF TWO BROTHERS:

Jim Morrison
and
Michael Hutchence

Volume One:

RENAISSANCE MAN

(The Memoirs of Jim Morrison)

Jim Morrison & Michael Hutchence

FOREWORD

As Jacquie and I worked together during our private phone conversations, it was clear to me that a higher power was at work and there were not just two of us communing, but rather, four. I sensed Jim Morrison and Michael Hutchence giving their approval of Jacquie's use of me as an intuitive and their happiness and encouragement from the other side about Jacquie's work. I would communicate what I was hearing from them on the other side and Jacquie would then confirm that she was hearing the same.

Our sessions were a lot of fun because both men have such distinct personalities. BOTH Jim and Michael were telepathically in touch with Jacquie during the day. Both dictated to her and watched over her shoulder while she wrote to make sure their voices would be heard and understood by their fans on Earth. I sensed an urgency that their truths be told and their certainty that Jacquie was the medium through which this would be accomplished.

There is no doubt in my mind that Jim, Michael and Jacquie were related one to the other in previous lifetimes, playing such roles as sister, lover, brother, beloved, and married partner. In this life, Jacquie has traveled through the portal of time to bring both artists closer to us.

Some icons of the music industry fall from grace, while others leave no footprints in the sand. The great ones leave their enduring music behind as their legacy. But Jim and Michael wanted to show the world a more intimate look at their lives as well as the Universal Truths they have come to understand on the other side.

We are reminded there is a heaven and their words comfort us. We are privileged that Jacquie has had this awakening of consciousness and chose to share her journey with us all.

Judy Hevenly,
Los Angeles, California

Jim Morrison & Michael Hutchence

Table of Contents

	Forward by Judy Hevenly	ix
1	Waiting for You to Come Along…	1
2	Is Everybody In?	15
3	Secrets Taken to the Grave…	33
4	It Happened First in Florida	47
5	When the Music's Over, Turn on the Lights!!!	55
6	Dance On Fire…	67
7	Other Voices: Notes on Vision	87
8	Blood in the Streets in the Town of New Haven.	113
9	Viva Las Vegas!!!!!	123
10	Lamb to the Slaughter…	129
11	There's been a Slaughter Here	141
12	No Justice, No Peace	153
13	Snake on a Plane!	161
14	I've got to go out in the Car with these People and get…	167

15	Under the influence…	179
16	The Dreamer	197
17	The Schemer	215
18	The Grim Reaper	225
19	The Mythology of Jim Morrison	253
20	In the Universal Mind	263
21	Wasting the Dawn…	279
22	It's Time to Live in the Scattered Sun…	287
23	Wake up Girl, We're Almost Home!!!	303
24	The Mystic Sees the Truth…The Rose of Mysterious Union	327
25	Rebecca	341
Final Thoughts	Riders on the Storm	349

CHAPTER 1
Waiting for You to Come Along...

"Ye shall know the truth, and the truth shall make you mad."

—*Aldous Huxley*

Jim Morrison & Michael Hutchence

A TALE OF TWO BROTHERS

Jim = Jim Morrison

Jac = Jacqueline Murray

Jim: Hi there, it's just me, Jim.

Jac: Jim who?

Jim: You know very well who, I've sent you enough signals and confirmations to make everyone around you believe I am around you...everyone but you.

Jac: Let's say it's true, you are around me and this is really Jim Morrison, the one who sang for The Doors. Why would you be around me? I didn't know you, I was too young to know you, and you probably already know, I was never a fan of you or your music.

Jim: You chose to be a channel when you were on this side, before you were born and you are operating at a very high vibration, which means your channeling is crystal clear.

Jac: I am operating on a high vibration? What does that mean?

Jim: You have to have a high vibration to channel us and we have to lower our vibration to speak to you. You earthlings don't operate in a very evolved way in the universe. (Laughs)

Jac: So even if I can speak to those on the other side, what are you doing around me? There have to be channels all over the world, and there are some very famous ones out there. I was never a fan. I am sure to some of your fans who worship you, it would mean so much if you came to them. I would think you have to have at least a few fans who are channels. I always hated "Light My Fire."

Jim: I hated "Light My Fire" as well, and still do. Jacquie, I am talking to my fans, through you. You won't put your own spin on it. It will be authentic, because you have the right intention and essentially, intention is everything. Your channeling is clear as a bell, and you have few preconceived notions about me. I have directed you to read a few things about me, but they could never seem to hold your attention. (Laughs)

You chose to be a channel, not specifically who you were going to channel. I didn't have to crossover when I did, it wasn't written in stone that it was my time. Unfortunately, there are many who believe they are channels but they aren't channeling me or anyone. They're not operating at a high enough vibration. They don't have the gift you have, be grateful, accept it and let's get ready to work.

Why I chose you, is because you won't try to tell me about my own life or act as if a certain book such as "No One Here Gets Out Alive" is my true story. You won't contend I must've died in a bathtub in Paris because it was in the Oliver Stone movie. You will make this about my voice, not your own.

Jac: Thank you. I guess that's true because I simply don't want to be a public person. You're the star, not me.

Jim: There are no celebrities or stars, as you put it, on this side. I didn't much like being a star anyway. Within two years I was completely over that trip. Jacquie?

Jac: Yes?

Jim: You hear my voice, right? It's not your own voice you hear but mine.

Jac: I hear a nice, masculine voice that speaks softly when you talk, but at night when I am trying to go to sleep, it goes on and on.

Jim: (Laughs) That's me. You are going to have to get your hands on one of my old interviews from Earth, and hear my speaking voice, so you can know this is the same voice you hear in your head. I will direct you to where to find one.

Jac: I actually think this condition may be called "schizophrenia," not channeling.

Jim: If you were schizophrenic, the voices in your head would be telling you what to do, what to say, and so on. I am here to offer you my words, my true story, as it has never been told or presented, but you can take it or leave it. I will not intrude on your free will.

But by your willingness to pick up the pen and write, it seems you are interested in working with me.

Jac: I am honored and humbled, though I do not understand it.

Jim: I am not the only one around your light, honey. If I told you how many there were waiting to speak to you, I am fairly sure you would try like hell to turn this off. While you are a very gifted channel, you have to be the world's greatest skeptic.

Jac: There are others?

Jim: About the length of a football field or so.

Jac: Whoa! So out of curiosity, why at this time, would you select to tell your story? I will have to recheck when you passed away,

Jim Morrison & Michael Hutchence

but I think it was around 1974. If that is so, why did you wait so long?

Jim: It was before that, you have to pay more attention when I show you things. There are a myriad of reasons why now, at this juncture I have opted to be channeled and tell it all, holding nothing back. Let me put it to you like this, Jacquie, I can't really say anyone really knew me in my entire lifetime as Jim Morrison or that I totally knew myself. Contrary to popular opinion, I wasn't surrounding myself in mystique. I was mystically kept from the true core of my being on many levels. I always knew there was something more, so much more to it, but I felt confined and trapped at times by what I saw. I often felt completely devoid of purpose in my life. I have worked hard on this side to evolve and heal and part of my karmic cleansing is to come clean about my past life, as so much of it remains unknown. I have huge regrets Jacquie. I also kept some dark, horrible secrets throughout my life that literally ate me up from the inside. I didn't just become a terrible alcoholic, there were reasons. And while some have guessed and hinted, the revelations have never truly been made until now.

Jac: I am very honored to be a part of this. I can't say I completely understand it, but I know when I have asked you directly for a confirmation, I have received it in some amazing ways and received it rapidly. You don't do small stuff do you?

Jim: Nope, I like to be big and showy. (Laughs) I was surprised how much confirmation you have required, but I will do my part to show you it's me, it's real, and we can work together if you so desire.

Jac: I will not decline to use a spiritual gift, as I believe it's a gift from God. I was trying to find out about this writing we are doing, and I found something saying it's called "inspired writing."

Jim: No it isn't. This is called "automatic writing." It's me literally taking over your pen when I carry on my part of the conversation. As you can see, the hand writing changes, even the way you hold your pen changes. "Inspired writing" would be more along the lines of me inspiring you to write a story or a poem. It would be a fusion of me and you, as if we were spliced together, but this is not what that is.

It's the same as you talking to a friend: you say what you say, they respond, and it's not you talking through them, it's them. Does that make sense to you?

Jac: I guess. I am a little confused about what you said, that no one really knew you. I assume you had close friends, family members and even the guys in the band who you were with for a number of years. They had to know you!

Jim: Actually, Jacquie, people decided who they wanted me to be, and many times, I became that for them. I kept the real me, the sensitive, shy guy with the dark secrets hidden the majority of the time.

Jac: Wow! I was wondering if you are with your girlfriend on the other side? I assume she was your soul mate, the one I saw in some of the materials you directed me to? I think her name was Pam, and she was a very pretty redhead?

Jim: No, I am not with Pamela, absolutely not. My eternal soul mate still walks the Earth. When she comes home, I will be complete.

Jim Morrison & Michael Hutchence

It's not anyone I knew in my 27 and a half years on Earth. It happens to be someone I would've met later in life. I charted it that way, we charted it that way to meet when I had learned some life lessons and dealt with a few things that are rather complex. Her soul is much more evolved than mine, so I had more work to do on Earth. I left her, I didn't have to, and it's my biggest regret along with wasted time, so much wasted time.

Jac: I am surprised you are not with Pam. The one thing that you directed me to that held my interest for any amount of time was about her. I felt so badly for her after you died, how she stayed with your body for a day or two and how she was so lost without you. I almost cried for her, and I assumed she went home to you.

It seemed that's all the girl wanted was to reconnect to you. She was beautiful.

Jim: The reason you feel that way, Jacquie, is because Pamela and I have been painted as these tragic young lovers. When you find out the truth about us, about her, you won't be shedding any tears for her, I promise you. As I just told you, my eternal soul mate never had the chance to meet me while we were on Earth, as she was only a baby when I met my untimely demise.

Jac: So your real eternal soul mate has no idea about you or about how she will be with you when she crosses over?

Jim: She knows more than she thinks. I have sent her signs, different ones than I send you, but I am slowly but surely getting her attention. She is not completely aware yet of what is going on, unlike you. (Smiles) I will do what is necessary to get this book in her hands so she can read my letters and poems, and she will know, she will just instinctively know they are for her. I will send her some dreams as well.

Jac: That's beautiful, but why does she have to know now? Can't this wait until she comes home?

Jim: No, not for me, it can't. I want the world to know how precious Earth life is, and how I left behind my one true love and wasted my time. She has never really found the right man, and I have to say, she wonders what is wrong with her. There is nothing wrong with her, it's just that she was meant for me and we were meant to have this beautiful life together. She was younger than me and could not possibly have known I was alive, because as I told you, she was a baby.

Jac: Oh, so you would've been the typical aging rock star marrying the beautiful young woman?

Jim: (Laughs) Yep, something like that. And we would've had kids, but she would not have had to settle me down, as I would've been quite settled prior to meeting her. I would've been ready for her and she for me. I want her to know I am here, and only want to be with her and long for the day she returns home to me. I will make-up for any and all lost time with her on Earth. I will shower her with love and my longing for her is beyond anything she can now imagine.

Jac: She sounds very loved and will be very happy when she crosses over.

Jim: Thanks Jacquie, I am being serious.

Jac: I know you are.

Jim: You are doing several things here, telling the world my true story for the first and only time, and that helps me with karma and healing. You are helping me connect to my true eternal soul mate, which means everything to me. You have the keys to unlock the doors for me Jacquie, because when we see you from here, we see your light, your aura and your intent. I have chosen you based on those things.

It's up to you whether you want to do this. I can find another channel, but the opportunity has been placed in your hands.

Jac: I am very humbled and happy to do it, thank you for this amazing opportunity. I will do my best not to let you down Mr. Morrison.

Jim: Thank you Ma'am. I will channel this book to you, my story, the entire truth. I am going to specifically concentrate on the falsehoods that have been told about me for many, many years. I am going to clear the air and offer pieces to complete the puzzle of who Jim Morrison really was, what he came to Earth for and what went terribly wrong. People may ask why was this part covered and that part wasn't. Because it's about what is important to me, not some biographer or ego driven movie producer. This is my chance to make it right. There will be those who will view this with an incredulous smile, but my dear, what do they have to compare it to? Someone writing about me who can only assemble bits and pieces, because that is all I ever gave anyone.

Jac: Thank you for the vote of confidence, but you channeled to others before, I am sure. You've been over there for awhile. Why aren't you still working with them?

Jim: Not as many as you would think. There are people who are mentally unbalanced and believe they have spoken to me or are speaking to me. Don't worry Jacquie, not you. (Smiles) There are many who think I come to them in their dreams. Why would I? They are simply dreaming of me, as they do other celebrities, from their own subconscious. It takes a tremendous amount of energy to come through like this to anyone, and truthfully, I have no interest really in being channeled that much. It would not be beneficial to *someone who is mentally ill if I came through to them, just as it wouldn't be in any way ingratiating for me attempting to evolve on this side to channel to someone with less than clear channeling and good intentions. Do you think I just come in for every fan, every group of kids who pulls out a Oujia board trying to contact me, or the ghost hunters who show-up at my old dwellings trying to pick-up my energy? (Laughs)*

It's wishful thinking honey, it ain't happening.

Some people in California, believe I hang-out in the men's room of a Mexican restaurant that was at one time, the very building I recorded "L.A. Woman" in, I have better places to go than a bathroom in a Mexican joint! Everyone assumes I only like Mexican food, if I was going to go back to a restaurant in California I liked, I am pretty sure it would be Musso & Frank's Grill. That's the kind of food I love Jacquie, even more than Mexican. But that's beside the point, just more people trying to cash in, saying my ghost is stalking around senselessly. What a sham!

Most people today walking around are programmed much like the movie, "The Matrix." That is what you are living in, Jacquie, an illusion — at least half the time. People can't really see, and they don't bother to look much. Those who are out in front of the psychic industry, and it is an industry of those in it for profit not to be genuine prophets, are not people I would waste my energy with. Some are just charlatans, and those with genuine gifts have often become jaded and greedy.

My coming through to you and telling my real story, is more than most people can handle, because it doesn't fit into their nice, neat little box they call their life. I always knew there was more on this side. I often rambled on to people about life after death, and I was fascinated about it. Turns out, I was right about something. I know

Jim Morrison & Michael Hutchence

some of this contrasts with your religious views, and I am sorry it's so hard for you at times, Jacquie, but you know you have this glorious gift, and you will not misuse it, that I am sure of.

Many will never obtain the vibration to hear me anyway or hear me clearly. There is no sense in coming through to someone who gets it jumbled. I have only come through to a few other people, and it was either on isolated occasions or for a limited time to accomplish something specific.

I am here to channel to you now, as we are committed to work together, Jacquie. You made your free will decision, and I have made mine. I desire no other channel at this time or in the future.

Jac: Ok but...

Jim: Be thankful, you have an enormous gift from the Source, and with it, comes enormous responsibility. Everyone has their own gifts, and for some, it's a struggle to find them. You are fortunate enough to have found yours.

Jac: Ok, but I still think that your fans will find it odd that you are not coming through to one or some of them.

Jim: I don't have any desire to come through to a fan. Let me ask you something, Jacquie, what are they fans of?

Jac: Well, that probably varies from individual to individual. I know there are hardcore "Doors fans," and then there are people who probably love you and your words.

Jim: Yes, but while I was on Earth, my fans were composed of mostly young people who wanted to drug trip at our concerts. There were women, and also some men, who wanted to watch me shake my ass in tight leather pants and sing your favorite song, "Light My Fire."

I now have a new generation of fans who go to the Pere LaChaise Cemetery. Cry at my gravesite, and leave joints and condoms. My fans who were with me while I was on Earth really didn't understand me while I was alive, and most of the younger ones, born after my death, have been polluted with the trashy books written about me and a hideous movie that had nothing to do with me.

Jac: I hate to say this, but it sounds like you have some bitterness toward your fans.

Jim: This is about truth, Jacquie, not trying to make my fans happy. I want my so-called fans to think for themselves and stop really being fans of anybody's. They need to be their own fans, and if they hold me out as any sort of artist, allow my words, lyrics and poetry to inspire them to create their own art. In my public life on Earth, I tried to get people to think, to push their buttons. Getting stoned and crying at a grave isn't paying tribute to my life or what I tried to do. Finding the artist within and opening the doors to show you life beyond the matrix you live in, is the real tribute.

I have carefully chosen certain mediums to help you with this project and provide you with a certain level of comfort of what you are doing here. Other than those featured in this book, I have spoken previously to a woman named June, and told her the truth of my death. She was very aware of my anger and that I didn't die in a bathtub.

I will also come through with brief messages to confirm what you have received here only to a few select mediums. One is named Darcy in California, a medium named Claudia Portugal in California and to a great medium named "MJ" so that you can have some solid confirmations of my truth Babe. But I want to be very clear Jacquie, my visits to these people will be brief, and they are only here to provide you with confirmation and another outlet to communicate with the woman I need to reach named Rebecca. Anyone else claiming to talk to me, outside of those in this book and those I just named, are liars. You are my true channel, the others are assisting you, as you are the world's greatest skeptic. You should become friends with the Amazing Randi.

Are you ready to take this journey with me, Jacquie, because it will infringe on your time and in many ways, on your life?

Jac: I understand the sacrifice, but it's a huge honor just to have this gift and be able to channel your story. I thank you immensely for this opportunity and the confidence you have in my abilities.

Jim: Just telling it like it is, from this side. I have no other agenda, but to tell the truth, it's time to slay the dragons, Jacquie, the dragons of the propaganda set forth about the man known as Jim Morrison.

CHAPTER 2

Is Everybody In?

"Facts do not cease to exist because they are ignored."

—*Aldous Huxley* (Complete Essays 2, 1926-29)

Jim Morrison & Michael Hutchence

I am here to dispel the many myths that have gone on about me, for too long and have been taken too far. My life as Jim Morrison was an ardent derision.

My fans are misguided for the most part. Many of them unfortunately saw a trashy movie about me that had nothing to do with who I was, and they read a couple of disgusting books that supposedly explained me. Some of them listen to the music I created with the other "Doors," and believe it's all about drugs in many cases. "The Crystal Ship" was never about tripping on acid. When I was a boy, I saw a paperweight, literally a crystal ship, that I would stare into and allow my imagination to run rampant. Later on, I told a groupie reporter "The Crystal Ship" was about staring into a glass of Cognac. Keep in mind, when I wrote "The Crystal Ship" I was in fact drinking out of a bottle or beer can, not a Cognac snifter, but "The Crystal Ship" became alcohol for me. I simply allowed people, even those closest to me, to think what they wanted about what inspired my lyrics. I never disputed them, because I could never explain where the songs or poems really came from, and it seemed futile to try.

I always felt, and still believe, it should all be obtuse. An artist may be inspired by something he knows specifically or not, but you the listener should allow the song, the lyrics, the poetry, the story, and the art to mean whatever it means to you individually. For years, people have asked, what was I talking about? (Laughs). I never really knew. The songs and concepts just came to me. Let the art that I have left behind, be what it is to you, not what you think it meant to me. I do not dislike my fans, I would simply encourage them not to worship a "dead icon." I was not an icon, and I do not want to be remembered as such. I was a man who lived a very messed up life and never truly found himself. I wasted so much time. My short life was a train wreck and a pretty bad one at that.

My fans need to understand I was a child of the oppressive '50s and the free-wheelin' '60s. I did experiment, and I was always curious. I had my own experiences, and I certainly wouldn't tell you not to have yours, but I did not enter into them with a sense of self, knowing who I was or what my purpose was. I caught some rare glimpses of the answers, but never fully accepted and embraced them. You cannot find wisdom or enlightenment in the emptiness within.

"The Crystal Ship" is not about a drug trip, it's about your trip — the trip you take to find yourself!

Those who wish to emulate me in some ways, are twisted. There is nothing to emulate, but if you use my poetry, my art to create your own, my words to inspire you, that's a tribute. Staring at a poster of me in what was termed "the young lion" bare-chested pose, where I was skinny is senseless. What is it you are staring at? Drunken Flesh? The Superficial? I was never about the superficial. I was drunk off my ass during that photo shoot, and zoned out, as I was for quite a few of them. I was starving when I had that look. I had no money after leaving U.C.L.A., and even when The Doors started, I had limited funds. In the early days, we played for food and booze.

When I wasn't starving anymore and could afford to go out and eat at any restaurant I chose, my weight climbed up the scale and few would want to put *that* poster up and stare at it.

Some fans even have copies of my mug shots from New Haven. This has perplexed me. New Haven was not one of my finest moments and not something I am at all proud of. There is very little of that life as Jim Morrison I am proud of. I may have not deserved the beating I got in New Haven, and while I still suggest people question authority, I was an immature screw-up. You don't have to receive bruises on your kidneys to make a point. There are incredibly thought provoking ways to go about things, versus incredibly immature ways, that wind up only causing you pain. My display in New Haven was not an intelligent, thought provoking way to go about anything.

My fans should find other ways to spend their precious time on Earth, rather than worshipping at the empty shrine, otherwise known as my grave in Paris. I am not there, and have rarely visited there. The energy you feel there is not mine, it's that of the mourners and other assorted folk who have stopped by. I am more alive now than I ever was on Earth. There is nothing to see at my grave, and it's not a tribute of any kind to me or who I was. My worn out body is indeed buried there, contrary to many bizarre rumors, but I have no desire to return to the tourist attraction from hell.

When it comes to accounts written about me or put on film, the lies, half-truths, and embellishments are quite a lengthy list. Concerning the accounts by other members of The Doors, I will not criticize them, because it's their right and their recollections. I may not share their perceptions pertaining to some of the events but keep in mind, from this side, your views of your past life are crystal clear. On this side, I have evolved, and it's fair to say one of the most important things I am here to reveal at this time. I am over The Doors. I realize The Doors were the public life I led, my claim to fame, and what most on Earth have to remember me by, however, I have grown tremendously on this side and no longer give any energy or real consideration to The Doors, because it is now for those who remain on Earth — Ray, Robbie, and John — to hold on to or to put aside. My personal belief is that it would have been best served to be put aside, but it's not for me to say.

From where I am now, there were many things I had to get over and heal from my past life. It's totally unconscionable that the crock of shit film, which was merely Oliver Stone's version of who I was, ever got to be made! I was a drunken degenerate at times, but there was another side to me, one that Oliver Stone failed to capture. Why was this film legally allowed to be done?

It was a boring, sloppy, untruthful mess. Oliver Stone should have retired from filmmaking after he had the unmitigated gall to put this nonsense out to the public.

I do not blame Val Kilmer for the piss-poor film. I stood behind him and helped with his singing, I am sorry he took part in that fiasco.

Some of the biggest myths of my whole previous existence were told about me and my so-called "wife," Pamela Courson.

Pamela Courson was a beautiful girl I met prior to The Doors getting their big break. She took to me when we were both starving, not knowing if I was ever going to truly make it, in the materialistic ways of fame and fortune. She took care of me early on, cooking for me and giving me a place to stay. I saw her as this sweet, innocent child, and I wanted to mold her, to educate her and

Jim Morrison & Michael Hutchence

teach her things I had learned on my own, to show her the world, or at the very least, my world. She seemed like a willing student in the beginning, and there is no doubt, we were both quite infatuated with each other.

There are many books that believe they are telling the true story of Jim Morrison and Pamela Courson. I am here to tell you my relationship with Pamela was far from the idyllic romance as it has been described. In fact, the best word for it would be, "toxic."

Almost anyone who knew me even slightly, would acknowledge I lived moment to moment. When I met Pam, I considered her a girlfriend and was not even remotely pondering thoughts of marriage or starting a family with her. Pamela was a nest builder, and the more she constructed her nest, the more I perceived it as a trap. I never once thought about the long haul with her, because by the time we got to the middle of 1969, I assumed it wasn't going to happen. I did call her my "Cosmic Mate" early on, when I was on an acid trip from another planet.

Pam was a child who never grew-up during our relationship, and I was a man, who never matured. It's important to understand, that even by the time I graduated from U.C.L.A. before I met Pamela Courson, I was already an alcoholic. I did not become an alcoholic during the years I was a member of The Doors, but my alcoholism certainly did escalate at that time. Before I met Pamela, I was not only an alcoholic, but I was complicating matters by dropping acid and smoking pot on a fairly regular basis. Acid was legal at the time, it was sold in drug stores just like aspirin. It was a fairly common occurrence for students of the arts in California to engage in the use of acid, and just about everyone I met in California was into smoking weed. I used these drugs, not so much for the high, but in the hopes I would obtain visions, as I was always attempting to "break on through to the other side."

Pamela picked a man who was already an alcoholic and using other drugs to complicate matters and his moods. Combining this with the life of a rock star, it's not a surprise I often acted like a 16 year-old, or perhaps even younger, on a maturity level.

Alcoholics and addicts often never mature and most rock stars tend not to as well.

A TALE OF TWO BROTHERS

It is well known and indisputable that Pamela herself became a major heroin addict during our time together. I did not introduce Pamela Courson to heroin, as I despised it. I did not ask Pamela Courson not to have a life or identity outside of mine. She had dropped out of art school right when we met, and I never asked her not to work or go to school, that was her choice. I actually would've preferred that she found something to keep herself occupied.

During the five years and few months Pamela and I knew each other, we were on and off, and sometimes, off for days, weeks or months at a time. I didn't stay in cheap motels just to drink or have a rendezvous with another woman, I was there much of the time because I could hardly stand to be around Pam. She was relentless and would show up anywhere and at any time. She would never give up or give in on the relationship and we both would've been better off if she did. Chances are, we would both still be alive and walking the Earth right now. Since Pamela latched on to me when we were both starving, she kept telling me I owed her.

Some of the biggest lies that have been told about me since I left the Earth are concerning my life with Pamela Courson. I ask those who have romanticized us over the many years we have not been on Earth, where was the love between us? Was it in the horrendous fights we constantly had up and down her stairs?

Did you find the love in the many times she shook me down for money? Since money meant essentially nothing to me, I was more than happy to give it to her. But where was the love in her using my money to get fucked up on heroin and trying to hide it from me, though everyone around L.A. basically knew her dirty little secret? Where was the love in all the affairs we both had all the time? I wasn't the only one having affairs, Pamela had more than has ever been reported. Where was the love when she repeatedly left me drunk and fucked up out of my mind where I could have hurt myself or another innocent person, because she was too embarrassed I was shit-faced again? I ask my dear biographers, do you honestly believe Pamela Susan Courson did not play major role in my death? Did you find her various versions of my final night in Paris credible? Why would someone who loved you so much be so concerned about covering up how you

Jim Morrison & Michael Hutchence

died, why you died, and not even bothering to inform your parents, sister or brother you were gone let alone your best friends back in L.A.? So this woman, threw the love of her life in a cheap box, hurried out of Paris only to fight the lawyers over money they were in fact owed?

Two addicts together are not love, and no one can make it so, no matter how many books portray us as madly in love or how many people say we were talking quietly in a corner at a party Maybe that was just done, because I had no desire to give others the time of day. Pamela and I were fairly good at putting on a public show, but it was, for the most part, a facade. After those parties, we rarely went home together. Pamela was a very effective propaganda machine. She was constantly pushing her agenda that we were inseparable, about to be married or that we were married.

She proclaimed to many that most of my songs, or that at least half of them, were about her. I was never the Jim she wanted me to be, and she never the woman I wanted or needed.

It was never what it seemed, and if it had been, my life would've been transformed. A woman that I was in love with may have very well gotten me to give up drinking. Instead, Pamela was the woman who made me feel like drowning my sorrows in a bottle, more often than not. She was a junkie running through my money like water – claiming I owed her, and she was using me more than caring about me. It's hard to face when you were with someone since the early days, that they were using you. And it's hard to admit it to yourself that you were never really loved or understood, but she had three loves in her life, her drugs, my money and in the last years I was on earth, her French Count.

If Pamela were in love with me, I can say without question, she would've been less concerned about her junkie friends, having affairs and spending money out of a vendetta – let alone getting high. If I had truly been in love with her, I wouldn't have wanted her to leave my side. I would not have been having affairs with women who were a short drive from Pam's place. Pamela and I were actually apart a lot and this has not been accurately reported because people want to believe that in 27 and a half years on Earth, I found real love. I am here to tell you, it wasn't so, but it would've changed everything if I had.

The question may arise, why did I stay with Pam so long? Why did I give her that white elephant boutique known as "Themis?"

The main reason was, I felt responsible for her. I believed for awhile I took a sweet young, runaway and turned her into an empty shell, a total junkie. There are no excuses, but as an alcoholic, I found one day running into the next quite often. I didn't take care of things in a prompt, orderly fashion and I allowed relationships in my life, quite a few of them, with people I should have never been around.

The song I should've written about Pamela was, "The Queen of the Guilt Trips." She tried to commit suicide twice in the years we were on and off and she made several false cries for help and attention as well. She made me feel like shit most of the time. I had confided to her about my darkest childhood secret, my excruciating private pain, and more than a few times in our turbulent relationship, she threw it in my face. She would scroll some unkind words on the bathroom mirror with lipstick, to insinuate that I had invited violations to myself while growing up, and that they were a part of my nature.

She threatened on a few occasions to go public with my deepest shame, and of course, put a different spin on it. The time period this all took place during must be taken into consideration. It was not an open society, it was not a time when people understood such things: the things that had been done to me before I graduated high school. I certainly couldn't afford this coming out to the public when I was already brought up on charges in Miami for public exhibitionism and facing three years in jail in a federal prison! This sort of thing could have lent credence to the fact I was a full blown pervert in the eyes of the judge, jury and public. Pam made her threats, after all, I was never going to marry her. She tried to get me to marry her a few times and brought it up often.

I came to the realization, after two years on and off with this woman, I was not in it for the long haul. It was just easier at times to placate her, because I couldn't handle the guilt trip if she tried to commit suicide and succeeded. She was hanging around really seedy people and shooting up heroin, anything was possible.

The true turning point for me in my relationship with Pamela occurred in 1968. I gave her a Euro trash boutique called

Jim Morrison & Michael Hutchence

"Themis" because a male friend of mine suggested, I find something for Pamela to do. She was showing up at inconvenient times, practically stalking me at times, and constantly causing scenes. Pam's friend Mirandi had opened a boutique and Pam wanted her own, it was a sheer envy thing. I gave her "Themis" with the hope she would find her own identity and something to do, instead of worrying about me. I wanted to give her independence at that time more than anything.

I want to categorically say, "Themis" was not my scene. I rarely went in there unless I was completely smashed, because I didn't like the energy. The famous publicity photo shoot that so many have seen, was the least favorite photo shoot I had ever done in my life for anything. I didn't dislike the clothes I was given to pose in, I detested them. I didn't like Pamela's friends who were in the shoot, and I could hardly stand the way she was acting, it all went to her head. I was compliant that day, was not up for starting trouble, in fact, I was quite hung over. It was all for nothing. "Themis" was like the Hindenburg, a huge disaster that went up in flames.

In the fall of 1968, Pamela left me for an actor named Christopher Jones. She ran off to London with him since I had no intention of marrying her, and her whole identity was based on that of a man, therefore a good looking actor would do just fine. Something went wrong in that relationship, and Pamela got her feelings hurt. I got a call from London in which she told me, in no uncertain terms, she was going to kill herself, and it was all my fault because I never loved her. She planned, or so she said, to leave a note behind specifying what a louse I was. The guilt and fear overtook me, and I left L.A. in the midst of The Doors' recording sessions, never saying shit to anyone and rushing to the rescue of the "Toxic Queen."

When I arrived in London, I discovered Pamela was crying wolf, as she was not at all suicidal. We had one of our epic fights that left me tattered and torn. She did not stay to try to restore my constitution in any way instead, she fled to find Christopher Jones. It was at that moment I realized that I was not in love with Pamela Courson. I loved the woman I thought she was, not who she was and I was never truly in love with her. It was all a mirage.

Upon returning to L.A., I went into denial about this for a few months, contending she had to love me and I had to love her. My denial didn't last very long but long enough for me to compose a will in early 1969 and leave her everything. The will is a complicated issue, but basically, I was feeling isolated from the other Doors because we had a bitter argument concerning the fact that three of them decided to use "Light My Fire" in a car commercial without receiving my vote. This came after the fact my greatest performance epic entitled, "Celebration of the Lizard" was not used in its entirety on "Waiting for the Sun." I had agreed it wasn't ready, but deep inside I was beyond disappointed as this was my masterpiece.

I felt alienated from my brothers in the group, and I had no inclination to leave my parents anything. I had no one on Earth I was genuinely close to, not even Pamela, but I knew a few things. She was completely dependent on me, and it didn't appear she was going to be able to stand on her own two feet any time soon. I felt guilty over this because she kept telling me how much I owed her, and whatever I did for her, was never enough. Also, I was well aware Pamela despised The Doors, and I felt emotionally detached from them because of how I was treated with the Buick commercial vote and "Celebration of the Lizard." This is all water under the bridge now as I put Ray, Robbie, John and all others who worked for us, through constant torment, and I sincerely regret it.

Later on, I regretted leaving Pamela anything, and by the summer of 1969, after I was facing the charges attached to the Miami fiasco, I felt differently about all the aspects of my life. I wish I had the emotional fortitude to end my relationship with Pamela Courson after giving her "Themis," as that should've been my parting gift to her. If I had not been in denial about her, about us, the Miami fiasco would have never occurred and my entire life would not have unfurled.

During some of the time with Pamela when we were off or on, I was seeing quite a few different women around L.A.— several of them but they simply didn't need to have their pictures taken with me or dress me up in clothes. I had a true aversion to showing off the boutique "Themis" she never intended to take seriously. I was careful to speak well of Pamela around L.A.,

Jim Morrison & Michael Hutchence

because I just didn't need any more drama. I would tell the women close to where she lived who asked about her, that she was a sweet child that I felt somewhat responsible for. Some of these women would just magically wander into "Themis" to see or talk to Pam. I had to walk on eggshells, because I didn't want her blood on my hands or any more dramatic scenes. I was much more candid with the women I was involved with in other parts of the country regarding my nightmarish relationship with Pam.

I had relationships with several women, and I am not talking about one night stands here, but actual relationships where I would be with a woman for weeks, months or see them on and off for years. Pamela just wanted to be in the spotlight and make sure everyone knew she was my old lady. Well honestly, she wasn't my only old lady, I had more women than anyone ever knew.

Not everyone who was with me sold me out and wrote their own book or contributed to one. Not everyone wanted to be famous for having some sort of relationship with me and looking like a glorified groupie. Each and every one of these relationships occurred when I was drunk or on my way to getting there.

When I was intoxicated or just waking up from a binge, sadly, I would lie to women and tell, almost every one of them, that I loved them. A sober Jim, not a drunk or hung over one, didn't do that, not even with Pamela. A sober Jim had such a hard time lying. A woman who wrote a book about me is named Patricia Kennealy. She has been cast out as a liar by many Doors fans, but I am here to say, I knew Patricia the last two and a half years of my life. We were friends and later became lovers. I loved her intelligence and dynamic nature. She was self-reliant and well versed, and honestly, I wasn't used to meeting such an ambitious woman. I enjoyed our interactions, her criticism of my poetry was mostly constructive, versus the personal assaults, that were generally thrust upon me.

The problem with my relationship with Patricia was the same one I had with every other woman, I was a drunken degenerate by the time we met. I was drunk off my ass the first day we laid eyes on each other, and two other women present, Diane and Ellen were more than aware I was sloshed. I would caution women to *never* believe the words of a drunken man.

I was drunk throughout my relationship with Patricia, and as she has openly admitted, she provided us with lots of drugs as well. I really see things differently than the account she has written about us, however, I did have a relationship with her and participated in a hand fasting ceremony in her small apartment in June of 1970.

I would like to explain that I was not involved in witchcraft and was not going to become a high priest, warlock or anything like that. Some of the Wiccan practices had been explained to me, but they really failed to intrigue me. I participated in that ceremony for a few reasons. I did have a love for Patricia, but I was going on trial in Miami for my life in just a few short months. By that time, I was pretty whacked out of my mind almost all the time. The night of the actual ceremony, I was both drunk and very physically ill, as I had pneumonia. I was so drunk I didn't even realize how sick I was or how high my fever was. I was, for the most part, completely out of it. And it's sad to say, but I probably would've participated in a ceremony with a frog that night. This ceremony occurred at one of the worst stages of my mental and physical state.

After I learned I had done it, I was basically surprised and truth be known, I could not remember the ceremony whatsoever. A year later, I would be out of my human body. On this side, the ceremony means nothing to me other than hurting someone again in one of my less than glorious drunken moments. I truly owe Patricia an apology for playing into the delusions of who I was and what we were. I created a lot of that myth, and after she had an abortion, she was angry and bitter because she was starting to see I wasn't at all who she thought I was. Patricia however, was not going to be the "one" because I hadn't met her yet. I had no future with Patricia and the eternal flame she holds for me should've been snuffed out years ago. I wish she would go on with her life and leave me in the past, where I belong for her. Taking my last name is not going to change the truth, she was just another girlfriend.

I realize my staunchest fans believe they know every aspect of my life, each microscopic detail, but where did you get your information? Certainly not from me, until now. I am here now to say, while it may surprise and shock some people, I did know

Linda Ashcroft (Ginger). There are a few key reasons Linda has not been believed or her story widely accepted as authentic, and one major one has to do with her timeline of our encounters, which is dreadfully wrong.

It has also been stated that no one else knew the Jim Morrison that Linda described in her teenage romance novel. Someone else did know that Jim Morrison, she was my first love and her name was Mary Werbelow. Unquestionably, I showed a much softer, more romantic side to both Mary and Linda, and I cared for them both very deeply. Linda had a fonder, more fabulous recollection of our relationship, because she was a young girl from an abusive home and she saw me as her great escape. I wanted to be her escape, because no one had given me a "get out of jail free card" during my somewhat tortured childhood. I viewed Linda Ashcroft and another teenager I befriended, named Danny Sugarman, in similar ways.

Linda and Danny were very bright young people who were raised in oppressive homes. I gave them both books to read to open up their minds and tried to intervene to be the freedom man for both of them.

Danny Sugarman is on this side now. We have communicated but have no relationship. He has work to do before that can happen. Danny sold me out. He has embellished stories and tried to attain fame and fortune based on knowing me. It's low and disgusting, but not surprising, since he needed money to furnish his lifestyle and spending habits. He has repeated things that were very private, taken them out of context, and there are some confidences that are meant to be taken to the grave, not sold to the highest bidder. Danny has hurt and angered me, but I do forgive him and believe he regrets his actions and words following my untimely demise.

Linda Ashcroft and I did meet in a deli the night she ran away from home. She was sweet girl, very intelligent, and very naive. I was around her only a few times, so it wasn't the great romance it seems like and we never had sex.

It astonishes me that Linda is not believed, and yet a self-proclaimed acid dropping groupie writes a book about me claiming we had a bizarre affair, and people buy it hook, line and sinker. Why is this woman believed? Most likely because people want to remember me as a lunatic rock star, and they can readily accept I tried to rape this chick. The truth is I did many things while intoxicated that I am not proud of, as they were beyond any semblance of decency. I regret them terribly, but attempting to rape anyone at any time was not among them.

Is it easier to believe I was this low-life who could hardly carry on a conversation? People may be surprised to find out the woman who wrote that book was a Doors groupie, and for a time, she stalked me. I did have two really freakish conversations with her, and she was completely gone during one of them on an acid trip to the point I wasn't so sure she knew where she was or who I was. She asked me some disturbing questions, and while I did end up with some freaks on certain nights, Judy Huddleston scared me and I didn't trust her. When I was around Judy, I felt like I needed to get away from her — run away would be more like it. As a groupie that was always around the band, and other groupies who knew us and assorted other people, she got some information and composed her fantastic work of science fiction. The only film she should've consulted on would have been anything having to do with outer space or anywhere but Earth.

As far as my genuine relationships went, the ones you form as an alcoholic are there to feed the addiction, not the soul. With all addicts, you gravitate toward those who will not give you a hard time about your drinking. Birds of a feather flock together, so to be around those who also want to drink, get wasted and not worry about it is ideal. But even if you are with a woman who doesn't really partake as much, as long as she tolerates you and your drunkenness, then it's easy to stay around her. An alcoholic doesn't want anyone around who will attempt to cut him off. "LAST CALL FOR ALCOHOL" is your least favorite thing to hear for the night, unless you have already passed out.

A huge myth without merit that has been perpetuated is that I would've been with Pamela Courson if I had lived in Paris. In truth, if I had survived that dreadful summer, all the relationships I had been involved with would have completely unraveled at one point or another, because they came about under false pretenses. Some of the women I knew were sincere and caring, but I was a terrible drunk. When you are a drunken degenerate, you meet people, you do things and you say things that would never happen if you were sober. The women I knew heard a lot fewer "I LOVE YOUS" and other assorted terms of affection when I was sober as opposed to being four sheets to the wind.

If I would have lived, I would've cleaned up my life, my health and most of all, my relationships. I would not have been attracted to the same sort of person, and God knows, they would not be attracted to me.

As a surprise to some, I will name two people in my past life who really "got me." These three people didn't need to know me for a long time or hang-out with me regularly to comprehend me, and they should've been consulted more since my passing, because, at least, they saw more of the real me than others did on Earth.

There was a friend I was fortunate to get to know during my last few years. His name is Robert Goldberg, and in an unexplainable sort of way, he understood me better than most. He is a man of integrity and tremendous intelligence.

Another person who was always honest about me, was my bodyguard of the last few years, Tony Funches. He has not lied about me once since my departure, and that's saying something! He gave literally the most insightful interview about me ever! I have incredible love and respect for this man, and he was with me on a daily basis the last couple of years. Yet others, who were around me constantly, never really read me like Tony did. I wish the authors who have written about me would've interviewed this man, as any book would've turned out to have a more balanced and precise view. Tony got a firsthand look at the everyday Jim, not just glorified incidents that occurred in the last years of my life.

The other person I wish to mention, is a journalist I had a great admiration for on earth named Salli Stevenson. After my guilty verdict in Miami, I began to speak more often to certain members of the press, hoping they would understand me. Salli Stevenson met me 6 months before I left for Paris, and I found her to be quite intelligent and enjoyed some of our conversations. To my utter dismay, since I have departed earth, Salli Stevenson has been gaining fame from our relationship which was purely platonic and short lived. Salli didn't know me well, she knew the compartments I opened up for her and I repeat, Salli didn't know me well. How much time do you actually think I spent talking to Salli? She has built this bizarre reputation on our friendship and it's a given she doesn't like this book because she wasn't asked to contribute to it and she wasn't paid for an endorsement.

I don't know who is worse, Salli Stevenson or Jim Cherry, the experts on all things Jim Morrison. Right behind Salli and Jim, the runner up has to be Sam Bernett, who claims 35 years later when he's in need of cash, I bit the dust in a toilet scoring drugs for Pamela Courson. Very entertaining Sam I must say, but the only problem with that story was, Alain Ronay and Bill Siddons both found a stash of heroin in the Parisian apartment, after I met the grim reaper. Why did I need to go and score drugs for her? She had a pretty substantial stash all the time. I couldn't speak French, and I wasn't one to score drugs in L.A. but suddenly I decided to get some more junk for Pam, even though her promise to me was to get off the smack? Anyone who buys that story, didn't know me at all, because heroin to me was garbage.

Salli Stevenson lost her journalistic integrity the day she began her endless gossip concerning her lame theory of my demise. Her insider source claims I was on heroin months before I left L.A. How strange Salli, who was supposedly so close to me never knew about my supposed heroin habit in those days? Her insider had a wicked substance abuse problem back then, great source to base a rather baseless theory on. Not to mention, my former bodyguard has been candid about the things I did and drugs I chose to partake in during the last months of my life, he would vouch for the fact, heroin was not one of them.

Of all those who abolish the truth in my case, and all the embellished and inane books published about me, the single one I find most offensive is in fact authored by a delusional woman named Patricia Butler. I of course find the book offensive when you take into consideration, Pamela Courson is the main reason I got short changed on earth and not being with my true love currently. So the alcoholic who was basically sleeping with every other woman he met and the heroin junkie made such a gorgeous couple, it had to be true love, that's why I didn't allow her to attend the single most important event of my life, my trial in Miami! I needed someone there with me, to be by my side, I didn't want Pam anywhere near me during the most crucial time of my earthly existence. Patricia Butler needs to rename her book to "Junkies dance and then they kill you."

CHAPTER 3
Secrets Taken to the Grave...

"No one keeps a secret so well as a child"

—*Victor Hugo*

Jim Morrison & Michael Hutchence

A TALE OF TWO BROTHERS

My childhood has been shrouded in mystery. No one really knew me growing up, or my family per se, and over the years, many who have been infatuated with creating myths about me, have done so about not only my childhood, but every aspect of my short life. Those myths have been copied from book to book. I was a military brat, who moved around and never truly made real friends, or if I did connect to someone, it was not to be for the long term. I was the class clown, so I was easily accepted and wouldn't be hassled. I basically created my own reality all through school.

I devoured books, and when I was old enough I went to places to see European art films. I was thirsty for experiences and reality beyond where I was. My thirst began at a very young age while living in Albuquerque, New Mexico. It's where I first saw reptiles, and in their colors, I saw the world. I started to believe the world has to be more colorful, more dimensional and more enthralling than where I was at any given moment.

My childhood has been described as not being typical, whatever that means. I can tell you about my earthly perceptions. I felt unloved, neglected, and yes, I was abused. It was not something you talked about in those days. It was shameful. Maybe for some people, it explains my entire adult life. It's not such a grandiose resolve, but it is a major contributor to my downfall with alcohol, and women.

I was a forward thinker, growing up in the backward times of the 1940s and 1950s. I was beyond different. In every school I went to I was a total outcast, and even with my attempts at times to fit in, I was not a part of the culture others were living. Even engaging in conversation with many of my school friends or some of my more educated teachers was somewhat tedious at times.

Many who have attempted to dissect me like an insect have noted my entire adult life was spent rebelling against authority. In putting two and two together, it's obvious the key authority figure was indeed my Father, the naval officer.

Jim Morrison & Michael Hutchence

My childhood was traumatic, because at one time I worshipped my Father. He was this larger-than-life, mythical figure who was rarely around. But when he was around, he dished out strict discipline. He was the ultimate authority figure, and it seemed to me, he rather enjoyed the humiliation that he put on me. It disturbed me, how much he enjoyed it, because I needed a father, a man to love me, understand me and want to make up for lost time. What I often got was a few hours with a military officer who treated me like a soldier in his ranks, not like his son. My father had a bad temper, at times, really bad. There were many incidents that left an indelible impression in the back of my mind, like the time he chased me around the house with a baseball bat or the time he went ballistic on me while we were playing catch and started hitting me hard with the ball. I guess he wanted to make a man out of me — his kind of man — one he could respect and be proud of, and he had this frustration about how different I was. He couldn't mold me to his way of thinking or liking.

It's true, my whole adult life was spent rebelling against my Father. I wanted to be the anti-thesis of who he was. I couldn't be him, and I couldn't please him, so I stopped trying. Yet, as an adult, I didn't care about being famous or necessarily got off on the trip the way people believe I did, I just wanted him, my Father, Steve, to notice me. I wanted him to look at me, Jim Morrison, the singer, the star, the talent, more than anything, but I never got that. The man I never really wanted to speak about much, caused more of my actions and reactions in life than anyone else.

After my Father returned from the Korean War, he was different, and he became violent on a regular basis around the house. It's been said that my parents had a policy of never hitting their kids, well at least not out in the open, behind closed doors is where it mostly took place. I always got it with a belt or whatever my Father had in his hand.

My Mother was the primary parent and disciplinarian for many years when my Father was away serving his country, not his family. My Mother and I became very, very close, and I resented when a little sister or brother came along, because I didn't feel I got the amount of attention from my Mother once there was a new baby in the house, let alone two. I felt replaced and somewhat rejected. My Mother would bitch about what a fuck-up I was to my Father when he came home. I would hear my Mother, who I thought I was so close to, bitch about me to the so-called man of the house, and I would be dished out a military style discipline.

I was told my parents were really embarrassed when I got arrested in New Haven and for the Miami fiasco. That wasn't the kind of attention I needed from them. I would tell reporters or others who knew me, I didn't want to involve my family, so I didn't mention them. But the truth was, there was anger, bitterness, resentment and much of that fueled my actions and shaped my life until July 3rd, 1971.

I need to say at this point, my Mother is on this side now. Clara is happy, we have seen each other, and I have apologized to her — and forgiven her as well. We are at peace. My Mother and I are finally at peace, and I look forward to the day I can do the same with my Father. I forgive him, and I need to apologize to him.

I have chosen to address things that I feel are proactive in nature to explain my life as Jim Morrison. There are many other things, that you may or may not care about, that you won't find in this book. This is my story, not the one you find in a trashy tabloid book or a big screen crock of shit, of who I was, what I did and what went wrong in my short, bleak existence.

This is the only time I am presenting my true story. I have channeled to others before but never in this much depth about anything. You are getting the whole story, as only I can tell it. People are so apt to believe what other voices say about me. Why?

Many of those that knew me to some extent, including some of the women, never sold me out. They never wrote a book or contributed to one. I compartmentalized my life and only allowed people to peek into one or two compartments, no one ever got that deep into any one of them. I didn't allow it.

When you are empty on the inside, what you show the outside world is a projection of what they want to see. It worked. As in the Universal Law of Attraction, if they wanted to see an egotistical rock star, I gave it to them. If they wanted to have an intelligent conversation or try to scratch the surface and find more depth to my soul, I let them scratch, but not very far. I never showed anyone all of it. If they wanted a one night stand and to be treated like a groupie, I was more than happy to serve it to them on a platter. If they wanted to feel special in my eyes, I gave them that as well. I was not intentionally out to hurt anyone, I was just so empty inside, I simply projected back what they wanted or what they asked for.

I never revealed much about my childhood, and yet, after my untimely demise, the vultures swooped in and tried to dig up as much dirt and endlessly questioned my family and even a kid who sat next to me in third or fourth grade. It was along the lines of…let's see what really made Jim the psycho that he was. It's really disgusting and grotesque on the actions of some who have bothered my family because they were silent for many years regarding my childhood and life. I was the one in a public life that started when I was 22 years old. I was estranged from my parents, and since my family really didn't know me as a person before I was estranged from them, what could they possibly tell anyone? I was secretive. It wasn't about mystique, it was about pain. I wasn't around them very much as a teenager, and for them, my Mother and Father, they had no idea how I ended up in a cheap box buried in Paris in 1971. It was hard enough for them to be estranged from me and really to never hear from me and read these awful things in the paper about my public exposure of a sex organ in Miami. For a family like that, a proud military family where my Dad had risen in the ranks, it was sheer, unadulterated hell, having a son like me.

But once I was no longer walking the Earth, you can't possibly imagine the pain my parents felt. The estrangement made it all the worse. I have come to see Earth as less and less of a decent place from this side. While I may have been on Earth to shake things up, and push people's buttons, I realized then, as I do now, there is a sacredness to many aspects of life. What I said about my childhood on Earth obviously wasn't enough for the vultures, who needed to feed their sickness with the prey of my family or anyone else they can bother for their fodder. Feast on what you have on Earth, for you cannot take my soul, but if you could, you would try.

I will now open the book on things no one knows about. The private world of Jim Morrison that has everything to do with who I was and what I became and nothing to do with what has been written or speculated about me.

I openly spoke and wrote about one of my earliest memories, involving the dead Indians on the road (Route 66 in New Mexico) when I was 4. I always believed that one or two of their souls jumped into me and somehow went through me. I thought one of the souls possibly belonged to a Shaman. What I have since learned on this side is, I had the ability to channel spirits and never truly realized it or brought it to fruition. It scared me, and it made me feel schizophrenic on more than one occasion. A few of those Indian Spirits came to speak to me at different times of my life. There were times, I thought it was a dream and other times, I just thought I was hearing voices. I was able to do on Earth what my channel is capable of now, but I didn't realize it and it scared me. It's one of the reasons, or excuses, I used to drown myself in alcohol. If I suffered from real, genuine schizophrenia, I reasoned that the alcohol could not shut off the voices. If I wasn't insane or close to it, the alcohol would kill the voices in my head. The alcohol succeeded, the voices went away.

My Father tried to tell me the massacre of Indians on the road was just a dream. They were screaming in an ungodly fashion and pleading for help. There was a river of blood, and I was being told this didn't happen, it was all in my mind. I knew beyond anything else, at that tender young age, it was not a dream, it was the realest thing I was aware of up to that point. It stayed with me my whole life, but at least now, I understand it. I was never consciously aware I was at times, channeling this side I am on now.

After that incident, a few things happened. I would have such disturbing nightmares that I became a bed wetter. My Mother did not look upon this kindly and tried to use it to shame and humiliate me. She would often send me back to sleep in the wet sheets, and I would end up sleeping on the floor. I don't think anyone intentionally wants to wet their bed at four or five years old, but her method of handling it scarred me emotionally.

I was a man of secrets, many of them, and many never appeared and will never appear in print, but for here and now, though some of these things were speculated about. My biggest, darkest, most shameful secret was that I was sexually abused not once, but twice, before I graduated high school. The first time, happened when I was 12 years old. I need to talk about this, because these incidents, in many ways ruined my life, and I gave them the power to do so.

The first incident, was done by a friend of the family's. I would say more, but my channel will be sued and we know with the current legal climate, any lawsuit is possible. This was not just a molestation, this was a full rape, including sodomy. I had no idea what the hell was going on and was pretty much in shock. This happened because this person also had a military background and had too much to drink. I told my Mother about this, but she simply didn't believe it and thought my imagination was running wild. After all, I was known to make-up stories to skip school, and they were quite creative. My teacher once called my Mother to ask how my brain surgery had gone, and that wasn't the half of the things I would fabricate to cut class. I felt, or at least had hoped, my Mother could tell I was telling her the truth, but it was too painful for her to recognize that this horrid act had been committed on her son by someone she had much faith and trust in.

This had to be, other than the rape itself, the biggest and worst let down of my life. I had no protection or love or any sort of understanding how to deal with this, and, in fact, throughout my entire life, was never able to deal with this. It was a complete rape, and tarnished me and my innocence forever. You will find that those who are sexually abused during childhood, tend to become overtly sexual beings as they grow-up. This is exactly what happened to me.

I would say, a good book that explores the theme of my childhood would be "Billy Budd" by Herman Melville. The theme being innocence versus evil, not necessarily good versus evil. When your innocence is taken in such a violent, traumatic way, it will stay with you for the rest of your life, whether you try to dismiss it or not. A healthy person integrates all aspects of their existence, does not compartmentalize it and act completely differently to the people in their lives. Wearing many masks, clearly demonstrates something is wrong with that persons' psyche' and they more than likely have some dark, deep secrets lurking within.

It got worse. When I was in Alexandria, VA during high school, I met a friend at a bookstore, and he was very, very intelligent and older than me, in his mid-twenties. I will call him

"Daniel," and I trusted him but didn't know him well. He invited me over to his place one time. I looked up to him. I was impressed by his intellect and his knowledge of philosophy and hoped he could take me under his wing. I was searching for a mentor at that time but void of finding one. The kids my age had never even heard of the stuff I was reading, the philosophers I was quoting, and weren't into poetry while I was becoming heavily into poets. "Daniel" held a knife to me and...um...had me perform a sex act on him. It was not a turn on, it was another case of sexual abuse. I never told anyone of this incident, but I went to the girlfriend I had around this time named Tandy, and she actually took me to see a minister because I couldn't tell her what was wrong. I was ashamed, and this was the second time in my life this happened to me.

For the record, I want to say, I wasn't gay — far from it — but I always thought that because these things were done to me by men, maybe I was gay or was being perceived as such by others. I kept asking how did this happen with another sick bastard? What kind of fucking signals was I giving out to make this happen?

I wasn't gay or bi-sexual, and if I was, I would wholeheartedly admit to it from where I am now. I was molested, abused, raped and no one ever understood or got close enough to me to understand. After all, if my own Mother didn't believe me, I always thought, no one else ever would. I drank so much of the time on my way to becoming an alcoholic to forget those sexual molestations and to forget my Mother's betrayal in her own disbelief this could have occurred. I drank to block it out. I had to block it out.

Sexual abuse left unresolved or at least partially healed, can ruin your life and certainly cause any relationships you have to be quite cluttered with baggage that should not be brought into a healthy, stable relationship. It was taboo to talk of it in the context of the times I grew-up in, and I really couldn't find an outlet or a person to speak to about it, only small fractions were revealed at any given time. I internalized the pain, hostility and rage, and in the end, I punished myself. I had a rage inside, and I tried like hell to dull it.

Assumptions have been made about me before I left the Earth, and now it's become a circus of the absurd. It's so contrived, as people give their own theories of why I was the freak and psychopath they describe me as. If sexual abuse doesn't clearly explain why I was dysfunctional as an adult, what does?

The first time I was abused, caused me to act out a lot but I also acted up prior to that just to get attention. This hasn't been reported very much, but I was a shoplifter. It wasn't just to get things I didn't have the money to buy. I would also stage these overdramatic acts, like collapsing and playing dead for minutes at a time, though I later learned at U.C.L.A., I suffered from Petit Mal.

I put my first girlfriend, Tandy, through a sort of hell. Tandy had no idea what was going on, I was so over the top, and I tried to use her to convince my Mother I wasn't gay. My Mother had questioned me to see if I was gay when I told her about the rape and thought it was my overactive, possibly homosexual imagination.

Tandy was at my house one night when we were in high school, and I ran upstairs and messed up my parents bed to give the perception that Tandy and I were engaging in sexual activity. I also messed up her clothes and hair, and Tandy was angry and freaked out. I smiled at my Mother as if I was proud to tell her, I wasn't gay. I really had a thing for Tandy, but I can't call her my first love. She wouldn't let me get close enough to her and I was pretty much overwhelming to her. She also had other boyfriends, so I didn't feel very special in her eyes.

My life was not as it was supposed to be, not even close. I was powerless as a child and a teenager, so to change it, I disowned it. This was not to hurt my younger sister and brother, who were both innocent involving anything to do with me, but it was certainly an attempt to put some distance between me and the world of pain I had experienced growing up.

I am somewhat surprised and find some disdain in the fact that my childhood drawings or things I created, must now be placed in the public domain. What I did with The Doors and in one published poetry book (the one I put together myself on Earth), was for the public to embrace, or piss on if they choose. What I did in my childhood, or adolescence or any other time, has no place being shown to the public, it's not my legacy, it's the mind of a child in pain. After the age of 12, it's the mind of a sexually abused child who needed help. Even from this side, I find the release of my childhood play to be basically deplorable. This is not a way to honor me or my memory. Is nothing sacred?

There are drawings that exist today that I did that were overtly sexual and the sexual organs are very exaggerated in size. It was because of what I had seen when I was raped. My attacker, as I will refer to him, uses a sexual organ that hurts so badly, you think it's huge. It was not just puberty or an overly sexually aroused adolescent thing at all.

I drew a picture of myself, very distorted with a crown on my head. Tandy held onto it. I drew it because I was the king of pain, the dark prince, and I hated myself. I hated Jim Morrison and even contemplated suicide one night, after the second molestation. A Bo Diddley song came on the radio, and it made me laugh. I have to thank Bo Diddley, because I could've easily ended my life that night. This would not turn out to be the first time I was suicidal. I almost took my life again when I was at the height of my fame.

For a kid who was a clown to cover his shyness and a true loner, moving from state to state, school to school could not have been worse. In 1955, I saw a movie in California that changed my life. It was called "Rebel Without a Cause," and it starred James Dean who became an idol. I was at one time quite obsessed with his character in the film and with James Dean himself. He rebelled against everything. Between seeing that film, and reading a book called "On the Road" by Jack Kerouac, at 12 years old, I just wanted to run, run, run. I wanted to stick my thumb out, start hitching, seeing the world, and making my own rules.

But as time went on, and this sick shit happened to me again, I was not very motivated. I was truly in a fog after the second incident of sexual abuse, and I found school to be such a waste of time. I didn't feel I needed the teachers, just the books, and the books I wanted to read myself, which I felt taught me more than any of the assigned ones I had.

I was already estranged from my parents before they enrolled me in college in Florida and packed me up to go live with my Grandparents. They thought the military would make a man out of me, and I wasn't going to be that man, that was for sure. Little did my parents know, I preferred my Grandparents, Paul and Caroline, to them. I didn't see much of my Grandparents while I stayed with

Jim Morrison & Michael Hutchence

them, and the little that I saw of them, they didn't understand me, but I loved them. My Grandmother would find beer cans in her trash can. I would taunt her, because this was like the old South back then and tell her I was going to bring home a colored girl as a girlfriend. She didn't find me funny but she loved me.

Freedom

The child ran away from home
he was tired of the totalitarian existence
that was a right of his birth

He thought he found freedom
stealing and shuffling
through the streets

But liberty does not seem authentic
when you don't know where
you will eat or sleep

You start depending on the kindness of strangers,
and the fact you cannot move through freely
becomes disorienting

Some strangers place no demands
others precipitate ties, it's quid pro quo
and now you no longer know
is it me, or the stranger,
all lines run together

You find many won't give
without wanting something in return
This is not freedom, it's parallel to the

A TALE OF TWO BROTHERS

same existence I had before
just more jaded, just more sleazy

You are reshaped again,
This time not as a soldier or a slave
but "the Browning version" of a whore

The child can go home again,
feel safe for the first time in a long while,
But he now knows
freedom in a world of Svengalis, gluttons,
and terminal Nazis,
is never free
and none of this is who I was supposed to be

—*channeled from Jim Morrison*

Jim Morrison & Michael Hutchence

CHAPTER 4
It Happened First in Florida

"The first time someone shows you who they are, believe them."

—*Maya Angelou*

Jim Morrison & Michael Hutchence

A TALE OF TWO BROTHERS

My college days truly amounted to an alcoholic in the making. I was an average student and really did most of my learning all through school on my own by reading, reading and reading.

I started drinking a little in high school, mostly beer, here and there, but my alcoholism truly took flight in Florida. I was drinking beer regularly when I lived with my Grandparents and attended school in St. Petersburg, but when I transferred to Florida State, that was it, I really started to get wasted on a fairly regular basis.

I used to hang-out at a coffee shop in Florida when I first went to college where there were poetry readings. People could get up in front of this small, but receptive crowd and be Alan Ginsberg for the night. I did this a few times and loved it. I came to realize there was a pretty good sized group of gay males who visited this shop. There seemed to be an interest in me from some in this group, and it mutually fascinated and repelled me. I got into a situation with one of these gay men, where I threatened him in a sadistic, horrible manner. I wanted to choke the shit out of him because I was bigger now, weighed more and was never going to be abused again by anyone. I am truly not proud of it, but gay men would continue to hit on me the rest of my life and it pretty much disgusted me. Of course, that was because I didn't realize a heterosexual man could have been molested as a child as well, I didn't know what to think or how to feel, so I tried not to feel. My uncle had to take care of the coffee shop incident, because, you see, it was scandalous. Why was I threatening a gay man if I wasn't gay and had not been involved with him? It was a time when things were still scandalous and your family could be shamed.

I got kicked out of an apartment I shared with a group of other guys. I was an obnoxious jerk to live with and was not used to having roommates. I had done my own thing in my parent's homes for a long time, living in a basement or an attic and spending most of my time as the loner I truly was. I was consumed

Jim Morrison & Michael Hutchence

by my own world and didn't have much respect for my first set of college roommates, but I didn't feel some of them respected me very much either, it was a no win situation.

My first arrest due to my drunkenness occurred in Tallahassee in September 1963. This should have been my last arrest, but it was the first of several. I was drunk off my ass and on my way to a Seminoles' football game with my friends when we were pulled over by a police cruiser. Smartass Jimbo just had to run his mouth, then I stole the cop's umbrella and, when he wasn't looking, his helmet. I spent my first drunken night in jail and was roughed up for the first time by the cops. It should've been a loud, intrusive wake-up call, but instead, it was only a taste of things to come.

I did appear in a play at Florida State and had been reading about what was termed "method acting," and I would say, that is where Jim Morrison of The Doors first began to play around with how far he could take it on stage. I didn't go very far, but I certainly did the unexpected, the unorthodox, and took the audience and the other actors on a different trip, each and every night.

I lived in a trailer park for a short time at Florida State and this is where my voyeurism took root, not on a rooftop in Venice Beach, California. I would peek into the girls' dorms and take notes. I remained a true voyeur, observing and taking notes for the rest of my life.

I also lived in my first of many motels in Florida, the Cherokee. I already liked motels in Florida, before I ever got to California. I later moved into an apartment with some art students and instructors to save money. This was a more sophisticated group of roommates than my original ones at Florida State. I could have conversations with them about esoteric studies, and I was on a completely different wavelength with them, so it was a more comfortable place to dwell. There is an event that occurred at this apartment which is worthy of speaking of. Someone brought drugs into the apartment, and for the first and last time, I tried opium. I hated the trip, I got nothing out of it but endless vomiting and nausea. This experience turned me off opiates for the rest of my life. I had nothing but disdain for opium, opiates and, what I call it's cousin, heroin, for the rest of my life.

A beautiful thing happened in college in Florida. I found my first love, and her name was Mary Werbelow. She was a Queen, and overall, I did treat her well. She had the most amazing figure and was beautiful beyond any words I can use to describe her. She was my Goddess. Mary was perfect in every way, and the first thing I openly admit I noticed about her, was her chest. Everyone used to call me the "Backdoor Man" when I became famous and thought I was looking at women's rear ends. Well for a man who was so into the backside of a female, I sure as hell spent a lot of time in strip clubs in L.A. watching the girls with big chests. I tried to just like a girl for her face and her personality, and if she liked me, that would usually be enough. When I was obnoxiously drunk, it didn't matter anyway, I could end up with anybody and usually did. But I can tell you, it all started with Mary, my love for an endowed upper body figure.

I showed my devotion to Mary by hitchhiking over 20 miles each way to see her on weekends in Florida. Mary reciprocated by showing her devotion to me by moving to California after high school to attend college there. You see, I became extremely interested in film and cinema arts and could not pursue that course of study on an academic level in Florida. I was drawn, literally, by some unknown force to attend U.C.L.A. That force now has an identity, it's known as fate. Mary attended another college in California mostly so we could be together.

Mary coming to California was a joyful thing for me, however, I had been engaged in some drinking episodes in Florida. My drunken antics did not go unnoticed by Mary as they were quite upsetting to her.

By the time I transferred to California, my dark side was starting to have a hold on me. I was becoming a rather heavy and frequent drinker and taking psychedelic drugs as the other students at U.C.L.A. film school were engaging in, and this was not at all Mary's trip. Mary began to feel she was losing her identity in me. I was just somehow absorbing who she was, and she wanted to pursue her own dreams and interests. I was helping her move into another apartment when she broke up with me, and my heart was broken...or more like torn apart. My ego was deeply bruised. I knew I could not hang onto the Goddess. I was going down my own path, which was quite self-destructive, whether I was fully aware of it at that particular time or not. I was young, my body could take it, but Mary didn't want to follow and I thank God she didn't. I would've done nothing but hurt her in the end.

I went back to see Mary after I became famous, and I did ask her to marry me. It may sound strange or rude, but I was curious about how she would reply and how she saw me after she dumped me and crushed my ego. I wanted to know, would she want me now that I have amounted to something and was making money? The answer was "No." She moved to India in 1968 and I never saw her again, and that is precisely how it was meant to be.

I would have left Pamela Courson, or any other woman for Mary, in a minute if she had even entertained the possibility of getting involved with me again. The reason was, I felt she could've saved me, saved me from myself. But it was not meant to be, it was just meant for the time it was. She was my first real love and I will always love and respect her. She is not, however, my eternal soul mate. Mary and I will not be together on this side. That's not how it was designed, and I don't regret a minute with Mary. But I am glad she got free of me, we were meant to come together and go our own ways. Mary, by the way, did not believe The Doors could ever work. Maybe I should've listened to her.

My days at U.C.L.A. were mostly about experimentation, and I did learn quite a bit about the filmmaking process there. It wasn't a complete waste of time. Contrary to that piece of shit, disgusting, inane garbage some call a film made about me by Oliver Stone, I graduated from U.C.L.A. — not that it matters now where I am. But I did follow through and matriculate, and this lends credence to the notion that my alcoholism had not yet reached full tilt. My student film was clearly an experiment of a montage of obtuse images. It was not received well, mostly with indifference, not disdain. People in the film school didn't truly understand me but many of them were pretentious and superficial, and I had most of them figured out.

I was a loner and that never helps you to be accepted in social situations. It wasn't a very good film, but it was definitely a project that was meant to stir emotion through images and take you on a trip…well…not everyone was willing to go. A few of my friends were willing to go on that trip, and went with me, and stayed with me, for the rest of my life. I formed just a few, very significant, relationships at U.C.L.A.

During the U.C.L.A. years, I had a friend who was older than me and he was more or less blamed by more than a few people for my continuous, outrageous drinking. Felix wasn't to blame for squat. I was already at the early stages of alcoholism well before The Doors were ever created. I was attracted to other drinkers or those who would go along with me and not attempt to get me to stop or end my evening of amusement. I was already on my way to the end, because alcohol began to dominate my life. Many people drink and party heavily in college and tend to overcome it, but it can take a lifelong path. I was already writing my story, and taking my path and not realizing how fatal it would all turn.

Goddess

There was a cult built around the Goddess Athena,
the Daughter of Zeus, an Owl was always by her side,
She was worshipped and wanted, to be a hero in her
eyes was greater than any amount of gold

But the warrior Goddess I most prefer is
Sekhmet, from her breath the desert was
created, the Scarlet lady, the fierce
lioness captivated me and still does

For you see my Angel, every Goddess
is in you and you are every Goddess to me…
Like the Goddess Isolde, you must choose
between two lovers, the King you serve on

Earth or this one, I am your Tristan and
you have bound yourself to me eternally
As I described the Goddess Guinevere
in a song I once wrote as she was the

Jim Morrison & Michael Hutchence

Ashen lady, it was you I always saw
and remembered in all other Goddesses

I searched for you in the faces of many,
but upon looking into their eyes, I came to
realize each and every time they were not you

Rebecca, and I worship you as one has
worshipped the likes of Athena, Sekhmet,

Isolde and Guinevere…my entire existence
revolves upon becoming the hero for my
Goddess…the true lioness of my soul…
I am your James…yes, I am yours, forever...

–channeled from Jim Morrison

CHAPTER 5

When the Music's Over, Turn on the Lights!!!

"I remember my youth and the feeling that will never come back any more - the feeling that I could last forever, outlast the sea, the earth, and all men."

–Joseph Conrad, Polish born British novelist and short story writer, author of Heart of Darkness and Lord Jim.

Jim Morrison & Michael Hutchence

A TALE OF TWO BROTHERS

  I do believe The Doors were indeed the four of us. After Ray's brothers dropped out, we formed our magical quartet of Ray, Robbie, John and I. If one member of this group left or quit, the energetic equation was going to change, and truthfully, it would never be The Doors again. I do understand and appreciate the desire to keep our music alive, and I am genuinely surprised from this side, that people on Earth still revere The Doors and that the songs have become classics.

  The continued commercialization of The Doors and our music makes me both saddened and disappointed. There was no need to take the music to the masses and sell it out, because those who were supposed to find The Doors will find them. What we created, at least to me, was sacred but became diluted with commercial hits like "Light My Fire." It may have made us sell out large concert halls, but my performances became more synthetic and theatrical in those bigger venues. The pure experience of The Doors had been lost.

  I realize now The Doors worked better in a small venue, where it was about more than chanting for me to sing "Light My Fire" or shake my ass in leather pants. A more intimate setting created more of a mystical experience for a limited audience than, for example, Cobo Hall in Detroit or Madison Square Garden.

  When I was starting out in The Doors, I didn't see it that way. I wanted to be a headliner performing in front of larger crowds. Now I see, our mystique was lost in those venues, but that was entirely due to my performance as opposed to my talented band mates.

  We didn't have a choreographer, and I never took voice lessons. We were all natural and no one taught me how to move on stage. I would simply trance out, and it wasn't all chemically induced either. It was our own creation, often copied but never duplicated.

  I do regret the pain, anxiety and confusion I caused Robbie, Ray and John. I owe them all an apology for putting them through the shit I caused due to my alcoholism, temperament and, at times, immaturity. They tolerated me well, my moods, my tardiness, whatever stupid shit I pulled on them.

Musically, Robbie and Ray read me so well and could understand exactly what needed to be done with every song. There was complete musical symmetry. While the musical chemistry was right on most of the time, my personal relationships with them over the years simply were fragmented. I take full responsibility for the lack of being able to maintain personal relationships on Earth.

I enjoyed performing live with The Doors much more so than the tedious studio sessions. By the time we got to the third album, it was a difficult ordeal. Paul Rothchild, our (uh-hum) humble producer, was a perfectionist but was never remotely satisfied when the takes were excellent. Paul never had faith in me as a vocalist, and this made the recording process grueling for us much of the time. When you know the man producing your records believes you can't sing a note and is used to working with real singers like Janis Joplin, who wants to show up for work?

I liked the live Doors shows where I felt we connected to the audience. I could always feel if we were or not. I didn't like to open my eyes and see people laughing, unresponsive or disrupting a show. I always cared what the audience thought and truthfully, was extremely sensitive to the group energy if I was inebriated.

The energetic connection I tried to make to the audience was serious, never an act. It became more exaggerated when I felt the pressure of performing in front of a larger audience. I regret that. I needed to stay pure to the essence of my soul on stage. I wasn't an entertainer, but the fans and critics alike wanted to see someone else. That was, at times, the ultimate struggle.

I feel those who are supposed to find The Doors will find them. I hope they allow the music and words to permeate their souls, inspire them and allow it to be whatever it is to them individually. They should not color their experiences by reading a trashy book about me or watching that disgrace of a film that Oliver Stone made. All of that was so far removed from what it was and who I was.

My lyrics and poetry mostly came from the subconscious, and I am now aware that some of them were channeled. There are assumptions that certain songs I wrote were about certain people.

Those in the studio with me will tell you, that so much was altered and the lyrical changes just happened randomly. If I had a love song composed for a certain person, why would I improvise and change it so that lyrically it was not the same song? A good example of a song being completely misconstrued would be "Waiting For The Sun," which according to some, was written about America. I would like my fans to keep in mind, much of the time, I often didn't know where my lyrics came from, and I didn't disagree with people who thought they knew. I just let it go, as I let so much else go in my life.

"Waiting For The Sun," as it turns out, was actually inspired by something known as the "Emerald Tablets of Thoth." I was a voracious reader, and I consumed some of the greatest literature the world has ever known. I embraced great philosophers, and so many of my songs were inspired by what I had read, not experienced. The rest simply came from the side I am on now. Few were from Earth experiences. but I was a student of the times. Literature, philosophy and art are timeless, and if anyone, for some inordinate reason, would like to really pay tribute to me, read more and open yourself up to great literature and poetry. Study various philosophers until you find one or two that ring true to your inner core. For me, it's well known Nietzche was a philosopher who spoke to the very essence of who I was, but I was never able to apply his philosophy. Go and see, with your own eyes, great art from many centuries long ago, and it will open your soul.

You may wonder, who was my musical muse? My muse was an unnamed woman with a face I could not see clearly. The moon was my muse at times, or she was a composite of all the women I had known and the fantasies they engaged in about me. My muse was so many things at different times, but to infer my lyrics were about one particular girlfriend is completely without basis. I now know my muse was my other half, my true eternal soul mate.

Is "Orange County Suite" about a particular girlfriend? Just because one of the girls I was with was originally from Orange County, why take it so far? I mention Chicago in there too, where Ray Manzarek hailed from, so is this song about him? I never planned to move to a farm with Pamela, marry her or have children with her. People take things even from a song and make them what they want to see. The truth can only come from the horse's mouth. Only I know who I was. While on Earth, things were quite jumbled, and I had this lackadaisical attitude about allowing people to believe what they wanted. But all that is over now, I can see it all more clearly than any day I walked the Earth.

I am not on Earth in a human body. Surprise, surprise, I really did "bite it" in Paris in 1971. Therefore, all control of The Doors must rightfully go to the three surviving members. It was incredibly wrong of my parents, or anyone, to sue The Doors. My work was art. The Doors were art. This should never have been about money. My parents, Pamela Courson's parents, and Pamela herself, while she was on Earth, had nothing to do with The Doors. I realize the mess I made with my legal will at the time of my great demise is the cause of much of the controversy, and this was not the way I meant to leave it. I may have been fatalistic at times and downright suicidal, but I thought there was time to change my will. My eyes were opened quite widely, even in my alcoholic haze in my final days.

I have not viewed the documentary "When You're Strange" and have no actual desire to do so. I am far removed from that life, and it's hard for me to accept that the story of the Doors needs to be told over again ad nauseum. Showing me in leather pants, and talking how about how drunk I would get, hardly needs to be rehashed.

Pamela's Father, Corky Courson has come to this side, I haven't spoken to him and don't plan to do so, I have no feelings for him and he should've never had my work or my money and of course, his daughter shouldn't have had it either. This man was clueless about what I left behind and it was a travesty anything was left to him.

I am not opposed to the other Doors making money from the legacy, they created and finely crafted it. In my opinion, the push to have the music saturated in commercial markets reduces the art and the vision. If I were alive, I can assure you, there would not be a Doors CD on sale at Starbucks™. It should be about art, not greed or the money. I was disappointed an unpublished poem was sold to a rock singer and used in a song. I do not consider it a tribute, because that was not how my work was intended to be used. I am rather disillusioned that my words, art and legacy are so easily turned over for money. There is no integrity or pureness in any of this.

My words were all I have to show from my wasted, messed up life. I would like my words to inspire others to turn them on, to bring out the artist in them. But when they are not used in the context for which they were intended, it's similar to spitting on my grave. The intent to disrespect may not be present, but you must be careful and delicate when taking someone's true legacy and trying to present it. This may be sour grapes, but I am opposed to The Doors continuing on with a new singer because of my perspective on this side. The Doors were the energy of the four of us, and I would not say it was equal. My band mates contributed more to The Doors than I ever did and were never given the credit of being such, talented, innovative and ahead of their time musicians. My view on this now is, The Doors were designed for a certain time period. While the music can still be listened to and appreciated, without one of us on Earth, the live performance simply will not have the same mystical dynamic we were destined to have.

The Doors were what they were, when they were, and that is how far it should've gone. But it is now up to Ray, Robbie and John, it's not for me to say from where I am.

I can look back now with a completely different perspective on The Doors and the music we created. Some will be surprised to find that my favorite Doors album is in fact "Morrison Hotel, Hard Rock Café," because we created our own musical cocktail of rock, jazz and blues. We did it without taking away from our creative and sometimes edgy lyrics. By the time "Morrison Hotel" came out, many critics, and even some fans, had written us off. And to me, it's the best studio representation of The Doors. Our songs were maturing. Our debut album was a good debut for any group, but at the same time, we did grow and improve and "Morrison Hotel" was a fine example of that. You couldn't really put us in a box, as a rock band, a blues band or anything else, we were our own special brand.

My second favorite Doors album may not surprise anybody, because while I was on Earth, I would often tell people how proud I was of "Strange Days." It had an ambience, a true ambience, not often found on other albums of that era or since then. Our world as

Jim Morrison & Michael Hutchence

The Doors was truly changing, and things, at times, could seem out of control. I felt it was unquestionably better than our debut album. There is a feeling to it that is unique and unpretentious. There is a motif to this album that something has changed and that something around us was not quite right. Some may feel it sounds dated, but listen to it again from start to finish.

I would have to place "L.A. Woman" in third place of my all-time favorites. The concept was to go more toward the Blues, as we all believed as a group, we did that best. I wanted to sing some old songs, like "St. James Infirmary," but I was vetoed and we went with fresh material. Paul Rothchild had finally fallen out with us, and it was a different and more pleasant experience recording this album minus him. I really do think we matured. My voice was rough from booze, cigarettes and cocaine. I was heavily into cocaine at the time we recorded "L.A. Woman" and had tried to quit drinking twice, to no avail, during the making of that album. I went through dry heaves when I tried to kick the bottle that would have knocked anybody on their ass eternally. I was really out there on the booze and the coke at this period in my life and some interesting and disturbing images came to my mind. "L.A. Woman" was a tribute to the home base that gave me so much joy, pain and lunacy, but I had very clear images of a woman in my mind while composing this song. I thought she was a love from another life. "L.A. Woman" was The Doors at their best. We weren't so psychedelic at that stage, but the times were a changing', and maturing in the musicianship and my lyrical repertoire was only increasing, despite what has been written about us repeatedly.

I would have to put the debut album "The Doors," in fourth place. It was very naive and very overrated in my opinion. It was a mere starting point, maybe a good one for any group, but some listeners never got past it! It was just a bunch of songs thrown together, lacking any sort of ambience that "Strange Days" later had. I hated "Light My Fire," and by 1969, I never wanted to sing it again.

I got so tired of the public never really getting past that song when I felt we had done much better songs. Robbie Krieger wrote that song, I only added one line. Robbie certainly wrote much better songs as we grew. I hated the album cover because it put me in a larger-than-life position over the other members of the group. I also could never outlive the look I had, starving at 22, when we got signed. It's hard to accept people always expected me to look like that, as if I was petrified wood from an enchanted forest. I don't think I really knew how to sing or use my voice when we recorded those early songs either.

I would have to place "Waiting For The Sun" in fifth place. It was too commercial, and it was basically a montage of songs we found to get an album done. And it took forever. I couldn't write songs I had written for the first album, hearing a concert in my head, starving on an abandoned Venice Beach rooftop. I couldn't write the same songs I wrote on "Strange Days," because we were past that. You evolve as a person, and things like touring and traveling weren't so new anymore. There were some new songs but plenty of recycled songs on this album, but as an artist, I got shot down on this album. I had written my best performance epic for that album called "Celebration of the Lizard." A section of it was used in "Not to Touch the Earth," which seemed so out of place, altogether. The lyrics to "Celebration" were printed inside the album cover, but it was something that was so special to me and so important to me as an artist and was just thrown out. I was told it wasn't ready, it was too long, it doesn't work, and on and on.

This was when I began this emotional split from the other Doors, because my art — which was indeed my soul — was denied for the more commercial songs and work. Richard Goldstein wrote a very truthful piece about it called "The Shaman as Superstar," and I felt he explained it beautifully.

My least favorite Doors album of all was "The Soft Parade," which could've been great but was seriously overproduced. It was in some ways, an experiment, but it wasn't at all what I pictured or what I wanted. It was for all intents and purposes, lame. Many people thought we were selling out, thinking we could do a "Sgt. Pepper's Lonely Hearts Club Band." We never imitated others. Maybe The Kinks on a song that turned out to be the music for "Hello, I Love You," but otherwise, we did our own thing. I was always a Brian Wilson fan but wasn't trying to recreate "Pet Sounds." There were a few good songs on "The Soft Parade," but it was, overall, a completely overproduced mess that also took forever to make. It wasn't worth the time or the effort.

The Oracle of Delphi

An ancient enchantress whispered in my ear,
The Oracle of Delphi appeared in a dream
She brought to me an amethyst, large and round
and clear

She told me to stare deep into it and allow her
to call upon her idol Apollo
She told me I was much like Alexander the Great

I needed to heed her warning before it was too late

No one could resist me but only for a time
the tides would turn and with them,
those who once clung to me would deem me insane
As they could not understand what went on in my brain

I would be called pompous, and a clown
one with a large ego and soon, no one would want
to be around, I would be turned on like a serpent
The Oracle came to say, I held my head low and asked her to stay

I asked, "Pythia, do you bring me this news
because I have not made an offering to Apollo?"
The Oracle came closer and laid down beside me
She told me to look into her eyes, for they told no lies

I saw Apollo, large and strong,
shooting a large serpent with an arrow,
Pythia whispered, "Are you not the Lizard King?
Did you not claim you could do anything?"

I told her it was not who I was,
I was trying to do satire and be
clever and she said "My son,
my utterances are taken as truth
by all the rulers in the world and creatures
Of the sea, what you said must be taken
literally."

Pythia stroked my hair and held her head high to
the sky, "You are what you call yourself, she replied"

She went on to say "The serpent tried to have
Apollo's Mother when he was in her womb, he will
never embrace you son, your time comes soon."

She gently wept as I began to kiss her
soft, wet lips

I fell under her trance though she had just
predicted my death, I did not care, the Oracle of Delphi
was in my bed, Apollo's need to punish me
circled in my head

As the night lingered, two became one
The serpent rode the enchantress
until I was done,

We became the two-headed beast
I bedded a high priestess and
had her with contempt, and she called
me her most holy Priest.

She told me she must return to
Mount Parnassus and her lair
I didn't want to let her go
I grabbed her long, dark hair

Jim Morrison & Michael Hutchence

She once again handed me an Amethyst
large, round and clear
she told me to look into it deeply

When no one was around
I would see what I most feared
then She quickly disappeared

I saw two eagles collide,
and I saw the large serpent die
an arrow penetrated his skin
he lay still, cold, hard and dead

I then saw myself, coughing up blood
I was that serpent, I was that arrow
that ended my life, the vision filled me with dread

I shrugged it off , wrote it off as just another dream
But the Oracle of Delphi mated with me, I knew it had
occurred and unlike most nights, it was crystal clear
not a blur, for I was not drunk as I was
so many nights before

I love you Pythia, I praise your sweet name
I have removed the arrow that took my life
I have ended the game. You shall not come to me
again, Apollo no longer holds my fate,
I have entered the heavenly gates and live in a garden
and wait for my Angel for I am no longer a snake

—*channeled from Jim Morrison*

CHAPTER 6
Dance On Fire...

"The worst tragedy for a poet is to be admired through being misunderstood."

—*Jean Cocteau*, French poet and novelist

Jim Morrison & Michael Hutchence

A TALE OF TWO BROTHERS

I know the words I provide to my channel are arbitrary, because so many of you will simply not accept or be open enough to the possibility I am speaking out from this side. I have always been about thinking outside of the box. Why can't I be about thinking outside of the cheap one they threw my bodily remains in?

The Doors were so unique because we seemed to invoke the darkness, night after night, of ancient ceremonies or rituals brought through in the psychedelic hot dreams of the '60s. Pan, the ancient Greek God, was a great influence on me. Many have derived pictures of Satan from Pan who was considered evil because he was highly sexualized. I was greatly inspired, and I believe rightfully so, by Greek mythology and literature. I did not take to the worship of Pan and was not invoking him on stage nightly, but the elements of the nightly ceremonies seemed to mirror things that many in the climate of the '60s deemed as Satanic, or dangerous. Just because someone reads a book by Alistair Crowley does not mean he or she is becoming a worshipper of the dark side. Perhaps they wish to find what all the hysteria is about. Perhaps they wish to open their mind and consider all the possibilities. Sexuality became associated with evil and the darkness, and the eroticism of The Doors, clearly scared more than a few.

Occult literally means "hidden," not Satanic. I suppose you may want to conclude the Rosicrucians, the Free Masons, The Knights of the Templar, even those members of the Skull & Bones have been part of the occult. You need to draw your own conclusions, as always, but Satanic worship was not a part of any of these organizations. Satanic worship was not a part of my life.

I had sufficient darkness in my soul, but I was not a practitioner of the dark forces, on stage or off.

Superstitions are dangerous and belong to the truly ignorant in society. I would like to compare myself with the pentagram. This symbol has existed since the beginning of the Earth and has been found in cave dwellings. The origins of the five-pointed star has roots in all major cultures, such as Mayan and Egyptian, where it is a secret symbol of the planet Venus in honor of a specific Goddess. This sign was found in the drawings of Babylon and throughout Greece.

It was thought at one time, mankind drew the pentagram to represent five visible planets. Later on, the ancient Greek philosopher, Pythagoras, believed the pentagram represented the five elements — which were air, water, fire, earth and what we called the psyche (energy). Early Christians wore the pentagram, and in the Renaissance, the pentagram was a great symbol of alchemy, and even ceremonial magic.

Ritual Magicians, centuries ago believed the pentagram to be a microcosm of the human body. Therefore, it was primarily used by ritual magicians to create a divine state or bring one closer to God. So the pentagram has represented true mysticism for centuries. Some certainly did engage in using it for black magic and to bring forth evil forces, but as with anything else, you can use it as you choose, but that was not the purpose the pentagram was originally intended for or initially drawn for.

There are numerous links to the pentagram and Christianity, and at one time, it was set in jewelry for Christians. Also, it could be drawn in one continuous movement of the pen, which would mean joining the Alpha and Omega together. It is strange that the pentagram is now a symbol that invokes fear and images of Satanic ritual, as this is a relatively newer use for this symbol. It truly is about immortality and individual choice, away from the divine to Satan Worshippers, and those who practice what is termed black magic. I am not an advocate of black magic. I encourage mysticism to directly connect to the divine in your own way and your own time. I do not believe the dark forces, which I am here to say do exist, will offer you anything but complete emptiness. But you must choose your own path. The darkness and light co-exist in every living person and in every living soul.

Even those enlightened ones will continually be subjected to the darkness and must learn to resist it and realize the path it leads you on will not bring any type of fulfillment or happiness in the long run. Members of Hitler's regime certainly did engage in occult practices pertaining to black magic and destruction.

Enlightenment leads to wholeness and perfection, the kind Hitler and his maniac psycho flunkies could not understand in any sense.

They were in some ways, the great purveyors of a Godless life, as it is clear, none of them were working with the divine.

Just as the pentagram is not understood, so many things in my life were not understood either. That includes what I was trying to do individually and as a member of The Doors. I was this old soul, this one who invoked the ancients yet it was all misinterpreted and still is. Hypothetically, I could've held a pentagram up on stage, and do you think the audience would realize it was the symbol of a Goddess or even represented the five elements? Or would they take it as a symbol I was invoking dark forces or practicing black magic with? The assumptions humans make are astounding. I have come to believe this is because they are not well versed or well read, for the most part, in terms of classical literature, ancient mythology or just relatively basic aspects of world history.

What tends to happen is people begin to believe old wives' tales or superstitions instead of reading a few books on the topic and doing their own research. This is by far one of the most frightening things currently happening on Earth. For example, the history of the Middle East is not clearly understood by those in other parts of the world or by those who decide to invade it or bring war upon it. How can you prevail or aid in a matter you do not understand with any in-depth knowledge?

I actually wrote a poem about the Middle East, and it has been released recently by a group. It's called "Woman in the Window." I dislike the arrangement of the song wholeheartedly. I would have never done anything like that with it, however, it got into the hands of another musician. I should not be surprised that my art, the words I left behind, are often sold to the highest bidder. I have concluded, nothing you leave behind is sacred.

I realize many think I wrote "Woman in the Window" about global warming, as if I predicted it. As I've said, allow my words to be what they are to you, but I wasn't referring to global warming in that piece. The woman is from Palestine in the song, and it's important to look at the context of what was happening in Palestine at the time it was written and what Palestine represented (what it was near, etc.) to understand what I was referring to in her garden and the evil man invading it. I did invoke many ancient images, and refer to mythology, and to the great books I had read, but I also was a voyeur of the times I lived in. My words should be taken in the context of the times, and this is why I have stated, The Doors were meant for a certain time. I am glad you still appreciate the music, however, Earth works on the linear timescale and we were what we were to a particular time. Keeping what I wrote in the context of the global time frame is most appropriate.

There is really no one on this side who doesn't have very real concerns and sadness for the Earth. The Earth is an extension of who you are. That being said, look around it, and tell me, is that who you want to be? We can discuss global warming, and industrial waste and the diseases plaguing the Earth, as the land that gives you life and light is being raped several thousand times a day. What is now needed is a reconnection to the Earth by all who live and thrive on it.

When I was awaiting trial in Florida, the most enlightening experience I had was not in the courtroom but scuba diving in the Bahamas. I was always quite the naturalist, and certainly from the time I was old enough to really walk and talk, loved to be outdoors. As I got older, unfortunately, I spent more time on a barstool, inside a dark haven with the less than enlightened souls than I should have. I would still travel to places: for example, I took Danny Sugerman to a beautiful waterfall and other times I visited Big Sur with other people, but I really didn't spend enough time reconnecting myself to the planet I lived on. I experienced an earthquake not long before I left for Paris in 1971, and to feel the force of the Earth, the power she exalts, is quite remarkable on many levels. I was sleeping in a chair when it woke me up, and for all I knew, it could've been the end of the world. But those things, earthquakes, and natural disasters in general, should cause all who experience it or are around it to reconnect and show a much greater respect for your abundant host.

When I went scuba diving in the Bahamas in 1970, I saw things under the ocean that surprised me: the colors of the aquatic life alone and the whole eco system that exists, is so separate from our land experience. If I had a wish, it would be that every human being go scuba diving and experience the life in the ocean, where we all originated from anyway. The ocean is not separate from the

Earth, it is a part of it, and when you experience the infinite mysteries of the ocean, it can be a life-changing experience. The ocean is pure energy. That energy can amplify your entire life force. People connecting to the ocean (through scuba diving or deep sea diving) may sound like a simplistic thing to suggest, considering the mass destruction and horrors of war taking place on the planet, but I feel it would make a good start. I lived during the Vietnam War, and the lessons of that war have not been totally revealed. Man still hasn't learned from the truth of Vietnam.

Contrary to popular belief, I did not write the "Unknown Soldier" to stick it to my Father. I wrote it because the images of Vietnam were all around us at the time. I certainly did have the military background I grew up with in the back of my mind, but that song was to reflect the times we were a part of. I had nightmares about napalm and dismembered bodies. I did not write this song to be political, but to be thought-provoking about what I saw during that time on Earth, as a citizen of the United States of America.

When I did perform my section during "The End" with my version of the Oedipus complex, it was almost surprising, but not quite, that few who heard it knew where it was from. It was shocking to many yet had been around for centuries. There was a strange connection in my life as Jim Morrison to the Oracle of Delphi, and "Oedipus" was a legend connected to it. Freud would undoubtedly say I added this section, because I felt the Oedipus complex. In some ways I did — desperately wanting the love of my Mother and her belief in me, but I believe the whole Oedipus thing was also connected to the great literature I read and directly to the Oracle of Delphi. Oedipus is mentioned in the "Odyssey" and "Iliad" by Homer, but it doesn't appear my audience was connecting to that or what was going on inside my head (although I had no real way of explaining it). If my recitation, "Father I want to kill you, Mother I want to fuck you," made people research or inquire about "Oedipus", I would consider that a good thing.

There were a few Doors' songs I was really proud of, as I attempted to take the listener on a journey. I really can look back and say, "W.A.S.P., Texas Radio and the Big Beat" is a favorite. I feel it takes the listener on a very unique journey, and of course, I loved the Mexican radio stations that were, in fact, broadcasting

Jim Morrison & Michael Hutchence

through Texas in the 1950s and not subject to American regulations. The W.A.S.P. was a station at Florida State University when I attended, and these types of stations, college stations and those without regulations, were so much more interesting and unpretentious. I wrote the lyrics to that song in 1968, and I am very pleased it was placed on the last album we did together. There were certainly other songs with spoken words, but I love the way it is mostly spoken with a small amount of singing. I also had envisioned a man in a room with a microphone and machines possibly, speaking or talking on a recording in the years to come. W.A.S.P. is truly one of my favorite Doors' songs.

There has been much speculation about another song I wrote the lyrics to called "Five to One." It's important to say I did use the statistic from something I saw in the news, but once again, just different sentiments and strange scenes from my life permeated through the song. I do believe it's a very reflective song about young people in the late '60s but I also felt that, by 1970 or 1971, the whole feeling that song represented was indeed gone. It had a revolutionary feel in one way, and that whole ambience was gone in just about two years. Once again, this song is a collage of drunken ramblings reflecting where I was and things being said to me, and even things I heard on TV.

"Riders on the Storm" is also one of the best songs I believe I left behind. Did Billy Cook inspire it? Yes. I was always interested in making a film about a dangerous hitchhiker on a killing spree, and I did live at the time of the Zodiac killer, which captivated most Californians. Charles Manson really had no inspiration in this particular song. I was going to make that film about the hitchhiker, but "HWY" turned out to be much more subtle and obtuse. I certainly would not have made a film like the current slasher films filling American theaters. It would have been much more of a psychological trip, not a graphic blood fest. "Riders" was the last song I recorded with The Doors, so I consider it very special. It has a really incredible ambience, and this song was one I am really proud of.

There are lyrics in "Riders" I wish to comment about, starting with "Girl, ya gotta love your man," and goes on to say, "Take him by the hand, make him understand, the world on you depends, our life will never end." I now realize, I was without a doubt, writing this and singing it to the unidentified muse in my mind, heart and soul, who is my eternal soul mate. I sang this to her, for her, and I know this now because my world depended on no particular woman, and I certainly did not see a future with anyone with I was involved with on Earth.

I wanted to be needed by a woman, and I wanted to need her. I suppose I did a lot of role playing about that with my many girlfriends and conquests. Truthfully, I didn't really depend on any of them and none of them really made me understand very much. Their guilt trips, desire to be the one with me and their enabling of my alcoholism was certainly not what I needed. If they picked me off of the floor and tolerated my behavior, maybe just maybe, they were following my creed about allowing me to be who I was. But I think I needed one of them to look deep into my eyes and see my soul, to recognize the pain, and all the damage that was done to me early in my life, that I just couldn't shake. But, this never occurred. I wouldn't let them because they weren't the one. My eternal soul mate can and, I hope more than anything, will heal me. I am over my life as Jim Morrison, but I need her to show me true love and help me heal from the pain, sadness and the burden of regret.

I wrote lyrics to a song on "The Soft Parade," and I hoped it would indeed be a single released from that album but it just didn't make the cut. The song was called "Easy Ride," and I do mention "coda Queen be my bride." This was just a poem or lyrics I wrote, I'm not sure where they came from. I could not see the face of my twin flame, the one I wish to be my bride for eternity. I did see a woman with red hair, and as she is now on Earth, like my own hair, in the sun, her hair naturally has reddish streaks. I knew in the deepest parts of my soul and my mind, the woman I searched for had some sort of reddish hair. How could I have known that? Now I see her and know, especially when she was younger, her hair had naturally reddish highlights, and when my hair was in the sun, it also had reddish highlights. I wish I could tell you my songs were about certain women, but in truth, the muse was unidentified then. Now, she is all that matters to me, as I wait for her in this paradise (that has turned into a prison) until she returns.

Many people have speculated I also wrote "Love Her Madly" for a particular woman on Earth. In fact, Robbie Krieger wrote those lyrics, so perhaps it would be best to ask him who it was about. Robbie wrote great lyrics and never got enough credit for them.

The time on Earth I had with The Doors was really wonderful — and I mean in terms of working with Ray, Robbie and John and being in the presence of their rare and amazing talent. I am over The Doors on this side because, I needed to evolve, and staying in the past, is a sure way for that not to happen.

I do give the other three members of The Doors ninety percent of the credit for the group, and for myself, around ten percent. This was not an equal situation, I contributed less to the group than the other three members, but I still contend, The Doors were the *four* of us and that has to do with my understanding of energy dynamics, and elements of synchronicity mixed with quantum physics. It's just not a personal bias, but how I see things from this side with a greater, richer understanding of all past life events.

I realize there are those who condemn and criticize the other Doors for not stopping or making more attempts to squash my alcoholism. I really do wish they had been more direct with me about the disaster I was making of my life and the group, but, once again, given the context of the time we lived in, not much was known or openly discussed about alcoholism. One thing that was known, it was certainly not cool. Truth be known, I had a rare enzyme condition, which did allow me to drink quite excessively without any kind of adverse effects. After a certain point, however, the alcohol would hit me like the mother load from hell and it was all over. The enzyme condition, however, did not cause me to become an alcoholic nor did any addictive gene. What caused me to become an alcoholic was nothing more than, me. I caused myself to become one. Of course, it's easy to say it was the whole rock star trip and the excesses that accompany it. But I was already an alcoholic before I ran into Ray Manzarek on Venice Beach, he saw something in me that caused the whole thing to happen in the first place. My alcoholism was in the early stages at that point, and the fame and ego trip fueled it, but I could've put on the brakes at any given time. It was more difficult to stop the train wreck when I tried during the recording of "L.A. Woman" and later in Paris because, physically, I was experiencing dry heaves and shakes that were really not tolerable. The withdrawal seemed to be just about killing me, but I should've never have gotten to that point.

When looking back at Ray, Robbie and John, I've realized they didn't know how to handle old Jimbo. I brought many things in with the drinking, bad recording sessions, disappearing acts, and often times, the other Doors had no idea where I was or what was going on. I did not discuss my moves with them, or anyone really. One regret I have is that I feel I should have let them in more. I brought people to the studio they had every right to not want around during our sessions. I know I drove John Densmore practically into his own nervous breakdown with many of my maneuvers, and rightfully so. I was a handful, but what we did together, was really, really unique, and magical. I am grateful for the opportunities and experiences and am sorry I wasn't more a part of it.

I would've conquered my alcoholism during my time in Paris as my friend Michael McClure had done. Just a year later, things would've been very different in my life. I would not be one for Alcoholics Anonymous, and I am not here to criticize them, as I am aware of the help and hope they have given so very many. I simply buy more into the Universal Law of Attraction, which has been called many things and has been around since ancient Egypt. My perception is that if I stood up before a group of others and called myself an alcoholic, I would've remained one. I have labeled myself and to break the identity of alcoholism, I would have to change my mind set and the idea that I can't live without it. The so-called relapse is a very real event for many, but when I conquered alcoholism, I would not consider myself a recovering alcoholic. I would support the notion you are either recovered or not. Cancer can be removed from your body, darkness can be removed from your soul, and I believe, addictions can be removed from your life completely.

I would've been a different man at the age of 30 — if I had gotten there — and more developed and thoughtful by the age of 37. I believe you are on Earth to evolve, to grow, and to become better over time, like a fine wine. I was attempting to grow up in Paris. Addictions are basically an immature behavior. A part of

Jim Morrison & Michael Hutchence

kicking them for good is growing up and leaving behind the self-absorbed ego that is indeed part of every addict. Have you ever met a mature alcoholic or drug addict? I haven't.

Life *is* too much because as an addict, you *made* your life too much. It's all perception, and in my case, the pain from my childhood engulfed me, the lack of any true love in my life ravished me emotionally, and the alcohol became all there was to me. Once, I roamed the Earth and danced on fire, that's finished now, I have gone home, and now it's up to you to do your fire dance and find the answers I could not, because you still have the chance, you still have the time.

You are simply in a stage of your life, this isn't your entire life you are now living on Earth. For some reason, many can't or won't cherish the stage they are in, obviously I didn't. I see things from this side in a new, mature and evolved way, and I am still evolving. While I was on Earth, I had numerous paternity claims. I look at that now and feel a deep sadness, because while some of them were blatant shake downs for money, why did anyone on Earth want to have my baby? Did you believe an immature, confused, alcoholic man makes a good father to your child?

I want to say, unequivocally, and this will surprise many, I have no biological children on Earth, not one. If I did have one, I believe you would see a legal action taken against my estate and a payoff would have to be given if it were proven. There is a man on Earth using my last name who has been led to believe he is my son. Biologically, he isn't. I would've liked to have known him, because I actually feel some remorse over this, to be raised to believe a complete lie is pretty devastating.

I know I would not have been a good father or even a halfway decent one in the 27 and a half years I spent on Earth. An addict can never be a good parent unless they kick the habit and leave it behind forever. Your first love cannot be your child, no matter how much you try to compensate. I believed, before I left for Paris, having a child may help to force me to change. I now believe that was wishful thinking.

I know many women have claimed to have aborted my children. I will not go into the specifics of this, as it is a private matter, and I am not here to out any of the women because abortion is really not a happy affair. I will say, I was asked for abortion money quite often, and as it turns out, I was not the most fertile fellow on Earth. I could've had children, but it wasn't all that easy to make it happen. I will go on the record and say, Pamela Courson asked me for abortion money early on in our relationship a couple of times, yet she was never pregnant with my child. She actually got pregnant during one of her affairs and had a miscarriage. A child would have never come to us, that is not how it was to be.

I would've fathered two beautiful children with my eternal soul mate, and we would've had a girl and a boy. The souls of these two children chose us as parents, and of course, I went and messed the whole thing up. Those souls could have gone on to incarnate on Earth to others, but have chosen to stay on this side with their Dad and wait for their Mom to return home, and wait they do. There are souls often waiting for parents on this side, of children who returned home before the parents, or miscarriages, or even abortions. I was an open minded, free thinker and could never tell a woman what to do with her body, but my view on abortion has drastically changed. This is not because of religious dogma or when conception begins, but because a soul chooses you to nurture him or her and give them an Earth life. You have accepted this before you came to Earth and then you turn around and basically reject the soul of your son or daughter. While many of them do go on to incarnate to other parents, I now have met my son and daughter and could never bring myself to reject their souls. You will not be condemned for rejecting a soul or that young soul will not be punished, but what greater gift could you be given but a soul wanting to be born to you and loved and taught by you?

When my channel was first exploring this whole phenomenon of channeling me, I would send her to certain psychics or mediums who could validate things for her, because hearing it from another human being always seemed to help. I sent her to one in upstate New York and when I showed this man who I was, I came in with a little girl and the psychic told my channel that I was trying to relay something to her about this child and that she was my child. I often have shown up with my children to the real ones who have connected to me, as I love them beyond what I ever thought possible. I am sorry I didn't give them the life on

Earth they wanted, but they are willing to wait for their Mother and to give me the chance to be their Father. Your life with your children, those you brought to Earth and those you didn't, due to your choice or a disruption of nature, will often times be on this side for you. Maybe people can't picture Jim Morrison as a father, and on Earth, I know I would've been a bad excuse for one, at least until I got older and sober.

Unless you plan to do it on your own, women need to make better choices in who they allow to father their offspring. An addict is one of the worst possible choices, as he will never have the maturity level to be a good Dad or have the sacrificial nature you must have to really love your child fully. A child not having food and water is a tragedy, a horrible death sentence as they must starve to death, but a child having the necessities of life, but the absence of love, is the most deplorable and preventable tragedy there is.

Magic Carpet Ride

Dreams are weaving in your sun kissed hair,
You think you know me,
You do, the question is -

Do you want to?
Do you care?

You smell the scent of Patchouli around you,
but you don't know where it comes from,
You feel someone touching your neck,
I'm kissing it, I'll kiss you 'till you're numb

I sing to you while you sleep
deep into the night,
"You don't know what you can find,

why don't you come with me little
girl, on a magic carpet ride?"

You toss, You turn,
Finally so bothered, you turn on the light
You ask "Who's there?"
I say "It's me"
You look around "Who are you? Who's me??"

I can hardly hold back

"Your eternal soul mate, I'm gonna set you free"
You grow anxious
"Why should I believe you?
Get out of my house"

I start smirking and reply
"Sorry baby, I'm actually
Gonna be your spouse"

You look partially frightened
as you respond "What do you mean?
I don't know you"

It's time to break the news
"In the Shamans' Circle,
You'll be my bride,
with a feast of friends,
we're taking a magic carpet ride."

I have to take charge of this situation,
This is obsession woman, not infatuation
"Get ready, pack your things,
I'm kidnapping you,

by any and all means,
don't change that Victoria's Secret nightie,

Jim Morrison & Michael Hutchence

it's sweet, I'll take care of you,
don't worry baby, if you're hungry,
we'll stop and eat"

You seem rather compliant as you say
"I'd rather wear jeans and a sweater,
my man will be home soon,
should I leave him a letter?"

The thought of him makes me see red,
"Nope, I'll make you forget his name,
I'm taking you right from his bed"

I take your hand
as we fly through the stars,
to the moon, all around Saturn,
finally landing on Mars

We danced, we kissed,
We took it all the way,
We had a picnic on the moon
We committed to each other for eternity,

I gave her a ring,
She said "Jim, I have to go soon"

A sadness came over me,
A loss like no other,

Rebecca woke-up in the arms
of another lover
She thought it had all been a dream,
but on her wedding finger,
was an unusual amethyst and diamond ring

She thought maybe the man who laid
next to her gave it to her instead,

But when she took it off, it was engraved,
this was not all in her head.

Inside the ring it read "TO REBECCA,
FROM JIM, ETERNALLY YOURS"
Now my love knows, she has seen me before

—*channeled from Jim Morrison*

Truth

The Santa Ana winds
are kicking up again,
I get more restless, more insane,
I am encapsulated in a mad man's pain

I go from woman to woman,
They're running all the same - cold,
The one I go to the Bronson Caves with
needs to be bought and sold

She is not my eternal soul mate,
She is not my twin flame,

She's a loud lesson,
I don't love her, it's just a game
The game's not fun anymore,
She's a burden and a half,
She lives to annoy me,
She likes to have the last laugh

How come I don't see a thing
different or special in any single woman?

Jim Morrison & Michael Hutchence

I am the same with each,
give them permission to write,
Tell them to sing
They look at me like I am their Shaman
Why do they think I am here to teach?

They want me to release some magical
being within, Instead, I'll probably
just pass out from the whiskey, beer
but hopefully not the gin

I wish I could find her - the mystical
angel I know is for me,
She'd fill my voids,
end my pain,
Set this poor boy free

But she remains a great mystery
What do I do?
Where do I go?
I want to make a film,
I want to stop
all the pseudo romance,

Not sure how,
I feel like I am in a trance
I was obnoxious again
on the strip,

I was talking out of my ass,
giving people lip,

I never know where I'll wake,
But why do I wake?
Let me stay
on the Crystal Ship

A TALE OF TWO BROTHERS

I want to do film,
maybe record a few poems,
to find someone I really love

who will take this lush,
give him a bath
and a hairbrush,
cleanse him, purify me

Turn this wreck into beauty
I haven't found her,
The Santa Ana winds keep blowing,
Am I supposed to care
that one of them overdosed again?
Or that one says she is pregnant?

Don't they understand
it's pseudo-romance?
They never stood a chance…
I am not real, I cannot feel

—*channeled from Jim Morrison*

Jim Morrison & Michael Hutchence

CHAPTER 7
Other Voices: Notes on Vision

"I offer images- I conjure memories of freedom that can still be reached- like the Doors, right? But we can only open the doors, we can't drag people through. I can't free them unless they want to be free. Maybe primitive people have less bullshit to let go of, to give up. A person has to be willing to give up everything- not just wealth. All the bullshit that he's been taught- all society's brainwashing. You have to let go of all that to get to the other side. Most people aren't willing to do that."

—*Jim Morrison*

Jim Morrison & Michael Hutchence

SECTIONS:

I. To the Other Side

II. Who Told these Dead to Dance?

III. Mr. Mojo Risin

I. To the Other Side

by Francine Milano

Jim Morrison: "Good Morning, Francine. I am glad you decided to contribute to the book. You know how I feel about most so-called psychics. Only a handful of them are truly using their God-given gifts the way they are meant to, and a few of them have let me down personally in a big way by using their own self-serving greed about the common good. As I've told Jacquie, your gift has come with good intentions, and I am grateful for all the help you have given us."

During the process of this book, I was honored to personally connect with Jim Morrison, Michael Hutchence and others on the other side to confirm certain articles of information for the author. She is an excellent channel who some might consider to be a natural without formal training, when in fact, she was blessed to be trained straight from the source. While Jacqueline Murray is truly the chosen channel for both Jim and Michael, I feel privileged to have access to them. In getting to know Jim in particular, his energies were not what I would have expected from

Jim Morrison & Michael Hutchence

a spirit whose last existence here was as an alcoholic rocker with a hell of a reputation. In fact, in my first reading with the author, he came across as a gentle friend and frustrated writer named Jim. Although I felt anguish, nothing in his violent lifestyle came through to me. In his afterlife, Jim has grown like we all inevitably do as evolving souls, but

I learned a lot about how deep his life as Jim Morrison really was. There was an esoteric side to Jim that was reflected in his personal work, and there were many long-forgotten articles pointing to the fringe of the occultism. Even the name of the group had esoteric connections of which many are still not fully aware. For instance, it is widely accepted that the group's name, The Doors, was taken from the title of Aldous Huxley's book, "The Doors of Perception," which explored the effects of mind-expanding drugs, but it goes much further than this. The book title was taken from a quote out of William Blake's "The Marriage of Heaven and Hell." "If the doors of perception were cleansed, everything would appear to man as it is, infinite. For man has closed himself up, till he sees all things through narrow chinks of his cavern." This literary work was not only influenced by alchemy and mysticism, but, in fact, it was actually channeled material. It seems that Blake had more than just a fascination with esoteric topics. His work inspired Huxley, and in turn, Jim was inspired by them both. Jim was also very deep into his own philosophy. While it often showed in his lyrics and poetry, even he did not know how "plugged in" he really was. He most definitely could have been a more active medium if he had chosen to go down that path. In digging deeper into many things Jim said, wrote or experienced during his lifetime as Morrison, he had many connections to alchemy and metaphysics of which he wasn't even aware.

For a general overview of channeled material, Jim has asked that I speak to the readers about channeling and mediumship. I know there are many related books available – some good – others, not so much. I'm not here to name names, critique books or change the subject of this one. I'm here to offer some simplistic information about mediums and psychics, how the process of channeling works, and maybe even dispel a few myths along the way. This is a fascinating subject to many people, but the more you understand how it works, the more your personal perspectives might alter and improve the quality of your own life.

We all have spiritual gifts. How is that possible? We all have the ability to shape our lives through goals and the discipline to carry them out. Sometimes we sabotage ourselves for a variety of reasons, and other times, what we *think* we want isn't actually what was agreed to before we came here. Before you were born, you sat with your guides and chose a route that would best serve your growth and those around you in this lifetime. Their job is not just to protect you, but to serve. They will get you to the right place and time, often causing what we might call a coincidence, but it's your choice what to do with the situation presented when you finally get there. You do have the free will of choice, but if you go against what your original agreement was, you may feel the gut instinct that maybe this is wrong. We always have the power of free will to change our agreements, but our higher selves — a part of us who dwells with one foot in the spirit realm — really knows that most of the plans we already agree to for this lifetime are still the best ones for us, unless we had previous decisions that steered us off course completely. It is that inner conflict that can often cause the most severe form of human suffering on a personal level as well as for the masses. While we all get messages that go totally ignored for the most part, it's the higher self who helps us keep it together with the aid of our spirit guides.

Many people ask me what the experience is like. It really depends on how I choose to channel. For instance, I tried trance channeling where I allowed the use of my body for physical communication. Trance and physical mediumship is a dying art once very popular in Western Europe, especially in England, but it's not nearly as practiced today. It definitely wasn't my cup of tea. The experience was totally surreal. Imagine sitting in the back of a cab where you have not seen the driver's face and can barely make out his eyes in the rear view mirror. You can hear him talk, but he's not talking to you. You aren't sure where you are, where you're going and how long the ride will be. The experience might be different for others, but giving up total control was frightening for me. The types of channeling that have become second nature to me are through the senses. Clairvoyant and clairaudient (the ability to see and hear) along with clairsentient (feel and sensing with emotions) are the methods that seem to be well within my comfort zone. The experience, for me, may be very different than for someone else. I tend to see a fog in front of me, and I get pictures through haze. When it becomes clearer, I can only describe it in human terms as recalling a memory and repeating it to a client. In automatic writing, many can shut their eyes and just let the fingers fly without even worrying if their hand is even on the paper. My style is to hear or see each word or phrase as I write them down. Mediums don't always choose how their personal channeling experience is executed, but we all share the energy, awe and jubilation of the spirit world.

When I do a private reading, or even a gallery reading, it is truly an exchange of energy. We are not only connected to the other side, but to each other as well. When two people have a conversation, they are exchanging energy back and forth through the eyes. I've always wondered why we don't stare at lips and ears during a conversation, but perhaps the eyes really are the windows to the soul. The difference in connection to a person and a spirit is that when we connect to the other side, the energy exchange is a lot higher. The level of vibration needs to increase in comparison to a typical conversation by phone or in person, and if I were to describe it in physical terms, I would say this place is a couple of feet above my head where I need to direct my consciousness.

That's part of the aura, so I'm not really projecting or leaving the body in any way, just meeting *them* somewhere in the middle as they too need to come down a few notches for me. I suppose if they came all the way down to eye level, I really wouldn't be needed much because we'd all just walk around talking to them. What I am doing is raising my awareness to a higher level, and this is something most of us actually do in our sleep. It has been said that we go astral projecting everywhere when we sleep. This is simply not true for most of us. What we do though, is levitate just a little outside of our bodies. We naturally shift our awareness, and it is precisely there where you are connecting to your own spirit guides, loved ones and even divine entities. Conversations in our sleep are not always meant to be remembered, but the higher self has it all stored in a file for safe keeping. If we knew everything in a wakened state, then we would not need free will and just ask for instructions. What would be the point in our lifetime here if all the answers were simply given to us?

The real training comes in for those seeking the full experience in a wakened state. Underdeveloped mediums still have experiences they just don't give credit to. Many people channel music, poetry and even ideas for screenplays. Yes, they are talented, but where do all these fantastic concepts come from? Aren't we co-creators of our world? In every development class I teach, I love watching gifts unfold. Some come busting out of the gate while others go at a slower but steady pace, but it's the diverse talents that always amaze me.

There are many types of mediumship: trance channeling, hands-on healing, automatic writing, spirit art, music, and more. You may have noticed I left psychic abilities off the list. Being psychic is not always considered politically correct as having a rightful place in the mediumship category, though I'm still on the fence about the issue. To be intuitive (psychic) is to get your messages straight from the gut, so are you really raising your vibration and communication beyond yourself? Science certainly has not done nearly enough to satisfy our natural curiosity, and that's a whole other chapter, if not a book, of its own. Medium or psychic, not everyone in my classes go on to do readings. That's not why the gift was given to us all. The gift's main purpose is to stay connected to the giver and each other. It is a personal connection home to the God source from which we originate, and it also serves as a reminder that we are all plugged into one another as a single unit. Everyone's gift is as unique as the individual. My students blossom and find their own niche. Often times the biggest goal for them is to help them make better choices in life. For many, that's a huge, life-changing achievement. I would love everyone to realize that they have abilities beyond the physical and intellectual scope and start giving these dormant talents some attention. Even developed mediums know that development is a constant. The ultimate side effect of the journey is a new perspective on love and your relationship to God, the Universe and everyone in it.

The question I think I'm asked most often is *what's the key?* Many people are immediately sorry they asked when I reveal the key ingredient. The dirty word is meditation. When I say that for the first time in class, some people look at me in total despair, as if I told them to get down and give me fifty push-ups. With car keys in hand, they seem ready to leave right then and there. Even the many people who think they can't or give up because it didn't work the first, second or even third time, need to consider that there are many forms of meditation. I always encourage people to try all of them, even if you make great strides from the beginning. More often than not, the trouble lies in quieting down the inner blabber that resides within us all. You know — the one that says, "What noise? I *am* being quiet!" Once this is achieved, you can make room for the more distant voices to come forward. Channeling can be defined as funneling of energy, and aren't we all made of energy no matter what we embody? What we are achieving as we develop is how to control what we funnel into our personal space.

Meditation brings forth the inner guide that will lead us there. Aside from the more popular guided CDs, which I certainly recommend for disciplining the journey and not drifting off to la-la land, there are also yoga meditations for centering the self, scrying (staring into water, candles, mirrors) to calm the mind, silent meditations for the intermediate levels, and one of the most overlooked and important forms is prayer. This is a tool like a cell phone to the other side — our gift in its purest form. Our direct connection to God and any entity dwelling in the divine realm through prayer is often taken for granted and abused. Whether you write in a journal, meditate on it or even sing it, you are heard on all levels. Every thought is a prayer in fact, so you must be careful what you ask for because you are the co-creator or your world, and the ethers take your requests seriously. But do consider the power of prayer and meditate! Also, please remember to ask for protection for your guides before any type of meditation. Opening yourself up to the metaphysical is like opening a door in which one can come or go. You must have a guard on duty.

The number two question I find myself answering repeatedly is *how fast can I do it?* The truth is that there are really no short cuts, at least that I know of. This truly depends on the individual and how well they are working with their spirit guides. Guides are not only here to offer direction and protect us, but they are also here to teach us and help us learn from ourselves and others.

When we succumb to our path instead of trying to fight it every step of the way, the journey is easier and the path is smoother.

This is not to mean that everything falls into place at the snap of your fingers. Most accomplished mediums will agree with me that it wasn't easy to stand in the shoes they wear now. We all put our dues in, just as we do with most things we earn here in the physical. Another determining factor is where we begin. We all start at different points of development for many reasons, such as the challenges we've been through in the physical world which can set us back from the start, and we all bring emotional scars to the table when we're finally ready to make changes. We tend to move at our own pace on the astral plane, just as we move differently here on Earth in our physical bodies. There is one last point I'd like to make on what can hold us back in development as well as in life: INTENTION. This word means everything to our personal growth and to the future advancement of our *oneness*. When we finally realize that we are all connected, we can all begin to heal as one. If it is not your intention to use your gifts for the betterment of yourself *and* mankind, then your development will either not progress or it will move in a perverse direction. No one can grow a beautiful garden with tainted seeds. This is not a self-serving gift that God has given us.

Like many other mediums, I might get some information to help me make good choices for my life circumstances, but I can't do my own readings beyond an occasional card spread to help me resolve a particular issue. Even the seasoned professional needs to go to others, just as a stylist would not cut their own hair beyond a quick snip here or there. So, you would think that a medium should know just who to call, wouldn't you? It's far from the truth.

Although I've had the advantage to know others in the industry, I've struggled many times in choosing someone from whom to get a reading, just like most people. Add the advantage of the internet and advances in communications technology, and today's choices are overwhelming. No longer are we limited to the lady in the neighboring town who sees people in her parlor. I had a unique opportunity this year to do some hands-on research and to share some interesting information with you about what to look for when shopping for a reading.

One thing I found recently was that readings are not as inexpensive as they used to be, so most people don't want to give someone a test drive anymore. They want to be sure they aren't throwing away their hard-earned money. I had gone a few years without raising my own rates, and in looking at the fees of the industry in general over the last couple of years, I was amazed at the hikes. I don't think it's because I've been under a rock. I believe that Hollywood has given some new credibility and heightened interest to the industry over the last few years that the charlatans have taken away for ages. Shows like *Medium* and *Ghost Whisperer,* as well as many ghost hunting shows that are gaining popularity have shown there is really a mainstream interest in the metaphysical and the paranormal worlds. Fame is available to many mediums now — good or even mediocre — with their own shows and books that are flying off the shelves. It all leads to supply and demand, and reading rates have doubled in some cases in a few short years. The problem to solve is how to get a quality reading and not waste your money. I've found there's no easy answer to this dilemma. One can only take certain precautions that might put the odds in their favor.

My goal of the research was to gain helpful knowledge about locating the best, yet I found myself at square one – despite the education I didn't quite expect. How *do* we make an informed choice? There is no scientific formula to the answer, but here are three important factors to consider when narrowing the field.

1. Referrals are one of the most powerful tools we have. Ask those around you if they know anyone they would recommend. Much of a genuine medium's clientele has come from friends and family, so if you're happy with your reading, don't forget to pass the word on yourself. It will be appreciated by your friends as well as the medium.

2. Look for credentials beyond certificates and fluffy claims. Most of them are useless to measure talent, while their bio and scheduled events might say much more. Even if they don't do a lot of events on a regular basis, see if they have ever done anything with the media or other events that someone of lesser talents couldn't even do. How long have they been reading? Do they have

endorsements? If their literature or web page is not revealing enough, don't be afraid to make inquiries. A genuine medium or psychic will be very happy to answer your questions, and those who aren't may have something to hide. 3. Rely on your own gut feelings. We are all mediums! Of course you should apply this to all areas of your life where things may not be black and white. In the gray areas, go with your instincts. There is always *something* talking to you. You just need to be still and listen to it.

Now more than ever, we must be careful, as this field continues to get saturated. Channeling, in any form, is an art that won't be going out of style any time soon, but I do agree with Jim Morrison on many points. There just aren't enough true mediums here on Earth. To the genuine ones, we must offer cheers and learn from them whenever possible. Mediums are leading the way to a self-discovery and a world within that has yet to be tapped into. Don't be afraid to discover yourself.

EDITOR'S NOTE: This conversation took place the night before Marjorie Augustine gave Jacqueline Murray an in-person psychic reading in 2006!

Jim = Jim Morrison

Jac = Jaqueline Murray

Jim: Before we commence channeling tonight, I would like to speak to you about what's going on tomorrow.

Jac: Good because, honestly, I am a little nervous about it.

Jim: Nervous about what, Jacquie? You'll find out I'm real? That this (pause) is real?

Jac: Maybe. I've never called a psychic in my area. It's very strange for me to ask for a psychic reading and I know you have come through for me to others, but that was by phone, this is in person.

Jim: Well then, let me show you. You don't know this woman, and she knows nothing about you. She can't possibly know I am going to show up or what I intend to say, and maybe after this, you can stop all the doubts and second, third and fourth-guessing yourself and we can get on with our work.

Jac: You seem angry with me, Jim, I'm sorry. I'm on Earth in a human body, and maybe it's easier to believe and accept if another human being communicates it to me.

Jim: There you go again, haven't we been through this, woman? I selected Marjorie, you didn't find her by accident, because there aren't any accidents, Jacquie. I believe she is clear enough and can get up high enough in vibration for this to work tomorrow, barring any disaster. This should help this process along. I can't always promise you the psychic will be able to pick me up, honey. They have to work from your energy, their own energy, and you have about a football field of us around you. I have to work hard to get up over the others who want to speak to you, including some of your relatives. Is it necessary to make me work so hard? Haven't I given you enough validations?

Jac: I apologize, this is an experience I can't really share with hardly anyone, as you know.

Jim: But people around you are noticing things, Jacquie, and they have been telling you they know something is going on around you.

You can hardly keep this a secret forever. You are going to have to come out of the closet. Are you ashamed to be channeling me?

Jac: No, I am very honored and humbled to be trusted with your valuable words and can hardly believe God blessed me with such a gift.

Jim: Thank you, as I am honored to have you as a channel. I've gone through so much to get to you Jac, eventually you'll find out.

There are no coincidences and nothing is random. This has been in the works for quite some time.

Jac: Thanks for sharing, too bad no one told me until it all came crashing in.

Jim: If I come through to Marjorie Augustine tomorrow, and you get your validations delivered by another human being, one you have never met, one who knows nothing about you or me or this channeling we are doing, will it make it easier for you?

Jac: Yes.

Jim: Then I'll do the best I can honey. It's time to rock 'n' roll.

Jac: Ok, but I have free will, so if I don't want to continue for some reason, what happens? Do you jump to a new channel?

Jim: It's not that simple, Jacquie. I told you about this before. You are a member of my primary soul group, and we have a unique relationship.

Jac: One I can't seem to remember or recall.

Jim: Not now, you can't, but when you step out of that Matrix, you'll get it, woman. I have spent a great amount of energy to make this happen with you, I can't just, as you say, jump to another channel.

What the hell do you think this is, like your remote control on your television?

Jac: Ok, I hear you.

Jim: Would you like to get to work? This is the appointment time you gave me.

Jac: Ok, let's go.

11. Who Told these Dead to Dance?

"Death makes angels of us all & gives us wings where we had shoulders smooth as raven's claws."

—*Jim Morrison, American Prayer*

by Marjorie Augustine

    A conversation with dead rock stars? Can it hardly be true? What benefit does this book offer? Jacqueline Murray has been offered a rare and accurate glimpse into the afterlife through conversations with several well-known friends. Many psychics and mediums have claimed to channel famous disembodied Spirits and have had marginal success in representing those Spirits.

    As a medium and teacher of the mystical connections to the world of Spirit, I have been honored to validate and observe this undertaking. I have been very grateful to be part of this unfolding story between Jacqueline and her Spirit friends, Jim Morrison and Michael Hutchence.

    My relationship with Jacqueline began in the winter of 2006 when she called upon me to do a reading for her. I was asked to travel to her café to do the session, and we agreed upon a time and date. I felt nothing extraordinary in our correspondence and thought nothing more about it until the day I was to travel to her shop. In the car on the way there I was concentrating on driving and was startled to hear a voice out of nowhere that said, "Hello, I'm Jim." I looked over to my passenger seat to see a full apparition of a man who looked slightly familiar to me, with long, wavy brown hair and friendly, gleaming, smiling eyes. I was taken aback by the presence and told him, "Jim, I am not working yet, and this is my quiet time before the session. You will need to go. Come back when I am ready for the reading." He obliged with a smile, and when it came time for the reading, he returned. I was given such wonderful affirmations from the Spirit Jim and his friend Michael that I felt honored that they were so clear and precise. I remember being told during the reading that Jim and Michael were speaking to Jacqueline and that she was a medium as well, she doubted it, but she was, in fact, a medium.

They told me that they had been dictating a book to her and that she would write this book about the afterlife and other spiritual concepts that they would share with her. I remember thinking how remarkable the session was in that they had been very specific about why they had chosen Jacqueline to write the book. As I recall, they had told me that, like in the car, I had told Jim to go away and that most working mediums would have done the same. They wanted Jacqueline for her purity of heart and intent.

I remember Jim being very clear about directing Jacqueline to write at specific times, and she confirmed the details of this with ease and acceptance. I did not know until months later, that the friendly Spirit named Jim was, indeed, Jim Morrison. It was also revealed to me that Jacqueline would proceed with the plans to publish this book upon completion.

Jim Morrison and Michael Hutchence both have very unique Spirit signatures. Jim, who came to me, has a very intentional, high-strung and somewhat demanding energy. He can be somewhat difficult to work with at times. He told me he has only come through to a handful of people with limited contact. He felt he needed to practice, since he was going to be giving material to Jacqueline to channel into a book. He did channel to one other medium named June from California. He told me he had given her a lot of information about his death, and she got some of the same facts that Jacqueline did, which are completely opposite to what each and every previously written book about Jim Morrison had stated. This is important, because he says that his life and his death were very different from how they had been portrayed, even by those closest to him. I have heard of many instances where mediums have claimed to be channeling Jim Morrison, and have charged outrageous amounts of money to say he is doing this or that, and has some mundane message for one of his fans. It is not to say that Jim wouldn't have something to say to one of his fans, but that he is better off appealing to them en masse, because he can reach so many with much less effort. Jim had explained to me that from the time he began contacting Jacqueline, she would become his sole Earth channel.

I remember during our past sessions when Jacqueline would grimace at the idea of this, but it is most certainly true. She came to learn the validity of many of Jim's and Michael's predictions. The greatest of which has come in the form of this book. Jim had an inner knowledge of a soul mate that he was hoping to find. He knew she existed, and he kept trying to find her. He had visions of her when he had been in altered states, and this was something that was both a blessing and a curse to him. It left Jim feeling empty inside, because he knew he hadn't found her. And there were times he carried anger for everyone around him, and yes, this included God. Jim told me he simply wanted to feel whole and complete and that unless God would unify him and his soul mate, he was lost.

Jim kept me informed of his soul mate situation and had told me that he made contact with her: Rebecca, that's her name. He told me he wouldn't divulge more information about her, because, while he knows the truth of the situation, she is yet unaware of the full scope of who she is in relation to him. He thought she might find it strange if some Spirit showed up out of nowhere to announce their everlasting love tie and well, by the way, I used to be known as Jim Morrison. He had made some initial contact with her and is protecting her privacy about the whole situation. I don't blame him as I could only imagine what type of controversy it would bring about in her life. He tells me he waits for her return to heaven and that until that time, he has begun a spiritual project that he hopes will be able to expand in his collaboration with her.

Jim told me his soul's desire is to help people know that there is more to life than meets the eyes. You (your soul, you) will one day transition into the energetic resonance of Spirit. You will be received into the glorious state of union that is Christ Consciousness.

There are a myriad of ways you can express your true gift and use it to better humankind. This is the way he is choosing to do it. This book is his gift to you. Michael Hutchence's Spirit signature is very distinct from Jim Morrison's. Michael's energy is more laid-back. Michael has a dignified essence that comes across in both his demeanor and his teachings. I found it interesting that both of these rock stars had died prematurely and had been objectified and mystified. They could not be more different in how they present themselves through spiritual contact. Michael made it clear, in his messages to me, that he has been lied about in the same manner as Jim has been.

Now it's time to pretty much reveal the truth, for the first time, about how he lived his life and how he died. He made me aware of the fact that he has come through to other psychics previously, not to channel his story but to try to communicate with his brother, Rhett. Michael is very much the perfectionist, and he wanted to make sure he could clearly communicate with Jacqueline. He had instituted a field of practice, as channeling a whole book versus a short appearance is quite different for a spirit.

Michael had, on one occasion, explained to me his understanding of the condition known as eternal soul mates; some refer to this as twin flames. This is the connection Jim Morrison spoke of when he mentioned his eternal love, Rebecca. Eternal soul mates have an energetic and romantic bond forged from the very breath of God which gave the souls life. They are the complete balance of yin and yang energy. They exist with and for one another. The purpose of their existence is to create a harmonious and peaceful connection to their world. Attaining a high level of energy allows them to reunite and then present themselves to the whole of soulkind to work in service to the creative force we call God. Michael Hutchence wanted us all to understand that Jacqueline is part of his and Jim's soul group, and that this is why he and Jim chose her to write this book. They have known her in many lifetimes. She is a soul group member to both of them.

Michael told me there would be fans and critics who would not agree with any of these claims, and to that point, he has emphasized his desire to share the truth as he knows it now. He understands that not everyone will agree with these teachings, nor accept them, but asks that we try to have an open heart, for that is the very key to learning the secret of life, Love.

As a witness to the unfolding of this journey that includes Jacqueline Murray, Jim Morrison and Michael Hutchence, I feel there is a true sense of serendipity here. I sense in my heart and soul that the truth which resides in these writings will be seen and hope that the intent with which the book has been written will find its way to you all. My hope for you is happiness and God's love!

Many Blessings!

III. Mr. Mojo Risin'

"As I look back...over my life...i am struck by post cards...ruined snapshots...faded posters...of a time...I can't recall."

—*Jim Morrison*

by Marjorie Augustine

Part of the reason that Jim chose me to work with Jacqueline is because I could relate to and subsequently relay the painful experiences he had in his life. During the process of receiving psychic information, the Medium must have a frame of reference in order to accurately decipher the message coming from the Spirit, because I believe it is difficult to do a reading for someone on a subject or understand symbols on a specific subject, if you have no point of reference. The brain will have no way of receiving or interpreting the symbolism into something you can understand, let alone relay to a client. In the case of Jim Morrison, he knew I could relate to his suffering and pain surrounding the subjects of his addiction and abuse.

You see, I tried to escape many things in my life, including the calling of my psychic abilities through the use of drugs and alcohol. I had tried to escape the many realities of my life, childhood sexual abuse, rape, disownment, a lost pregnancy at age 18 and psychic abilities that caused me extreme shyness and social anxieties. Alcohol and drugs were a perfect escape for me. They were dependable and accessible. I was a full blown alcoholic before I turned twenty-one. I just sort of drank my way through my early twenties, and before I knew it, I had hit rock bottom. I had lost my family, my self-respect, my job, my relationship, my driver's license, any of the real friends I had ever had and any spiritual connection that I can recall. I had nowhere to go but up.

I found sobriety at 25 and started to explore spirituality. For 11 years I pieced my life back together, believing that I would forever suffer from alcoholism. This all changed for me during an enlightening exchange with Jim during the summer of 2007. I have been cured/healed spiritually, and I am no longer an alcoholic. Jim wanted me to talk to you all about this so that he could share his highest truths. Jim asked me to talk about his abuse, his alcoholism and his relationships.

Jim told me that he was abused as a child. This was a very painful memory for him to share with me, but he wanted to share this experience because he knows how frequently this type of situation affects young people, still today. There is such a stigma that surrounds sexual abuse that so many young people are lost within its secretive world, and he desperately wants people to know that he was abused twice before he left high school — once by a family friend and once by a mentor.

Jim Morrison had witnessed a terrible accident when he was four years old, as many of you already know. It set a pattern for him of disassociating with his pain and holding a silent vigil for it at the same time. When Jim was victimized at the age of twelve by his first abuser, he solidified his belief that life was about suffering.

His family friend had robbed him of his innocence, and then Jim suffered the further insult of sharing his experience with his mother who chose, not only to disbelieve him, but to alienate him and force him to believe he was dark and strange. As a result, Jim turned to books, philosophy and ideas. This was a place where he felt safe.

Another four years would pass before Jim would meet "Daniel," a man ten years his senior. Jim met this man in a bookstore and befriended him. This friendship was important to him at the time because Jim had never connected with kids his own age. His peers were not into the same books he read nor had they heard of the philosophers he talked about. One of the alluring things about his mentor, "Daniel," was that he knew so many interesting things. This was the friendship Jim had waited for his entire young life. It all went awry the night "Daniel" invited Jim back to his apartment, held a knife to Jim's throat and forced him to perform a sex act on him.

Jim's life was turned upside down yet again. His sorrow went to a whole new level. He began to believe that he was in some way attracting this type of experience. He had begun to feel abandoned by the people who were supposed to protect and guide him. He knew he couldn't turn to his parents since he had already done this once and had been chastised and blamed for his horrific and traumatizing experiences. He then decided he wanted to be numb.

Isn't this a common reaction from children who are obviously unequipped emotionally to deal with the violent and perverted ways that adults rob them of the very essence of their childhood? Jim explained to me that what was most puzzling to him was that the abuse would happen twice. He couldn't help but to surmise that he must be doing something to bring this on. This was where Jim Morrison's life took a tragic turn. He turned his back on his own pain and began, instead, to seek oblivion. He began to drink alcohol. When he got drunk for the first time, he felt the power from which he had been separated. This was his first brush with the seductive allure of being "turned off" completely.

He became very comfortable in the booze-induced haze that would become a major part of his life. Jim became an alcoholic. Alcoholism is often quoted as being a chronic disease characterized by the individual's impaired control over their own drinking, a preoccupation with alcohol, the use of alcohol despite adverse social and physical consequences, and distortions in thinking. Jim shared with me his very serious association with each of these behaviors. Jim also says that alcoholism remains very misunderstood. Not many health care providers or spiritual leaders have related to the fact that alcoholism is more than a physical disorder or disease. It is a spiritual depletion.

Jim told me he chose me because I can relate to his experiences enough to translate them for you. He explained that he was sick and broken inside. He was unable to see past his own suffering to really connect with the people who entered, and in some cases, stayed in his life.

He said he especially had a difficult time maintaining his relationships with women. He said that because he was so broken, they wanted to take care of him and fix him. He said it was easier sometimes to let them try, because he was unable to be reached.

He was weak and he fell into patterns of behavior and attention seeking because of feeling so empty. Everything he did in his life was an attempt to fill the hole he felt inside. He just wanted to be loved, to be truly loved, and he couldn't do it. He couldn't accept love in his life and in his heart, because he didn't love himself. If he did, he wouldn't have allowed himself to become so deteriorated – inside and out. He wasted away. The thing is, he wanted so badly to be different and later in his life, the fame was a huge illusion to him. He couldn't believe that people actually cared for him, and he hated it because he knew inside that if they really knew how broken he felt, they would turn on him. Fame was fleeting and it meant nothing!

He had disdain in some ways for his own fans and the women who loved him, because he was a sham. He was lifeless inside towards the end. He used escapism, drugs and alcohol to feel numb. He didn't have to think about how much hurt he had inside, the things he had done, the things he said, the way he felt for people who were around him, the anger, or the fear. It was a downward spiral. Jim sadly admitted to me one night that the best sexual encounter he had was with two L.A. strippers. He had slipped so far away from any real emotion that being with women who actually cared for him or wanted to care for him, exhausted him. The two strippers he had found in L.A. wanted nothing from him. He could let his hair down and be uninhibited. He wasn't that drunk that night, as he just had a few beers, and it was the best sex he had in his life. He told me it was very important to include this to show his emotional attachments to women weren't really deep or strong.

He was so far gone in his alcoholism that his deepest sexual connection came from a mere tryst. He told me this was a sad testament to the quality of his life as a rock star. He laughed when he told me he really did have a thing for strippers. He said they were so cool in the way that they (and most other types of sex workers) can simply let you be who you are, as messed up as you are, and can make you feel like you aren't a monster. Everyone deserves that. An added piece of information Jim shared with me was that as an adult, he had two sexual encounters with male sex workers. In both of these instances, Jim was drunk. He was attempting to sort out his residual questioning surrounding his sexual identity. Jim had, since the time of his molestation and sexual attack, been feeling as if he had done something to attract these experiences and needed to follow through with being on the giving rather than the receiving end of a homosexual encounter.

Jim told me that the graphic nature of both of these experiences were not pleasant to remember. Jim further added that he felt the comments made to him by his Mother had left him festering inside for most of his young adult life, and he needed a way to end the torturous ambiguity he had about his sexual identity. Jim was not gay. He made it clear to me that while he had been afflicted by these attacks, he was, in fact, a heterosexual male. Jim had not sought to attract the initial encounters, nor did he wish to live in the agony of wondering if he was gay. Jim had not wanted anyone to know about this, and he told me there was only one person who did, his friend and lawyer, Max, who, in fact, had to deal with one of the prostitutes who wanted to blackmail Jim after their liaison. Jim explained to me that his sexual problems, in addition to his alcoholism, left him feeling so empty and as if he really had little for which to live. He knew he was so straight, yet he felt so disconnected from the women he had been with as well.

Jim explained to me that he did feel like a monster most of the time. He felt trapped, not loved. He felt abandoned, not loved. He felt crazy and depressed and alone, not loved. He wanted to feel loved, but nothing he did really brought that about because he hated himself inside. He is saying it was so easy to carry an aloof and detached demeanor on the outside because it would appear he had everything and because he had fame. But you know, his fame in some ways was an armor he could not shed, and it kept him from allowing anyone in or letting himself out. He didn't like who he had grown into because when he was young, he didn't feel so dark and weird. Jim said he became what he considered strange, and he tried to just hide, in plain sight. Jim told me he was always pretty much a vagrant, and, he said, don't let anything fool you about the fact that he was a nomad. He couldn't put down roots...he felt damaged. Drunks, especially the damaged kind, don't put down roots.

This is my story too...just like Jim's. Molested, raped, drunk, druggie, a lost child, no stability. I hid in my strangeness. I hid for a long time, in plain sight. I have carried pain, and what Jim showed me is that I have let it carve me into a sensitive and compassionate woman. I have chosen to take all of the things that I drew into my life, and use them to help others. Jim is saying that so many people carry pain and that this pain is what transforms us. Alcoholism, abuse, negative deeds, lies, tragedy...we can overcome it. Often times, we cannot control the terrible things that are perpetrated against us, and sometimes the people who are supposed to guard and protect us, fail. They fail miserably. They will hurt us, abandon us, forget us and hold us back. They can and do abuse us, rape us and refuse us the dignity of human existence. We will often walk down a path of self-destruction and do worse things to ourselves than someone else ever could.

Jim says that he wants his pain and his suffering to have done some good. He wants his story to be passed along so that others may benefit from it. He wants to express his desire to encourage people who are trapped in the cycle of abuse. It may have happened long ago, it may be happening now, it may be that you too have decided to seek oblivion and are abusing yourself now with alcohol, drugs or even by recreating the cycle by abusing others. He wants you to know you can heal from this. You can shout louder than the pain, you can enlist the help of anyone who will listen. You can be bigger than the fear. Alcoholism can be defeated. It can be healed – completely cured. God can remove this depletion and fill it with something larger — LOVE. Abuse can be replaced with something larger, LOVE.

His message is simple but profound. Don't let your pain wither you. Don't let your circumstances diminish you: scream, pray, open yourself to the fear, talk to your soul, take your own hand and walk towards the light, let God fill the emptiness of your existence with joy and peace. Your life begins now. Use this moment to seek a different ending. Don't go with the alcohol. Don't do the drugs, don't abuse yourself, your senses, or your fragile body.

Your spirit is eternal. Jim has shown me that we recreate our lives every moment, and with each new step is a chance to let go of the past that haunts us. Don't give up, don't give in. The things that define us are not permanent, they are fleeting, and the only thing that really matters is what you aspire to be. You have a unique opportunity to lay the burdens of your pain at the feet of God. God can handle it, believe me. You wouldn't be giving him anything he can't handle.

Jim says we all have a story. They tend to be very similar. We all want love, we all have pain, we all search for something, we all feel alone, and we are ALL connected to each other. Seek healing, and accept love. Don't settle for anything less! Jim wants me to tell you that it is important to question every aspect of your life, your beliefs, your actions, your feelings, and to seek to heal those aspects of yourself that bring you pain. It is something you want to do before you pass on to the other side of life. The physical body will inevitably pass away, but the spirit lives on, intact. If you have unresolved pain and suffering, you will carry it with you to the divine realm, where you can continue to heal. Jim knows, because he is working on all of this now. He is saying that no issue, problem or pain will just dissolve. We all are existing in accordance to a higher law, which in essence says that we are responsible for our own actions and that there is no heaven or hell. Our own conduct leads to our rewards or negative situations.

In this sense it would be easy to understand that heaven is a state of our own contentment and hell a state of our own discontent. Each soul makes it so for themselves and so begin now to seek healing and to seek happiness in balance to harm no other.

Jim is working on developing the qualities of his soul. He is awaiting the return of his eternal soul mate, and he feels he will be most able to heal once she is reunited with him in the divine realms. Each soul has the choice as to how to make his/her own conditions of happiness. Jim wanted you all to know that you have the choice to be happy, beginning now. The cultivation of faith and knowledge leads to serenity and peace of mind. If you know what you believe, then under any circumstances, even the most sorrowful conditions, you can find peace. Jim is seeking to be fully healed and enlightened. Jim wanted me to close with the sentiment that we often feel small, broken and alone, but we are not. We are on a path of evolution. Open your eyes to possibility. You can begin your healing now.

Many Blessings!

Jim Morrison & Michael Hutchence

CHAPTER 8

Blood in the Streets in the Town of New Haven.

"Most middle-class whites have no idea what it feels like to be subjected to police who are routinely suspicious, rude, belligerent, and brutal."

—*Benjamin Spock*

Jim Morrison & Michael Hutchence

A TALE OF TWO BROTHERS

There are many myths I would like to dispel about my arrests and the police brutality I was subjected to. My civil rights were actually violated several times by American police officers. When I saw a police officer, or anyone in an authoritarian type of uniform, I saw my Father. Granted, I would've been a psychiatrist's dream patient if I would have fully realized the truth about how most everything transcended back to my childhood.

New Haven, Connecticut, brought fascism to me personally for the very first time, outside of the home I was raised in. It was surreal at the time. "New Haven" occurred the day after my 24th birthday, and birthdays were always depressing, downtrodden events in my life. Years later, I would spend my last two birthdays with my poetry, feeling that was more productive and meaningful than reliving my childhood birthdays. I had one really awful childhood memory that occurred on a birthday and I thought that maybe now that I was Jim Morrison, the rock star, my birthdays would improve. But it appears my emotional state was still that of a 10-year-old child on that date. I didn't have true love, family or anyone that was all that close to me on my 24th birthday either. The night before, on my actual birthday, we played Troy, New York, and I have to say, it was the worst experience I had connecting to an audience since The Doors began. It was similar to being in a glass booth, banging on it and yelling loudly, and no one hearing me. It was a terrible, suffocating feeling and it left me in a dark, dark mood before entering New Haven the next night.

It was better to play for five people watching us at the London Fog than the show in Troy.

Girls were always backstage, of course, and on this night in New Haven, I felt like I needed a girl. A pretty little college co-ed was hanging out with me, and we couldn't seem to get any privacy.

We went into the shower room. I was just talking to the co-ed, and we kissed. The police presence was very visible and while this had been debated, the fascist police officer who came into the shower stalls did not know who I was at all. The co-ed and I were fully clothed, and there was no oral copulation or anything close to it going on when the police busted in.

It has been repeatedly stated that I was belligerent to the officer, Lt. Kelly. I actually attempted to identify myself, but upon his initial reaction of not caring whatsoever about what I had to say, I got angry. The cop assumed I was a hippie. Supposedly, I just started swearing at him, but I tried to speak to him and straighten it out. That was completely useless, since he was a man who beat you down first and asked questions later. The officer actually swore at me first, but I did engage in using some profanity in retaliation, which was plain stupidity. I was not aware that New Haven had a sizable record of police brutality, and when I began this little exchange with the fascist cop who would have rather have been anywhere else than at the hippie concert, I got maced in the face and it burned like a motherfucker.

My eyes were stinging and tears were running down my face. Curtain time was getting close, and there was some question as to whether I could go on that night or not. I tried to get it together as quickly as I could, but I was fuming. My eyes were still burning like a brushfire in the Santa Ana winds. I wasn't arrested at this point, in fact, I was apologized to when the fascist cop learned I was the main event.

During "Back Door Man" I decided to talk about the incident of being maced. It was because I was still pissed off, and for the first time, I had an audience to recite a diatribe to in front of concerning my outrage. I thought, and still do, what happened to me in the shower stall was bullshit. The girl and I were barely even making out, fully clothed when the cop came in, and there was nothing provocative about the scene, and I belonged backstage. We always improvised, and I didn't plan to go into my rant in the concert that night, but it just came out. I merely pointed them out, the police, the authority, and all hell broke loose. I wasn't at all aware I was pointing out the existence of these brutal, unfair fascists. All the cities we were playing were melting together. I could basically tell when I wasn't in Southern California or New York City, and that was about it. Obviously, my story during "Back Door Man" was not well received, and I not only got arrested on stage (which I had not planned at all), but I received a terrible fucking beating and no one knew how bad it was once I got to the police station.

I thought I was going to die that night, but I took it like a man. Every time I stood up to an authority figure, mind you, I was standing up to my Father. I couldn't do it or didn't do it in real life, so this was my way of compensating. My arms were held back, and I was kicked and thrown down steps. When I fell close to the police cruiser, I was kicked in the ribs repeatedly. My kidneys were actually bruised from the beating, and this was prior to entering the police station. There were witnesses outside the venue, and they had every right to fear for me.

Down at the station, the beating continued. And while I was on the floor, unable to get up, I was spit on and one fine police officer took the liberty of urinating on me. It was not only humiliating, but I am sure this was almost typical behavior of the police in New Haven at the time. After all, I was anti-establishment, and, God forbid, I pointed out their existence. I was lucky to have been bailed out when I was, because I am sure it would've gotten a lot worse.

I could trance out during a beating as not to connect very much to the pain, and this is what I did. I had learned this from childhood, but the next day, the physical pain and bruises were pretty disturbing. In fact, if you saw me with my clothes off, I was covered in bruises from New Haven.

It was a pretty severe beating, and I felt it for a long time, but tried to downplay it to those around me. It was totally degrading, but all it did was anger me and that anger turned inward and became depression. It only fueled my drinking binges. I felt like my Father had beaten me down again, and once again, I was powerless. There were fans waiting to get me out of jail, and I can tell them now, thank you. Because you were a voice, and if I had stayed any longer, my career may have ended that awful night in New Haven. New Haven was much more significant than has been told. It wasn't so much that I was literally, the first U.S. performer arrested on stage, but it started a very public unraveling of the very private childhood drama of Jim Morrison.

Perpetual Notions

As I read in the old bookstore
My Rimbaud and the works of Jung,
A possessed looking woman sat down beside me,
I got up to leave, I was done

She asked me to wait a moment,
Her eyes were blue like the ocean,
She said "you don't know, I'm a mystic
and I need to speak to you of perpetual notions"

I looked at her in true amazement,
Her eyes hypnotized my soul,
She said "Open the Kabbalah,
read the book of Zorah, in order to become whole."

I told her I was done reading for the day,
There was somewhere else I needed to be,

She smiled wistfully, her blue eyes darkened
And she said "Jim, please listen to me"

She said my name and I asked her
"How do you know me, why are you here?"
She replied, "What mystic doesn't know you Jim?
Perhaps I should make myself clear"

She continued on "You are an old soul,
You can access the wisdom of the ancients,
You must not waste it"

With her words, I grew restless and impatient
I asked her to stop,
I told her, I can't hear anymore,

"Don't be surprised Jim" she told me,
"If I knock on your door"
I left the bookstore,
went straight to the bar,
returned to my room late,
walking back I gazed at the stars
The mystic stood at my door,
She whispered "The stars represent the souls who died,"

What are you doing here? I snapped
"Trying to save you" she replied
Save me from what? I asked in my drunken state,
She got louder "From what will happen to you if you
don't heed my warning, from the destruction that awaits"
I opened the door, sat on the bed,
told her to pull my boots off
if she wanted me to hear what she said
She started "In New Orleans,
your career will end,"

Jim Morrison & Michael Hutchence

I started to laugh and told her
it's hardly begun lady, guess again!!!
She proceeded "you'll collapse on stage,
Your band mates will say it's done,
this is after your trial,
I think it's best you run"

A trial lady?
I laughed in her face
What do I do wrong?
Already been drunk and maced

She went on "You'll be railroaded,
it won't go well"
Well since my life is going to hell
Do you mind if I sleep?

With all this to look forward to,
I might as well zonk out deep
She got angry "You can stop
the insanity, if you hear me out"
I told her Lady…, I'm tired,

What's this all about?
Her eyes were filled with fire when she said
"Stay out of New Orleans,
Even the airport will do you in"

I drunkenly slurred Alrightee,
I'll remember that, as the room started to spin
I passed out for the night
I woke in the late morning light,

There was a note on the table,
It read "Don't go to New Orleans,
Napoleon in Exile is no fable"

A TALE OF TWO BROTHERS

The note was signed "Cat"
And I threw it away,
I had things to do,
didn't care what the possessed female
demon had to say
I walked outside,
gonna get some beer,
The motel manager ran to my room
Muttering "Morrison better be here"
I was already gone,
But I turned back around
and asked, what's wrong, where's the fire?
The Manager said "Morrison, no pets here, you're such a liar"

I laughed and said
I had some bad dates
nothing else, he said a black cat
ran out of my room with a collar full of bells
I didn't reply,
Just went on my way,
He screamed "Morrison,
no pets, the cat better be
gone today"

Was the mystic a shape shifter?
Was I too drunk to know?
A spooky black cat
had written me a note?

Maybe I should've given up drinking,
but maybe at times,
it's better than thinking

—channeled from Jim Morrison

Jim Morrison & Michael Hutchence

CHAPTER 9

Viva Las Vegas!!!!!

"Las Vegas is a society of armed masturbators/gambling is the kicker here/sex is extra/weird trip for high rollers...house-whores for winners, hand jobs for the bad luck crowd."

—*Hunter S. Thompson, Fear and Loathing in Las Vegas*

Jim Morrison & Michael Hutchence

A TALE OF TWO BROTHERS

Robert Gover, a one-time writer friend of mine, gave a very accurate, first-person account of what went down in Las Vegas in January of 1968. I won't dispute a word of Robert's recollections. But I would like to include a few things. Las Vegas was, by far, the worst beating I had ever taken — not only by cops, but by anyone in my entire life. I had a weekend night off, and I was supposed to go to Vegas for some fun and relaxation with Robert Gover, his girlfriend, and Pamela.

Pamela and I had one of our infamous fights. At this place and time, I have chosen to come clean about the content of our confrontation. I had contracted a venereal disease called Gonorrhea and was being treated for it. By the time I saw Pamela, honestly, it was safe to be sexually active. I unfortunately contracted venereal diseases twice in my life, a fact I am not proud of, but luckily, they were both treatable.

The real story was, I wasn't interested in having sex with Pam. I know how this sounds. She was a beautiful girl, the loyal girlfriend waiting at home and putting up with all the shit I caused her over and over again. I admit it, I wasn't a good man to her or really to any woman. The open relationship Pam and I had was not what ruined us. It was the fact that I was not in love with her. I realize now that if I were in love with her or anyone else, I would have wished to have a monogamous relationship. Though I lived in the era of free love, and wished to be the antithesis of my parents and how they lived (not to mention the fact I had women throwing themselves at me on any given day and certainly almost every given night), I had jealousy issues. If I were in love, I could not stand to be apart from my other half, even though I was truly a loner. I was only that way because I never found the "one." I wouldn't have been able to stand my woman, being with other men, and I had minimal jealousy with Pamela. I even became rather close buddies with someone she had been involved with, an actor named Tom Baker, and it never bothered me. She had even taken Tom to meet her family. I am not proud I wasn't in love with this woman, it's very, very sad, but it's also the bona fide truth.

I wasn't in the mood to be physical with Pamela, so she decided to get a reaction out of me, by bringing up my darkest secret, my deepest hurt of being molested as a boy. She said, since it was done to me, I liked boys. She called me a "fag," and claimed that is where I contracted my case of V.D. When she said things like this to me, I was seething inside. Just for the record, I had contracted my case of V.D. from a female stripper in L.A. It was cruel on my part to tell her that I had a venereal disease, and I couldn't be with her. I knew it was probably more than safe, however, she fought back with spewing her disgusting, low vile at me. We just loved to hurt each other but couldn't really seem to love each other.

I was not in a good mood, obviously, and I was the one who decided I didn't want Pamela to go to Vegas. Truthfully, I hadn't wanted her to go. I wanted to have a good ol' time, drinking and finding a new lady for the night. I had a very hard time revealing my true feelings to Pamela about anything and I withheld so much from so many others I could've been closer to.

Robert, his girlfriend and I headed to Vegas in his Olds, and met up with another cat who was Robert's friend with his lady.

We went to dinner and then on to a strip club called "The Pussy A Go-Go." I was drinking, highly agitated, and really was in the mood to start some shit, but I never thought it would escalate into what it did.

Outside of the club, I took out a cigarette. Keep in mind, many of the unfiltered cigarettes in those days resembled a joint, and I cuffed this cigarette to make it appear I was smoking a joint.

After all, in my case, nothing was ever what it seemed. I did this prank for the benefit of the male security guard, the uniformed flunky who I thought would be appalled until he found out he was mistaken. The end result was that I took a horrible beating.

I was hit in the head a couple of times with a billy club and it was, of course, humiliating as this was done in public. When Robert and I were taken to the police station, I was beaten some more and blood was just streaming down my head.

Robert and I were made to strip in front of a whole room of people, men and women, and we were taunted about our sex organs. Then, we were sprayed with roach powder, and I even got roach powder put up my ass. It was so painful and degrading, I zoned out and didn't give a fuck.

I only cared about the beatings in New Haven and Vegas the next day when I would be covered in bruises and in extreme pain.

I have no doubt that Robert and I could've been killed or seriously injured if a guardian angel, Robert's girlfriend, had not shown up and bailed us out. It was clear, some of the cops couldn't wait to get off duty, and we were in for it. Thankfully, our torture was over for the night.

I had no idea at the time what was fueling my demons, but now I see it clearly. It was another time I went up against my Father without the results I wanted. This night from hell ended my association with Robert Gover, and I am sorry for the shit I caused him. He was a very decent and intelligent man, and I enjoyed having conversations with him and raiding his book shelves.

I still don't know why I was beaten that way. Was I beaten by those cops because their wife, daughter or girlfriend would find me sexually attractive? Was I beaten for my behavior or my lifestyle?

You think about it. The police in America, absolutely scared me during my lifetime. It goes to show, nothing is what is seems. The illusions in your life are much more than you now realize.

Jim Morrison & Michael Hutchence

CHAPTER 10

Lamb to the Slaughter...

"Every event needs a sacrificial lamb. They'll be serving portions of me, I understand, for lunch."

—*Michael Tanner,* Author of Nietzsche: A Very Short Introduction

Jim Morrison & Michael Hutchence

A TALE OF TWO BROTHERS

Miami was indeed a turning point in my life. It made me truly see what my life had become and how to some extent, I misunderstood myself and what I was doing.

Did I expose myself in Miami? YES AND NO! During the actual concert in Miami I was full of an alcoholic, visceral rage. All of my anger boiled to the top. At that point in time, everyone wanted a piece of me, and I couldn't come to terms with who they thought I was. Fame was destroying me, turning me into a cartoon character of sorts. I was criticized, though the music was getting better and more interesting. I didn't look like a Greek god anymore, as if I should have frozen myself in time. All they wanted was a sex symbol with sunken cheeks, and all I could see, night after night, were all the girls wanting to fuck me — and some of the guys too. I felt I had to sing "Light My Fire," because night after night, that's what the crowd wanted to hear. By 1969 I came to hate that song. My concerts were for me an experience, a ceremony of sorts, and I wanted each member of the audience to be engaged and affected. I wanted to make people think, to come out of their shells and open their minds in ways they were not accustomed to.

I wasn't there to strut in leather pants and sing "Light My Fire" for the rest of my life. I had more and more to say all the time, contradicting what has been written that I supposedly stopped creating, that's complete bullshit. My writing was deeper by now, and it was much more interesting. There were pressures put upon us by the record company for a hit, and we never seemed to pick the single that would become the hit. We were bashed for "Waiting For The Sun" by the critics. I understood that at the time but I wrote "Unknown Soldier" and "Five to One," and I thought, that was some pretty thought provoking stuff for that album. But I was already a has-been by the time I got to Miami...so many had already written Jim Morrison off.

Before departing for Miami, The Doors, all of us, had a planned vacation in Jamaica following the concert. Everyone was bringing their old ladies, and I was expected to bring Pamela. Some of the other Doors, of course, preferred me to bring her so their women wouldn't want to hang-out and go drinking with me. Sincerely, I didn't wish to bring Pam on this vacation. It was just another time I didn't want to be around her. By the time I had given her "Themis" a few months back, I felt differently about her, about our relationship, and seemed to be only able to take her in small doses. I should've been honest with her, once again, but instead, before leaving for the airport, I instigated a fight. I didn't want her going along, but she did make it to the airport before I sent her back. It may have been cruel, but she started pulling the "fag" card again, telling me she didn't like this or that. It was complete bitching and moaning that I wasn't giving her enough, and she made a threat against me, saying she would tell the world I had been with young boys and got diseases from them. I sent her away from the airport and it was my fight with her that caused me to miss my plane.

I can look back now and say, without question, if I had ended my relationship with Pamela when giving her "Themis," as I had contemplated, the Miami fiasco would've never happened. That was the day, that sealed my fate on earth. My love for Pamela Courson was gone, all gone but I didn't know how to get rid of her. A holiday to Jamaica that was beginning following the Miami concert would've been one I would've wanted someone to come along with me, someone I was into, someone I loved. I didn't because I knew that very day, I was not in love with Pamela Susan Courson and I didn't have any amount of love for her anymore. March 1st, 1969 was the day, I started to reveal my truth for the world to see. The interpretation of my release of the bullshit, was of course, severely twisted. On that night in Miami, the anger came out, the false image was ripped away and the woman everyone claimed I love so much, was not there, because I didn't love her and that was my truth as of that date in my short life.

I got pretty toasted on the plane I eventually caught and was laid over in New Orleans, where I spent the whole time in the bar getting lit. By the time I got to Miami, I was way over the intoxication level to perform. The concert, however, was oversold and fears of a riot existed if I didn't go on. I went on and they got what they got.

What they didn't get was exposure, not of my private body parts, but they blatantly heard how I really felt. I no longer wanted to be a rock star, and in my highly intoxicated state, I used an overabundance of profanity and was full of emotional rage. But I never pulled my pecker out for the crowd. I teased them, I taunted them, but I never did it. I was the one accused of public exposure, but just with the power of my drunken suggestion, plenty of girls and boys took their clothes off and left them in piles on the floor.

There were literally hundreds of pictures snapped that night from various sources, yet there was never any proof or one picture that exists that shows I did the act. Many people who knew me just assumed I did it, without asking. People wanted to believe it, that I was crazed, out of my mind to make them feel better about the shit they were doing pertaining to drugs and alcohol in their own messed up lives. This way, they could point and say they weren't as bad as I was.

Despite being heavily intoxicated, I was more in control in Miami than anybody realized. I was up on the balcony after the show and wondered if I had gone too far with the profanity…little did I know, that was the least of it. I was painfully unaware that in four days, someone would decide to bring a complaint against me that would result in a huge lie and practically ruin my life. Miami took a year and a half away from me. It also took away the naivety I had about the American legal system, the government and the truth about the Constitution of the United States. The Constitution only applies to the citizens the government wishes it to apply to. My lifestyle was persecuted, and *it* was on trial. I tried not to take it personally. Perhaps the true concern was the power over the kids who took off their clothes in droves that night at the mere suggestion of a drunken, enraged rock star. I am sure there was concern about how gullible the youth was becoming, like complete dupes at the time.

I was painfully surprised more of the so-called civil rights people of the day and other rock groups and performers, did not seem to care at all what had happened to me in Miami. It was for them, both fear of the government and (mostly) that I was a drunken, has-been who deserved it.

There was a cornucopia of issues in the fiasco that were — and still are, rather significant in American society. This trial, however, was not covered very much at all, and it got reduced to Jim Morrison whipping out his cock on stage! It was all political, not sexual.

The Doors were never political but were politicized along the way. There was a film done in London called "The Doors Are Open" for television that had a very political slant, and many misconceptions about the group were drawn from that. The makers of that particular documentary had their thesis already written before we showed up, we were just placed in their film to give us exposure to the European market. Certain songs we sang were given political connotations, and that was never intent when I wrote lyrics.

Regardless, I became, and quite unwittingly so, a symbol for the hippie movement. I was about freedom, but I was not political. Yet I was built up by the press as this ultimate hippie, here to lead the children away from what was good and holy. I was living the lifestyle more of a beatnik poet than a hippie. But the press never allowed truth and discrepancies to get in their way.

Miami changed me so much, it changed The Doors, and it could've changed minds, but the popular culture wasn't so interested in this trial. The Doors were declining because I wasn't strutting around with the Alexander the Great haircut in tight leather pants and I was no longer starving. I weighed about 145 pounds when The Doors began, because I didn't have money to eat. I didn't want to starve the rest of my life to maintain a look that brought hordes of groupies who never gave a fuck about my words or the message. They never got beyond my body, and they never cared about my mind or looked into even a small piece of my soul that I was willing to reveal to them.

I was the personification, in the minds of authority figures, of anarchy, chaos and revolution, because they believed I hypnotized my audience with dark and disturbing messages. It was dangerous, they thought, to make people aware of or to think about things their parents, schools or politicians were not engaging them in. This may sound ludicrous to you now as many recall the late '60s as a time of free love, but I assure you, America was still quite conservative. I was one of the scapegoats they wanted to hang for it.

During that unforgettable evening in Miami, I had a lamb in my arms that a friend named Lewis Marvin had brought along. It was actually incredibly symbolic, as I was the "sacrificial lamb" that night, in more ways than one being, led to the slaughter.

I can look back now on this clearly, see the identity crisis America was going through and how threatened some were by someone shaking things up and/or stirring the pot in young minds. My performances were not just concerts, they were, in fact, like a ceremony of sorts or like a performance I used to attend called "The Living Theater," they would fascinate some, disturb others.

I tried to push buttons, I tried to wake everybody up, and I tried to make people think outside the box they thought they lived in. It worked sometimes, and when I could get some of the stoned or drunk people in the audience to receive the vibrations or have an actual thought beyond what they saw, that was an achievement.

The Doors were marginalized after Miami. We lost concert dates, we lost incomes, and I will never accept the other Doors weren't majorly pissed off at me because I was drunk off my ass again and took it too far. They never knew exactly what I was going to pull, and while it kept things interesting at times, it was wearing each member of the band down somewhat. The other Doors knew wholeheartedly I didn't expose myself that night, but they also knew, I was drunk, obscene and over the top. So their feelings were mixed, and there was fear the group would never be able to recover. But at least the other Doors stood by me.

I was surprised I got such little support over Miami. I was surprised when someone was clearly being railroaded: people, fans, other artists, even John Q. Public in general, could accept such bullshit. By then, I was so despised, even the few who thought I wasn't guilty felt I deserved it. With all the photographers there, where are the pictures of the exposure?

I admitted to being drunk and using profanity, but I never exposed myself. Was I capable of it when drunk? Yes, without a doubt, but for some reason, I stopped and didn't go through with it.

Jim Morrison & Michael Hutchence

Pamela took is as a joke, but once the trial started, she was highly embarrassed over this and terrified, since The Doors concerts were being cancelled left and right, that her financial support for her decadent lifestyle and smack would come to a halt. She asked me if I did it, if I exposed myself. I told her I did, just to piss her off. I could've cared less what she thought or how she felt at that point.

I internalized my pain and one night in Miami, it resulted in an outburst. I regret that night for the pain it caused others and the lost and wasted time. I spent a year and a half simply dreading, fearing and trying to forget Miami. I regret hurting the other Doors, it was really a debacle, and it hurt each of them personally. For a year and a half, I drowned my sorrows so heavily, it's amazing I lived to be 27. I would desperately try not to think about the trial, but three years in federal prison were hanging over my head so I could only block it out so much.

The interesting part of Miami that fateful night was that I was saying quite embarrassing things to the crowd that night, but the majority who attended the concert, didn't give a rat's ass. Most were ready to ask how high, when I said jump. This is one of the aspects overlooked about that night, crowd control, rather mind control, and that someone as loaded as I was could cause so much havoc.

Freedom of artistic expression was on the line with this case. The bigger picture was being railroaded by the government because they fear or despise your lifestyle because it contradicted traditional American values. I was surprised at the time that this was not a landmark case of some sort, not because my ego was hyperextended, but because I truly believed other artists in particular would rally for this cause and support me, not as an individual but the principals involved in this mockery of justice. None of them came, none of them showed, none of them cared. Many of them had plastic beliefs and were not willing to put their money where their mouth was. I was always willing, but it wasn't understood.

Even the fan support of the trial wavered, because to many of the fans, I was this clown, this joke, who took himself too seriously. And since I put my black leather pants away for the court dates, my razor and my expensive L.A. haircuts, I was simply not relevant to them anymore. I am not sure what the most absurd lie told about me is, that I showed the crowd my cock in Miami, or that I died in a bathtub, smiling, of a drug overdose.

My attorney Max Fink was as close to a Father as I ever had. He mounted a brilliant defense in Miami, but his hands were tied, and rather unfairly, by the judge. I told Max about the molestation I was subjected to as a boy. Max already knew when he began to interview me for the trial that something was not right about my childhood. He found it fascinating I selected the state I was born in, Florida, to allow my rage to flow, before a packed audience. I shared with my lawyer my darkest secret, for I trusted him more than almost anyone. This kind of secret can destroy your life and aid you in becoming an alcoholic or a drug addict, among other things. I want people to know what happened to me and why I was the way I was. I wasn't a bad person, but I became a lunatic in my own right and was unable to compartmentalize the pain and cope with it. I handled everything the same way, in the bottom of a bottle, onto the next bottle then onto the next one. I told people during the years I was in the limelight, not to hide your pain, to wear it proudly, but the pain of my childhood, I could not allow myself to wear, let alone permit hardly anyone to see it.

Press Rewind

Push the envelope
Go out on stage boy,
Wake the Stoned hippies up,
Wake-up the dead.

You're a Shaman,
Lead the Ceremony,
You're the devil,
Is Alistair Crowley still alive?

Groupies love you,
And you like young sluts,

Jim Morrison & Michael Hutchence

You treat women like garbage,
You're not even any good in bed,
Your haircut looks ridiculous

Oh, you've gained weight
You looked good for about 5 minutes
No more sunken in cheeks
No more leather pants

Your beards' a mess
You don't look like a rock star anymore

You're not Norman Mailer
You're not Allen Ginsberg
You take yourself too seriously
Your poetry's lame and so are you

You're drunk again?

You showed your meat in Miami
Cause it's all you had to show,
You can't sing for shit,
but you think you can,
You're in love with yourself

You're strange,
You should get off the drugs,
What are you trippin' on?
Can I have some?

You're a has-been,
You're drunk again?
You stink,
how long has it been
since you had a shower?
Did I mention you stink?

A TALE OF TWO BROTHERS

You're a fag.
You're married,
"No, I'm not,"
Your songs are all about...
What are your songs about?

You're going to Paris, why?
Are you going to France to avoid Jail?
You want to write poetry in Paris? HAHAHAHA
You're drunk again?
You stink.

I've heard it all before...

—channeled from Jim Morrison

Jim Morrison & Michael Hutchence

CHAPTER 11
There's been a Slaughter Here

"The crisis of today is the joke of tomorrow."

—*H.G. Wells*

Jim Morrison & Michael Hutchence

A TALE OF TWO BROTHERS

Before I ever got to trial in Miami, the sacrificial lamb known as Jim Morrison, was slaughtered emotionally. I placed myself on the table as an offering. Without going into tedious details, it is well known the charges in Miami were not filed until days after the concert. When I returned from vacation, I had to arrange to turn myself in. When I got booked in Miami, it was a short process, not more than 15 minutes. Yet, during those few minutes, I was threatened by the police. I was told they couldn't wait for me to go to jail, they liked long hair, etc.

For someone who was sexually assaulted twice, by two different perpetrators, prior to graduating high school, it's difficult to imagine what this threat did to my nervous system and mental state. I knew what would happen to me if I did time. I had no doubt of the horrors and violations that would take place against me, and yet, on the outside, I didn't want anyone to know my deepest pain. My deepest fears were in front of me. I told friends, if I had to do time, I would get some great writing out of it. I couldn't begin to speak aloud the truth that another episode of sexual abuse would ruin what was left of me.

I was already a hardcore alcoholic before March 1st, 1969, and there is no reason to think otherwise. But now my life went into the dumpster in ways I couldn't handle or comprehend. I was 25 years old and should've just been beginning my life, but instead I went from hardcore alcoholic to hopeless alcoholic. There seemed no turning back. I was striking out at people I knew and complete strangers in drunken stupors, and sometimes, even drunken rages. I heavily regret the pain I inflicted upon others and myself, as none of it was necessary.

I knew the truth before I got to my 25th birthday, it began to become clear to me after a long concert in July of 1968 that took place in Houston. It was as if the fog was lifted. I didn't like where my life was going or who I was, and instead of getting in the driver's seat, I was once again the passenger, the hitchhiker, who allowed myself to be steered right into the oncoming bus.

I was a loner surrounded by people who wanted to hang-out with a rock star and see how crazy things would become. I was more than willing to give them crazy. I was aware the woman, my cosmic mistake I had been with on and off for the past three years, was a heroin addict, and I didn't recognize her anymore. She was like a shell most of the time.

I was searching for love, for acceptance and for validation that I was a decent human being worth loving even though I drank too much. I never truly measured up to any woman I was with, beyond the sexual part, and that varied depending on if I had passed out on them or not. It was my fault in almost every case that I never showed them who I really was. I was too afraid to bear my soul, because if I did and got rejected, I would be finished. I just couldn't do it. I couldn't connect, I couldn't find the right one. By 1969, the many women in my life were driving me up a wall, and I felt more of a void than ever. I had one at the home I paid for, bitching at me and nodding off in her dinner, and a few of the others, getting angry at me for not fully being what they wanted.

Pamela and I never really had romantic moments, and I was looking for that in other places. What Pamela and I did was to try to put on pseudo-romance or what we thought romance was. The happiest I was with her was when The Doors toured Europe and we spent time in London, but it wasn't enough to sustain anything. I wasn't just an alley cat just to sooth my libido, to the contrary, I was genuinely searching for someone I could be loved and accepted by, and not made to feel like running to the next bottle every time I was around her. I did give other women some genuine pieces of my soul, and some authentic romantic moments, but they were few and far between.

I believed in the months prior to the Miami trial, that this nightmare was a manifestation of the fact I no longer wanted to be a rock star. I can now look at it from a more enlightened viewpoint and acknowledge that in some ways, it was what I thought, but there was more.

The true story of Miami, which has not been fully told, has more to do with the toxic relationship I was still involved in with

A TALE OF TWO BROTHERS

Pamela Courson. I had tried to repress the anger, hatred, shame, confusion and horror of the sexual molestations I suffered as a child and young adult. Pamela's words to me before leaving for Miami drove me as close to insanity as I could possibly come. I am not denying I was an alcoholic, and would've been drinking prior to that show. But by missing my plane and how completely turbulent I felt emotionally following my fight with Pam, I drank myself into a blind rage. I take full responsibility for my actions.

After a series of events in 1968 when Pamela left me for an actor, went to London with him, had a fight with him, then called me to say she was going to kill herself because I never loved her, I should've just ended the relationship with her. When I arrived in London, it turned out she had cried wolf just to test me, and she then left me in London in a complete emotional tailspin to meet up with the actor. I was also thinking about it right after I gave her "Themis." But she kept coming back, and I kept allowing it. We had broken up before and would continue to break-up, and there were times I really thought it was over. I had her cut off financially from The Doors office for months at one point. Deep inside I wanted out, but the guilt got the best of me over and over.

If I had taken control of my life in 1968, when I felt it began veering out of control, and ended my toxic relationship with Pamela, it's safe to say, the whole incident in Miami would've never occurred. I would not have been as enraged that night or nearly as drunk. The profanity and piss-poor performance would not have taken place and I am doubtful anything would've come from it.

It hung over my head how I had brought the careers of The Doors to a screeching halt in one asinine rage. It is said my visits to what was known as "The Living Theater" were the direct cause of Miami, that is not an accurate assumption though they had an influence on me. Before we even got to Miami, I was destroying The Doors, slowly but surely. What once was improvisational magic between the four of us, turned into who knows what Jim the lunatic is going to pull tonight. Will he end up getting arrested and getting the shit beat out of him again or will he cause a riot? Never knowing what to expect from me was draining my band mates, and I could see it and feel it. I would bring hangers-on to the studio, show up late — and I mean really late (if I showed up at all), and the entourage escorting me were not exactly people I would trust to stand too close to me if I had been sober. I was open minded but the others involved in the recording process were right not to be happy with the unusual guests I brought to the sessions.

Now I had done it in Miami, I had put an end to the whole shebang. Ray, Robbie and John didn't deserve this, they were each extremely talented and they put up with more from me than they ever should've or had to. It weighed heavily on my mind what I had done to them, and I didn't know how to tell each of them my true feelings. I didn't expose myself, and yet, with my lifestyle choices, I had brought pain and uncertainty to each of us.

Identity Crisis

Circles go round and round,
Slow down, pause before you speak,
Say each word deliberately,
reflect before the syllables pour from your lips

You will find you can slow
everyone and everything down
around you, so that time no
longer controls your brain

Once the constraints of
the clock have been sufficiently
neutralized, consider these questions:

Did you really know your parents?
Or the secrets they covet?
Who were your parents before you were born?
Why did they get together?
Was it out of lust and a few too many drinks?
Sure you've heard stories

about them but they are not
what they appear.

The child (you) is forever
traumatized by the
imbedded images,
the loud conversation
or strange stories you have
come upon via your caregivers

You never knew much
about them, did you?
But if you had love,
you thought that was enough.
How much love is enough?
How much love do you
need to forget?
How much love
heals the emotional scars?

A psychological battering
occurs every time a child
learns how to communicate,
as you guess at what
your baby desires but
yet struggle to meet
their needs.
Do you give them
what they want
or what they need?
Is there any difference to them?

Once they botched
the job in raising you,
Does anything else they

Jim Morrison & Michael Hutchence

do in their lives
really matter?
If they succeed with
their other children,
should they be proud?
They desensitized you
for life, now they give
more to the other
eggs they hatched
so they feel pride?

When one child is damaged,
no healthy children can prevail.
You cannot assume
the role of the dutiful
Mother or Father to
some of your children
and leave one out to
fester in pain and believe
you've done anything
worth mentioning.

They have provided
you a roof over your head,
but emotional abandonment
makes you wish you were
cold and hungry,
as there is no blanket
or plate of hot food
that can provide
the sought after quick fix.

When you have given this ample analysis,
your whole identity comes undone.
You will have to start

from ground zero to
rebuild, and the circles
you use to see, dissipate,
you have opened
them and walked away
from what you used to believe.

—*channeled from Jim Morrison*

New Orleans

I came to the French Quarter
to see a gypsy woman known far and wide
I knocked on her door, she hurriedly brought me inside
She spoke of death, magic stones, lost love
and my strange ride

She threw the bag of stones on her table
closed her eyes and saw murder and mayhem
surrounding me
She said she would speak of more
when she was able

With tears in the gypsy woman's dark eyes
She predicted someone I loved would soon die

I didn't have to ask, I already knew
I couldn't even cry, for that someone was me

So I asked how does it happen?
How does he go? I told her don't
make such a prediction, and say you don't know
He dies of a broken heart she says,
on a warm Paris afternoon

Jim Morrison & Michael Hutchence

I look puzzled and say
but we are in New Orleans gypsy woman,
tell me how soon?

She grabbed her magic stones
from the table and retreated to the other room,
I followed and pleaded for more information
about my impending doom

She turned back around, her eyes full of fear
he crosses to the other side by dawn's early light
But I remind her, she just said warm Paris afternoon

She whispers he gives up by then, he knows
he has not found his true love and it will end soon

He starts to shake and shiver
She spells out my fate
He gets very nervous
for he knows what awaits

The woman must be insane, I tell myself
I run from her door, but by the next
nightfall, I return for more…

She continues on as if I had not left
He thinks he found her, she says in a harsh tone

He has only found deceit
His bitter ending will be anything but sweet,
He'll die alone

She looks at me sternly
and announces I would warn him
If I were you

A TALE OF TWO BROTHERS

But I think to myself
what she says can't be true
Paris is the town of my rebirth
the city of poets, where I will thrive

I feel you are wrong ancient voodoo Queen
I will stop drinking, I will stay alive

I spend the night
under her flickering candlelight
while she reads to me
from the Egyptian Book of the Dead
A book no living person has entirely read

I fall off to sleep
in her gilded golden chair
I dream of Spain
and of all the earthly delights I'll find there

I wake in the morning
The sun streams in like a bad burn
The gypsy woman is braiding her hair
She asks during sleep what I have learned?

I do not answer, only block my eyes from the sun, for it is on fire
She persists, did you dream of Paris?
I tell her no, of Spain and I hope she is a liar
She says you'll go there one day
and onto Corsica and for 10 days it will rain

I leave her house without saying a word
I think she must be wrong, Paris is the town of my rebirth
not the city which will bring my hearse

Jim Morrison & Michael Hutchence

I return later in the day, I need to ask her
Can she cast a spell, so I may find my woman
my true love and not rot in hell?

The gypsy woman turns pale and gray
She declares there is no spell strong enough
to stop my fate, it's over and done with,
For it's too late, I must go away

She orders me to leave and slams the door
I knock again loudly for I need to hear more
My rage goes on for a considerable amount of time
but she does not come back

My knuckles become red and sore
My hands covered in blood
spilling over to her garden
what has this she-devil done?
How do I get a pardon? This can't
be so, what do I do? Where do I go?

I wake early in the evening
in a motel in L.A. realizing
I was only dreaming, or was I?
I am not in New Orleans
Where then is the Gypsy Queen?
Was I dreaming of a past life?
Still searching for my wife?

How do I stop it from happening
all over again?
I'll go to Paris, be reborn and find out then.

—*channeled from Jim Morrison*

CHAPTER 12

No Justice, No Peace

"In vain we chisel, as best we can, the mysterious block of which our life is made, the black vein of destiny reappears continually."

—*Victor Hugo*

Jim Morrison & Michael Hutchence

A TALE OF TWO BROTHERS

Anytime an injustice is corrected, or clarified, it's very good karmically for the planet and everyone who was personally involved. The Governor of my birth state has granted me a pardon, for a crime I didn't commit, imagine that! While this is a very interesting development, I am not at all energetically connected to it and am extremely surprised there is now an interest in this case.

While I am giving this channel all the information necessary to set the record straight, I don't have an interest in changing anything in a legal sense because I am no longer on Earth. The energy and time could be invested in other ways that would be more helpful to the injustices taking place currently, not just in America, but all over the vast planet.

I was disappointed more people weren't interested in the case when I was alive and going through both the trial and appeals. It was a real let down. But I don't think it's important to clear me from anything at this stage, because the legal system in America is not unbalanced, it's completely bent.

In an essay I was writing in Paris about the trial in Miami, I spoke about it personally but also made observations concerning how the legal system in America really operated. If I had not have had the money to finance a defense, I would've been in jail, not in Paris. Of course, it was my lifestyle and the money that was included with it that got me arrested in the first place, but it was shocking to me and my idealism went out the window. It was entirely based on politics and economics, not truth or fairness in any sense. I was asked the most innocuous questions, but it was a valuable experience as an observer.

I am sorry my essay written in Paris may never see the light of day. There are others who sit in the justice system who are not famous and don't have the finances to fight verdicts or appeal, so they can't go to Paris or even to their own homes. I would much rather see those who fought for me, fight for them, the nameless, the ones who can't afford good attorneys to put on a good defense or halfway decent defense. There are plenty of innocent people in jail, and this has been seen repeatedly in recent times when some were freed from death row after several years of sitting in rancid cells without hope or help. Clearing my name is a nice gesture, but it's a moot point. You can't really clean-up my image after the damage that has been inflicted upon me. I can't quite understand why anyone would want to make a movie about me, but if it was to happen, at least portray it with some air of truth. I don't see the reason so many books were written about me, but if you believe any of them are really all that accurate, that's unfortunate.

I would rather see another Jim, who has no money nor a famous name to get people excited, have citizens who never met him spend their time and energy to free him from jail or clear his name. A Jim who is still on Earth, one who it will mean more to than it does to me, and more to his family as well. If you want to battle injustices of the system, you need to start with the people who couldn't stay out on appeal or leave the country, as I was legally allowed to do.

My Mother and Father are on this side now and I do not have a relationship with them, but I am sure the pardon means nothing to them. I am on this side now, not walking around running some bank or living in Africa, so I am not entirely sure what this was done for. Miami was a true catalyst for my downward spiral, and clearing my name now won't change a damn thing for me on Earth. Once again, I see my fans are misguided.

I know some of those who worked on this legal effort are intelligent, good people, but what are they doing this for? With all the problems the Earth currently faces, what will clearing a charge that I was convicted of in 1970 do for anyone? There are more constructive ways to spend your time and energy to empower others. If people wanted to help me or be involved, this should've occurred in 1969, 1970 and even in 1971, while I was out on appeal. The time for that is over, and I am over my past life as the drunken degenerate who took the stage in Miami, gave one of the worst performances in my life, and should've never gone on because I was so disgustingly lit. It's over, let it go, and spend your valuable energy on things that matter. Earth operates on the linear time scale and everything has a place and time. My time to clear my name or clean-up my life is gone, and it won't be coming back. Thanks for the thought, but no thanks.

Dinner in America

I disliked soup, not the way for me to start a meal,
give me a hot burrito and a cold Mexican beer
and that was dinner for me in a small joint
with college students or aspiring poets.

You eat dinner with images
of war and zoned out
starlets too stoned and needy
to leave the circus they have caused
with the ruckus of their
frenzied libidos and thirst
for the engagement of
souls in their debauchery
of the cesspool they have
invited you into.

You eat dinner with a cell phone
that has somehow attached itself
to your ear, in the oblivion of the
somewhat startling
realization that all the other diners
are lucky to hear your conversations.

You eat dinner as just a matter
of routine on the go, in your
fast food heaven with plastic
utensils and ignorant, snot nose teenagers
capable of inciting a riot.

Jim Morrison & Michael Hutchence

You eat dinner when you are invited
to a restaurant and you talk
of politics and taxes for that
is all you have. You wonder
if your friends had any work done
on their wax museum faces and
talk about the weight you lost.
Is that all there is?

What's for dessert?
I always had an aversion
to watching people eat
ice cream. How about a nice
piece of pie to go along with
the lies your leaders tell you
ostensibly, to control you
with fear and conspiracy theories
about the Mossad because
it always comes back to them
when there are no apparent
explanations.

Freedom fighters no longer
Fight for anything you can identify,
so they never enter your pretentious
conversations.

Storm Troopers are now
cartoon characters in a movie,
instead of in Nazi Germany to your
children and their sewer culture minds.

Maybe astrology has your answers,
but your Zodiac has 12 signs,
Nostradamus had 13, what

happened to the 13th sign?
It connects Sagittarius and Scorpio,
but no one ever told you about it
so you always believed there were 12.

You see a snake, a lizard, a serpent,
So you say, look, the devil's on his way,
but isn't he already here? He's at your
dinner table, he's in your evil, greedy
world leaders, your pseudo news about
some no-talent celebrity who duped you
into thinking she is important, and your
hypothesis on who killed Kennedy, or
Area 51 or how many really died in the Holocaust?
Does it matter now?

Your 14-year-old daughter, just bought
a pregnancy test, your Father
is being abused in the home you thought
would be so good for him, your husband is engaging
in a hot and heavy affair with a co-worker,
your 11-year-old son tried speed for the first time
and liked it.

Would you like another piece of pie?
Is that show on tonight where the doctors all play musical
beds?
Or what about the one featuring the corrupt,
depressed lawyers with the actor who used to
walk around on a plastic space ship?

Give me a hot burrito and
a cold Mexican beer and I'm good.

—*channeled from Jim Morrison*

Jim Morrison & Michael Hutchence

CHAPTER 13
Snake on a Plane!

"Betrayal is the only truth that sticks."

—*Arthur Miller*

Jim Morrison & Michael Hutchence

A TALE OF TWO BROTHERS

After Miami, it's no secret my life was a mess, and I actually got into more serious trouble in November of 1969 in Phoenix. I would like to mention that the Phoenix arrest occurred only two days after I visited Dade County, Florida to be booked for the Miami hanging. In a few short minutes during the Miami booking, the police had transported me back to being sexually victimized as a child and adolescent, and they gave me a very profound hint what I would face in prison.

I couldn't handle what was hanging over my head, so my way was to do whatever I could to not to think about it. I was eager to engage in another drunken escapade, just to have some fun and not have to deal with the guillotine, I felt I was facing in my state of origin.

I got on a plane to go raise havoc at a Rolling Stones concert. There was nothing innocent about this, as I knew I would be trashed and wildly obnoxious. God only knows where my mind was, because I was quite crazed at this point. I was on this flight with an actor named Tom Baker. The self-proclaimed Lizard King was not the snake on the plane that night, but Tom Baker was the slithering asshole.

Tom Baker was a fellow alcoholic and birds of a feather, flock together. He would never cut me off or get on me about drinking too much, and that is what mattered to me in so-called friendships in my adult life. It was also quite easy to be around Tom, because he was an even bigger jerk than I was when drunk and I could always say, "Well at least I wasn't as bad as Tom was."

Tom was absolutely jealous of my money and fame and was always left with my leftover women for a night. He was a struggling actor that never really made it, and because I was always the passenger, taking the ride, not driving my own car, I allowed Tom to cause me some unnecessary grief on a few occasions. He was someone who stirred up a lot of shit, often just for the sake of watching me go down and burn, because it made him feel better about the fact his life was in the gutter. He was not a real friend to me, but I forgive him because I allowed it. I wanted to be generous to people at times and a decent guy, but I bet on the wrong horses in the race several times over.

Phoenix was a classic example, almost too classic, of mistaken identity. Tom Baker was seated in my seat (the one assigned to me) on the plane, and I was in his. I was getting smashed, no doubt about it, but I was mellowing out and not causing any trouble. I am sure I was saving my antics for the Rolling Stones concert.

Tom took it too far that night, and it's not that I hadn't taken it too far on many occasions. But if Miami was a serious legal matter, interrupting a flight, which is a federal charge, was even more grave. Considering I was already out on bail for Miami, this was really going to be the end for me.

I was not harassing the stewardess, or anyone, for that matter that night. Granted, we were in the wrong seats, and the things Tom was doing to this poor stewardess were just beyond childish and stupid. They stopped being funny after the first five minutes. But the stewardess later had to be coerced by my legal team, because she damn well knew it wasn't me harassing her throughout the flight. Tom Baker and I didn't look alike, but I was the famous one with the money. There was, without a doubt, thoughts of a lawsuit on its way for this one, and if it could be proven I caused all that trouble on the plane, they would have owned me.

Tom Baker had no money, so I graciously posted his bail. The snake decided to let me take the rap for it and said nothing about the mistaken identity; he was going to let me go down in flames knowing the serious trouble I was already facing for Miami. He figured I had the money and I could get out of it, but it wasn't that simple. An interesting debacle occurred when we went to court for this unbelievable mess. I was clean shaven for the court appearance on the suggestion of my lawyer, and Tom had a beard. This had been the complete opposite on the plane. Needless to say, they still knew they had the wrong guy. But my legal team worked very hard, and in April 1970 I got a huge relief when those charges from Phoenix were dropped — no thanks to Tom Baker.

People were able to run all over me when I was intoxicated, and I was seen as a "mark" at those stages. I take full responsibility for that. I had very few real friends and even fewer that understood even one or two aspects of who I really was.

Jim Morrison & Michael Hutchence

CHAPTER 14

I've got to go out in the Car with these People and get...

"My fate cannot be mastered; it can only be collaborated with and thereby, to some extent, directed. Nor am I the captain of my soul; I am only its noisiest passenger."

—*Aldous Huxley*

Jim Morrison & Michael Hutchence

A TALE OF TWO BROTHERS

I never clearly understood how my life on Earth got so tangled and twisted, but from where I am now, it's crystal clear.

Throughout my adult life, I took a ride with anyone, to anywhere. I lived moment to moment and while that in itself should not be condemned, always allowing others to call the shots in my life was a serious mistake (with sometimes difficult consequences) that I made over and over again. I took a ride with The Doors, and while that was truly my destiny, I was not actively involved with the business end of it mostly because I didn't want to be. I should have contributed more about the direction of the group and offered more well-thought-out suggestions. I wasn't in any way or shape prepared for this ride even though early on, I thought the group would take off and become huge. But for a shy, sensitive soul like mine, I needed to take the steering wheel on this wild ride others only dream of.

I took a ride with male drinking companions, and basically anyone else who would tie more than a few on, for the night or for a day with me, for that matter. As long as I could get tanked, and they didn't care (no one seemed to mind I was being a belligerent jerk off and treating others like shit). It's amazing I didn't end up dead sooner than the age of 27, hanging around half the people I spent time with.

I took a ride with practically any woman who was available for any given night who was even remotely interested in me. I was around psychotics and freaks. And could've ended up dead more than a few times (or damaged in ways I won't explain), but that didn't stop me. My attitude was: you drive, I'll sit in the back seat fucked up.

I took a ride as a victim of sexual abuse as a child and adolescent and turned my anger, shame and depression into alcoholism. I punished myself for what others had done to me.

I took a ride with a woman who was self-absorbed and, later on, became a hardcore heroin addict and didn't want to let go of me. I became so apathetic about the relationship, I allowed her to drive my inner demons instead of ending it two years after it started.

I took a ride with the limits others placed on me as a rock star, those who believed I could never be taken seriously as a poet or writer. Seeing "The Lords and New Creatures" published was a great high in my life. It was unfiltered, but it was also written while I was in college. It should've been primitive work, as I should've grown as a writer, visionary and man.

In the film "HWY: An American Pastoral," I went from being the hitchhiker to the driver. I got rid of what was giving me trouble, I killed it or the never seen on screen character in the movie, and I buried him in the desert. At the time, this film was just basically making itself, going its own way and I never made the conscious leap to the fact I had to also take over the driver's seat in my own life. I had to kill what was giving me trouble, bury it somehow and start to control my own destiny. Fate had brought me to where I was, but I needed to take charge of my destiny. I was never able to do that, even though I was making attempts to gain control of my life in Paris. This is what lead to my undoing, not becoming the driver in my own life.

I hope you can benefit in your life from the huge mistake I made in mine.

Diner

Late one afternoon, I was just hanging out
back at the motel with a six-pack near the bed,
My friend came by, he knocked so loud,
he could wake the dead,
I answered the door, he said he was bored,
"There's a carnival on the edge of town,
get up man, let's go." he said,
"let's see what's going down."

A TALE OF TWO BROTHERS

I threw on a t-shirt and
a pair of jeans,
my worn brown Frye boots
always made the scene,
We drove to the other end
of town, it was eerie,
deserted, not a creature
was stirring, not even a sound.

The carnival was enclosed
like a tomb, the tents hid
everything including our
impending doom. We paid
our way in as a man at least of
a hundred let us through,
"It's been slow." he said
"Nice to see you two."

A very tall woman of
at least seven feet two,
pulled me into a tent to Tango,
She nearly broke my neck,
what could I do?

She danced on and said
"You waltz very well."
my ribs were bruised,
my spine ached, she was
the dance partner from hell.

The Tango, the Waltz,
The Fox Trot and more,
I told her my friend couldn't
find me, as I searched for a tent
opening or some kind of door.

Jim Morrison & Michael Hutchence

She laughed as I searched,
but I found another room,
it was a hall of mirrors,
I hoped I could get out of there soon.

One mirror made me look
short and fat, the tall
lady just laughed and laughed.
One mirror made me appear
ten feet tall, the room was now
spinning and I started to fall.

A midget grabbed me before I
hit the floor, he told me to run
for my life, the carnival is haunted,
He said "Wait, there's more"
my dance partner was a demon,
She taunted me because she wanted my semen.

The midget then told me,
I was the She Devil's groom,
I started to shake and knew
I had to find my way out soon.

Two fire eaters surrounded me
and caged me to a wall,
I heard my anxious friend call
and call.

"JIM, JIM, WE HAVE TO GET
GOING, THIS PLACE IS INSANE."
He yelled out much louder now
"THE TALL BITCH IS DERANGED!"

The fire eaters wouldn't leave me,
they were guarding their prey,

the tall she devil emerged in a
black bridal gown, I screamed
"DON'T I GET A SAY?"

She emerged with her maid of honor,
a goblin from hell,
They paraded down the aisle
to a song I knew well,
"STRANGE DAYS HAVE FOUND US"
she was a Doors fan, I could tell.

The minister showed up,
but he was a mortician so he said,
he smiled and asked me
"Aren't you the young man
who says bring out your dead?"

I turned pale and felt faint,
the mortician said
"Is everybody in? The
ceremony is about to begin,
this can't wait."
My bride grabbed me by
my neck "Say what I tell you,"
she whispered "or you'll feel worse
than if you were in a car wreck."

We got to the "I do's" and I
couldn't reply, I heard my friend
screaming, he was being tortured somewhere
nearby, the bride from the gates of hell
began to cry.

I told her let my friend go,
it's not his fault I won't
perform at this show.

Jim Morrison & Michael Hutchence

The bride in black said
"When I first saw you Morrison,
I thought you were the one,
I have chosen you to give me a son."

I told her no way,
I've not yet found my bride,
You can't be it - you demon,
let me go or you'll die!!!

The fire eaters beat me,
and the world's strongest man
came in and with one punch,
knocked me out, I woke up the
next day in New York City,
thinking what the hell was that about?

A knock came at the hotel door,
my friend Leon who was just with me
at the Carnival from Hell, walked in and
said "Jim, I'm bored, I've got a car,
Want to take a spin? Man, you don't look well."

I said "I don't know,
you were just in my nightmare,
let's hang here, I'm still
shaken and scared."

He said "Remember that carnival
we went to before on the edge of town?
Remember the crazy tall bitch always
hanging around?"

A carnival? I asked,
When was this?
"Last September Jim,

A TALE OF TWO BROTHERS

The chick was seven feet tall
that you French kissed."

I hoped he was joking,
it couldn't be true,
I told my friend Leon of
my nightmare I had, through and through.

He said "Jim you always
wanted to break on through,
I guess you got what you wanted,
as women of all realms consider
you the hunted."

I told my friend I needed
a beer, let's go for a drive,
I'm losing my mind, my brain
was becoming numb with fear.

We drove all day to Niagara Falls,
and drank and drank until nature called,
I headed to the men's room at the hotel bar,
when I returned my friend was gone and so was his car.

The brunette female bartender
asked for my room key,
she said she was off soon
and would like to get to know me.

She came to my door at 3 a.m.,
She said her name was Rosemary,
I said "Hi, I'm Jim."
She unbuckled my belt,
threw me on the bed,
all those drinks at the bar
were surely going to my head.

Jim Morrison & Michael Hutchence

She said "Jim, I don't want to get
married but If I'm lucky, your baby I will carry."

I told her, no wait, hold it,
Rosemary's Baby? NO, not tonight,
I grabbed my belt and shoes
and ran out into the darkness,
I couldn't find any light.

I walked to the falls,
but didn't want to get too close,
I walked and walked but I saw this chick,
she saw me and made a u-turn mighty quick.

She was a girl with blonde streaks in her hair,
very pretty, she asked me what was going on?
I said "You don't want to know honey,
take me anywhere, the country, the lake,
The beach or the city."

She laughed and said
"Baby you talk in riddles,
want some pancakes hot
from my griddle?"

I said, sure thing,
I'd love to see how
hot your griddle gets,
we drove to this diner,
she made me pancakes
and they were the best.

Never tasted pancakes
so fluffy and hot,
with all the butter,
and blueberry syrup on top.

A TALE OF TWO BROTHERS

She served me coffee,
the best I ever had,
I look into her blue eyes,
fell in love, I wanted her so bad.

She said her name was Rebecca,
she literally saved my life,
first there was a she devil that
wanted to be my wife and this Rosemary
chick tried to get her claws into me,
but it was with Rebecca, that I was meant to be.

I kissed her pretty mouth,
fell deep in love,
my heart went south,
she was an Angel sent from above.

My heart broke when I woke up
again in New York City,
no Rebecca, no pancakes,
the back of my neck felt dirty and gritty.

There was a knock at the door,
it was my friend Leon who kept showing up,
I pulled the covers over my head,
I'd had enough.

My friend shouts through the door,
"Jim, open up, I'm bored, I know this
great little diner on the other side of town,
where we can put some coffee and pancakes down."

I race to the door,
but wake up once more,
I am in Philadelphia,
with The Doors, on tour.

Jim Morrison & Michael Hutchence

The diner I met Rebecca in,
is the soul kitchen of my dreams,
and I will return there by all
And any means.

I actually searched for this diner,
for a few years,
I kept on looking in between
all the beers.

I finally got myself a map,
and when your shift ends
Rebecca, I'll be back, you can
count on it. Angel girl, I've searched
for your sweetness all over the world,
you are my only bride, let's go on a magic carpet ride,

all the other women tried to get me, but I will only be your groom if you let me.

Rebecca, I love only you…

—*channeled from Jim Morrison*

CHAPTER 15

Under the influence...

"A book is a garden, an orchard, a storehouse, a party, a company by the way, a counselor, a multitude of counselors."

—*Charles Baudelaire*

Jim Morrison & Michael Hutchence

A TALE OF TWO BROTHERS

The Treasure of Sierra Madre

Jim: What are you reading?

Unknown Male Voice: The Treasure of Sierra Madre.

Jim: Do you like that book?

Unknown Male Voice: Yep, I'd like to find the mother load like these three did, too bad greed got the best of them.

Jim: (Laughs)

Unknown Male Voice: What's so funny?

Jim: The gold, it's fools' gold, it's not the real kind of gold like you find in Alchemy.

Unknown Male Voice: If you say so, uh you know a little something about Alchemy? Is the Philosopher's stone real or made up?

Jim: It's real.

Unknown Male Voice: Oh yeah, where is it?

Jim: It's esoteric, but you bet it's real.

Unknown Male Voice: See now you are talking about something you can't see or feel and I am talking about buried treasure, something you can hold onto and cash in.

Jim Morrison & Michael Hutchence

Jim: (Laughs)

Unknown Male Voice: What exactly is so funny?

Jim: When I was on Earth, people thought I was that treasure, they thought I was gold (Laughs), the prospectors were all over me.

Unknown Male Voice: Lots of people have made money off you, maybe you were and still are the gold.

Jim: No, not even close. I became none of what I wanted. All of what I despised. Emotionally unattached to everything and everyone, so no one could hurt me again, I didn't make it go away, I made myself go away.

Unknown Male Voice: Sorry to hear that friend, I still want to be Humphrey Bogart in the movie version.

—*channeled from Jim Morrison*

    The highs and lows in my life were not as a rock star, they were simpler things. At heart, I was a poet, some may not think much of me in that regard — and they are entitled to their opinion — but when I was performing my poetry, was when I was the happiest and at peace. I am speaking about when I did it early on, before anyone knew who I was, at a coffee house in Washington D.C. during high school, and later on, at a coffee house in St. Petersburg, Florida, while in college. My poetry didn't rhyme, it would mostly reflect those things that influenced me during the time, such as the type of philosophy I was studying or what I was reading.

    I worked from the genre of Jack Kerouac and Allen Ginsberg. Dylan Thomas was also an influence on me, and I found him to be a bit more magical than the others. I always thought I was a beatnik or a bohemian — never a hippie — and it's quite interesting in ways that I am often associated with the hippie movement in America. The culture puts labels on everyone, it boxes you in, and more often than not, people become a slave to those labels and to the false limits they perceive as truth. It's well known that William Blake had a great influence on me, and most especially, what he wrote about perception. What do you see in a grain of a sand?

I was interested in breaking through the standard culture of the times I lived in, as opposed to being part of the counterculture. Nietzche was indeed one of my favorite philosophers while I was on Earth, but his philosophy was something he could not implement and was one of only many I studied and became somewhat well versed on. I read most of the major philosophies in the world, and for a time — several years actually — Frederic Nietzche captivated me, because his philosophy was something I had not yet encountered — let alone read about. His philosophy didn't kill me or ruin my life. Playing the endless role of "The Hitchhiker" and not allowing myself to get into the driver's seat but for only very short periods of time ruined my life.

While there are many who have been fascinated with my fascination with Nietzsche or the boring comparisons to Arthur Rimbaud (God knows I was never on the level of Rimbaud), I was deeply influenced by many of the books I had read and some of The Doors' songs were a direct result of what those amazing authors had written. I was extremely influenced by T.S. Eliot and James Joyce much more than most discussing my life have ever picked up on. "Finnegan's Wake" started over at the end, just refer back to the first Doors album. I was also inspired from a young age by Norman Mailer and was a big fan of "The Naked Lunch," and so on. I had a variety of literary influences and was always taken in not just by poetry, but by a great novel, as I wanted to write one, or two, or three in my lifetime.

Anais Nin had a great influence on me as a writer, as the raw emotion she presented swirled around in my head. There were so many books I dearly loved, but I basically read less and less the more famous I became, which was truly a mistake. Great writers often start out as readers, and I would read anything and everything, as it got me through the roughest spots of my childhood. Reading is a gift, a present you give to yourself that you will perceive differently than the next person.

Jim Morrison & Michael Hutchence

Eastern philosophy did have an influence on me. Shamanism certainly caught my attention, and I believe my fate of becoming famous was a calling, not a deliberate act of wishing to become some sort of cultural celebrity. There are no such things as coincidences, and I didn't accidentally run into Ray Manzarek a couple of months after my U.C.L.A. graduation one day on a beach with songs playing in my head. I had planned to go to New York after graduation, but something kept me in California, it was my fate, my true destiny. I didn't grow up planning to become a rock singer, and I didn't plan on it at all in college. It was a calling of electric shamanism and, little did I know, that plan was to create a following, an audience of young minds that would grow with me and experience my later in life, new found spiritualism, wisdom and enlightenment. This was the goal that I had set for myself before December 8th, 1943 when I arrived, kicking and screaming, in Melbourne, Florida. The goal was forsaken because I didn't take too kindly to the ride, and I wasn't at all prepared for the fame. The quiet garden I sought to cultivate, became a jungle. Predators of all kinds stood around me, some quite enticing and beautiful.

I sought to get in touch with my spiritual side throughout my life. The taking of such drugs as peyote and dropping acid were simply to give me visions, not just to trip. Like Crazy horse, I wanted to receive visions of the real world, beyond this one. I got high on weed to get visions, as it was often used for spiritual awakenings. You do not need drugs of any kind for true spiritual awakenings. Trips like that can cause you to become a victim and even to harm yourself or someone else. My mind was so restless, meditation was obscure to me. You must do something I was, more often than not, unable to do during my time on Earth, and that is quiet your mind to clearly hear the messages and perceive the visions. There are a multitude of distractions on Earth to stop one from being able to truly hear the message. The veil between the so-called worlds is thin, much thinner than you think. Heaven isn't thousands of miles away from Earth. Nothing is what you think, you live in an illusion, and you can't comprehend it at this stage.

There is no time; there is no space. I was never good at adapting to linear Earth time. It's true, an alcoholic loses time —

sometimes a day or days, but linear Earth time was always a struggle for me as I always knew there was more than what we can see with our eyes. I searched for what was on the other side of the thin veil my entire life. I am here now, on this side and it is beyond describable or anything I imagined or dreamt of on Earth. When I broke on through, I had true regrets of wasting my Earth life, wasting so much time and not leading those who would follow me to a higher plane of freedom. For we had just begun our journey together, and then I had left, with so much work undone, so much time wasted. I had only just begun.

My biggest single regret will always remain not sticking around to be with my true eternal soul mate who would not have come along until later in my life when I was more together and capable of true love. I was half a man when I came to this side, and my spirit was in many ways broken, trying to recover, trying to redeem itself, trying to find the path and wondering what went wrong.

I did more introspection in the last few months in Paris than ever before. It may have seemed much of the same as my life in L.A., one drunken episode to the next, but I was ready to make changes, major changes, and shed my skin. I did end up shedding my skin, but not in the way I had planned. When I crossed over and left my battered body, it was a loud, disturbing, rude wake-up call that painfully came upon me.

A spiritual transition was about to happen for me one way or another, on Earth or away from it. You have the chance while you are still on Earth to evolve spiritually, and I cannot emphasize how much better off you will be if you begin this process while you are still attached to a human body. The programming you receive on Earth is what is dulling and damaging your spirit. Truth and wisdom are not found in prepackaged, modern cultural images cultivated strictly for greed. You must seek to find and you must not allow yourselves to find in vain. Use what you find for the greater good of yourself and all mankind.

I thought I had foreseen my death, and this is interesting because for a long time, I actually believed I had this correct. I had these visions, and I told several people around me about them at different times. I had read about a book that kept track of every day of your life. It was called "The Almanac," and so I wanted to be able to utilize this book, my book, to see certain things, including my own death. I had thought I had visions of my own death a few times, but I was wrong. I was sure I was going to drown — and not in a bathtub. This was surprising because I was an excellent swimmer, but even the best swimmers can go out that way. I saw this drowning happening while I was still quite young, but by the last year of my life, I really wanted to alter this and live to be quite old. I didn't want to die at 27, but perhaps when I was 23 or 24 I was more accepting of it...the whole live fast, die young James Dean thing. I was having visions of drowning and thought it was me but could not fully determine who was drowning. It's rather complicated, but I actually was seeing my true eternal soul mate (as our souls were so bonded) and not myself. I had no idea exactly who I was seeing so I thought it was my death. Now I know it was my twin flames' exit point I was shown, not my own.

I speak of this now because when I tried to bring up my almanac, or Akashic records, as they are actually called, I got some jumbled information regarding my other half. I was not quite able to zone in on it or make sense of it. I was never meant to drown, and I was actually not meant to cross over when I did in Paris. I would like to caution anyone seeking such visions to do so in a clear, unpolluted state of mind, unaltered by substances. It was my use of alcohol and other drugs that prohibited me from tapping into my spiritual gifts in a clear and accurate sense. It was the complete opposite of what I had believed on Earth, for I was so eager to break through, open the door and see beyond the ordinary, mundane illusions painted around me.

I actually did believe in this so-called almanac and that it listed every day of my life. When I got really drunk, I would take my Shelby Mustang and drive fast and carelessly around dangerous roads like Topanga Canyon and thought I may go out like James Dean. I took the possible exit point of drowning to heart, and I wanted to test the almanac. So sometimes I engaged in extremely reckless behavior while intoxicated: driving like a maniac with nothing to lose or climbing up to windows, on roofs or ledges (which I had already began doing previous to believing I was reading my stored life's history in the almanac). Someone could've gotten hurt, and I look back at the drunk driving and it infuriates me because I could've killed someone easily. I truly regret driving drunk, as I never wanted to hurt anyone else but myself. I was always testing things out, pushing the limits.

James Dean became an idol of mine at 11 years old. He always fascinated me all through life and personified not only rebellion but "cool intelligence." You have to understand, as a pre-teen in the 1950s, "Rebel Without A Cause" was the most captivating film I had yet seen. Like many of my generation, I grew-up wanting to be a "James Dean prototype." The last five years of my life in California gave me the opportunity to visit the site where James Dean crashed and died. I do believe I made a spiritual connection to him a few times as I stood gazing where my idol lost his life. I actually saw him vividly once, with a broken neck. This vision horrified me, as opposed to fascinating me. I did have the ability to channel the other side, just never really understood it. James Dean was constantly in the back of my mind, and for a few years, I considered making a film about him or a character that was, in fact, a sort of prototype of him. I wanted to verify some of the details I saw in my head of what he was wearing that fatal day he crossed over, and things like that…another project left unfulfilled.

Another idol in my past life who inspired what I consider to be my absolute best poem that has been made public was Brian Jones, the founder of "The Rolling Stones." I found him to be similar to me, a true introvert with some other complicated sides. Brian, as it turns out, died at the hand of someone else. His death, like mine, was not the way it has been told for many, many years. Do you think it's a coincidence Brian died at the age of 27 just like me? Or that he died on July the 3rd just like me? It was two years later on that same date, it would all be over for me on Earth, and my life turned out to be this fast blur. The poem I wrote for Brian, was called "Ode to L.A. While Thinking of Brian Jones, Deceased." I composed this poem at a girlfriend's place named Raggi (Peggy). This work wasn't done obviously until the summer of 1969, when many contended I had no creative juices left. My work only got better and stronger, but so much of it was left in bars and restaurants or not recovered from Paris. What was recovered, ended up with the wrong people from the beginning. Pamela should have never been left my work, Michael McClure should've had it! I believe he was the only one who knew me who would do it justice and release it properly.

The world I created for myself while on Earth was not as beautiful as it could've been. Perception is everything. I did find the most incredible beauty in works of art. I could sit and look at a great painting and truly believe there was a God. I searched for God throughout my entire life, but never found the one I was looking for. The God of fire and brimstone could've never been my God, I wanted one who was loving and compassionate.

I could find beauty not only in art but in music, though I was not a connoisseur of any kind of music. I loved the blues and felt if I was born to sing any type of music, it was truly the blues, which were created and recreated nightly. I loved old blues singers like Muddy Waters. I was a great fan of jazz and of Miles Davis. I had a friendship and professional relationship with a very intuitive, musical composer named Fred Myrow. He was a student of an absolute genius and musical pioneer named Darius Milhaud. Both of these men are on this side now, I have not made contact with them but truly respect their work. I made plans to do some very intense and new work with Fred in Paris, late in July of 1971. I was composing a rock opera of sorts, he was going to score it. I was preparing to make major changes in my life and the Doors had closed behind me and I was ready for some radical changes, so I could shed my skin and become the man I truly was, not the actor in the Greek comedy/tragedy that was playing out.

Ghosts

Do you like ghost stories?
I know a few but I can't share
them, or I'd have to take your
life and make you a ghost

I don't think you'd
want to rattle around
an old attic, although

you'll find some interesting
family relics there

Maybe you'd choose
to haunt a ship
because it's so traditional,
maybe something along
the lines of the Queen Mary

Maybe you should
think of haunting
a library where
you can push the books
off of the shelves that
some poor student
really should be reading
as opposed to their
school assignment

Where would you
like to haunt?
A cemetery is too
predictable, you've
got to be more
inventive than that

I have an idea,
I will keep my
ghost stories to
myself so you
don't need to
become one

You were made
to dance in the
light and welcome

the dawn and I was
made to see the ghosts
and know their stories

—*channeled from Jim Morrison*

"True love is like ghosts, which everybody talks about
and few have seen."

—*Francois de La Rochefoucauld*

Validating Your Existence...

The movie is over,
the lights came on,
we can discuss the
plot, maybe even the
subplot, or we can
just go home.

After all, we have our
own movie to live out,
a comedy of errors,
a tear jerking drama,
a mystery with more
twists and turns than
the world has ever seen.

It's our lives,
for when we come back

to heaven,
you will watch every second,
every nuance that came
out of your mouth,
and you will feel
the way you made
each and every person
feel that had the misfortune
of interacting with you.
You've never seen
a movie like it,
You'll be angry
when you learn,
you wrote the script,
you'll criticize the acting,
the direction, even the screenplay.

Do you want your money back?
Was it worth the price of admission?
You will discover everyone around you
was an actor, some more
technical than others,
some more seasoned,
or natural as opposed to
trained. The hardest
realization may even be
that you were just an actor,
and how terrible an
actor you really were
as you muddled through
your lines, often blowing them.

You often missed your
cues, but every once in a while,

Jim Morrison & Michael Hutchence

there was a great ad lib and a few scenes
that you played out that could earn you
the pretentious Academy Award.

You'll become sullen
with the realization,
you can never make
the movie over again.
Production has ceased
and it is perpetually stored
on reels that will live in infamy.

I always wanted to make
films, my scenes of
eternity turned out to be
experimental, with a lousy ending.
It wasn't a full length film
and it wasn't short.
I suppose I wanted it
to be a beautiful art house film,
but it became appalling and loud mid-way through.

The subtle images
the film opens with
seemed to magically fade away,
and the mayhem of a strange circus as a
backdrop began to take center stage.

My film turned out
so hideously, I wish
I could burn it so that no
image remains of it, or of me
in the deplorable existence I
rummaged through. My film
turned out so misunderstood

even to me, there is little if anything
I can appreciate. I always wanted
to make films, just not this one of

James Douglas Morrison,
Born December 8, 1943 in Melbourne,
Florida and died July 3, 1971 in Paris,
France. That Jim Morrison has died,
the real one has emerged.

—*channeled from Jim Morrison*

EDITOR'S NOTE: This conversation followed Jacquie's psychic reading by phone with Kathleen Tucci, a psychic medium in Dallas, Texas. The reading took place in March, 2006.

Jim = Jim Morrison

Jac = Jacqueline Murray

Jim: Were you satisfied that both I and Michael Hutchence came through to Kathleen today? She even knew who we were. She met Michael in person before, and she has brought me through several years ago for someone else.

Jac: That's what she said. She gave me very specific confirmations, it really helped me a lot Jim to continue this work, thank you. I don't feel like a complete crackpot now.

Jim: Are you curious as to who she read for before that knew me?

Jac: Not really, that's your businesss, not mine.

Jim: It's a woman named Candice. I came through on the phone and then in a gallery reading. It was minor, Jacquie, nothing significant, and I basically did it to connect to Kathleen as Michael and I felt you would cross paths. None of this is a coincidence or random.

Jac: I guess I figured that out when I was googling something else completely. Her website came up, and then I couldn't find it again.

Jim: But I helped you remember her name. She knew who I was, and she told you Michael and I are around you and we want you to be our main channel and write this book. I don't like all the psychics you cross paths with, lady, but I come through to the ones who can pick me up for you, because you are a hard sell, a real pain in the ass sometimes.

Jac: Didn't think you had an ass anymore.

Jim: I have an ethereal one, Jacquie. Seriously, I only do this to validate our work. I give them stuff so you know you are on the right track and channeling clearly. They are here to confirm what we are doing, as you are the main channel.

Jac: Ok you keep telling me that.

Jim: You need to believe that, and at this stage, I only come through to psychics for you. And if my eternal soul mate should go to one, I will pretty much step over all the other energies around her to be heard.

Jac: That's understandable.

Jim: Another test passed, let's get on with the show.

Enter the Mystic

by Kathleen Tucci

When speaking with Jim Morrison he seemed determined to discuss information about his soul mate. Although much has been reported about Pamela Courson, Jim has been specific about explaining the difference between infatuation when maturity is still developing and truly knowing that you feel a void, searching for that special connection with someone that then completes you. He makes it known that Pamela was not his soul mate, as so many times is reported.

It starts with the lyrics of and what was in 1968, The Doors began recording the album "The Soft Parade." The recording process was a reported mess. The sessions for this album were out of control and took way too long. The Doors worked on the album for nine months, and in June 1969, the album was finished and published in July. Jim states that during this period he was very fragmented and feeling seriously depressed. He would struggle each day to make it to the next, hoping the nightmare would end. He says this frustration is what led him to befriend people who would later take advantage of him and his warm generosity.

He was a deep thinker and a scholar of romance, yet at the same time, desperate, lonely, and searching to fill the void that only his soul mate could. Having not found her, certainly not in Pamela, he says, and stating he was never close to any other woman either, that prolonging pain endured despite his attempts to drown his emotions in alcohol. As he spoke of that album, "The Soft Parade," Jim then began reciting a poem:

"Animals, Animals everywhere
The lost world must atone
For the love of nature is all there is
In the deep recess of our mind
The answer lies to annihilate
Can't get enough of the sweet taste
Where all comes together in this place
We will live in harmony one day
Only to be the host of all endings

Jim Morrison & Michael Hutchence

We are our own demise
Yet we share with nature
Ability to reproduce from nothing"

By the time The Doors third album, "Waiting For The Sun," was released, Jim's popularity had begun to waver somewhat. His fans began watching him become more and more reckless and out of control. After Jim's arrest in Miami in 1969, soon a nationwide ban began on The Doors, with many states not wanting to host the group's performances. Jim's emotions continued to spiral, and he began to rebel against the image others in the media had created, hanging out with folks such as actor Tom Baker, and others. There was an incident he brings up with regard to a plane ride he took with Tom Baker. He describes how he and Tom were traveling to see a Rolling Stones concert and then were arrested for "interference with the flight of an aircraft" after an altercation ensued when Tom got nasty with the crew and blamed it on Jim. Jim explained that he was minding his own business, sipping his booze and enjoying its numbing characteristics. He describes a turquoise ring and explains he was in a dazed funk, looking down at his hand, turning and twisting the ring on his finger. The ring appeared to be a chunk of raw-looking turquoise stone set in a silver base, flat against his finger. He had been rather low-key on this flight, when Tom decided to make a stink about the service they were or were not receiving from the flight staff. Once the authorities were summoned, Tom blamed it on Jim, and Jim acceptingly took the heat for his companion Tom, including picking up the financial responsibility involved. He was that kind of guy, a stand up friend in the time of need.

In December of 1970 he spent his last Christmas at the Hotel Chateau Marmont in West Hollywood, CA. He was not with Pamela Courson, and the holidays to him were not important. When I ask him why this is significant to his details about his health and subsequent death, he responds with this, "Tell them that I was not in love, but that I could relate to and understand deep love. Holidays were wasted on me...I was alone." Jim brings up suffering a fall at Hotel Chateau Marmont in Los Angeles not long before leaving for Paris. At the time, he suffered a bruised rib and muscles.

CHAPTER 16

The Dreamer

"This whole creation is essentially subjective, and the dream is the theater where the dreamer is at once: scene, actor, prompter, stage manager, author, audience, and critic."

—*Carl Jung*

Jim Morrison & Michael Hutchence

A TALE OF TWO BROTHERS

The reason so much has been speculated, fictionalized, rumored and exaggerated over my final days in Paris is quite simple, an elaborate cover-up was staged surrounding my final gig on Earth. Few people knew where I went or what I did in Paris, unlike L.A., and many have attempted throughout the years to fill in the blanks. I want to make it clear, as I lay out the true account of my final days on Earth, I did not die from a drug overdose. There were many contributing factors to my death which I will explain once and for all.

I did bask in the quiet of Paris, but the rumors surrounding my death have been greatly exaggerated. I did cross over in Paris on July 3rd, 1971. What you call "DEATH," freed me from a worn and tortured body and an equally distorted and painful existence.

This is rather an important part of my story to many, because they have made so much out of less than four months of my life. It has been truly fictionalized, and at the end, supposedly, I took my own life or decided to suddenly get into heroin, a drug I long despised. For those who do not wish to believe the truth, my voice, my story, then you may continue to indulge in your glorious romantic fantasies of me dying with the woman I loved, with a smile on my face in a bathtub after taking a fantastic drug trip. The truth is stranger than fiction, yet much more believable than the lies that were given in the name of self-preservation on the part of Pamela Courson.

I know a milestone for me occurred after the Miami incident. I self-published a two volume book of poetry. This two-volume book, was to be dedicated to the my authentic inspiration for publishing it, a person I respected at the time more than anyone else, Michael McClure. The true story is, I decided to dedicate this book to Michael and Pamela went ballistic on me, suggesting maybe I was gay with him. She threw a total fit and while it's true, she detested the Doors and claimed I should've been a poet, truth be known, the only reason was, the Doors gave me access to many women, one who could might just end up replacing her. She ran through money and without the life of a rock star, she would've had to find another wealthy man to take care of her and her expensive habits she developed once I became famous. She surely didn't want to go back to her life before. My money gave her the clothes, the cars, the drugs and all the trappings that made her who she was — a shallow, self-indulgent, mentally-ill bitch. Once again, I gave in and dedicated the poetry book I was so proud of to "Toxic Bitch", and it would be one of the many things I would change today. The person who encouraged me to publish that poetry, was the one who it should have been dedicated to, Michael McClure. Most of it was composed in college, before I ever laid eyes on Pamela Courson. She was truly not the inspiration. But she was, one of the most manipulating women that walked the earth and I was simply too worn down to handle it.

After the trial in Miami, I was a broken man, and I knew I needed to get out of L.A. Miami had drained my life force almost completely. I had worn out my welcome in L.A. and would continue to flock to people and places there that would enable my hardcore alcoholism. I wanted to mature — at 27 — I felt too old to be a rock star, and I also believed my poetry and writing would never be taken seriously or given any real recognition or consideration by those in honorable literary circles. I was also quite heavily into a cocaine habit for the months prior to leaving for Paris. I thought cocaine would give me energy and help my writing, but it's really a monster that didn't help my creativity at all. I went to Paris to go into a self-imposed exile and to stop drinking. My true motivations for going there were to dry out and become disciplined about my work. My attorney, Max Fink, got a warning in February of 1971, that if I had to serve prison time for the Miami injustice, I would not survive prison. There were also concerns my passport may be confiscated. Max got this warning from a colleague of his while playing golf. Pamela was on her way to Paris at this point searching for a place for me to write yet for someone in danger of losing his passport, I was actually in no real hurry to leave L.A.

I spent a month after Pamela left for Paris leading the life of a bachelor on his last binge. It was a blur of alcohol, cocaine and women, many women, and I loved every minute of it. As much as I wanted to return to Paris, I was in no hurry to join Pamela.

Contrary to rumors and assumptions, I did not leave the United States to avoid jail time. I was assured I would not go to jail as long as my case was on appeal, therefore, I did not exit the U.S. illegally. There was no extradition agreement with France at that time for alleged "sex crimes," which was what public exposure was said to be.

Before I went to Paris, I was quite physically exhausted but decided to go out as the ultimate frat boy. I was partying as hard as I ever partied with my male companions and had so many women in just one month. It was my ode to being a rock star. During that final month in L.A., a woman I had been involved with informed me she was pregnant. This may shock a few, but I really wanted her to have the baby. I had known her for a while and cared about her, but beyond that, I had heard the grueling details of Patricia's abortion. In all honesty, it made me sick to my stomach. I didn't want that to happen again, and I wanted to mature and to have something in life to force me to grow up. I wanted something to look forward to, and stop going from day to day, moment to moment. I had seen people I knew have kids, and it had altered their priorities and realities. I actually asked this woman not to abort my kid, and she told me she had made up her mind and was going through with it. I helped her through the abortion, and I was actually quite saddened by it.

If we would've had that child, I am certain I may still be on Earth. I would've gone to Paris but my stay would've been shorter, and I would've taken care of things in a more timely fashion. I do not believe I would have been in Paris on July 3rd of 1971. I am quite sure the public embarrassment of me fathering a child and admitting it was to a woman who lived not that far from my supposed wife would've ended my pain and suffering with Pamela Courson. It wouldn't have been pretty, but it may have gotten the job done of ending something that should've long been over.

Unfortunately, that child was not meant to be. That baby, that promise of a child, my child, could've saved my life, but it wasn't going to happen. To me, that child represented hope. Patricia's pregnancy was thrown on me during the Miami trial; the timing couldn't have been worse. This pregnancy, in early 1971, came at a calmer time.

After a month, I finally knew it was time to go to Paris to write and to try to let go of some of my numerous demons. My first time in Paris was actually in the summer of 1970, and it was not with Pamela Courson. I found the city to be exuberating, was enthralled with it and could not wait to return. Pamela had been in Paris and Morocco for months in 1970 with her French count, Jean, and had returned to L.A. in terrible shape, as she had gotten dumped by her drug dealing lover. Pamela kept talking about getting clean in Paris — finally going off smack. I was not buying into it, but she begged, and I had planned to return to Paris after the Miami trial — with or without her. I didn't go to Paris to chase Pamela, I went to Paris to chase my dreams. I sent her ahead to find a place to rent so I could write and focus. It was sheer torture being around her after she got dumped by the Count. I had developed an apathetic attitude about her and about us, which truly meant, the relationship was over. Pamela tried to convince me she was quitting smack to keep me around and keep her funds flowing. She clearly knew our relationship was on its last legs. It was a ruse, and I basically knew that before my plane ever touched down in Paris. I was really sure there was no hope for the relationship, and this would be our final break-up in Paris.

It was another part of me I had to let go. Pamela never really had me, maybe in a materialistic, bang the door down, cause enough of a problem way, but she never captivated my soul. And her soul, was a dark empty place at that point. This is not the truth many wanted to see when writing their trashy books about me, but there were a few people who certainly knew some of this. Some of my closer male companions saw this and had a few discussions with me about how to end it with her. I was always concerned Pam was going to overdose in Paris as she did in L.A. and, in fact, once I had gotten to Paris I was fairly convinced Pamela was going to be the one to overdose and end her life there, not me.

My bodyguard Tony certainly knew the truth of my relationship with Pam. Some of Pamela's own girlfriends knew the truth, as she admitted to them a few times she was in love with her French count and wanted to marry him. She still had a love for me but was quite sexually attracted to Count Jean and relished in the idea of marrying royalty and getting a title. Pam's life wasn't working for her, at least not in L.A., not her life with me. Why do you think she wanted to move to Paris? To be closer to the count and treated like a star, that is what she really cared about. I was pulling stunts in the United States, like in Miami or getting arrested with Tom Baker in Phoenix, so I was embarrassing her. She was treated differently in Paris, no one really knew about me there.

I was her meal ticket, she felt I owed her and she felt she owned me like a possession. Jim, the I don't give a shit alcoholic, allowed it to go on and on. I know that many have painted the picture that I was the one who poisoned Pam. But in all fairness, the relationship was toxic in every given way, and the biggest mistake I made was allowing it to go on for the length of time it did. I should've ended it in 1968 and got my head out of the sand. "Themis" should've been my parting gift to her. My money should've never been used to allow her to become a heroin junkie. I take responsibility for funding her lethal habit, even though I didn't endorse it, and she continually tried to hide it from me.

Pam tried to replace me on a few occasions — and I mean genuinely replace me — and I am sorry she didn't. I do believe things would've worked out better for all involved. I was a hardcore alcoholic, how could the relationship we were in ever be healthy for her? I could never be what she wanted, and she could never have my soul.

Pamela was simply what I was to her, a lesson to be learned. I remained in denial for quite some time and was also the great procrastinator in what had to be done with the relationship and other facets of my life. An alcoholic has a very real way of losing track of time and putting almost everything off. I wasted so much time, and it's truly one of my biggest regrets. When I sat at the airport in L.A. with friends, I told Frank and Kathy all I wanted to do in Paris (and it was more for my benefit than theirs) was to try and give myself hope and try to bring myself to a point of great anticipation, instead of the daydream I was creating after visiting Paris with Leon several months back. I was done with L.A., I had lost my emotional attachment to it and was really just as burned out on it as the City of Angels was burned out on Jim Morrison.

I didn't miss my first plane to Paris intentionally, but I was too busy trying to get psyched up about the possibilities of who I could recreate myself to be. When I got to Paris, mid-March 1971, I had periods of hope and hopelessness that yo-yoed back and forth. Mostly it became hopelessness. It was so strange. I knew the break-up with Pam was well on its way, because I didn't feel an emotional attachment to Pamela Susan Courson any longer. I realized this as soon as I got to Paris. I didn't feel much of anything. I had mourned our relationship, what it was and what it had become in 1969, and now in Paris, I was completely over it. I knew I had to deal with it, but after all the emotional battering she put me through, all the drama, her continued stalking of me and her overdoses, I was putting it off as well. I was not in Paris to fuel the romantic flames of a dead relationship.

Pamela made threats against me in the past to tell the press I was gay, because I had told her of my abuse and how gay men continually hit on me. Pamela accused me of contracting sexually transmitted diseases from boys, but actually, I got them from girls, strippers to be exact. She would write "FAG" in lipstick across the bathroom mirror at her place to get to me. Pamela preyed on my darkest secret, because I was so apathetic about her and our relationship. I would've been ruined if she went public with any of her falsehoods, and since I was trying to become established as a serious writer, I didn't need any more of this shit. I was trying to get my films shown, my books published, and I had planned to do so much writing and wanted to be taken seriously. I was well aware, Pamela would sabotage my plans if I had just dumped her. She would've been, and was at times, the ultimate scorned woman.

Pamela was good at wearing a mask, but by 1971, I knew who she was and I also knew I had to leave her behind if I had any chance of going forward. She was like an anchor around my leg, and I was just filled with frustration over how to free myself from the mess I had made without having to go through all the inevitable, over the top, emotional drama. I felt too exhausted for any of it. I know it sounds like I am bashing this woman from beyond the grave, but it takes two to tango. I do own up to the fact that we brought out the worst in each other. I was as no good for her, as she wasn't for me. All she wanted was to be loved, and she didn't know what to do but lash out in some crazy ways to get me to love her. She had given up her entire identity for me and had hung all her hopes on me — on us — and here I was, becoming more of a sick lush every day and not being honest by ending an already dead relationship.

My state of mind before going to Paris, no one can truly imagine. Basically, the fear of going to jail and the knowledge I had on some levels, ended The Doors, was heavily on my mind. Not only because of that night in Miami, but the last concert we did in New Orleans was always there in the back on my mind. I may not have expressed much to the other Doors, but it was like an albatross I could not dismiss. When I ended the image of Jim Morrison that blissful night in Miami, I always questioned if I damaged The Doors' legacy. I know it always seemed to be about me and/or I always seemed like an egotistical jerk, but more than anything, I was very, very private. No one on Earth ever heard what I really thought most of the time, and I always was fully aware, The Doors were not only the four of us in the group, but all the people in the background who worked hard for us. I cared about The Doors on the level of the people I was hurting along the way, not what a critic thought, although I did read the critical reviews all during my years on Earth and some of them stung. I did take some of them personally and to heart, though I was well aware most of the time that I shouldn't have done such a thing. I continually felt misunderstood, but looking back, I have only James Douglas Morrison was to blame for that, because I made some very futile attempts to become understood, by anyone. My void inside was too great, most of the time, to overcome.

The day I boarded the plane for Paris, I felt completely emotionally detached from everyone — my family, my friends, Pamela and all the other women — even The Doors themselves. I felt emotionally detached not just from everyone but almost everything. I was still very much attached to my true love, which was a bottle of scotch, whiskey, dozens of Mexican beers or any alcohol I was in the mood for — on any given day or night or could get my hands on. I always put alcohol before any human beings, and as an alcoholic, I obviously had problems maintaining relationships.

I did not find true love in my life as Jim Morrison or anything even remotely close to it, other than some romantic illusions perpetrated by the women around me. I loved many women but was never really in love, and I know that is hard to believe, but I had no love for myself. I truly never found the one who could complete me, and would make me want to change and give me hope.

Anyone who stays around an alcoholic and pretends it's a normal relationship or a healthy one, is indeed enabling him to continue down his own self-destructive torment. My only marriage on Earth was to a bottle of Irish whiskey or whatever I was in the mood for at the time. It's pretty much next to impossible to have a sincere relationship when you are constantly drunk, and the events of the night, the week or several days before remain a blur. It's surprising some of the women around me never cared about my drinking, as they seemed to enjoy me half-crocked some of the time.

At this point, I want to make a few things clear. My friend Patricia has been criticized quite a bit for the book she wrote about me, and about us. I do want to say, it wasn't a total work of fiction. I was much more intoxicated around her than she realized, but I had a gift of hiding my level of drunkenness from people — unless I was bombed beyond recognition. I could put down 20 shots, literally, and not be what you may consider shitfaced because of my enzyme disorder that allowed me to stay sober until the alcohol caught up with me. This doesn't mean my brain wasn't entirely affected by the alcohol, but I could hide it fairly well, especially by the time I met Patricia. I could be hitting the bottle not to extreme excess, but certainly could have quite a few drinks before I saw someone and they would be none the wiser.

An incident that occurred in December of 1970 that Patricia reported in her book is absolutely true. This event was certainly one of the reasons I am not here on earth now, someone was becoming scared out of her fucking mind I was really going to leave her. Patricia came to confront me in L.A. after I did not show up for her abortion in New York. She did show up at the apartment below Pamela's to visit a woman named Diane, who was a mutual friend of all of ours. I worked with Diane professionally as well. Patricia did have a nice woman-to-woman chat with Pamela about our relationship, and perhaps it wasn't the nicest thing to do but as the night wore on, I chose to spend the night with Patricia right on Diane's floor, instead of going upstairs to be with Pamela even though the next morning was Pam's birthday. This may sound as if I was the coldest bastard on Earth, but before I am judged on this choice I made, I want to make it known, being around Pamela at that time was like fingernails on a blackboard, she was dumped by her French count and an impossible bitch to deal with. At that time, I cared more for Patricia than Pamela and this happened often with other women. I stayed with Patricia that night to show her I did care about her. After all, I had shown her so little, and I was readily looking for a way for Pamela to walk away from me and stay away for good! I was hoping this heartless event, of spending the night right before where she slept, with my lover from New York who had aborted my child, would make her determined to leave me. If Pamela walked away on her own, then she may not pull the dramatic stunts she threatened every time I left her. I was actually surprised she came back from her many months with the Count. I had thoughts such as, "She's his problem now" and it was a relief. I didn't miss her at all by this time, not even for 5 minutes, I was over her and I was actually quite unhappy she returned to L.A., dumped, angry and miserable.

Proof of my feelings for Pamela can be factually supported by the fact, she ended up in the hospital during the Miami trial on a heroin overdose and I didn't fly back to see her on a weekend break, or even rush back after the trial was over. I decided to drive back from Florida to California with Babe Hill, see the country, party it up and pick-up women. I was in no rush to return to a woman who had just made a suicide attempt while I was on trial for my life! Why? I knew she was the catalyst that caused this whole fucked up fiasco to take place. I was so past her games, her lies, her schemes and demands, it was obvious.

Pam was not in L.A. when I returned, I received a long note of how she left the country with the French count. He had been seen around Janis Joplin the night of her fatal overdose, so he had to split. Pamela was in love with him, not even the drugs, or just the money but the title, and the lifestyle. She was into him sexually way beyond what she had ever been into me. I was into other women sexually more than her, so we were even. I had just been convicted in Miami of a so-called sex crime that could land me in prison for a few years, and Pamela took off with Jean and people still believe we were in love, going to stay together? Despite what some have written, I wasn't distraught she had left with him, it was actually a relief. Miami was overwhelming for me, the mockery, the madness, and the sheer fact I did not receive the public support I felt most assuredly would occur. I didn't receive fairness, justice or even impartiality. I had to sit through a sham with my life on the line. It was easier for me that she had left with him. I was no longer hung-up on when she would be found dead, it was more along the lines of when. I felt it was out of my hands and later in Paris, told my friend Alain, we could not save her if she overdosed or threatened suicide, she made her choice.

So now, there we were, December 22nd, 1970 and Pamela parades in Diane's apartment, as I lay sleeping on the floor naked with my lover from New York. Pamela stated that I always ruined her birthdays, and there is some semblance of truth to this. We did not spend holidays or birthdays together except but for only in the beginning of our relationship. I did not celebrate her birthdays (or other holidays) with her for the most part and she did not celebrate my birthdays with me. In regards to holidays, I gave a few other significant women gifts on their birthdays, at Christmas and, at times, random gifts just to show I was thinking about them. If they were not in or around L.A., I would send their gifts through the mail. I would also hand deliver gifts at times. I would send very thoughtful gifts to other women. I do believe this illustrates that a man truly in love with the one who told everyone she was his "wife," would not do such things. Patricia was one of those women who did receive birthday, Christmas and random gifts. I did put time and careful thought into these gifts I gave others; I did care about a few of these women — I was never in love but for the most part, cared more deeply for *them* than I did Pamela Courson.

To be clear about this, keep in mind, that from 1968 on, Pamela was looking to replace me and not just to make me jealous or to give her some attention, but to literally find a new relationship and man she could cling onto. It seemed like an easier way out for me, if I could more or less replace her. Patricia was telling Pamela to her face about our torrid affair and the subsequent abortion, and Pamela didn't flinch in front of Patricia, but secretly on the inside, her anger was starting to rage, her fear, beginning to mount I might actually be leaving her.

She was getting her sexual kicks elsewhere, as I was getting mine.

The relationship Pamela and I supposedly had was such a façade it even shocked Patricia. I was the one who ruined my relationship with Patricia because by the time I met her, I was the hopeless alcoholic, and shortly thereafter, the Miami Fiasco occurred and I was teetering on the edge of disaster. I really was very cold to Patricia when she came to visit me during the Miami trial, but I was becoming emotionally unattached to everything and everyone around me. I was lost.

I did actually invite Patricia to go to Paris with me, for a couple of reasons. I felt I owed it to her, and I wanted to show her I was not such a bad guy. She did speak French, but that wasn't nearly as important to me as to have someone with me who would help me achieve my goals while I was there. Patricia did do drugs with me but had her feet on the ground, she wasn't an addict and I truly needed a coherent individual with me. If Patricia had gone to Paris, I am 100 percent sure I would still be roaming around on Earth at this time. I did not invite her there to be the other woman, but I did invite her there to be my companion in Paris. Keep in mind, Pamela was going to Paris with or without me, it was easier to send her ahead to find a place in which I could write, but she would've gone back whether I went or not. She was losing her grip on me, her guilt trips and tantrums ceased to spark any emotion in me, and basically, she made a plea to get off smack in Paris. I wasn't at all hopeful about this and in the most intrinsic way, didn't really care if she did get clean or not. I believed Pam, and I would continue to lead our separate lives as we did in L.A. But I really wanted a companion with me who I could explore Paris with, as this was the second time I was going and I was truly captivated with the City of Poets. Patricia declined my invitation, and I can hardly blame her. I intended to see her when I returned to the States, probably toward the fall, and I was hoping for at least a friendship because I did view the relationship we had as over. I wanted to stay in touch with her because of my guilt at that point. Things had ended badly when she visited me in February of

1971 before I left for Paris. I wasn't a bad person and I feel remorseful about it.

As a result of going to Paris minus Patricia or any other coherent companion, I preferred to take my long walks around the city alone. Pamela often wanted to go, but I turned her down. I was trying to write and not be bothered. My friend, Alain, would accompany me at times or I would visit my friend, Agnes. I think if anyone else had gone to Paris with me other than another addict, I would still be alive and on Earth.

My relationship with Patricia would not have worked out even if I had lived, because the relationships I formed as a hardcore alcoholic would have completely unraveled, and honestly, mine with Patricia had already unraveled.

I never knew what to think about the Wiccan practices and no matter how unconventional I was, I could not call what Patricia and I had a marriage. Patricia and I lived on different coasts, and I spent time in New York without her and with other women. I was at home in California, and if not staying at Pam's place, I was often with other women. Who with any amount of self-pride would deem that a marriage? If Patricia was really my wife, where was she? Why didn't she want to be with me? She was a writer and truthfully could've written anywhere in the world, including California. I look back on my life as Jim Morrison and realize I wasn't the only dreamer, they were all around me with delusions of grandeur as to who I was and what I would give them. They all seemed to want to be the "ONE," and yet none of them ever could be or would be. I was a loner, end of story.

Paris was to be my rebirth. I told Salli Stevenson on October 13, 1970 that I would've chosen a calmer, quieter existence, and I truly meant it. I actually believed that away from my male drinking buddies, all the places I would go and get trashed in L.A. and all the excesses around me, I would sober up. I look back now and realize I could not run from myself, the demons weren't in L.A., they were on the inside. My life was in shambles, but I was not suicidal — depressed, yes. I had been suicidal in 1969 for brief periods, but I was past that now. I knew it would take every last ounce of energy I had, but I fully intended to change my life, become the disciplined writer I wanted to be and knew I could be if I rid myself of alcohol and Pamela Susan Courson. These were all the desires of a true dreamer.

The dreamer tried twice in Paris, and for a period of several days each time, to quit drinking. I was successful but it never lasted. The second time was longer than the first time, but I could not seem to maintain sobriety, I felt as if alcohol had beaten me.

I need to explain the path of destruction, which I, the dreamer simply tried to ignore. In June of 1970, I contracted pneumonia while in New York with Patricia. She got me some antibiotics, but I didn't allow myself ample time to rest from the illness and darted off to Paris with Leon prior to my trial in Miami. I did go to a doctor when I returned from Paris, as I was ill again and put on more antibiotics. After the emotional toll of the Miami trial, my immune system and health were declining. I was not one who liked to visit doctors, as I was very negligent about my health, and the fact that I went to see one, should make it clear, I was really, really sick.

I had a fall from the Chateau Marmont a few months before leaving for Paris. I absolutely coughed up blood at that time but was told by the doctor, I didn't break any ribs as I thought I had. I was never truly right again after that fall. In April of 1971, while in Paris, I coughed up some pink sputum and went to American Hospital and was given some anti-spasmodic medicine. I was told to cut back on alcohol and cigarettes.

In May of 1971, I accidentally fell off a terrace of my room in L'Hotel in Paris and onto the hood of a parked car. This aggravated my medical problems and my limp had returned that I had from the fall at the Chateau Marmont a few months earlier. Alcoholic Jimbo brushed it off, as I had done so many times before, and ran to the closest bistro for a drink. I wasn't dead yet, so I was going to drink.

By June of 1971, I developed two serious health conditions I was unaware of. One would be pleurisy, and the other I have learned was a duodenal ulcer. The truth is, neither of these conditions I developed should surprise anyone, and they absolutely explain the symptoms I was living with night and day.

In London in early June, 1971, few know of the near death experience I had and went into denial about afterwards. Let me see if this sounds familiar, my lungs were full of mucus one night in

London, and Pamela did have a hard time waking me. She slapped me and threw a glass of water on my face. When she did wake me, I stunk, I reeked worse than anything I could ever remember and actually did want to take a bath. Pamela was also yelling at me, and I simply wanted to go in the bathtub to get some peace. I got into the tub and I coughed up some pink sputum. There were no clots of blood and it only happened once, and she came in and cleaned out the basin for me. I really almost didn't wake up that night, and Pamela called the hotel operator to get a doctor for me. The doctor came to see me early in the morning and told me I was on the right medication I was given in Paris and to get some rest. The events of that awful night in London would be greatly embellished a month later and used to explain how I ended up dead in Paris. They were the outline of the cover-up story that would be given, which was completely unbelievable from the beginning, but it got even more so as time went on and the story changed.

I saw a doctor once again when I returned to Paris, believing I was only suffering from asthma flare-ups as I did suffer from a minor form of asthma. The air quality in Paris was very poor at the time, and this can be validated. I was consuming large quantities of alcohol on and off, smoking cigarettes (sometimes like a chimney stack) and I was taking my anti-spasmodic medication. My medication bottle had a label on it and it was, of course, written in French. I couldn't read or speak French, I was the typical stupid American traveling abroad, and the medication was not to be mixed with alcohol — or so the French label said. I was not properly diagnosed or treated for either pleurisy or the duodenal ulcer I was suffering with. I had serious chills on and off for two weeks before I met my great demise and would build a fire in the apartment we were renting in the Paris heat. My health had been terrible for a year before I left the Earth, yet after these incidents of being sick as a dog, I would go into denial that I would shake off whatever it was since the grim reaper didn't take me yet. I had told many I would not live to be 30 or would die young, and I had seem images of my own death.

But truthfully, I wanted to live a long life and go out quietly in my sleep. It turns out, I did anything but that. My death was not easy.

I was a poet and, of course, what more serious place for a poet to cultivate his art than Paris? My poetry was not conventional, and because I was a rock star, it was highly disregarded by the critics. I truly wanted to be recognized as a poet, and I was not given that recognition during my Earth life. I wasn't Chaucer and didn't pretend to be, I was an American writer and poet. Some say I was a hippie, but I contend I was an absolute beatnik poet. I lived without worldly possessions in ways that some find incomprehensible. I had all this money, but the material things meant little or nothing outside of my books. I wanted to be accepted as a poet, a serious writer, not a rock star. I never truly got the acceptance, but it would've come later on…if I had stayed on the Earth.

"The Lords and the New Creatures" were very early ramblings for me. I did most of it while still in college, it wasn't a very enlightened work, but I still thought, in some ways, remotely interesting. I left some of my best work all over California in notebooks, and I even left some fine work in Paris. Much of it was never recovered, some was destroyed. I wrote more in Paris in the four months that I was there than anyone realizes. This nonsense that I wasn't writing just because I was depressed and physically ill is simply bullshit. My work did mature and ripen, it was not as naive and contrived as it was in the early days. I still had good writing days in Paris and much to say. I was writing a rock opera, new poetry, and an amazing essay on the Miami fiasco. I was also working out storylines and concepts for a great American novel, not "THE" great American novel, but one of them. I was terrible about leaving my writings behind at all kinds of places in California, and that didn't really change in Paris. Some of it is gone, never to be seen or heard from again.

Some of it was burned in the fireplace of the Parisian apartment the night before my death and even more letters and notes, immediately following my death by the "Toxic Queen." She was angry, she was full of fear and she was, the ultimate woman scorned and I hadn't even left her yet, but she knew for a fact, it was coming soon, very soon.

Jim Morrison & Michael Hutchence

CHAPTER 17

The Schemer

"There are two things to be considered with regard to any scheme. In the first place, "Is it good in itself?" In the second, "Can it be easily put into practice?""

—*Jean-Jacques Rousseau*

Jim Morrison & Michael Hutchence

A TALE OF TWO BROTHERS

In Paris, as in L.A., Pamela Courson and I often lead separate lives. That's not really how she wanted it initially in Paris, but in all truthfulness, regardless of how asinine this sounds, at this stage I could handle her better on her junk than I could when she was not using heroin. I needed to be alone and take my long walks, and to find inspiration and write, write and write. She often wanted to accompany me to places like the Place Des Vosges and on my many journeys to the River Seine, other assorted sites and cafes.

Much of the time in Paris, Pamela was consumed by her French Count, Jean de Breteuil, who was actual royalty, and Pamela was one to assume her identity from a man. If she couldn't be my wife, Count Jean would fit the bill nicely. He had a title, he was rich and — better yet — all the heroin she could ever want. Pamela had been involved with him for a couple of years on and off in L.A. and had just spent some months with him Paris and Morocco at the end of 1970. She came back to L.A. at the end of 1970 pretty messed up as the Count apparently had moved onto his next conquest. Yet, Pam remained infatuated with him and hung her hopes on some kind of a possible future with him. At this point, she wasn't banking on a future with me. After all, she had promised to get off the smack in Paris, that wasn't happening and she knew I may finally be ready to throw in the towel on the relationship. She could see how apathetic I was about it.

Pam was, for the most part, in love with Jean, and here I was, trying to figure out how to end the relationship with her in a nice, quiet way and treat her with dignity and respect and here she was, thinking about the French Count and if they could be together. I didn't see the writing on the wall about Pam and Jean. I guess because I was so wrapped up in the world of Jimbo the drunk. I had met Jean and I thought he was pure scum, but I generally didn't like any of Pamela's friends who were just with her half of the time because I was her old man or because she had my money.

In April of 1971 Pamela initially wanted to travel to Cotes De Azure where the Rolling Stones had houses and hung-out on occasion. This was a ploy to find the Count who was now involved with Marianne Faithfull, a former love interest of Keith Richards. Pam was already getting heroin in Paris from one of her many male friends, so there was no need to chase down Jean for any other reason beside the obvious one, she wanted him back. We didn't make that particular trip.

Pam and I took a road trip for three weeks to Spain, Tangiers, Marrakech, Morocco, and Casablanca. I know that Pamela painted a romantic picture of this trip, but it was anything but idyllic. This was the first time we were together in such a confined space, meaning the rental car we were traveling in, for that amount of time, in a long, long while. We flew back to Paris thankfully. Pam didn't have any of her smack with her, and by now, she was a hardcore junkie. We fought about anything or next to nothing, and on the way out of France I actually picked up some female hitchhikers to shut her up and piss her off. I could only take so much.

I was on the trip of my lifetime, seeing things I had always dreamt about and going to places I had long awaited to visit, and I would go and often zone out to be in my own space. I was unaware, for a time, that while I was going on the greatest travel adventures of my lifetime, Pamela was on a wild goose chase for her French count. We stayed with people connected to the French Count so she could ascertain where he was or what he was doing, and conveniently, they might have access to some smack. I cannot condemn Pamela's sexual relationship with the Count. After all, I was having so many during the years with her, and considering for a year and a half at this point, we were not engaged in any sort of physical relationship, it only made sense. Our sexual relationship did not resume during our time in Paris or any of the trips we took while there. Sex with two addicts was never all that great.

In Tangiers, Pamela and I stayed with Paul and Talitha Getty. Talitha was a lover of the French Count and sadly, quite hooked on heroin herself. Pam wanted to know how serious the relationship was or had been. We also stayed at the home of the

A TALE OF TWO BROTHERS

Count's Mother in Marrakech; that is where my relationship was with Pamela, we were staying with the Mother of her French lover. She was searching for Jean, in a time when no one had cell phones, so it was pretty much hit or miss.

In Marrakech, I told Pam I wanted to go swimming, and I was moving to a hotel for the pool. She came with me, but the real reason was I caught on and grew tired of Pam's obsession with the French Count. She wanted to put this façade of romance on in front of other people or in front of any camera snapping pictures of us, but she could hardly follow through with it.

When we returned to Paris at the beginning of May, 1971, we took up a temporary residence at L'Hotel. I realized how hard the three weeks on the road with Pamela had been, even though I visited some of the most amazing things I would see in my lifetime and had drawn tremendous inspiration for them. My drinking became extremely heavy at this point, I wanted to zone out on this relationship, as much as possible.

In the middle of May, Pam wanted to go to Corsica. The day we went to get on the plane, I just couldn't do it. I needed a drink, for one thing, and wanted to go back to a café or bistro in Paris by myself. I simply couldn't go on with her that day, I couldn't take it anymore. I told her I was going to the bathroom, and I did something so childish but it was the easy way out. I threw my passport in a trash bin along with my plane ticket, wallet and other things I was carrying. I know this was really a desperate move, but I was always losing things so it wasn't hard for her to fathom. I kept very few possessions on my person, and yet, would lose them all the time. I told her someone may have stolen it or that I had accidentally lost it. There was nothing accidental about this act.

I had gotten out of going that day but had to go to the American Embassy in Paris to get my papers replaced. To my rather unpleasant surprise, they issued the passport and papers very quickly, and I felt stuck to take this trip with her. I didn't want to tip my hand that I was figuring out how to end the relationship, because she would've flipped on me. For those who do not believe I deliberately lost my passport, wallet and plane ticket, it's kind of interesting that the passport was later found in the airport and returned to my parents after my abrupt exit from the Earth. If it had been stolen, I don't believe they would have it, but it probably would've turned up later on the black market or eBay™. Passports were valuable things in a time when they could be so easily altered. I also still had possession of all my money, I had taken it out of my wallet before I threw my stuff out.

When we went to Corsica, I want to say, categorically, it was an awful trip. It rained for 10 days, and Pam was in need of her heroin. To say we were both bored, was a terrible understatement. We had nothing to discuss anymore, or did we really ever? For the last two years, Pamela had told her close friends I had outgrown her, and she told me the same. She had also told others she had outgrown me. She was right, we had outgrown living in delusions about each other.

My friends Frank and Kathy wrote about taking a trip abroad and invited me to go. I did write back and reported to them that I had lost my passport and wallet to keep my cover story to Pam. She was always going through my mail. In L.A., I got my stuff at The Doors' office so that made it more difficult, but in in Paris, she would read all my stuff . I really didn't want to tell my friends, what I was doing to avoid being around my so-called "wife." I didn't want anyone to know how bad it was for me in Paris. Frank and Kathy were making this trip at the end of July, and I had told them they could stay at the apartment we had rented. I did not answer their invitation about taking a trip with them to Turkey and Greece, and that was intentional. I was making plans to leave Pamela, not just for a short time, but permanently and leave Paris for a few weeks. I intended to return, after visiting Rome by myself and take up a new residence and meet a friend named Fred Myrow, so we could work on the rock opera I had been writing. I was serious about pushing myself and I was serious about ending it with Pamela for good. I did not want her to know where I was going or what my future plans were. I just wanted to be free.

On June 28th, I had only a few short days left on Earth. Pamela and I went with my friend, Alain on a day trip to Chantilly. This was a very hard day for me, I was not well physically and I had to play a role so Pamela would not suspect what was coming. Pamela had spent most of the month of June away from me and with the French Count as Marianne Faithfull must have been busy. She had hopes of winning the Count back and clearly that didn't happen. She returned to the Parisian apartment, and I had Alain staying with me at the time. Alain left and Pam was clinging to me like I was her best friend. She had suffered public humiliation with me for years with the other women cropping up, and that face to face with Patricia back in December still bothered her. She was angry, I didn't love her and my biggest mistake, was being unable to play the role of nothing being wrong between us long enough to get out of dodge. The same day we went to Chantilly, I had written the Door's accountant Bob Greene.

I began to scheme, as I needed to find out what I could afford to give Pamela and have her sign something from my attorneys stating she would not do the things she had threatened me with so many times, like making false claims I was gay or liked boys. Miami was still on appeal, and I didn't need any additional bad publicity. I had turned my life into a circus act and was trying to restore it to something with some kind of semblance of dignity.

Pam held so much over my head, along with the fake suicide attempts, real overdoses and other strange cries for help. I needed to get her to sign off . The times I lived in were quite different than where you are now in America. While allegations of homosexuality may not be viewed by many as perversion at this stage, it was viewed quite differently in the late 1960s and early 1970s. Of course, anytime molestation of children is brought up, you would be deemed a monster, and rightfully so. Such an allegation, even without merit would ruin my life forever, and I knew it. People already believed the worst about me. I planned to leave Pamela with a credit card in her own name, have her return to L.A., meet with my attorneys' and sign a statement that she would not speak publicly to anyone of my molestation as a child or present false rumors that I was gay or involved with young boys. She would be given a monetary settlement, to shut her up about our relationship and that would be it...or so I hoped.

I wanted to see what I could give her, and I wrote to the accountant from The Doors office, Bob Greene. I did not tell him of my personal situation or my plans, he was an accountant not a confidant. I wanted credit cards in both our names, so I could leave Pam in Paris and take off, possibly to Rome. I also kept thinking about going all the way to Mexico to meet a female friend. I was considering meeting a female friend there. I was even thinking of going the July 4th weekend. I was too physically ill, it turned out, to go that weekend, and besides, I was waiting a few days to get Pamela her credit card and get some cash and a credit card for myself for traveling, and had thoughts of going in the next few days, as soon as the credit cards and cash arrived I was going to leave.

    I figured I could leave Pam with a credit card, hopefully, she would not attempt to bother me. Then I could have my attorneys prepare a settlement. I was prepared to leave Pamela with $100,000 for the pain and suffering of being with me. What she did with it was not my concern, I was going to wash my hands of her and the toxicity which permeated our entire relationship. One-hundred thousand dollars in 1971 was a more than a fair and decent settlement as far as I was concerned. I was checking what my finances looked like to see if I could do it, give her the 100 grand and to see if I could buy a place in Paris to live on and off by myself. I did tell Bob Greene we wanted to clear out of "Themis" and give it to her sister. This was my way of not having to put another penny in the white elephant Pamela insisted on having. Pam was not serious at all about it. It was a huge waste of money I regret, because the money could've gone for so many things and creative endeavors.

    I told Bob to give "Themis" to Pam's sister and her sister's husband, as maybe they could make a go of it. If I was staying with her, I would not have cleared out of "Themis" or given her dream boutique away. Pam had never told me she was not returning to L.A., the rent on her apartment was still being paid there and she still owned "Themis" at this point, so I assumed at some point, she was going home. I was anxious to find out about the finances and to get those credit cards in both our names so I could leave her for awhile and get a settlement drawn up by my attorney. My attorney had handled some sticky and difficult situations for me in the past, I didn't see this one as any more challenging.

    I was ready to make a serious move in my life. You may think you have the time to change things, but tomorrow is never promised. Pamela romanticized our time in Paris to feed her own delusions. A male drinking buddy, and mutual hell raiser, named Babe Hill, initially gave me the idea of a financial settlement for

Pamela, and I thought it was the best idea he ever came up with. I was ready, it was time, and I was so close to changing my life, but my time ran out and a huge mess was left behind, for no one knew the private pain and plans I was scheming in my final days in Paris. I was not suicidal, I was methodical at this point, preparing for a fresh start, a bright morning and new future. I must have been a dreamer, for none of this would ever come to fruition. I regret my wasted time, my procrastination and above all, my wasted life.

All Roads Lead to Mexico...

The chameleon chirping on the side of the road,
told me it was time to go...

I've been there before searching
for a Shaman and returned once
more to sing a few songs...
the land of the ghost of Cortes,
Montezuma's revenge,
the Aztecs dream gone wrong

I met a woman who guided me
on a tour of the Mayan ruins
I knew I had been there before
the macabre chamber of my sacrifice
instantly transported me to another life

I've seen the Aztec gold
and felt more akin to this place
than any other at 25 years old

My tour guide was a gentle lover,
she reminded me of another
who remained unseen, but for only in my dreams

Jim Morrison & Michael Hutchence

As I searched the ancient ruins
and received a visitation from fine art
I realized this place, was deep within my heart

In the Parisian summer
the memory of Me'jico burned
Why would a poet leave Paris for Tijuana?
Because my soul yearned and yearned

All roads lead back to Mexico
The land of my birth a thousand years ago
I long to return to a place
I felt most at home

In the middle of July 1971,
I would've been downing Mexican beers
in the sweltering sun
while gringos sang their songs
and told their tales
that go on and on

I would've returned to the Ancients
And learned their secret language
But I didn't have the patience
So I went home in anguish
I saw the chameleon,
and knew it was me,
I've changed so many times
In this strange vortex of energy
A cyclone of all my days

In Mexico, my heart often stays

All roads lead to Mexico…

—*channeled from Jim Morrison*

CHAPTER 18

The Grim Reaper

"I can remember how when I was young I believed death to be a phenomenon of the body; now I know it to be merely a function of the mind — and that of the minds of the ones who suffer the bereavement. The nihilists say it is the end; the fundamentalists, the beginning; when in reality it is no more than a single tenant or family moving out of a tenement or a town."

—*William Faulkner,* As I Lay Dying

Jim Morrison & Michael Hutchence

A TALE OF TWO BROTHERS

A turning point came for me that no one on Earth really knew about. After a concert that went longer than it should've in Houston in 1968, I was backstage and there were all these people around, and yet I was in one of my moods. I didn't want to be bothered, yet no one was leaving me alone. I didn't lash out, like Jim the drunk often did on innocent, random victims. But, I became aware that night in Houston that if I remained a public figure and if I continued to be the lead singer of The Doors, I was going to end up selling out my soul or my life was going to end by my own hand...or it would end because of the lifestyle I signed on for to cope with never being understood. I felt no one understood me, and I wasn't being myself anymore in front of the audience because they would never get it anyway. Houston was a turning point, and it began a downward spiral, as I was depressed.

All the women were no longer a power trip for me. Some were cute, some downright pretty, and others, just complete freaks but they were women who would've never looked at Jim Morrison before he donned a pair of leather pants, got skinny and grew his hair. By Houston, the more women I had, the more of a void they left. In just three years, from this concert and my realizations after it, it would be all over.

As I fast-forward to Paris, I am fortunate to have seen things in those last months that left a lasting impression on me. I finally got to visit Andalusia, which I had written about in "Spanish Caravan." There were films shot of me visiting Spain. My physical body may have been there, but I felt transported and as if a new spirituality was awakening within. Before I left the Earth I finally got to see this work of art in person that had deeply inspired me called "The Garden of Earthly Delights" by Boesch. I sat and stared at it for quite some time, scrutinizing small details of this painting. It really had this mesmerizing affect on me, it was as if I was touched by something not of Earth, something divine. I felt as if I was time traveling when I visited Morocco, it was my second time there, and I had this strange déjà vu feeling both times, but could never really find what I was searching for. These trips were very special to me, as they inspired Jim Morrison to become more spiritual. It would not have mattered who I had taken these trips with, someone I knew, someone I didn't know, someone I loved or someone I could hardly stand, the experiences were absorbed in a private place in my soul, as so many things in life were with me. I would be in my own world anyway, regardless of who else was there or not there.

I was on this newfound spiritual quest of sorts after these trips, so how did I end up facing the grim reaper?

My death was simple, the complexities of the lies around it, were not. It never had to be that way. To understand how it all fit together, I refer back to June of 1971. Pamela dragged me to London under some guise, but as it turned out, I wasn't really up for the trip. Count Jean was in London at the time staying at the home of Keith Richards, because the Count was with Marianne Faithfull. Once again, I felt duped because I had no idea we were going to London to find the Count. I was in no condition to argue, and I gave in to the trip, as I took a fascination to London since The Doors played there. However, I went against my better judgment. As soon as we got to London, Pam took off to see the Count and get her smack. I would say it was the final nail in the coffin of our relationship, but in truth, the relationship was already cremated and the ashes spread all over us and everything we touched.

In the middle of the night in London, Pam could hear my breathing was shallow, and I sounded as if I was about to die right then and there. She tried to wake me up in her heroin stupor, but it was difficult. She slapped me across the face and threw a glass of water on me. I did wake up, but it took a while. My lungs were full of mucus. After a point, post waking up, I realized I reeked. I smelled as bad as I ever smelled, and Pamela was in between coming in and out of her stupor, screaming at me about not waking up and trying to shake me while I was awake. I didn't feel well enough to even go out and have a beer, or a few shots of whiskey, so that should say something as to the condition I was in.

But I couldn't handle being slapped and yelled at so I retreated to the bathtub...

While I was trying to enjoy my bath I began to cough up pink sputum (mucus mixed with traces of blood). This pink sputum had been coming up here and there for awhile. The first time this happened was in February of 1971 when I took a bad fall at the Chateau Marmont, I should've given up the high-wire acts long before then.

Pamela cleaned out a basin with a small amount of this pink sputum in it. I had called her to come in the bathroom, as I was feeling very sick. I was having a coughing fit from hell in the tub, and she was clearly falling back into her stupor, as if she didn't hear me. After I called to her a few times, she came in and she took the basin and cleaned it out for me. I did feel somewhat better after coughing up this goop. She called the hotel operator to summon a doctor, because there were traces of blood coming from my lungs and there was a strange gurgling sound in my breathing. I was sick, weak and felt as if I was going to die that night, but after the coughing fit, I did feel somewhat better.

A doctor didn't show until the early morning hours, and by then I felt halfway to alright. He told me I was on the right medication, the one given to me in France and I should rest and follow-up with my doctor at the American Hospital. I did follow-up with the doctor a week later in France. I was not on the right medication as it turns out, and I also needed an antibiotic as pleurisy and a duodenal ulcer had now taken hold of my body. I went into denial that I had almost bit the dust that night in London, because it didn't last very long — but the intensity of it truly rocked me.

It was this incident, only a month prior to my final departure, that Pamela Courson constructed her cover-up story. She took real events, embellished them and inserted them into her storyline. It really was her storyline. No one else could vouch for it. Fire department rescue workers did find me in a bathtub on the morning of July 3rd, 1971 in Paris, France, but did it ever occur to anyone, I was placed in that bathtub when I was already dead?

My final days in Paris were troublesome. I was not physically well, coughing, spitting up sputum, and having no lung capacity to make it up a flight of steps without being out of breath. At 27, I felt 72.

The last time I was truly around Pamela Courson was the evening of July 1st, 1971. We went out to eat and had gotten into a fight because I was not feeling well at all that evening and some drunken German students recognized me. I couldn't speak German, so I could only imagine what they were saying. I was generally not rude unless I was drunk off my ass, and I could be a fairly obnoxious, degenerate when heavily intoxicated. I simply wished to switch tables because I just wanted to eat quietly. When I wanted to change tables, Pamela began telling me to fuck myself, so I left. It goes to show, at this stage, I could not eat a meal with this woman without arguing.

As I left the restaurant, she followed me back to the apartment. That night, July 1st, 1971, I watched the movies of our trips to Morocco, Corsica, and Marrakech. I also listened to The Doors' music, "L.A. Woman" and some earlier stuff as well. I was just going off in my own world while she yelled and screamed at me and even ripped up some of my more recent work. She made confetti out of it and threw it in the fireplace. There was certainly a lot of work preserved from Paris but not all of it. Pamela went on and on, about how I owed her, I could never leave her or I would be sorry, how I wouldn't fuck her and I wasn't able to fuck anyone because I was a fag. Pamela tried to resume a sexual relationship with me in the hotel in Marrakesh, only to be rejected. I was not physically attracted to her at that point and just told her I wasn't feeling well.

The night of July 1st, I showed her my hand, which turned out to be the biggest single mistake in my life. In the Parisian apartment, Pamela went on and on and I couldn't take it anymore. I told her, I didn't love her, and we were going our separate ways. I called her a few names I am not proud of, but after being called a fag who liked little boys over the course of a few years, I told her she was a junkie and a whore and I had someone else I wanted to move on with. At the time, there was no one woman in particular I wanted to move on with. I didn't just make that statement to hurt the "Toxic Queen" but to hopefully make her so disgusted or upset, she would let me leave, not try to follow me this time and let this end as it should've years earlier. She started to pull a huge dramatic scene on me and we had been fighting for 3 hours. I had to get away from her, so I went out around midnight and I got myself the French version of a grilled cheese sandwich (croque monsieur) and some beer. That was the final time I had any real conversation with Pamela Courson before I met the grim reaper. She knew, she really knew, our relationship was going to end and rapidly. She decided not to mention this to anyone after I took my final curtain call for reasons only she can explain.

I was truly ill the next day, July 2nd. My friend Alain came by and wanted to get me out in the warm air and thought I may feel better if I had gotten something to eat. Alain knew, something was really bothering me and it was this final showdown with the Psychopath I had been supporting for years. That altercation, made me wonder what she was going to pull, and I wasn't sure what to expect. I had to stop a few times on our walk with severe hiccupping fits. Alain and I did some walking, but I had to sit down, which was unusual for me during a walk, and we stopped by some shops. I was shaking, literally shaking, at times during this, my final day on Earth.

I stopped by a jewelry store and bought a red carnelian Star of David pendant. I told Alain it was for Pam. I simply lied to him, because I didn't feel like explaining my situation with Pam and I actually bought it for Patricia, as a peace offering, a way of saying let's be friends. It wasn't a pentagram but I thought she would like it none the less. I was always giving ladies I was involved with jewelry, and I tried to find really special pieces they could remember me by.

I felt I had given Pam enough. My thought at that stage was, she may end up hocking any gifts I gave her for drugs one day. I had a strange and unusual nervousness that day. It was the weirdest feeling I ever had on Earth, and I had experienced some truly bizarre things in my time. This wasn't anything like the shakes alcoholics get or the freaky feeling I got on acid or strong weed in the past. I tried to get Alain to stay with me, as I was so incredibly nervous and disturbed, but I didn't know why. I made excuses of things I wanted him to do or help me with, but he pretty much saw through it. We were having a drink, and that is where Alain made his exit to go meet our friend Agnes. If he had known

I would cross over soon, I am positive he would've stayed with me and called for medical help. He was a great friend.

Alain told me to go see a western that night called "Pursued." I want to make this clear, I was too ill to go out, I barely made it back to the apartment and up the steps and Pamela was not around. I never went out after returning to 17 Rue Beautreillis that fateful evening of July the 2nd, 1971. I don't know exactly why Pamela lied to Alain and others the following day, saying we had seen the movie and I didn't like it very much. It was a western, and I had a fondness for them. It was slow and a bit obtuse in some not easily seen ways, actually I would've enjoyed that film. Alain asked the next day if we had seen the movie and Pamela said we did. Later on she told people, and several of them, I went to the movies alone that night, and the film, which was "Pursued" was even changed to "Death Valley."

I had some more drinks after Alain left, and I slowly made my way back to the apartment, struggling to even make it up the steps. I was not well enough to go out for dinner, see a movie or visit the Rock 'n' Roll circus for some smack. Pamela was not at the apartment when I returned, which was a relief. I couldn't have handled another fight with the Orange County bitch. When I got to the apartment, I laid down, and I was half out of it. I had been drinking, I was really sick and so I was not the most coherent at the time. I had planned to be a man and own up to my death, because the way I lived my life, who I allowed in it and to be privy to my private world, ultimately contributed to my leaving way before my time. I had decided for legal reasons, not to reveal the name of my murderer I was going to own up to my own mistakes from this side and let my murderer off the hook.

I have since decided, the truth needs to be told and the way photographs of my murderer (alone or with me) are continuously displayed, is fucking horrific to me and how she is called the love of my life, or anything close to it. You see, as a lay sick as a dog in the bed in Paris, my murderer walked in the apartment, on a heroin trip, and decided to inject me with poison. It was done without my knowledge or consent. I was unaware it was done until after I left my body. Why did she do it? To keep me in Paris, to make me stay, to cause me to get hooked on the poison that ruled her life, so why would she do that? Because she could not accept I was leaving her for good, she could accept the truth and she was angry. I felt a terrible numbness in my right arm. I had the most intense pain in my arm I had ever felt, and I could not move it. I could not get off the bed or call for help. I was also going into a semi-conscious state at this point from the pain and physical illness. I then got the worst headache of my life, the pain was a motherfucker, I was absolutely passing out. My chest was tight, I felt as if I couldn't get any air. I knew something was happening but was too weak to move or speak coherently.

No one was there when I passed away, I was found a couple of hours later, laying dead, on the bed in Paris, after spending nearly five hours breaking on through the other side. These were five painful hours, and I want to make it known, I struggled to hang on and tried to stay on the Earth. I took no drugs of any kind that night other than the five little pills of prescribed medication earlier in the day. I did have several drinks that night before returning to the apartment. What killed me, Jim Morrison was mixing heroin with alcohol. Keep in mind, as a non-heroin user, it was a perfectly awful death. The American Government didn't have me waxed, it was not a staged death so I could continue to live on and have everyone think I'm dead (Laughs). It was a painful death, unnatural, and unnecessary. A simple autopsy would have proven to the world, and I sincerely wish one had been performed. I had almost succumb a month earlier from natural causes, but I didn't and I would've lived for 40 more years!

After I was injected with a large dose of Chinese heroin, the woman who killed me took off, with a man who later became a French TV star. This was a crime of passion, there were a myriad of thoughts running through her mind. This was a way to get me to stay in Paris, she hoped, in another way, undoubtedly she wanted to see me get hooked on her drug of choice so I would never leave her, and a part of her, even wanted to see me dead, as payback for the hell I put her through. She was in a rage, and later returned in utter disbelief, she had actually caused my death that fateful night.

I died alone, and I will later discuss what I saw and experienced on my way to this side. I did not die in a bathtub, I wasn't well enough to take a bath or make it out of the bed. Pamela came in during the early morning hours of July 3rd, 1971 and found me already deceased on the bed. She desperately tried to wake me up violently, and she went into a state of pure panic. At first, she thought I was playing a joke on her. It took her awhile to wake me up in London, but she still succeeded, so she was hoping beyond hope that I could be revived. She did use heroin that night and was quite stoned, as well as scared out of her mind, I was dead, I was gone, what was she to do? What would happen to her now? How would she explain it to anyone we knew? How would she explain it to the French police and officials? How would she explain it to the world?

My murderer realized she ended my life. She was now in a mode of self-preservation. Pamela immediately phoned the French Count. I was already gone, medical attention was not necessary, but she still hung onto the hope I would suddenly wake up. The Count rushed over and was told what happened and Jean put Pam into a further state of hysteria. Jean was as scared, if not more so than Pamela. It was *his* smack that was in the apartment I died in, and if anyone found out what happened, he knew he would be sitting in a French jail cell, opposite of Pamela Courson for a very long time. Count Jean was being looked at under a microscope at this time, because of his alleged involvement in giving Janis Joplin her fatal overdose, which I refuse to address at this time. It's not as if he wasn't a known opium and heroin dealer in Paris.

Jean told Pam to listen to him, and listen, she did. After all, I was now her past, Jean was her future, or so she hoped. The two of them, together, placed me in the bathtub. WHY? Back in those days, you treated a drug overdose at times by placing someone in a tub and filling it with ice. Ice was not readily available in those early morning hours in Paris. They were still trying to wake me up. Pamela was also flashing back to the night I almost died a month earlier in London and remembered how ill I was but felt somewhat better in the tub. Pamela could not have placed my body in the tub by herself, and the French Count could hardly do it with her, but somehow they managed.

The Count told Pamela to keep my death a secret for at least a few days, as he had to get out of the country, and to be sure to flush her stash. Anyone who knew me at all in my last life would have to admit I was not a heroin user, and I had nothing but disdain for the drug. I tried to help a singer/songwriter named Tim Hardin get off heroin, and I certainly, on several occasions, told

Pamela to stop using it. That is why she tried to do it covertly, it was not my bag. I did not intentionally take heroin in Paris, and anyone that genuinely knew me on earth would never believe I did.

I did not mistake Pamela's heroin for cocaine either. Pamela did use cocaine early in our relationship, long before I did. But for the three years before I crossed over, she was strictly a heroin user, joint smoker, lude taker and user of other assorted downers. I would have never believed she had a stash of cocaine in the apartment, not in a million years.

She gave several people several different stories surrounding my untimely demise. Some have never been printed, and the ones that have are so full of discrepancies and contradictions, why would anyone believe them? It was no secret Pamela Courson was a heroin addict, and I am puzzled as to why anyone would believe an addict.

Why didn't my parents request or demand an autopsy? If my son had died in a foreign country, under mysterious circumstances, even if we were estranged and I was not notified until after he was hurriedly planted in the ground, of my death that fateful night." I would have wanted to know if he was murdered, committed suicide, contracted a disease of some sort, or whatever else may have occurred. It would not bring him back, but I certainly would rather his early demise at the age of 27 not remain a mystery, for I would always wonder. An autopsy would have confirmed I severely abused my body but I did not commit suicide. I was murdered. I am rather unpleasantly surprised that Pamela Courson seemed like a reliable source of information pertaining to my final hours on Earth.

Pamela was a young, scared, American woman. The man she felt she owned like a possession was now dead, and the heroin injected into him without his consent, did him in. Pam had very little money left. I had written The Doors accountant to get us more money and credit cards, and she did not have a credit card at that time. Here she was in France, and she had been out all night with another man, not her so-called "husband," and also doing smack. How was she going to explain this? How was she going to make it back to the United States without sitting in a Parisian Jail cell?

She simply went back to a night the month before when I had been ill. The interesting part about her initial story to the French police is that it wasn't at all believable or even plausible, but it was readily accepted. Pamela claimed I went out to dinner alone, we went to a movie, and I was just fine. Alain had been with me all day and knew I was far from fine, so right there, the story was bogus. I then, according to Pamela, watched our movies from the trips and played Doors songs. She then couldn't wake me up, but when she does, I go take a bath. During the bath, I supposedly cough up three bowls full of blood and blood clots with pineapple mixed in, but she doesn't think I need medical attention and goes back to sleep. Who would leave their so-called husband, or even a stranger in a bathtub, coughing up three bowls of blood and blood clots? That has to be the most absurd story imaginable. She goes to sleep with me being that ill in a bathtub and comes in to find me with a smile on my face, dead as a doorknob. Why was any of this believed? Pamela was out of her mind the night I died and she lived the rest of her days on Earth overwrought with guilt, and her mind played tricks on her pertaining to my final hours.

In several other versions Pamela later gave several other people, I came into the apartment and saw her doing lines of heroin, I asked what it was, and she tells me coke. So I supposedly want to do lines with her after not having coke for months since I left

L.A. I was a glutton when drugs were put in front of me, but I would never believe Pamela was snorting coke at that stage, never. SO, I do some lines and can't tell it's not coke and then get up and do some more, even though Pamela cautions me that it's rather potent. Pamela Courson was fully aware if you were not a heroin user you could die by ingesting the amount of heroin she said I did. So she just goes to bed afterwards, supposedly seeing me snorting lines and lines of heroin? Once again, this is more bullshit shoveled at people and some of them bought it.

Then there were other assorted versions of how I spent three days doing heroin with her, knowing full well it was heroin. I could've done heroin for several years before, and I didn't want to do it then, so why in Paris, after being so physically ill, being off drugs for months other than alcohol and cigarettes, would I suddenly want to indulge in heroin use, especially after I had seen its adverse effects on so many, including Pamela herself? With how deteriorated my physical health had become, and I believe evidence still exists of this, in the final pictures taken of me just days before my passing, it wasn't even a remote possibility for me to ingest a drug like heroin, one I did not use, for three days and live until July 3rd. I would've been dead in hours, not days. Another one of the great fables to emerge from corners in Paris suggests I died in the men's room of the Rock 'n' Roll Circus. Supposedly, I went to score drugs for Pamela and ended up sampling the goods. I did not score drugs for Pamela Courson anytime, and certainly not in Paris. There was one incident on the trip where we took a ferry boat during our three-week excursion.

Pamela was truly jumpy and in need of a fix, and she could not obtain heroin in front of me. A Middle Eastern drug dealer offered us hash, and I agreed to it because she wanted it. We ended up getting beat on one hundred dollars. We never got the hash, and that was the closest I came to scoring anything for Pamela. Also, do not assume I would've smoked the hash myself. I didn't really care for the strong stuff in other countries. I had a bad experience with some strong marijuana while in Jamaica in March 1969 and was strongly thinking maybe I shouldn't indulge in this hash, as I knew it had to be rather potent. My only addiction, at that time, was truly to a bottle of Cognac, scotch or any kind of alcohol that was available.

There were secrets stashes of Chinese heroin all over the Parisian apartment, hidden in jewelry boxes and drawers and other places. There was absolutely no need to score any drugs for Pamela, she had a vast supply. I was not supposed to know of her supply, but I did and in truth, that was something that was really bothering me as I tried to sit in that place and write, the heroin and the fact it was there would randomly come into my head and really fucking unnerve me. I now know the real reason for that, it was going to be the substance that ended my life.

When the French Count was unavailable to supply Pamela with drugs, she had an endless supply of androgynous friends who were heroin users. She would always have her drugs.

I personally considered scoring drugs sleazy, and in a town where I didn't speak the language, I wasn't about to go out and find drug dealers to hook me up with smack. The story of me suggesting I should score drugs for the "Toxic Queen," comes from a woman called Zozo, otherwise known as Elizabeth that we rented the Parisian apartment from. Just for the record, I actually told Zozo I found it quite seedy when women went out and scored drugs and never suggested I was going to go out and do it for Pam. Incidentally, my last sexual experience on earth was in fact with, Zozo. Even though she had a boyfriend, Zozo knew Pam and I weren't real. Pam had talked to her of her sexual encounters with not just the Count but other men in Paris and we were alone in the morning and things happened. Elizabeth was my last sexual experience on earth. I doubt she will ever tell anyone and that's precisely how it should be.

The Rock 'n' Roll Circus tale was another one spun that had some basis in truth. In L.A., I was always passing out in places from being the drunken slob I would easily become. But in Paris, many didn't know much about me. One night, at the Rock 'n' Roll Circus I was completely shit-faced from drinking all night at several places, and I had this extremely bad coughing fit. Looking like death warmed over, I passed out one night in the bathroom. Pink sputum was coming out of my mouth. A couple of guys came in and carried me out and put me in a taxi. This didn't occur in July of 1971, but in May of 1971.

Some of the people at the Circus were the young "in" crowd and had seen me with Pamela and her group of Euro Trash heroin users and suppliers at such places as the Café De Flores. I couldn't speak French, and I was passed out anyway, assumptions were made and rumors started after my death. It was more fiction, and I certainly was carried out of places on other nights in Paris, but I am not at all proud of this. If it had happened in L.A., nothing would have been made out of it, because everyone knew what a lush Jim Morrison was back at my home base.

I would like people to know the truth, we were two addicts who could not trust each other and cared more about the things we were addicted to than the other person. We were both looking for love and never found it in each other — or anyone else for that matter. To say she was the love of my life is tragically absurd. The love of my life was alcohol, pure and simple, after that, my written words, and in third place, the books I cherished. I didn't even love myself. There was no fairytale, just wasted time and a wasted life.

I had a fucking hard death, it was not the way I wanted to go, it was not at all what I thought it was going to be by some visions I had earlier in life. At first, there was complete darkness and silence, and I had no idea what happened, but I was screaming on the inside until I saw three faces I recognized and realized, I had done it, I had actually done it. I had crossed over. I had broken through. I had been obsessed with death in my lifetime as Jim Morrison, as I always believed there was another side without boundaries, and I always felt confined on Earth. It turned out I was right about something. I saw Pamela and Jean drag my dead body to the bathtub. The water turned pink in the tub, because I had blood on me, I had internally hemorrhaged. I did fight to remain on Earth for nearly five grueling hours, but now, I was out of my body, free, no more pain. I can honestly say upon seeing this scene of my so-called "wife" calling her French lover and drug dealer concocting a plan, I had no wish to return to that body or the fucked up life of Jim Morrison. I was happy it was over. I was free. But I was fucking enraged about what was done to me.

Pamela's biggest fear was that an investigation would take place once someone found out who I really was, the American rock star, and an autopsy would be launched. Her mind ran wild with the jail cell she would be locked away in for the rest of her life. An investigation would certainly turn up Pamela's habits and who this American woman associated with in Paris. She was initially going to have me cremated, but an autopsy would have been required to do so in Paris, so she couldn't do it. Her thought was, if she did cremate me, my parents, or The Doors could never request an autopsy, since nothing would be left.

Pamela didn't give the French officials my real name, and of course, it would be rather hard to exhume a body under a different name. She claimed she was my wife, which she wasn't, and then my cousin to get me buried. It's interesting so many believe I wanted to be buried at Pere LaChaise. I was into cemeteries and liked the peace and quiet I could find there, also the historical essence was of interest to me. I had gone to Pere LaChaise a few times with different people and even alone. It had this incredible tranquility in the middle of a city, and yet I found it to be horrifically haunting. It really was a spooky place. (Laughs).

Jim Morrison & Michael Hutchence

I had made a comment in jest one time, I would like to have been buried in Pere LaChaise in 50 years with the likes of the important and significant figures in residence.

My body had to be kept in the Parisian apartment for two nights and Pamela didn't dare look at it. She did not sleep next to it contrary to popular belief. She wasn't able to handle it.

What sanity was left of Pamela Courson by that time, quickly deteriorated. She was never the same, and she cried, yelled and screamed in pain as she paced in the Parisian Apartment asking, what would happen to her and why did I leave her? She was angry with me and blamed me for everything. My friend Alain helped her cover up my death without full realization of what had taken place. He saw her burning papers in the fireplace, and trying to steal Zozo's fur coat. The woman was gone, she was out of her fucking mind.

Pamela did inherit my estate legally which was something else that has disturbed me from beyond the grave, and that was my own fault. Pamela could've had the money in a more timely fashion, but she tried to deny the monies my legal team was owed. My lawyers deserved the money, and Max Fink was more of a Father to me than anyone had ever been to me. Pamela made things more difficult for herself than needed be, due to her total greed and her claim on me. She produced phony marriage licenses I never signed, one from Colorado and later one from Paris I knew nothing about. She had taken a file on me to Paris, with legal papers in it detailing my arrests and convictions. She had in her possession a copy of my will. Why? What was she planning? What was she thinking? She was really scared I was going to bail on her in Paris. She knew the end was coming and so did I, before my plane touched down in Paris. Perhaps she thought she could get me to hold on a little longer but I had taken all I could take. Many people saw me act on earth, play roles for what they wanted me to be and I was doing this during my final days in Paris with Pamela, so she would not suspect what was coming. But on the night of July 1st, I no longer had the energy to live a lie.

I believe Pamela was emotionally and mentally broken and should've gone home to live with her parents for a few years instead of staying in L.A. spending my money, becoming a junkie and stalking me. That's how it turned out, she may have been a sweet runaway when we met, or so she considered herself but she turned out to be a cold, manipulating, scorned woman.

Following my demise, I didn't follow Pamela around in my spirit form, I was angry, I was bitter and just had a hard time coping even though I was out of that tortured human body I had occupied. I was hoping however, the truth would come out. I was there once when Pam was with Danny Sugarman, and to set the record straight, I didn't care if they had sex or ended up getting married. I just wanted her to tell the truth and in a way she did but ended up embellishing the story once again. I didn't snort anything that night. I was laying on a bed half out of it when I was injected. I hated needles and would never inject myself with anything. I was killed by what I despised, heroin, injected through a needle.

I would like to speak about my grave at Pere LaChaise. It's a complete abomination. It's a place of disrespect toward me and the memory of my life. The Doors song "Strange Days" should blare from loud speakers at my grave site night and day! My bodily remains are there, but my spirit is not there, and contrary to many reports, you won't feel my spirit anywhere near that place. There is nothing there for me. There is no death. My bodily remains were shoved in a cheap box and planted in the ground. I didn't care if I was given what is termed a "proper burial," but it was a true example of the relationships I had in my past lifetime, very inconsiderate and void of thought or emotion. My grave site is the sideshow at a bizarre circus. It's not a way to honor me, and I could not be more saddened and disappointed with this so-called tribute in Paris. The true way to honor me is to read my poetry, to listen to my music, my words are my legacy, not a graffiti riddled, empty shrine. Whatever you are looking for there, you will never find. The answers to my life are being given here and now (on these pages) and the questions surrounding my death never needed to be asked. A simple autopsy should've been performed, and the suspicious blackout that occurred in the days following my death, which most felt was from some sort of debauchery, and yet, people should've found this much more suspicious. To believe I killed myself even unintentionally is completely asinine, why would it then need to be covered up?

Many people saw my dead body, besides Pamela, including the emergency workers, French investigators, a doctor who signed the death certificate and received some money, and even a man who lived in the building of the apartment we rented — not to mention the funeral director.

The neighbor who saw my body, by the way, was later interviewed by a small, independent book writer about my final days in Paris. If the author of that book could find him, it's quite interesting other authors never tracked this man down. This man came in to see what the commotion was, and my body was laying on the floor.

I realize Bill Siddons was blamed for not viewing my remains, but he was doing the best he could and in shock himself. Incidentally, his wife Cheri knew I had crossed over. She is a very gifted intuitive, and she knew I had gone over and also knew what had happened to me that very night, whether she recalled those precise details or not.

Those left behind truly never knew what to think. I can't blame them, and I suppose the few people who knew me truly had no hope I would clean up my life of my bad habits. My death remains as much a mystery as my life, and my hardcore fans think they know every aspect of my former life (laughs), how could they? I had believed Jerry Hopkins had Pamela figured out or so I hoped.

Everyone has individual beliefs that suit them, but I am here to tell you, when you cross over, you should know, anger, bitterness, guilt and resentment, go along for the ride with you. What you do not work out in your present lifetime, will be worked out eventually one way or another. You have to pay the piper sometime, and the more you can work out where you are now, the better off you will be. You can heal on this side, but it's a choice and the ones you wish to heal with may or may not make that same choice. Free will exists here as well.

Regardless of all my talk of dying young or my fatalistic outlook, I did not believe I was going to die in Paris in July of 1971. I did foresee my death years earlier, not in Paris, not in that way or close to it. I saw myself drowning, not in a bathtub either.

I had my bouts of depression in Paris, but my spirit did not give in, my physical body gave out. Because I died young, I was made into something I was not, but even during my life, I was continually portrayed as somebody else.

I created some of it myself with buzz words and the fun of creating an image for myself and the other Doors as "erotic politicians" or calling myself "The Lizard King" in a somewhat tongue and cheek sense. I wasn't any of the things people thought, I was just Jim, a poet, a writer and a dreamer. The day I ran into Ray Manzerek on Venice Beach was destiny, there is no such thing as coincidence.

My fame was my fate. But if I had to do it all over, I would've stayed on Earth — by any means possible. I would've waited as I would have met my true eternal soul mate later in life and fallen deeply, and truly, in love. I would've had a family and for once in my life, a home. I did not meet her while I was on Earth, as she was only a baby when I exited the train. I see her now, I look at her, and know that someday, when she comes home to this side, I will make her fall in love with me as I would've on Earth. And I will give her all the things I can't give her now. I missed the very best part of my life, for it wouldn't have been being a rock star, or being in The Doors, or anything other than finding the one who completes me and could understand me like no one else could.

She is still on Earth, and I live for the day I will see her face-to-face on this side. My biggest regret is leaving her alone with all the time I wasted, so much unfinished. You never know what is around the next corner, just when you think you've seen it all, you ain't seen nothing yet. I have been shown my life if I would have stayed on Earth. I would've gotten so ill in Paris, I would've passed out on a street. I would've been taken to a Parisian hospital and stayed for several days. I would've been given the right medications finally and gotten lots of rest. I would not have chosen to stay in the hospital but would've had no choice, as I would've been much too weak to leave. Obviously during this time, I would not have had been drinking and this would've given me the impetus to stop drinking all together as I had truly wanted to in Paris. The hospitalization would've scared the fuck out of me and I would have felt more confident I could survive without alcohol after I was of my hospitalization and recovering my health. This was the way it was going to go folks, and I would've slayed the lion attempting to eat me alive once and for all. Cigarettes would continue to haunt me on and off the rest of my earth life. A good cigar once in a while would also be a temptation. I was on the verge of a major life change and would've thrown myself into my new work, it was taken away from me, all of it and it's been a source of true anger, sadness and near insanity since the day I crossed over.

I finally would have been accepted as a writer, and been able to live the life I long aspired to.

I would have met the one and never been a loner again. The Doors would've been a beginning, and my life would've gotten so much better with time, age and understanding. I would love nothing more than to go back and fix it all but I can't. So I wait for her to come home and join me, so that I can make up all that I never gave her and hope and pray she decides I am worth spending eternity with. I am not the drunken degenerate rock star I was on Earth. I was not a bad person, but I have buried all traces of my ego with my leather pants. There is always a Plan B, and if that doesn't work out, there is always Plan C, and if that doesn't work out, a Plan D, and so on. Don't give up on your life, your dreams or on conquering that which is destroying you. You are worth it, life is worth it.

Ode to Paris

He left the rooms he once occupied within
Walking distance of his whole existence...
He was anxious to say goodbye,
yet afraid at the same time

The beatnik poet who threw tantrums now
had to mature; He could no longer act like
the sulking child he had been since the
European tour

He now had to find himself in the incognito
of freedom of the city that enchanted
him most.

A TALE OF TWO BROTHERS

He did not go there for a woman, he did
not go there to stay, he went to find
sanctuary from himself with the ancient
gothic oracle played an eager host.

But it wasn't quite the same as when he
went the first time, he felt much older and
the atmosphere seemed much colder

As he walked down the streets and soaked
in the architecture of centuries past, he
could hardly recall where he had been last,
it was surreal, a blur of a dream, in Paris,
nothing was what it seemed.

Nicolas Flamel liked to visit cemeteries too,
Perhaps you took in the same view,
the ghosts who spoke to Napoleon
Surround the city still,
What did Charles De Gaulle feel
that you couldn't feel?

He was the same drunken bore
They knew in L.A.
No one really knew where he would
end up at night, no one
cared at who's abode he'd stay

The city did not transform his heart,
the magic eluded him,
he could not find his soul in Paris
for it was already buried before he
could make a fresh start.

If he had to do it all over again,
he would not have gone to the city

Jim Morrison & Michael Hutchence

of his great demise, he'd stay in L.A.,
Roam through New York, but stay the
hell out of the city whose air is thick with lies.
He knew what he had to do
but could not follow through,
Paris ruined him, and his chance
to find happiness, and self-worth,
he went home now, to experience
his true renaissance, his cosmic rebirth

He doesn't look back happily on those,
his final earthly days,
they are like a great Greek tragedy
like the death of Agamemnon in
a whole new light, but in strange and twisted ways

He should not have been entombed,
in the city that did him in,
He was told if he was to end up
Like Oscar Wilde it would surely be
a sin, for some Paris is
enchantment, and forbidden romance but
For him, it was an ungodly end

—*channeled from Jim Morrison*

Autumn

Summer Days came to an end
I miss swimming on the shore
I walk the beach, a cold chill in the air
The Autumn of my discontent is upon me

A TALE OF TWO BROTHERS

I was searching for her
and will forever more
I can't have a house
a real home without my bride

She radiates through the night
with stardust in her hair
She walks the days
alone and forbidden to enter

A mad man asks how will you find her?
How will you survive?
I remain cold, callous and silent
Survival is not an option
without finding her

I sink into the sand
no castles are built here
No fortress to ease my pain
My soul cries out, I am no longer silent

I am shouting, screaming, mumbling,
talking, just talking
I ask how do I find her?
How do I survive?

For I am the mad man
and I remain silent,
there is no answer
Surviving is not an option
without finding her

—*channeled from Jim Morrison*

Jim Morrison & Michael Hutchence

The Mystic Sees Paris

by Kathleen Tucci

I believe Jim went to Paris in 1971 before he died because he was searching. He says he was searching for renewed inspiration where French symbolic poetry and surrealism reside. That Paris resonated with him and that being away from the "Hollywood" lifestyle would allow him to quiet his mind, regroup, and cultivate his craft (albeit poetry or song-writing) once more to a level he was pleased with.

He then says the following prose explains it in detail as he would say it today if he were still here:
"The length of the shadow is greater than you think, stronger than it had portrayed itself to be and definitely within this moment. You understand that you may see it within your mirror and faces without a great noise for announcement. Recognize it because it silently sneaks into your thoughts, your worries even your concerns. Realize it is no longer necessary within your purpose, for the truthfulness is coming closer each and every day. It will not be hidden from you, it will be as normal as the breathing of acceptance. Allow your miracles to shower upon you, for there are no limitations or higher relief than these that are in front of you. Upon seeing the shadow in the mirror, simply state the limitations and there is no longer an acceptance in this manner. It will then remove its own pulling for it is only a shadow."

Jim then acts out playing air guitar when referring to singer Phil Trainer. He is reminiscing and says many were present when they were together on this occasion in Paris, not just he and Phil, as if to imply they're in a jam session, because he then shows me many guitars are around, he, Phil and several others, all playing guitars. He speaks about having to break in the middle of songs with long bouts of uncontrollable coughing. Jim was vastly deteriorating physically between the continuous heavy drinking, not eating a healthy diet and his diverse bohemian lifestyle. In late April of 1971 Jim finally sought medical treatment for his ailing chest.

When visiting the American Hospital of Paris, 63 Bd. Victor-Hugo, Neuilly, he was prescribed an antispasmodic medication to curtail the coughing spells. Jim says he was warned to not only cut down on his drinking for the medication to work, but also to stop smoking as well. Of course, he wasn't about to give up two friendly vices that provided him solace from his despair. The unfortunate fact is that many antispasmodic medications which are also used as heart stimulants can be truly poisonous when taken in excess.

Jim speaks of recording his own poetry in a sound studio not long before he died and says personal friends were present. One day around mid-June, Jim says he went out walking. He found himself by the Left Bank and made his way to the Odeon, where nearby he saw a recording studio. He describes it as being on a second floor, having to walk upstairs to reach it, and that he'd come across it days before on an earlier walk. Jim says that while there he originally hired the studio in order to listen to some of his poetry tapes. He talks about a necklace he wore at a later date in this same studio when he returned to do a recording session, and that the necklace was a round silver medallion with a star in the center. Others had remarked of its beauty, he says, and they'll remember this necklace. Jim says Some of these poems he left behind, were even under his bed in Paris when he died. There were also poems, he says, in what appears to be a large tin can of some sort in his apartment. There was a fine desk in a corner of the room, which he happily sat at while writing, gazing out a window. He also is specific in saying that on July 2nd, 1971 he was totally under the weather.

Pamela came into see him, but Pamela elected to go out again and party with someone who would go on to become a French TV star. He has not given me the name of the star. But he does say that there are witnesses who are still alive that spent time with them that evening, and that Pamela and this man went driving for some time and came to rest at a café on the left bank. He shows me what I know to be a famous café there called Les Deux Magots. It's popular with both tourists and Parisians, and has a long and colorful history as a meeting place for famous writers and philosophers. It is located at the intersection of the boulevard Saint-Germain and the rue de Rennes. They smoked and drank there for some time before heading to the Rock 'n' Roll Circus Club (now called the "Whisky A Go Go" at 57 rue de la Seine) also on the Left Bank.

As Pamela entered the apartment early in the morning, she saw Jim strewn across the bed with one arm dangling over the side. He says he is on his stomach. He says he was already dead when she found him, and that had searing pain in his chest and throughout his body. His breathing became labored and so stressed that he was unable to move. His death, he describes, was slow and wrenching. He gives me the feeling of my throat swelling shut. I believe he is doing this (using clairsentience) to portray what it felt like before death, that he eventually just stopped breathing.

Pamela called the Count and when he arrived they dragged his body into the bathroom and laid him in the tub. She had seen him relax in the tub before when he had been under the influence. His tone is very direct when he refers to what happened that night. He insists that he was extremely unhappy and that although he was working hard to "clean up his act", he was exhausted emotionally. He stresses again about being so lonely and that he could not bear to be without someone to love him as a soul mate should. Pamela, he says, was not it. Three years later, on April 25th, 1974, Pamela died in Los Angeles from a heroin overdose. Ironically, she too was 27 years old when she died.

He had every intention of composing a second will while in Paris, days before he died. He even mentions Michael, who Jim says is a "fellow writer". When I asked him for more information about this Michael, he showed me the Golden Gate Bridge and mentioned this man to be a poet like himself. He refers to Michael writing about spiritual awareness, weaving his magic into a stream of higher consciousness thinking that, he says, most don't get or even take time to contemplate. Jim goes on to say that he enjoyed Michael's company, and they had a rare kinship, that he misses him greatly and that he's sorry for the lost time caused by his quick departure from this life. Jim insinuates had he lived, they would have spent much time together experiencing the path of existence here.

After some research, I believe Jim is referring to Michael McClure, an American poet, playwright, songwriter and novelist, who lived in San Francisco as a young man. He found fame as one of the five poets (including Allen Ginsberg who is also mentioned in this book with ties to Michael Hutchence) who read at the famous San Francisco Six Gallery reading in 1955. McClure's first book of poetry, "Passages", was published in 1965. His poetry is heavily infused with an awareness of nature, especially in the animal consciousness that often lies dormant in mankind. McClure has since published eight books of plays and four collections of essays, including essays on Bob Dylan and the environment. He currently also performs spoken word poetry concerts with Doors keyboard player Ray Manzarek. When speaking about a second will that he was putting together, Jim talks about not only the many lyrics and poems he has stashed around in many places, but that he had come to the realization that he needed to get his work, should anything happen to him, out of the hands of Pamela Courson. He had created the first will in anger, and therefore had left nothing to his parents, Steve and Clara.

Jim Morrison & Michael Hutchence

CHAPTER 19
The Mythology of Jim Morrison

"Every violation of truth is not only a sort of suicide in the liar, but is a stab at the health of human society."

—*Ralph Waldo Emerson*

Jim Morrison & Michael Hutchence

A TALE OF TWO BROTHERS

There are the 14 most popular myths created about me, and it's time to set the record straight:

1) That I died in a bathtub in Paris, France.

My body physically gave out on July 3rd, 1971 in Paris, France but not in a bathtub. I was placed there later.

2) That someone was with me or in the other room when I died.

I died alone, Pamela Courson was not there, no one was there.

3) That I had to die on July 3rd, 1971.

I was quite physically ill but an injection of heroin caused my death, nothing else.

4) That I was so depressed, I was suicidal in Paris.

Truth be known, yes I was feeling rather depressed in Paris but I was also constructing a new existence for myself, free of the ball and chain around my leg known as Pamela Courson and free of my rock 'n' roll days. I was making major plans in Paris and was actively writing quite a bit. Some of those writings were destroyed, some showed up later in books I would not have approved of called "Wilderness" and "An American Night" and others are yet still unpublished and they should be put out for public consumption, free of charge.

It was a difficult but productive final few months of my life. I did contemplate suicide once during my childhood and again during 1969 but I was not suicidal in Paris, depressed yes, about to take my own life, no.

5) That I died doing heroin at the Rock 'n' Roll Circus or the apartment in Paris from doing lines of smack.

I had gone to the Rock 'n' Roll Circus a handful of times in Paris. To be clear, Sam Bernett was not a personal friend of mine and hardly knew me. Also, I had been thrown out of there one night and one night, like I had done in L.A. many times over, I had passed out from drinking. I was physically ill and beyond intoxicated. I looked like death warmed over and was coughing up pink sputum, this was May, 1971, not July. I was carried out and placed in a cab. I was not dead and didn't die at that night club. The French Count spread rumors about it to a few people and it exploded over the years, to take any involvement away from him.

6) Possibly my favorite lie, that I mistakenly took Pamela's heroin believing it was cocaine. Supposedly, I snorted it and died.

Pamela had a heroin stash inside the apartment the entire time we were in Paris, I never saw her run out. I wasn't supposed to know about it, but I did. We were in Paris for nearly four months, I knew she had a heroin stash so what would possess me to believe it was coke? As shocking as I know this is, after I left the states, I didn't do any drugs other than my drug of choice, alcohol. I was quite physically ill the last few weeks of my life and on doctor prescribed medications for breathing problems from April 1971 on. Nicotine, alcohol and doctor prescribed drugs were the only drugs I existed on in those last few months of my life.

I always believed scoring drugs was sleazy and the truth was, Pamela Courson tried to convince me she was in Paris to finally get off smack. She certainly didn't want me to think she was still using it while we were there, why would she have asked me to go out and score it for her? She knew better than to have even asked me to do such a thing. Pamela was friends with a good many Parisian drug dealers and users, and I was not a part of this crowd. She had an easy time scoring. She didn't need me to do it and I had no reason to do so. *7) That Pamela Courson was my cosmic mate and true love.*

I did not find true love in my last life and never gave my soul to anyone. I called Pamela my cosmic mate early on while extremely high on an acid trip. By the end of 1968 and into 1969, I knew I was not in love with her. I felt I owed her because this innocent child from Weed, California had turned into a heroin junkie living in L.A. with my money. I felt responsible for this. I was planning on leaving her and helping her financially in Paris. She had already overdosed on drugs twice and came close to death. I couldn't handle the guilt but I also couldn't handle the fact she kept acting as if she owned me. I never met my cosmic mate in over 27 years and she would've come to me later in life, but I checked out too soon. I will be seeing her here and living happily ever after. It wasn't Pamela or any other woman I met on Earth. Pamela was a difficult, learning lesson as were some of the others. I could never give any of the women what they wanted, my soul, because it was hidden.

8) That I was a drug addict and always stoned on the stage.

I was a hardcore alcoholic and while I did experiment with drugs, keep in mind, acid was totally legal and sold in drug stores like aspirin in my day. My experiments with acid and peyote were not so much to get me high but to have visions and be able to leave the constraints of my body and break on through to the other side.

I was looking for freedom, to see what was beyond, not so much to trip. Before going to Paris, I was quite into cocaine because I believed it would help me gain energy to write, write and write. It was a very empty and very deceiving drug. I regret using them all but I wasn't a drug addict of any kind, I wasn't hooked on any of it and could easily do without it and many times, I did. Alcohol was my true love, and the one thing I could never seem to stay off of, I felt powerless over it.

9) That I exposed my genitals in Miami.

I was drunk in Miami, belligerent, angry, hostile and frustrated and couldn't sing for shit but I never exposed myself on stage. There is no photographic evidence of this because it never happened.

People were anxious to believe it because they saw me as a burnt out, has been.

10) That I was a complete, egotistical jerk.

This is of course, is a rather subjective issue but I would say, I was a loner, and also quite shy unless I was drunk off my ass and during those times and they were frequent, I could be quite obnoxious. My ego wasn't as pronounced as it has been written.

I never thought I was good enough or that I could sing, or really write and I wanted desperately to write but my confidence wasn't always there with it like people thought.

11) That my songs or poems were about certain people generally. Like to suggest I did many songs about Pamela or others is absurd.

My songs came from the subconscious, and to be honest, I had no real idea where the half of them originated but it's safe to say, the inspiration from books is apparent. There was a song I did called "Indian Summer" and supposedly this was about Pamela and I wrote this song and had it in my head before I ever met her.
It wasn't about anyone I am sorry to say. I now realize I was indeed a channel to the other side and I was writing about many things I could not understand on Earth.

I also am aware I did have a muse, one I could not identify during my life as Jim Morrison, but she is my true eternal soul mate and twin flame who still walks the Earth. I will come face to face with her on this side in the not too distant future and every song and every poem was, in fact, for her.

12) That I said my parents were dead and cut them out of my life to save them from the public eye.

For the most part, it was personal issues I had with them, not saving my Navy officer Father and his wife from embarrassment. I had hoped one day they would come around, I carried so much anger and frustration toward them but the day never arose. My Mother reached out to me at a concert, I wasn't ready to deal with it and later on, I composed a letter for my Father at the Miami trial but it wasn't really what I wanted to say. I regret never working things out with them while I was on Earth but I was hurt by them, deeply bruised and part of my identity, if not the major part was to be who my Father wasn't. It's not a pleasant story but so often, the truth is hard to embrace. If I had wanted to keep my parents out of the public eye, why didn't I just go see them secretly? I saw lots of people secretly, I could get away with it back then. How come I didn't call them after I became famous or write my Mother a letter? How come I didn't see my Mother and brother privately in Washington D.C. the night they came to the concert? Why did I see my brother a few times but never my Mom and Dad?

I pulled off seeing Andy and Anne in private or calling them so why never my parents? Because, I didn't want to speak to them, it's not hard to figure out. They are on this side now and I don't have any sort of relationship with either of them, it's free will over here too.

13) That my will was left the way I wanted it.

This may surprise many but it really shouldn't. By the end of 1969, I had taken the advice of a male friend to heart. He suggested I seriously contemplate cutting all ties with Pamela Courson and leaving her a financial settlement. It was simply a toxic relationship and later on Pamela pulled an overdose stunt while I was on trial for my life in Miami. She thought Miami was not all that serious and this was upsetting to me. She wanted to attend the trial to get her picture in the paper, but I couldn't handle her in Florida so she stayed behind in L.A. and indulged in heroin without food or much water for eight straight days.

Obviously she had to be hospitalized and this particular stunt was just too much for me to bear. My friend told me to give thought to my will and I listened. I was feeling pangs of guilt over the fact I was never truly a big brother to my younger siblings. I felt like I had abandoned them and wanted to leave them the money that was left from my career provided there was anything to give them at the end. I wanted to leave the creative control of all my writings to my friend and mentor, Michael McClure. I drew up this new will and as the alcoholic that I was, it was stuffed in a notebook somewhere and never made it to my lawyers office. I truly did not want my parents, Pamela Courson or her parents to get anything from my estate. I am truly dismayed at how things turned out. It's about how much I was worth as opposed to the artistry of my work.

14) That I wanted to be buried in Pere LaChaise.

WHERE DID THAT COME FROM? I visited it and many other cemeteries in my lifetime as I was into them and the spooky tranquility I found there. I find it rather disgusting when people visit my grave smoking joints and leaving condoms there. All these tourists want to be part of the circus and they create it in my memory which is not at all who I was or what I wanted. They cry at my gravesite while they believe the tawdry trash written about me or the deplorable movie made that supposedly captures my essence. It's very strange, people didn't know what to make out of my essence while I was on Earth. I feel this way for the fans, if you were alive when I was, you had me on Earth, and maybe you could've met me, talked to me, seen me in concert, etc., but that time is over. If you were not on Earth during my lifespan, that's unfortunate but that's the way the cookie crumbles so get over it and move on. My legacy is my words, not a freak show in an ancient graveyard. My gravesite is not a suitable tribute but it lends itself to my own take on my life, I wasn't understood.

My Awakening

I now see through your eyes...
Mine have never seen such beauty honey,

You are so alluring,
that the very essence of grace opens
to you
You notice the roses, the fleur de lis,
You notice when someone is hurting

and you bring them comfort and shelter
from the pain

I never touched grace before,
I saw so much, but I realize I saw nothing,
I witnessed the dark corners of the soul,
You my Angel have none of that.

This is my awakening,
Seeing the Earth once more but
this time through you,
It's never dull, because all
that you see, beguiles and fascinates me
I finally see the light of God...

Thank you Rebecca for doing what only you, could possibly do.

—channeled from Jim Morrison

Jim Morrison & Michael Hutchence

CHAPTER 20

In the Universal Mind

I was doing time
In the universal mind
I was feeling fine
I was turning keys
I was setting people free
I was doing all right
Then you came along
With a suitcase and a song
Turned my head around
Now I'm so alone
Just looking for a home
In every place I see

I'm the freedom man
I'm the freedom man
I'm the freedom man
That's how lucky I am

I was doing time
In the universal mind

Jim Morrison & Michael Hutchence

I was feeling fine
I was turning keys I was setting people free
I was doing all right

Then you came along
With a suitcase and a song
Turned my head around
Now I'm so alone
Just looking for a home
In every place I see

I'm the freedom man

I was doing time
In the universal mind
I was feeling fine
I was turning keys
I was setting people free
I was doing all right

Then you came along
With a suitcase and a song
Turned my head around
Now I'm so alone
Just looking for a home
In every place I see

I'm the freedom man
Yeah, that's how lucky I am
I'm the freedom man
I'm the freedom man

—*lyrics to "Universal Mind" by the Doors*

From "The Lords: Notes on Vision"

By Jim Morrison, 1969:

_ Few would defend a small view of Alchemy as "Mother of Chemistry," and confuse its true goal with those external metal arts.

_ Alchemy is an erotic science, involved in buried aspects of reality, aimed at purifying and transforming all being and matter.

_ Not to suggest that material operations are ever abandoned. The adept holds to both the mystical and physical work.

_ They can picture love affairs of chemicals and stars, a romance of stones, or the fertility of fire. Strange, fertile correspondences the alchemists sensed in unlikely orders of being. Between men and planets, plants and gestures, words and weather.

_ Cinema returns us to anima, religion of matter, which gives each thing its special divinity and sees gods in all things and beings. Cinema, heir of alchemy, last of an erotic science.

Venice Beach

On the beach in the summer
of 1965, a bottle washed up,
with a scroll rolled up inside,

Jim Morrison & Michael Hutchence

I felt electricity go all through
my veins when I began to
uncork this cosmic
communication

What could it be?
A message from the Ancients?
Similar to the dead sea scrolls?
or the loneliness of a sailor
missing his bride?

The paper was tattered
and torn and it read
"Whomever finds this,
spend time in the universal
mind, ask to find the keys,
and set the people free,
by finding this bottle,
you have now become
the freedom man."

I carried this paper with me
for all my remaining days,

something within me changed
upon reading it, some spark
ignited upon touching
the discolored parchment
that appeared that day at
my feet on Venice Beach.

Two years had passed and
I took out the parchment again and
noticed something I had not
previously seen. There was

writing on the other side and
it said "This is the strangest
life I've ever known."

—*channeled from Jim Morrison*

I want to talk about the spiritual gifts I had during my life as Jim Morrison that I would constantly try and ignore. When I was four years old and my family came upon the dying Indians scattered on the highway, I continued to hear their anguished screams long after the incident. I grew up with the belief that one or two of the spirits of those dying Indians had somehow jumped inside of me.

After I crossed over, I was surprised to learn this was not the case. No spirits had jumped into me or absorbed my soul, but I was able to channel spirits and never realized during my Earth life I had this gift. I did hear voices in my head at times, and one of the major reasons I would drown myself in a bottle of whiskey or scotch was occasionally related to the fact that I was afraid I was schizophrenic. And I would test myself to see if I could turn the voices off with alcohol. The alcohol calmed the craziness and voices inside my head, so I didn't think I suffered from schizophrenia. It was an actual relief to numb out what I now am aware were spirit communications with alcohol.

I had chosen my life as Jim Morrison to become famous, because later in my life, I would have grown spiritually, had taken my fans on the journey with me and showed them what I had found. My goal was to help them discover the true meanings of their lives. I failed miserably at this predetermined assignment, because I simply couldn't see the forest for the trees. Not to mention I allowed alcohol and apathy to rule my world. Life was just constantly painful for me, and while I would tell others to wear their pain and be proud of it, I was a true hypocrite in this area.

My soul was crying out in pain and crying out to be heard and loved. It was heard sometimes, misinterpreted and never truly loved by me or the eternal soul mate I left Earth without finding.

I was a channel. I was able to do the same thing that I am doing now from this side, but I didn't understand it and I didn't want to be too close to it. I studied paganism, the occult, magic and most of the great philosophies of the world. I was interested in the dark side, but never really walked on it like it is claimed. The dark side scared me. I would get so close and have to back away from it like a beautiful snake. Snakes are beautiful to look at, but I had a problem getting too close, actually touching one. The dark side was the snake to me, I was fascinated with it, but didn't want to own it. I was not into witchcraft, which is yet another ridiculous myth put forth about me. The ceremony I did with Patricia must be put into context, since I was both drunk and very ill with pneumonia including a high fever. I told Patricia I didn't really know what the ceremony meant to me, and I can tell you now, upon the day I crossed over, I had never figured that out.

What have I learned on this side? I searched for God in my Earth life more than anyone knows, it was most of the time a very private quest. I was looking for a loving God, one who understood me, and a passionate God, but not of fire and brimstone, and certainly not the ultimate authority figure or judge. When I read certain philosophers, I began to question God's existence or just started to think the religions of western culture had it all wrong.

When you are molested as a child you may feel God has abandoned you, and since I felt alone most of my life — even around other people, it was fairly easy most of the time to feel the abandonment through and through. I am not here to preach, I am here to do what I was trying to do on Earth but could only take it so far. On Earth, I was held back by my own personal demons and interior and exterior struggles. My goal is to truly open your minds and free you from the false constraints the culture has placed on you. Maybe your own family is trying to tell you what is right for you and what is wrong for you.

Speaking from experience, control is not love. Control is absolutely suffocation. I was tired of being suffocated and expected to be who I wasn't as a child and young adult, so I got away from my family of origin. I was tired of being suffocated and expected to be all the things I wasn't even close to as an adult rock star, so I left it all behind and went to Paris.

Most of you are being suffocated, if not in your own homes, by the culture itself and the advertisers and marketing think tanks who are now dictating who you should be to have this so-called perfect life and be fulfilled. Most of you know better and yet continue to submit to this dream of being someone who is happier because you have a certain look, certain clothes or just got ten years zapped from your face at lunchtime. I look at the world today, this vast, spectacular, glorious planet Earth, and I look at the country I was a citizen of, which is supposed to lead the rest of the planet, and sometimes the word *pathetic* is the best way to describe it. How can you lead the planet when you are being led yourselves?

One thing I was never a victim of was being led by the culture. I wasn't a dupe of the '60s because being an alcoholic, and not a full-time acid dropper or weed smoker, was anything but cool. I banged my own drum and walked to my own beat, and I certainly made a mess out of things. But it was my mess and I take full responsibility for it.

I am happy to report I have found the God I searched for on and off for 27 and a half years on Earth. God is true, pure energy, and he is true, pure love. You are connected to God whether you believe you are or not, whether you like it or not. You can choose at any time to shut down the connection and most of you have pretty much sidelined it, knowingly or unknowingly. I challenge you to explore God, his existence and the truth about the Source, as we often call God on this side, and I challenge you to do this by having a direct contact with him (or her if it suits you).

I am suggesting firsthand knowledge of God and not who others say God is or isn't. What would Jesus do? Why don't you ask him and find out for yourself. I am not going to condemn or support the Bible, the Torah, the Koran or any other so-called Holy Book or what is considered sacred scriptures. I am going to say it would be impossible for God or the Source to contain all he wants to tell you in one book. There is much too much to squeeze into one book or a few and through self-discovery and a personal connection, you will be astonished at what you may find.

I was involved in the study of nature and mysticism, and I would like to urge those reading this to find their own transcendence and their own mystic state to connect themselves to

God or the divine. Mysticism is all through the Bible and in the early Christian churches, among other beginnings of organized religion, so there is nothing new about this. I was on the mystical realm more often than not, and many around me felt I wasn't of Earth — or on Earth — half the time. And I have to agree, my body was on Earth, but my soul was often in other places.

I devoured so many books, so many teachings, and while some of the books about my past life supposedly explored me, they only contend a few authors had a great influence on me. This is far from accurate. I was a complete composite of so much information and so many teachings. Some had a greater impact on me than others during certain periods of my life, but to summarize my life by one philosopher or one philosophy is shortsighted.

In order to open your minds, I encourage you to read, read and read some more. Read what is known as classic literature, the great philosophers and as much timeless poetry as you can get your hands on. The more you read, the more your mind will open, and you will discover yourself in those writings that have survived lengthy periods of history.

If you are searching for a connection to God, I would not condemn any religion, but I will say, it can go either way. Religion can either bring you closer to God or it can damage your soul. When you begin to allow others to connect to God for you, and you lose your direct connection, this is where damage permeates. If you are filled with memorized teachings and you do not question or explore, then someone else is leading you to God *their* way, on their terms. And from this side, from what I have learned, I encourage you to find your own way. Mysticism can work for anyone at any time to achieve a direct connection to God, the universe, or the divine if you desire.

William Blake is difficult for some to understand, because he was a mystic poet as was I. I am not placing myself on the level of William Blake by any means, and some may argue and rightfully so, that I wasn't the best mystic poet, but the language and symbolism I used should give the reader different meanings each and every time he or she reads my poetry or listens to my lyrics. For example, the use of animals is highly symbolic, I used horses, lions and even intrinsically reptiles. Some of the actual meanings may be derived from mythology, ancient history, philosophy and alchemy. Instead of giving you specific meanings or what I meant at the time composing my poems and lyrics, it's up to you to open the doors and look beyond what you think you see. It's all in a secret alphabet, not generally written about one person, one woman or anyone I actually knew.

You can't rush mysticism. Mysticism is achieved in stages. Your soul can undergo this revolution on Earth or when you leave your human body. If your soul undergoes this while on Earth, you will see, feel and experience much more than what is in front of your current domain. I experienced some mystical experiences while on Earth, but I did not adhere to the stages to truly achieve the final state of communicative closeness directly to God. If I had, every aspect of my life would have been enriched, including my writing, and my personal relationships — which were my weakest point.

The connection to God brings you closer to the truth about yourself as to and why you are here and what you choose for your path in life. There is so much more than what is in front of your face. Mysticism is the road to enlightenment. This is a fascinating road and one that will take you places you cannot now comprehend, but you need to experience it personally. You are the only one who can take yourself on this magical journey.

The initial stage of mysticism, as with any process used to transcend from what you see through human eyes, is known as purification. Your soul must be purified of all things that are not useful to it in reaching a higher frequency, vibration and plane. Essentially, this means the possibilities are limitless to seek and find God and to find the light, but my contention has been and remains that, you must know the darkness to truly know the light.

I have experienced numerous occurrences of what is termed as "the dark night of the soul," and I would suggest, it's natural and almost unavoidable too, at times, to find yourself in a state of complete despair.

Have you ever noticed, that black gives all colors depth? The darkest night is illuminated beautifully with the moon and stars, the background changes the perception. The soul can only be purified when you have experienced the darkness and there is something to purify. I did, at times, choose to dabble in the dark side, but while it intrigued me, it scared me. I was not the dark prince as I have been described as, but I had sufficient darkness in my soul to require true purification on this side.

Once purification is achieved, your light begins to shine, and you enter into a stage of illumination. I can best explain it as a spotlight, shining on things you had a hard time seeing in the past, and that spotlight comes directly from you, from your soul, your energy field and your aura. Questions in life about people, their attitudes and actions you formerly didn't understand, become crystal clear and you begin to see God and where he truly exists and what it all means as opposed to what someone told you it means behind a pulpit or in a cathedral. The cathedral is within you, and you must learn to speak your truth from behind your own personal pulpit. The great love of God creates greater love of self, plain and simple. But you must come to it in your own way, on your own terms. No preacher, priest, rabbi, minister, or bible-thumper can bring you to what you need to find following your own path.

The next stage is that of the union with the Source, and there begins a sense of oneness that is both exhilarating and divine in nature. You begin to experience God within. This will lead to a natural progression of what is termed as spiritual bonding or marriage, which equals your soul in union with the divine source you may call God. This is a process some will achieve on Earth and some will achieve when their soul comes to this side, however, not everyone will achieve it in either dimension. You must seek to find and continue down the road, regardless of the fact, others will not go through the same experience or even begin to comprehend it on Earth. So-called spiritualists may try to give you set precepts of how to experience mysticism, or achieve it. I suggest you disregard this and fly your own plane. It's your journey, no one else can take it for you. I have simply offered suggestive guidelines that will hopefully help you begin the mystic process, if you so choose to take the journey.

There are many ways to mysticism and many known and unknown mystics. There are certain mystics and their stories that I treasure, and their published works, I truly believe, will help open your minds. A great philosopher, known as St. Thomas Aquinas used the teachings and ancient logic of Aristotle and combined them with certain church doctrines and questioned, questioned and questioned some more. He was one of the absolute most important mystics who found his own way and has continually enlightened others. I am not suggesting you become engrossed in church doctrine, unless you find it supports your own trip, but I would say the writings of Thomas Aquinas are incredibly enthralling.

The life of the great Italian poet Dante reminds me of my very own, as he wandered around seemingly endlessly searching. "Dante's Inferno" is, of course, a classic literary work but it also gives depth to the entire "Divine Comedy." I believe the "Divine Comedy" should be read in its entirety without "Dante's Inferno" being separated from it. Dante was an amazing mystic who was not only a great inspiration to me, but to William Blake.

I have been accused of trying to imitate Dionysius, the son of Zeus. I was even referred to as the "Bozo Dionysius." For the record, the Dionysius I would like most to be compared to, is Dionysius the Areopagite. Dionysius the Areopagite is the ideal study for the student of mysticism. He brought forth the concept of Neo-Platonism in what I believe to be its most ideal form. Neo-Platonism is the philosophy I should have subscribed to while on Earth in the fullest and truest way possible. It is an ideal and metamorphic find for those seeking to understand their own truth. This philosophy stems from Plato but intertwines some rather thought provoking theological teachings of Plotinus, introduced in the third century. It went through a revival in the Middle Ages, and rightfully so. I can tell you this, the teachings of Dionysius the Areopagite are some of the most significant I have come across that are available to you now. He's the Dionysius that best represents me, not the drunken, enraged maniac I once was.

I would also highly suggest the study of Alchemy in its purest application, which is not as the "Mother of Chemistry," per se, but in its mythical form. I do not dismiss the physical science of Alchemy or what it has contributed to the principles of chemistry, but once again, the physical concepts are what are easily seen by the human eye, not the soul. The study of Alchemy that I find most fascinating is related to a society of mystics known as the Rosicrucians. Many of their teachings have been condemned and misrepresented by some so-called "historians" and "experts." I want to be clear about this, Freemasonry held different ideals and I want to point out the true teachings of Esotericism related to the

Jim Morrison & Michael Hutchence

Rosicrucians. The writings and teachings of the Kabbala and Hermes are well represented in the system of Alchemy the Rosicrucians employed.

My personal road of choice, as Jim Morrison the eccentric rock star, for mysticism was found through Native American traditions. If you listen to "Ghost Song" and listen to it not just with your ears but all your senses, you will be taken on a mystical journey if you choose to go. The use of peyote when employed in a sacred way can lead to mystical visions. That is precisely why I used it, not to get high or block out my life but to experience what was on the other side. I can tell you now, no drug is necessary to achieve mysticism and in fact, you need to watch the visions you receive while under the influence of alcohol or drugs. They may be more frightening than helpful.

Once you begin to see the truth, you will also begin to feel as I did, as if you never fit in or even belonged on Earth. Mine was a combination of not knowing love on any true, intimate level and also having some experiences that led me to feel quite disconnected from the everyday world I saw people casually and easily fitting into. I experienced what many call "the dark night of the soul," and while this is not an uncommon experience, I had no real sense in how to cope with it. This "dark night" can go on for weeks, months or, as in my case, for years. Mine went on for the last couple of years before I exited Earth, and it completely manifested with the Miami fiasco. I felt abandoned, without God, a guardian Angel or even a divine presence. My dark night was finally subsiding while I was in Paris, but I was too physically ill and too much of an alcoholic to ever see the dawn. If I had made it to the promise of the new day, the dark night would have given me a heightened awareness to my mystical experiences. My illumination would have been brighter and more meaningful, because I had something to compare and contrast it with. I never made it to my personal renaissance on Earth, but I am here now.

I suggest mysticism to everyone and anyone, but I especially encourage it for anyone attempting to write. To stay creative, I suggest you remain the outsider, looking in. If you are the one being dissected and studied by everyone else, your viewpoint will be slightly — if not very — limited, and therefore, your art will be as well. Opening the box and seeing what makes it tick, will make you a much more interesting writer. Try studying the compartments, as opposed to being contained in one compartment inside the box. Insiders' views of the box are a dime a dozen, while the observations from outside the box and outside the culture, are more precious and innovative.

I suggest each of you research what is called Metatron's Cube. All the universal answers are basically contained in Metatron's Cube. It is the perfect blend of science and mysticism.

Science and mysticism can be, but should not be independent of each other necessarily.

The idea of geometry as the secret language of creation goes back at least as far as the Pythagorean school. You'll find examples of this thinking in Da Vinci's work, particularly the design known as Vitruvian Man. You can produce some cool art without being a slave to scientific veracity.

Newton was steeped in esoteric thought. Gravity was conceived as a mysterious divine force in place of the crystalline spheres the earlier cosmologists had thought held the celestial bodies fixed in the sky. It wasn't until the early twentieth century that this force was explained as the distortion of space-time by mass.

Science does not have all the answers and it never will. You must not only think outside the box but understand the absolute illusions science has caused you to live in.

Ghost Dance

Awake my child,
did you sleep well
under the northern
sky? Did you dream
of heaven and hell or
did I?

I shall tell you of
Handsome Lake and

Jim Morrison & Michael Hutchence

his sky journey and
four angels who
surround him
Would you believe,
one of those Angels is around me?

Wovoka brought the ghost dance
to heal us from all ills
the golden angel showed me
if it was used wrong, many of
our tribe would be killed

Mormons say the clothes
We use are shields, it is not so,
this is our dance from the Ancients
what could the Mormons possibly know?

The Lakotas say this dance
will wash all evil away,
but they will be filled with hatred
for those who don't do it their way,
Wovoka taught harmony and peace
and with those things the expansion
for our land would soon cease

Sitting Bull died for this dance
how soon we forget that we
are given the glory to continue
by fire in a trance
the ancient ceremony
The Navajo leaders
could not see

For we know,
to unite with our relatives

and friends on another plane
is righteous, proper
and has been ordained

Who the white man
calls ghosts are not our ghosts
at all, we saw our Father and Grandfather
we saw the Earth tremble
we saw Rome before it's fall

My Father walks beside me
I saw his eyes in the fire
why would I fear my own Father?
He is here to guide me
now free from his body he never tires

The vision Wovoka saw
was not of this Earth,
all the Indians who have gone
to the other side and the Buffalos
have found rebirth on the new Earth,
a higher plane, our land is fruitful there
but there is no rain

The Angel told me of my journey
and reminded me of Handsome Lake,
how the road to heaven is narrow,
the road to hell is wide and full of snakes,
do not allow your pride to be your mistake
I was told this by the Angel in the sky blue robe
A Bible passage appeared to me from the book
of Job

Find divine providence
though your suffering may be great
dismiss the adversary,

Jim Morrison & Michael Hutchence

the celestial prosecutor
before it is too late

In the ghost dance,
your visions are clear,
your Father can walk beside you again
Your Grandfather can talk to you more
now, then when you were young,

We shall not stop the dance
our ceremony has only just begun

—*channeled from Jim Morrison*

CHAPTER 21

Wasting the Dawn...

"Death is not extinguishing the light; it is only putting out the lamp because the dawn has come."

—*Rabindranath Tagore,* Indian Poet and Playwright

Jim Morrison & Michael Hutchence

A TALE OF TWO BROTHERS

There is something that is popular on Earth now that is called "The Secret," which is no secret at all. In fact, it came from the same place that in some obtuse way inspired song lyrics I wrote. The lyrics to "Waiting for the Sun" were actually inspired by something I read about called "The Emerald Tablets of Thoth," and this is precisely where this so-called new found secret originated from. You see, the Universal Law of Attraction is contained in those Emerald Tablets. I drew inspiration from mythology many times over and no one should doubt that.

Thoth was a real person who walked the Earth. As with many spiritually gifted former rulers of ancient lands before Christ was born, he was immortalized following his death. The Emerald Tablets of Thoth contains some of the most important wisdom for the new renaissance that is about to take place on the planet Earth.

What do you think you become, all your thoughts are actually prayers and intentions, and every utterance that not only comes out of your mouth but each is thought in your mind, manifests itself to what you perceive as your reality. Some are obviously more powerful and predominant thoughts than others, as they are repetitive, instead of just being dismissed or overruled in your psyche.

I attracted many things and people in my lifetime that I brought directly to myself, so I must take responsibility for the unfulfilled destiny I lived as Jim Morrison. However, there are areas of this so-called "secret" that are not explained properly or fully. While you are drawing things and people to yourself — and its manifesting almost like making a stew or fine wine, really slowly, the truth is, you are also living on a planet with millions and millions and everyone has free will and makes their own choices.

I am going to say here and now, I did not draw the sexual abuse I suffered as a child — no how, no way. Many proponents of the new found "secret" would suggest I did. I am not denying for some souls walking the Earth the abuse is actually charted before you are born, which is really hard to understand, but in order to become healers on Earth, some believe they need to experience deep, emotional pain so that they can go through this process of healing themselves and then others in their lifetimes.

This is not what happened to me at all. This was not in the plans and it pretty much threw me off balance through the rest of my life. The mind of a child can attract many things, experiences considered both bad and good out of fear or curiosity, but I was not attracting this abuse and, of course, deep down inside, a part of me believed that I did bring it to myself or cause it to happen, as with all other things in my life. I would think things like, "If I were a good boy, worth loving, this would never have happened to me. I must be sending out the wrong signals, because I don't like men that way."

Each of us KNOWS instinctively that the Universal Law of Attraction is real, and so each and every thing that happens to us, even as an innocent child, we feel we must own. It was more or less the free will of a demented predator that finds a child to abuse, not the other way around. The child is an innocent pawn in a sick, twisted game. You can only attract what you think of, or speak of, not what you don't know of. However, I believe, the victimization role should be a temporary one, because it can help you understand the feelings involved in being powerless so that you can rise to a state where you don't allow yourself to become duped again.

It's obvious now, that I went about things the wrong way in handling my abuse. I know there are thousands upon thousands who have done the same thing and continue to do the same thing: suppress the pain and harm done to them instead of healing from it. I coped with being a co-dependent soul minus my other half and also became sexually abused through my infamous addiction to alcohol. There is no one reason for addiction, and those who claim there is are truly misguided.

Yes, you bring addiction to yourself, as with any other behavior, but only you have the power over that addiction, as with any other behavior. There isn't one way for each person to cope with their situation.

Every thought is a mirror, a reflection of you and you will see that reflection manifest itself. Every thought is also a prayer, and it's what you are giving God and the Universe. Negative thoughts do attract more unwanted things in life, but what is left out of the mass-marketed version of the Universal Law of Attraction is something called intention.

Your intention is every bit as important as the thought itself. If your intention is self-centered, or mean-spirited against another, you may be surprised at the ugliness you attract in your life and the karma you are collecting, and surprise, surprise, you will have to deal with that karma later. It won't be pretty and it sure won't be fun.

The Law of Attraction does work on a time delay on Earth, so most of the time, the manifestation isn't instant. But it can be if you understand your own power and work on becoming more spiritually gifted. This is precisely why some of the figures you have come to know from ancient times were immortalized. They were capable of rapid or instant manifestation, so they were considered Gods, Goddesses, prophets, magicians, great alchemists, etc.

If your intention is to bring more peace and light to the universe and healing to your fellow man, as opposed to stuffing your mattress with your millions, then you may not be living the lifestyle of the rich and famous anytime soon. But more importantly, you are working toward the greater good, and since your thoughts are prayers for the universe and all those living in it, they are every bit as powerful as when you sit down to formally say a prayer. Your intentions and your wishes and dreams do count in the universal mind more so than your vote does on election day.

What I am suggesting, which will be taken with a grain of salt — but shouldn't be, is the ugliness on Earth was manifested by man, not by God. The entire collective of the population on the planet and their mind sets, limited, enlightened or of another kind, are bringing forth what is happening right now on Earth and for future generations. You must think differently to live on a different kind of planet. Your intention in those thoughts is the master key behind each and every one of them.

I realized I lived in a very materialistic country, and it's your trip, you design the flight plan, and if you want comforts from minimal to extreme, then do your thing.

My vision of this situation is that all the creature comforts you enjoy don't seem to be breeding a stronger, wiser species of creatures. If anything, the luxuries seem to make humans complacent and docile, and when you are not a searcher, it's pretty hard to find anything new of any value or substance.

If your intention is to find truth and understand the universal mind, you will be given the keys to do so. If your intention is to become wealthy, you may also be given the keys to do that, but you always need to ask yourself what is it you are contributing to the planet or the greater good? As many of you know reading this, I was not materialistic, that was not my bag, but I also knew that being a part of The Doors gave others employment to feed and clothe themselves and their families. I was more than satisfied existing in a small, less than luxurious motel room, because I knew the mind has no walls and that physical reality was all an illusion anyway.

Humans crave comfort, but it's in pain and suffering that you learn who you are. The true self comes through, for better or worse, when you experience those low points that cannot be forsaken. You discover what you are made of and who your true friends are. It's important to find truth in every aspect of your life, and so finding out who's who in your life and who is there for you when the chips are down is one of the most important lessons to learn. The trick-or-treaters who disguise themselves as people who love you or care about you, can only hide behind their masks for as long as you allow it. You are giving them the power to play a game with you and it's hurting your soul the more you let them roll the dice. I took a ride with others driving throughout my life, and I can tell you now, it was a huge mistake. Stop allowing others to be your driver, take the wheel, and control your own destiny.

Many people claimed I was always testing those around me, and I was. I would push people to the limit, push their buttons, in order to see who they were, and better yet, who they were in life. These tests never seemed to produce the results I sought, and I was more disappointed than pleased with the outcome. It was thought I was playing head games, but I was actually testing those around me.

You will be able to gather information on those around you by witnessing their actions, as opposed to listening to their words. Don't believe their rhetoric, believe what they are willing to show you, willing to do and not do for you. Take it from a man who was drunk and told many, many women he loved them. Talk isn't just cheap, it's often a pile of complete bullshit. The proof is in the pudding. It would be a wonderful thing if people would take more responsibility for what comes out of their mouths, but it seems less and less likely that will occur on Earth or that the human race will become less tolerable of lies and deceptions.

The dawn is the most important time of the day, because it's the hope of that day, the promise of a new beginning and the possibilities that rise with the sun that gives each of you a clean slate so you can begin again. I wasted many dawns, too many, so I want to challenge each of you not to do the same. When you wake up in the morning, before you do anything, think of what you want to transpire that very day. Your thoughts are transmitting to the Universe, and you are writing your own pages in your own chapters each and every day of the huge book of your life.

As the pyramids were great transporters that magnified energy and prayer, you are in fact, your own pyramid walking around on Earth. Thoth built a pyramid called the Pyramid of Giza, so I have a question for you, what's in your pyramid??? What do you want it to say about you — if someone walked in and was able to look around, what would they see?

Now here's a little secret I will let you in on, Thoth was not only a real person but so was "Themis." The boutique I wastefully paid for was named "Themis," and yes, the name was used at my suggestion. She was a real person, later immortalized, and she was someone who was actually connected to my eternal soul mate and to me in a past incarnation. She was also heavily connected to the Oracle of Delphi. Not only was everything in my past life actually about my unidentifiable muse, it now shows up all through the existence of Jim Morrison.

Interestingly enough, I used the name of something connected to my true eternal soul mate when I was giving something to another woman who was just a learning lesson. Did I believe at that place and time that the learning lesson, known as Pamela, was my eternal soul mate? No, not at all. I believed the relationship was going south, but I was searching for the unknown and when you search you find. I found my woman now and have manifested the amazing life I want with her by my thoughts and intentions. It will be beyond anything she can imagine, so the concept that it's too late, I left her and it can't come to be at this point is all wrong. You can manifest anything by thoughts, words and intentions. You will be given the keys, and then it's up to you to unlock the doors.

CHAPTER 22

It's Time to Live in the Scattered Sun...

"I spent a long time trying to find my center until I looked closely at it one night & found it had wheels and moved easily in the slightest breeze. So now I spend less time sitting and more time sailing."

—*Brian Andreas*, Story People

Jim Morrison & Michael Hutchence

As I am not on Earth at this time and — astonishingly to many, have no need or desire to return, I see much of what will happen to the planet that gave me so much; and my eternal soul mate still inhabits Earth and it causes me and many of us on this side, a heavy sadness. Many have been waiting for the apocalypse or Armageddon and many from centuries past, such as the fourteenth and upward, have had this great sense of disappointment that their preachers and leaders had it wrong, and the world is still rotating.

I really don't feel if you have a fixed mind set on what is going to take place in the coming years, that this will be of any interest to you, but for those of you who would like to know more, I will offer some of my insights.

I contend that the so-called second coming of Christ will not be what people have been led to believe or believe by their own perceptions using strictly black and white guidelines. There will be a spiritual renaissance that will take place on Earth in the next several years, but the second coming will actually be of the Holy Spirit, which is the true essence of the Christ Consciousness, as it will permeate the souls of many and fill the world with incredible light. Those that are looking for a physical manifestation of Jesus will be sorely disappointed. But those who understand the true nature of Jesus, will be filled with great light and will be beacons that light the way for the world.

The veil between the dimensions is getting thinner and this, of course, will continue. While there is no real separation, just a perceived one of heaven to Earth, it will become more and more apparent, the dimensions are not encapsulated within themselves, but they coincide together at all times.

Earth will experience in time, something I refer to as the scattered sun, meaning more and more people will become truly enlightened and be in accordance with other dimensions, acting for the greater good at all times and serving man and God. But these golden rays of light will be surrounded by darkness, this is why I refer to the sun as scattered. The darkness will be those who are filled with fear, jealously and envy of others and who knowingly, or unknowingly, push back the enlightened ones and despise the fact that those around them are on the path to wisdom.

This wisdom fills the darker souls with fear, therefore, they reject it without attempting to understand it. The light will be bolder and brighter, yet the darkness, greater, and it will try to encompass all of the light.

There are lower energies, dark energies and, of course, dark entities, and they do have a mission, whether they recognize it or not. This is to cut the light coming through to Earth, by those who are enlightened or are on the path to enlightenment. Beware of those who remain stagnant, not growing or evolving, for they are on the path to nowhere.

I believe you have come to Earth to grow and evolve, not go along with these so-called status quo and be content with where you are — I was a nomad in my past life, and I now understand it's a very useful thing to be a spiritual nomad, always searching for answers to matters of the soul, always posing questions, because if you become too comfortable in your acquired knowledge, you stop moving, you stop growing.

If you're walking around in colder temperatures minus a coat, you tend to move faster and desire to get somewhere fast, because you are not comfortable or satisfied with freezing. When you are all warm and cozy inside your house in a comfy chair, when the weather is inclement, you may end up taking a nap. You fall asleep because you are comfortable and safe, as opposed to a place where you feel you have to keep moving. It's better to be out in the elements when conducting a spiritual search, there is always room to grow, things to learn and room for improvement.

The changes on Earth are going to be extremely overwhelming to a great many, but not to the spiritually enlightened. Those that are seeking to live in wisdom with compassion will come through all conflicts and times of strife virtually unscathed. Those who are not making spiritual connections and nurturing the soul, will end up finding the coming times on Earth unbearable, not just uncomfortable.

There are energies on Earth — and in this dimension — that are not evolving, and that are dark and unhealthy. As the veil gets thinner, many of you will want to become more engaged with making direct spirit contact. I would advise against it unless you have made true and substantial contact with those in the divine realm through mysticism. You need to connect to that realm, and ask and receive ample protection before you start to try and bring in a friend or family member, or anyone else for that matter. Lower energies are basically in the dimension Earth resides in, they are very, very close to you and waiting to be heard.

Many of them long to be connected to a human body again and this is why when children or teenagers pull out the old Ouija board and start to play around with it, they bring in entities and energies that are really undesirable. There are documented exorcisms worldwide, and many times a dark entity has connected to a child or teenager after the use of a Ouija board. That does not mean the Ouija board is the tool of the devil, but a tool can be used for either darkness or light, depending on who is using it and how it is used. A Ouija board is best used in the presence of someone who has been connecting directly to God or Jesus or at least the Archangels and has some experience with mediumship or channeling. Many of you who utilize the internet are aware of how easily it is to become deceived by others on the web who suggest they are someone they are not. This happens with darker and lower energies as well, with tools like the Ouija board. I have never come through to anyone through such a tool, and I never would, because it's not my bag. I don't find it necessary, since I have a clear channel now.

Be clear about with whom you are communicating, and if they are of darkness or light. No one of the light will ever suggest you do anything detrimental or try to infringe upon your free will.

Many have come to believe a final battle will ensue between good and evil, and I am here to tell you, to open your eyes, it's already taking place. It appears evil is winning, or at least overtaking, more of the souls on Earth than we had hoped would happen. Many souls are in the abyss, simply lost in the darkness, and these souls emerge into evil. It's all around you, each and every day. It's in your neighbor, the good family man, father of two, who goes to work every day and spends evenings on the internet, operating as a child predator, lying about who he is, trying to lure children into his evil web because they are vulnerable and will satisfy his disgusting desires. While his children and wife sleep, he sets a trap for a child he can have his way with. Evil is in the man who divorced his first wife, married another one, had more children the second time and happily lives with and raises his new family, while the children from his first marriage hardly know him. His own children were discarded for the new ones, how can a child cope with this? How can this not be evil? Yet he is not murdering anyone or dealing them a fatal drug dose. However, it's this more subtle, harder to detect form of evil that does the most damage. The damage you do to a child cannot be repaired, or undone, it only can be healed and that may take a lifetime.

Evil comes in heavily disguised and sometimes hard to distinguish forms, yet it's all around you, so much so, I contend, most of you don't recognize it in the people who are a part of your everyday lives or who live close by. True evil is taking advantage of people's weaknesses, preying on the elderly, defenseless, or the children. These things are done every day, but by what are regarded as established and well respected cultural institutions. It's time some of you considered re-examining the meaning of evil, it doesn't have to appear as an all-powerful world leader like Hitler, or a new version of the so-called anti-Christ, it's in your culture, it's a part of your world and you easily dismiss it, because you have lost the notion that intention is where evil and light stem from.

An act can be of an evil nature even with the best intention, however, it is what is in your heart, and a part of your soul that you act on that manifests itself in evil or light. It is hard to judge what is in the heart of another, and so, at times, intention is very hard to comprehend. But when you learn to read people, to read their character, their motives become crystal clear. I was a good judge of character in my past life, yet as an alcoholic, allowed people to walk all over me who I didn't want to be around very much in a sober state. I was always interested in what made people tick, and if you seek a more spiritual existence, you will easily be able to read the intentions of others.

When you go down the road to a more spiritual path, it's pretty much the same as an alcoholic embracing sobriety. The people you once associated with will not be any good to you at that stage. And chances are, many of them will not want to see you evolved and lose your old habit, because your vice, more or less justifies their vice. The places you once spent your time in may not serve your more spiritual path, just as a bar or party where everyone is getting trashed, would not be the best choice for a newly sober alcoholic to hang-out in.

For many with addictions, they have to change their social habits, and lose their old set of friends, because those friends will not cater to their new sobriety. This may be the a harder part of the transition more so than going cold turkey. Sometimes those closest to you were a part of the old you, and the new you, the one choosing a different path, has outgrown these people — and possibly even significant others. It's pretty much the same as if the group of people you are around now were your friends in fifth grade, and now that you are in high school, maybe you'd like to hang-out with a different set of friends with different interests. Evolving does often mean leaving friends, family and even your significant other behind if they are attempting to hold back your spiritual growth or don't support your quest for enlightenment. Your path can't be their path, and I feel it's a mistake to try to bring anyone on your path, as they have their own path and you must honor that. But at the same time, if you are with someone who wants to hold you back on your own path, sometimes you need to make a hard, but critical choice.

More and more you will need to make choices as relationships that do not allow growth will need to be discarded. Sometimes, when you are going forward and evolving, you notice you have to leave some people behind. Many of you that will become more enlightened will find others around you who may not be, and when someone of a darker energy is around an enlightened one, the darker one acts as an energy vampire. That's probably the best way to describe it, as they drain the energy and light from the enlightened one. When you are around someone you were once close to, or still think you are, and feel emotionally exhausted, chances are you are dealing with an energy vampire. I had few of those around me in my last existence. As the Earth moves into new times, it's the last thing you need, because you will really want to. And moreover, need to shine your light, not be drained by others who feed off you because of their own darkness.

What it all comes down to is there are people in this world you can help and others you can't help, no matter how hard you try. People have to want to go forward, and that was something I really did want to do in Paris, but I was so emotionally exhausted and physically ill, I could not overcome my own dilemma. Each person does have to change on their own, by their own intentions and actions, and you can't shape a single human being into what you want. It's a pretty substantial waste of your time and energy.

Mysticism is the true way to enlightenment. I know it can be a lengthy journey, and what I would like to do, realizing how much I needed this in my last lifetime, is to offer portals. You could call them short cuts, but I prefer to refer to them as direct connects. There are channeled works of art all over the Earth. I want to mention a certain artist and his paintings, because one of them would have been the most suitable artwork for the cover of this book. The artist's name is Lowry Burgess, and he was born a few years before I was.

This artist is literally channeling his works from the other side. While there are other channeled and amazing artworks, his are very unique and special. The first one I would like to speak of is called "Vision Portal: Rose," which is a painting about purification, one of the first and major steps in mysticism. This painting is so breathtaking, it's the painting I most wish to show my eternal soul mate, the butterflies in it will mean something to her.

The painting that would most fit this book is called "Vision Portal: Crocus," which uses various images to fuse philosophy and physics and literally takes the spectator to the infinite. If you were to meditate on this painting or any of Lowry's divine work, you would find a portal that would transport you to another dimension in a much shorter amount of time. His inspiration and divine artistic vision can now inspire you. I love this man's work and cannot talk enough about it.

I made a brief appearance in 2006 when his work was shown in Paris in a solo exhibition and at the London Roadhouse. I rarely go to Paris, because it is not the best place for me to be. I have gone there to analyze what went wrong, but I do not regularly go there. I went when Lowry's work was exhibited, and I will build new memories of Paris with my eternal soul mate and expunge those recollections of my final days there as Jim Morrison. They were not beautiful, but lonely and depressing. I am over them and only wish to create new memories with my woman when the time comes. If any fan of mine would see one of the paintings I mentioned or some of Lowry's other works in person, they would understand why I am such a huge fan of his.

There are many other types of portals and not only divinely channeled art. Portals are prophecies sometimes, but prophecies are not usually portals. American President Abraham Lincoln had what he thought was a vivid dream about his own death and funeral just a few days before it actually occurred. This wasn't really a dream, or just a premonition, but Lincoln was taken forward through a portal to see his fate and destiny played out in a very frightening way. Lincoln's destiny was predetermined and although something could have gone awry to change it, by the time he was allowed to step through this portal to view the future, the cards were on the table.

During my lifetime as Jim Morrison, I lived through the murder of another president, John F. Kennedy. Many will acknowledge I wrote about this in "NOT TO TOUCH THE EARTH," and of course, that was only a part of "Celebration of the Lizard," as I was a student of the times. I was in college in Florida when the President was assassinated, but regardless of where you were or what you were doing at the time in America, a great fear and sadness permeated the landscape. It seemed as if the world could end any day. It is not at all a coincidence that these two presidents were murdered when they were, and Kennedy's funeral was made to duplicate that of Lincoln's. Both of these men had a vice-president named Johnson who took over the Presidency but failed to heal the country. Almost 100 years to the day of the delivery of the Gettysburg Address by Abraham Lincoln, President Kennedy was murdered. One of the most interesting things about both of these murders is that in each case, their wives sat next to them while they were shot and had to continue their lives after witnessing the murders of their husbands on an up close and personal level, while a country mourned in great fear. Lincoln was given a portal to see his future to prepare himself and those around him. It would not be the first time he was given such a portal, but it would be the last time on Earth.

Some connected souls like Abraham Lincoln are given portals right in their dreams, but most of you will need to seek them out and open the connection. Most of the time, dreams are just manifestations of your subconscious, but there are times when they are actual visitations of loved ones from the other side, or even portals to the other side.

There are various types of portals many don't think of or recognize in their daily lives. Each of you can create a portal through meditation, but there are some tools that aid in this. Much is said about crystals and stones used as portals. My own belief is that the art of scrying can be conducted in crystals and even in the stone known as amethyst. You should be very careful since crystals are tuned with frequencies, and for someone starting out on a spiritual journey, I wonder how wise it is to seek to use something full of encoded information you could not possibly understand until you are further along. Scrying, however, is a powerful tool and portal, and one of the best places to do it is actually in a body of water, such as a lake. Water is a portal, and this is why meditation near a body of water is really recommended. The desert is a portal that can transport you into time travel, if you allow it to. You can go back in time and receive fascinating visions, but I suggest you do it with plenty of fresh drinking water and no chemical enhancements. Be of a clear mind.

The portal I now see in America I should've connected to while on earth, is located on the borders of Arizona and Utah, and it's called Monument Valley. If you want to connect to the Ancients who went before you, this is the true holy land in the U.S.

The energy vortexes in Sedona, Arizona are portals. It is suggested you connect to the elders of Sedona or some other wise spirits when you are in Sedona. But really, you can easily have some of the most memorable mystical experiences there, and many have come to see an Ascended Master known as Babaji there and many, many others. The Ancients, as we call them on this side, are all around Sedona. If you are seeking answers to questions, ask them with a clear mind and a sincere heart in the vortexes of Sedona. My personal favorite vortex in Sedona is called "Red Rock Crossing" or "Cathedral Rock." The energy there is nothing short of amazing, and it's the perfect transport where many receive answers and incredible visions. I believe many who go there will soon see alarming visions of things to come on Earth in the next few years.

I have given my channel visions and they are truly upsetting to her, so much so that she asked me to take these visions to another channel and have her record them. Michael Hutchence and I have been showing our channel things, but we realize they shake her to her very core and she can hardly function after seeing them in meditation or in a dream. We have gone to another gifted psychic, Francine Milano, because our channel wished us to.

I really have only one channel now and will not be switching channels any time in the future. I have chosen her, she has made a spiritual agreement and the other gifted individuals who appear in this book are there to support the channeled words I give to my sole channel, Jacquie. I have independently gotten others to back up, almost word for word in some cases, things I had channeled to her weeks or even months previously about my death and other aspects of my life. I did this to confirm she was hearing me clearly and putting it down on paper precisely as I was giving it to her. We have decided some others could add small pieces to this book, that we thought would be interesting or helpful, not just be placed in the book to verify all this information. While I am grateful to each of them who has made a contribution, my sole channel is the main author of this book and the only one I have given it all to, the information, my story and my truth.

I think the poetry in this book makes more sense and shows a more matured version of who you thought you knew on Earth. If you visit a psychic or medium and try to bring me in at this point, only unless you were a close male friend I am trying to reconnect to or my eternal soul mate, you are wasting your time. They won't be able to pick-up my energy and may not even tell you the truth that nothing is coming through, so you may get a pack of lies. I want to confirm to one male friend in particular, this is really me, and I intended to leave him all my raw, unpublished and unedited work. I want to confirm to my eternal soul mate that she is everything, and I need her to start really connecting to me and our upcoming life on this side.

Instead of trying to channel me or bring me in to find out something, I suggest you start to connect to the divine realm in some form and pursue true mysticism. It will surely help your soul and your life better than attempting to channel a dead rock star or have some psychic verify for you I didn't die in a bathtub. You had me on Earth, if you connected to me, that's great, cherish the memory, and if you didn't, you now have this book, these words, and that is all you will have of me. For all the others who know me on Earth, there is no sense in visiting a psychic or medium to bring me in, our business has concluded but for the fact I owe many of you a heartfelt, or maybe I should say, soul felt, apology and you will receive it and we will move on. Once again, I am over my life as Jim Morrison, it's time for all of you to get over it and move on. There is more to life than visiting a hollow grave in Paris listening to "Light My Fire."

Safe Passage

I bring you safe passage to the new world,
Time wept for what was lost but not forgotten.
Where we once were is no more and never again
to be seen.

The other side of the mountain
brings new hope and promises,
complete transformation for stepping
on the soil.

If your heart is heavy,
you should not go
It's only for those who want to vanish to be born anew

if you stay behind
I cannot help you my friend,
I must go with my torch to bring
the others to safe land

I can only serve the brave,
the explorers, the pilgrims who

A TALE OF TWO BROTHERS

want to begin again
and take no prisoners

We went to the wake
for the dead
their loved ones got drunk
under the moon and cried and howled

They are buried on the hill now
with elaborate gravestones,
just above the catacombs we
once explored

They cannot go with us
their ghosts stay behind
this town has nothing to offer
so I tell those who come along
it's time…it's time

Pick up your torches
mine shines brighter and I will
lead the way
do not fear the dark unknown
fear what will happen if you stay

Your growth has been stunted here
Your eyes were cursed
they can't see past the mundane
where nothing is fruitful

I offer you safe passage to the New World,
one you can make it be whatever you wish
you will create it, mold it and shape it,
it will be your wet dream, your nightmare,
your heaven, your hell and everything in between

Jim Morrison & Michael Hutchence

But the only thing it won't be is…mundane
not more of the same, it will change and reshape
every other day

Your eyes will view things differently
in this vast kaleidoscope,
randomly changing by proxy
if you don't shake up the realm
of possibilities

You will not see it the same
way twice, you will not see
him the same way anymore
she will not be who she once was

This is the brave new world
It will bring out the truth in each of you
I am just the torch bearer
I will lead you and return

To bring more to this side
those who dare to see
what their life can become
When they no longer know what to expect

Our journey will begin tonight
close your eyes and hold on tight
You'll begin your travel as soon as you see
my bright light

Do not forget the moment
You left apathy behind
Do not allow the past
to enter your mind

A TALE OF TWO BROTHERS

Are you ready to rise from
your own ashes?
Are you ready to see what
has always been there?

I am ready to take you,
it's my pleasure sir, Ma'am
Just remember you can never
go back again to the lost
but not forgotten

I bring you safe passage…

—channeled from Jim Morrison

Jim Morrison & Michael Hutchence

CHAPTER 23

Wake Up Girl, We're Almost Home!!!

"That was the day the ancient songs of blood and war spilled from a hole in the sky
And there was a long moment as we listened and fell silent in our grief and then one by one,
we stood tall and came together and began to sing of life and love and all that is good and true
And I will never forget that day when the ancient songs died because there was no one in the world to sing them."

—*Brian Andreas* (Traveling Light: Stories & Drawings for a Quiet Mind)

Jim Morrison & Michael Hutchence

Jim = *Jim Morrison*

Jac = Jacqueline Murray

Jim: Jacquie, some of this information has truly shocked you, and I am sorry it was so emotionally heavy. It's quite contrary to the materials I have directed you to read about my life.

Jac: Yes it is. I really didn't know much about you before we started this process.

Jim: I know, and that's refreshing.

Jac: You weren't exaggerating Jim, you've really been lied about, it's really disgusting in some ways. But this wasn't about my opinion of you or anything related to you. I just wanted to get your words, and what you wished to convey to the public, as clearly as possible. This is your story, yours alone.

Jim: Is there anything you want to ask me, Jacquie, now that we're done with my story?

Jac: I guess I want to ask about going to the other side and how you reconcile the life you lived on Earth and the choices you made during your Earth life?

Jim: It's not easy, Jacquie, and the one thing I would urge you to do, as well as anyone on Earth, clean-up as much of your mess as you can before you cross over. Time is not an issue on this side, but on Earth, time is of the essence. I would also say seek out true relationships, not ones of convenience, but ones that allow you to be true to yourself and to the other person. Make sure you're not involved in a charade with others. Is there something else you want to ask?

Jac: You seemed to have conveyed a sense of anger and sadness over your last life and you do, take personal responsibility, but I got a sense even before you said so, that you are so far removed from your past life, you are really over it. But I was more or less shocked at the reaction to your fans. I was just wondering, is that what happens to everyone when we cross over, do we put that past life completely behind us and do you resent your fans?

Jim: I am over my last life and wish nothing more than to put it behind me. It's quite individual over here Jacquie, some hang on to their past life, their past identity and even cling to the Earth and others evolve.

Regarding my fans, it's not a question of resenting them, but too many of them have bought into the myths, misconceptions and fallacies created around my image. I am to many, a false icon. I realize there is little else to go on for the true fan, because I internalized so much and never let anyone else know what was really going on inside my head, or for that matter, my heart. I gave people bits and pieces, never the whole picture, and many people have taken a small piece of my life, the puzzle that it was, and filled it with pseudo pieces that do not belong.

Jac: I absolutely got that.

Jim: What the fans that worship at the altar of Jim Morrison believe, are true illusions. When you are living in the matrix, however, you don't have much to go on. And by the way, the theory of the Matrix first came about in Germany, the year before I was born on Earth. You must look beyond or you will remain a slave to things that are not real and never really were.

Jac: Ok, well, I thought I was living in an illusion when you first began talking to me.

Jim: Yes, you did, and it made my job harder. You are truly a skeptic, Jacquie ,but that's a good thing, and it serves you well. It prevents you from being gullible. I am fairly certain if you were to make up my story from your imagination, not receive it from me, that your story of my life would be totally different.

Jac: Yes, a happier one. I am a romantic at heart. I would tell a romantic love story.

Jim: My story is anything but that. Before we conclude, is there anything else?

Jac: I feel like asking a question for your fans. If a fan of yours, wants to make contact with you, even on an energetic level, where would you suggest he or she goes?

Jim: I have visited Pere LaChaise in the past, Jacquie. I don't go there now so if I have fans or curiosity seekers who believe my ghost is hanging around my graveside, please don't waste your time. I was startled to see the number of people there, not at all happy about it, and I kept asking myself, what were they hoping to find?

Jac: Ok, that's a closed door for fans then?

Jim: Yes, these people come to Paris and go to my gravesite and cry and laugh and try to bring me in and ask me questions. If they want to make it a more fitting place, they should play The Doors song "Strange Days" over an intercom system day and night. If they believe they are connecting to my energy, they are not, and basically, they are connecting to the energy of the many others who venture there.

Jac: So you are giving me a place they can't connect, I want to know where they can connect, what about in California?

Jim: No, why would they be able to? I do not hang out in my old haunts, pardon the pun. Why would I, Jacquie? What would I be there for? To remember my drunken escapades or yelling obscenities on Sunset Boulevard or all the wasted time and energy of my last life?

Jim Morrison & Michael Hutchence

From this side honey, the memories are not so sweet. Those who think they are contacting me at the places I used to live, stay, record or hang out, are not speaking to me. One psychic, and only one, in California ever spoke to me before and her name was June. She spoke to me over several months in 2000 and 2001, and I was in California at that time. I spoke to her for a variety of reasons, and one of them, my dear, was to practice so I could channel a whole book to you. It takes a tremendous amount of energy to do this for me and for the channel, as you know. This really is work. I gave June some information back then that you can check for yourself, as she was in the media, on TV, and in various places including "Time" magazine sharing the details of my death I channeled to her. I will show you what I told her, Jacquie, it's still publicly available and you will see it's exactly what I told you. It says I didn't die in a bathtub, I am not with Pamela on this side, and I didn't kick the bucket from a drug overdose. I actually allowed June to feel my death, which I realize is horrible, however, I needed her to really understand how I died. She had the ability to do that. I didn't give her my life story, Jacquie, that was for you, for our book. I don't channel to anyone but you now Jacquie. It would be a waste of my energy if I did, and it would dilute my messages. I know you are clear and not spiking this with your own input.

Jac: Thank you, Jim. I was just trying to give your fans something: they love you and I feel some of them want to be closer to you.

Jim: I am a huge proponent of free will, but I am trying to caution my fans, the worship of me is nothing but an empty vessel.

They believe things about me that were not true, therefore their whole belief system of me is hollow. Simply put, I was a sexually abused kid who grew up to become a hardcore alcoholic. Unfortunately, this all too common a story I share with far too many, Jacquie.

My fans think I found true love and a cosmic mate, and in reality, it was another addict who left me for dead. They believe I was wandering around the desert for months at a time finding myself. I never found myself. They believe I died in a bathtub of an *accidental or intentional drug overdose, I wasn't trying to checkout, Jacquie, and I was trying desperately to change in Paris. They believe I had an enormous ego and it was really more along the lines of tremendous self-hate. They believe I exposed myself on stage in Miami, it never happened. So I ask you Jacquie, who do they think they know? Who are they worshipping?*

Jac: We have gone over this so many times in the book, and I do understand this very clearly. I guess I was just hoping your story would be a little more fan friendly.

Jim: I want to make this clear, I am proud of The Doors as we were quite unique, and in America presently, there is such homogenized music. I was fortunate enough to be mixed with a group of incredibly talented musicians and I would give them more credit than I give myself for our songs. But I would've gotten past The Doors, and they only would've been a chapter or two in my whole life. I screwed up, and I refuse to stay attached to a wasted life. It would not be healthy or help me evolve.

I only channel to you because others who would call me in, that could communicate with me, would try and keep me attached to something I have to move on from now that my true story has been told. So for those who have their Oujia board out or are visiting places in California where I used to stay and are holding their séance or whatever, you might as well pack it up and stop. I will not be coming in for you and you may, in fact, be put in touch with another spirit, but it will not be Jim Morrison.

Jac: That's an area of confusion for some, so you can be communicating with a spirit who is impersonating a spirit?

Jim: (Laughs) Yes, but once again, it takes a huge amount of energy to penetrate this dimension, and I have yet to know of a spirit who has impersonated anyone in order to write an entire book. If you go directly to the Source, whom you call God, and ask who this entity or spirit is you are speaking to, I assure you, you will easily determine if you have a so-called impersonator. Tell them to leave if they are not who you thought they were. I was always quite surprised at the long-winded ritual you will conduct every time before we started a session of our work. You would invoke various Archangels, Saints, Ascended Masters, not to mention your Spirit Guides, and by the time you got to the Holy Spirit, Jacquie, you were more than safe. Was all that necessary?

Jac: I wanted to make sure I had the right Jim Morrison. I don't want anyone else coming in but who I ask for, and I wanted to make sure I only channeled you each and every time.

Jim: You got the direct connect, honey. There was never a reason to worry. You have strong spirit guides and you enlisted their help so no one gets through who shouldn't. Did you suspect you started with the real me and at some point, an imposter would come in to continue my story? (Laughs)?

Jac: I just wanted to be very, very sure.

Jim: But do you think if an imposter came through, I, the real Jim Morrison, wouldn't have come in and told you? Do you suppose some kind of demon would suggest to his fans that they are worshipping a false icon?

Jac: I think you would've told me if I had an imposter at some stage and, no, I would think a demon would encourage your idol worship.

Jim: Yep, and probably suggest everyone devour peyote buttons, while downing their whiskey in front of my grave, invoking my dark spirit. But I want to caution you Jacquie, you will hear all sorts of stories of me being channeled and most of them are false. There are stories of these two women in the Valley in California who claim I am married to them from the other side (Laughs) and I guess I shouldn't laugh, as they need help. I don't communicate with anyone in California or anywhere else presently, just you though I am actively around my true eternal soul mate.

Jac: So spirits don't often cling or show up where they used to live?

Jim: It varies. Each spirit is truly individual and some are still very attached to their Earth lives and those they left behind, so to

A TALE OF TWO BROTHERS

speak. I am attached to the woman I did not meet on Earth who would've been my wife later on, my true eternal soul mate, or as some would call her, my twin flame. She is presently in Canada, and so I am there, around her at times.

Jac: I think with all the poems and references in this book, everyone will know her name is Rebecca.

Jim: Yes, you know her last name also, Jacquie, but let's leave it at that.

Jac: She's a brunette with highlights in her hair?

Jim: Yes, she is. Since you are a romantic, Jacquie, you have to think this is a truly beautiful story, that I am waiting for her on this side.

Jac: Yes, but it's so sad, Jim. This is such virgin territory here, everything I was directed to read about you, suggests Pamela was it for you.

Jim: Jacquie, if I had lived and you fast-forwarded to a year to the day I crossed over, the world would've known Pamela and I were permanently finished, without question. Once again, I was 27 years old and though people did marry young back then, I was such a free thinker, that wasn't truly in my realm of possibility. I was infatuated with many other women, and I am glad some never sold me out by writing a book or contributing to one. My drunken escapades soured many relationships with the more together women I had in my life.

They caused the break-up of my relationship with Mary Werbelow and Patricia who certainly saw what a dirt bag I became after a drinking binge while she was in L.A.

Jac: Anything else you want to say about your true love,

Rebecca? Does she have an inkling you are around her or what is going on here, Jim?

Jim: She can feel me touching her arm or her face sometimes, and I kiss her eyelids sometimes when she is going to sleep.

Jac: She feels it?

Jim: Oh yes, but sometimes she thinks it's a bug (Laughs), wait 'till she finds out what it really is!!

Jac: So with all the beautiful women on Earth, she is the only one for you? You are into monogamy now Jim?

Jim: Yep, listen from here, we look at the souls of those on Earth, and you'd be surprised the most cosmetically beautiful people don't always have the brightest soul, in fact, much of the time, their souls are quite dark actually. It's your light, your aura, we look at.

Jac: Really?

Jim: The beautiful people tend to spend their time on superficial bullshit instead of growing as a person and becoming enlightened. Remember what I told you, honey, mysticism leads to enlightenment.

Jac: Yes, I've been reading more about mysticism, as you probably know.

Jim: You have, but not enough, your soul is very, very bright and really lovely. Now in the case of my eternal soul mate, the light around her is so bright, it's blinding to us on this side.

Jac: That's beautiful Jim.

Jim: I would've fallen in love with the whole package on Earth, but now you know, despite her good looks, it's about her soul from here, because I don't occupy a human body anymore and we have ethereal bodies here and are attached to the bright lights and beautiful souls. Someone with big boobs or a nice ass wouldn't do much for me here. (Laughs).

Jac: I guess not.

Jim: So I just happened to have selected the woman with the brightest soul imaginable but considering where I would've been in my life and how spiritually evolved I would've started to become, it makes sense but she sure would've outshined my soul, even in it's more evolved state.

Jac: This is really interesting, Jim, so when she dies, or exits her human body rather, what will happen to the two of you? Will you come up and introduce yourself as her eternal soul mate or what?

Jim: She will see me and know me, she'll just know, and be overwhelmed with emotion and we will both finally get the happy ending we've been waiting for. But it won't really be an ending, because there is no end, there is no time.

Jac: I am glad you will finally get some happiness. This wasn't the easiest story to channel Jim. Someone like you, with so much talent, not to mention intelligence, and how things went wrong, and how you never found true love or any of the things you were seeking, is really, really sad. I am relieved you will finally be fulfilled.

Jim: Why thank you, darlin'. I know I am not the easiest to work with, but you have handled me pretty well. I know you have a hard time understanding you are the chosen channel for me, more accurately, the sole channel now, and we have other work to do and more things to talk about, but I am grateful to you. You put up with my shit very well. (Laughs)

Jac: Thank you. Apparently I signed up for this. Next time, I am on the other side I better hire a lawyer to negotiate my contract.

Jim: I'm not that bad, Jacquie. Do you remember the song you heard over and over in your head for two months when you would wake up in the morning?

Jac: It was "Roadhouse Blues," but I wasn't familiar with it or who sang it.

Jim: Well my eternal soul mate hears a song in her head over and over, it's called "Blue Sunday."

Jim Morrison & Michael Hutchence

Jac: I wonder how she is handling that, I thought I was going crazy hearing "Roadhouse" constantly.

Jim: She is asking herself what's going on. I'm going on. My life went by like a fast blur, Jacquie, I was in a haze. I can see it all clearly now from where I am. I am over it, I am just waiting for my woman. When she comes home, when she comes to me, I will be complete, the nightmare will be over.

Unchained Melody

I woke-up tired, thirsty, drained
of all bodily fluids,
dreaming of the Ancient druids
staggered into the bright sun,
it stung my eyes, the nightmare has begun

I was in this dirty, cheap motel,
it was worse than my usual rooms from hell,
I heard the desk clerk speaking Español,
I knew I was in Mexico
I couldn't find my friend,
he left me, so did his car,
I asked the man at the front desk,
Did my friend say he was coming back,
did he say he was going far?

The clerk's eyes looked opaque,
I did a double take,
beads of sweat surrounded
his thick, overgrown moustache
He said loudly "Friend,
what friend, you came alone"

great, I checked my pockets
I had no cash

The clerk went on "maybe you
need to call in a guide,
you're confused man"

I shot back Do I look like
I want to sight-see? I don't
think you understand,
what are you smoking man?
I was hot, thirsty and
staggered from the motel
I kept thinking, Dear God
I must be in hell

How did I get here?
I was supposed to be in
the studio on Monday,
Paul would be there,
I had to do vocals
Last time I checked, it was Sunday

I stuck my thumb out,
I began to hitch,
a dangerous, enticing game
I played when I got left or stuck,
the sun was a bitch
as usual I was down on my luck

Oh man, I craved a beer,
I want a nice girl
to show up and pick me up
and let me curl up

Jim Morrison & Michael Hutchence

until we get back to L.A.
on this sizzling hot day

A truck pulls over, opens the door
I think this will do, as I climbed aboard,
the trucker looks like someone I know
but I didn't care, just wanted to go

"How ya doin' son?" he yelled in my ears
I told him, good, better now,
but I really needed a beer,
he smiled slightly, and
proceeded to say
"I don't want to hear your story,
they all have one, nothing personal son,

I'd rather not know, how you got here or
where you'll go"

I told him ok, but do you have a smoke?
He looked at me strangely
with one eyebrow raised
"That won't do you any good here,
in fact, it will go right through you"

The truck flew down the road,
never saw one go so fast,
I shut up but he continued on
"I've seen you before son,
it was in Babylon"

My head was pounding,
Babylon? I asked quizzically,
Is that near a town where we played?
I know it's not in Cali

A TALE OF TWO BROTHERS

Is that in Ohio?
Are you a fan?

The trucker looked at me
Dead seriously,
"Where you played?" he asked
Yes sir, I am in a band

The trucker shook his head
from side to side,
and said "Son, you were in a band,
don't know why but you don't yet
understand, you are having
trouble assimilating"
I was tired, thirsty and my head
was going to implode, it was getting
frustrating

He pulled his rig into
the gas station,
"This is as far as I can take you,
God speed"
I got out of the truck and thanked
him, kept thinking a beer
is what I need
My headache is getting worse,
the sun is burning my face,
this little siesta in Mexico
was a curse and now I can't
get out of this place
I hitched for miles down
the road, when I couldn't walk
another step, two chicks stopped in
a sweet Chevy, wanting to give me a lift

Jim Morrison & Michael Hutchence

Hi Ladies, nice to see you
The redhead chick in the passenger's
seat turns and speaks "You look dehydrated,
and weak" then she asked "Where are
you going?" and she looks at her friend
and laughs, I respond it's not funny girls,
I've been walking for an hour and a half

I told them I need to go back to L.A.
"L.A.?" the blonde driver asks,
as they broke out in silly girlish giggles,
she slams on the brakes and I tell her
not to give me whiplash, as the desert
sun sizzles

They looked pretty good,
so I told them it's ok if you ladies
aren't going that way, how about
we just get some beer and tequila and
hang out tonight and party in the
moonlight?

I got only silence
so I asked with a raised voice
where are you ladies going?
the redhead turned to me again,
her lips were moist

"Away from guys like you"
she snaps back
excuse me, do you know
me I ask? What are you
implying? They are silent
but I keep trying

A TALE OF TWO BROTHERS

The blonde driver tells
the redhead to show me,
the pretty little passenger
turns around and reveals
a huge scar, strange since she
doesn't know me, the scar
would be personal I thought,
it went from her neck
down to her heart

It was grotesque,
but as with things so disturbing,
I chose to stare,
I ask her who did that to you?
she shoots back with an icy glare
She said "a guy like you"
I got mad and said you don't
know me, that's not my scene,
I may not be a Prince but I am surely
not that mean

"He was just like you" she
said in a determined voice
"Didn't love me, didn't love himself,
was drunk and cruel, a complete asshole,
a total fool and if you had
stayed where you were,
no telling what you would
have done to her"

You don't know me,
I got as loud as my headache,
Can we stop for a beer for Christ's sake?

Jim Morrison & Michael Hutchence

The blonde driver replies
"you won't need a drink,
your destination is close,
you need a chance to think"

I was relieved,
we must be close to the border I thought
but no specific information
is what I got

So we are close to the border?
I ask to be sure,
the blonde says "yes,
close to Canada to be sure"

Canada? No I need to go to L.A.
Can we stop for a drink?
I needed it quickly, I was in
No mood to play

The blonde driver turned around
purple bruises on her face and neck,
who beat the hell out of you?
"No one did" she tells me she
was in a car wreck

I had nothing to say
but wanted to be kind,
I told her at least you lived
she looked in the rearview mirror
at me like I was out of my mind

The chicks looked like I felt,
I wanted to be polite and told them
if they wanted to, they could kidnap me
for the night

A TALE OF TWO BROTHERS

They said nothing more,
we pull into a coffee shop
I tell them sorry sisters,
I really wanted a beer,
the redhead said "You're nothing
but a bore, you're here,
go inside and find out
what you left behind,
what a fool you were,
in your case the truth
is unkind"

The blonde driver chimed in
"You need to go, we're not like the
girls you used to know, you can't seduce us,
with your voodoo talk and your bad stage show"

I open the door
wanting to scream at the
battered whores who left me
in Mexico, at the end of the road

The coffee shop was empty,
nothing around but unending desert
I walked in and the guy at the counter
said his name was Kurt

My head was exploding.
this vacant place was my worst fear,
no women and most of all, no beer

I asked Kurt to use the pay phone,
I need to call my friend Babe for a ride
he smiled and said "I'm sorry Jim,
there's no phones on this side"

Jim Morrison & Michael Hutchence

I tell Kurt, my head
really hurts, and he hands
me a small prism, made of glass,
I told him, don't know if this will
help Kurt, do you have any beer
or grass?

He holds the prism up to the
window, where the sun had begun to set
I could see L.A., Sunset Blvd.
and Kurt told me "Jim, you ain't
seen nothing yet"

I suddenly see my liquor store,
my bars, my strip clubs,
even my car

I want to get in the blue lady,
get some Mexican food and beer
and be left alone, I really
just want to go home

Then I see her,
a woman I never knew
I look at her hard,
realizing she was actually my muse

Her hair is brown with sun streaks,
her blue eyes could make your knees weak,
Kurt who is she?
He looked morbidly at me
and said "She's your better half,
I am sorry she's all alone, Jim, you
can't go back"

A TALE OF TWO BROTHERS

I have to go back, I said emphatically to Kurt
I need to meet her, seeing her without
me is starting to hurt, I want to meet her,
I know she's the one, Kurt began to wipe
down the counter, and said "You can go back,
but they won't hear you or see you, I am sorry
Jim, right now I know it really hurts to be you"

I got angry, my voice became raised
man, stop talking in riddles, my head hurts
where the hell am I Kurt?

Kurt was cleaning coffee cups,
though no diners were in sight
He said "Jim you fell asleep in Paris,
on a hot summer night, you ended up
here, this is the coffee shop at the
road that goes nowhere."

He continued on "Your head
doesn't really hurt, you're confused
is all" I was getting antsy and said
Kurt, I really need to make a phone call

A van pulled up, with two men with glowing
white light, Kurt said "Jim that's your ride,
you'll heal and be fine, you'll like the other side,
but before you go, you may want to
check in here every week or so, your better half
will be here, though she has some time to go"

As the men come to retrieve me,
I remember being in bed in Paris,
couldn't move, couldn't talk,
couldn't call for help, couldn't walk,
OH MY GOD, it's true,

Jim Morrison & Michael Hutchence

I am on the other side,
OH MY GOD, what do I do?
I think I left my bride
The glowing men
come in and tell me it's time to go,
So every week I come back and visit
Kurt, write her letters she will get
when she comes home, I bring her
purple roses and always look my best,
As I wait for our first date, until then, I
cannot rest.

The jukebox will play
"Unchained Melody" as we have
our first dance, and for the first time
since I came here, I will know heaven,
for this is my one and only chance.

—*channeled from Jim Morrison*

Divine Channel

All the lies they told,
All the mud I have been dragged thru
will be rectified, by you, only by you

I trust my teacher more than any
other, we've known each other
for what seems like forever,
you are my sister, I am your brother

I failed you honey and I failed
myself, you taught me well,

A TALE OF TWO BROTHERS

but the promise of a new dawn
turned into hell

One day soon, You'll have me
in your classroom once again,
I'll be a better student,
more learned, so I can truly
ascend

You are my teacher, my channel,
above all my friend and I'll be
nearby until you find the Rainbow's
end, and class will start a new
session and I will be forgiven
for my horrific past life
transgressions

When you need me, I'll be around,
for you have been there throughout
my soul's history, teacher of the
mysteries, reader of records,
divine channel of God, you are
an old soul, one many of us
recognize and know,
and I thank you for all
you've given to me and
for presenting my truth
for the world to see.

—With love, from Jim for his channel, Jacquie

Jim Morrison & Michael Hutchence

CHAPTER 24

The Mystic Sees the Truth...
The Rose of Mysterious Union

by Kathleen Tucci

Jim Morrison & Michael Hutchence

In my past lifetime as Jim Morrison, I gave many women bits and pieces of me. Not one woman truly had the whole me, and none of them ever had my soul. The woman thought to be my "Cosmic Mate" should have been called a "Toxic Mate" and the others who think I married them or were in love with them, should never trust the words of a drunken man. I never had one woman I was really in love with or wanted to give it all to, because I had not met her yet. She would've appeared in my life like clockwork many years later, but unfortunately I got sick and didn't take care of myself. I ended up on this side, alone. When I first learned of her, and what I had missed on Earth, I was filled with anger and remorse. Then it turned to guilt, overwhelming guilt, because I had left her behind and she doesn't even know I exist. I should be the one holding her hand, running my fingers through her hair and holding her while she sleeps. I would do anything to turn back time and never leave Earth, only for her, not for the drunken degenerate rock star I once was. I would stay, only to reach her.

I must wait for her on this side. I must watch her, with other men, and she tells this guy she loves him and it kills me all over again, each and every time she says it. When she cries, I cry. Her tears hurt so much because I am not there to calm her and wipe them away. When she feels alone, I ache, yes your soul can ache on this side in the deepest, truest vibration.

I am here waiting for her, to give her the life I never did on Earth, to make it all up to her, because I must. I cannot evolve until I give her what I took away from her on Earth, without her ever knowing it. She was for me and I was for her. I messed up, I messed up. I never knew I could love anyone like this, or what was in store for me. I would've stopped drinking, more out of necessity so I could stay alive and become more spiritual and focused on my work. Jim Morrison would've finally grown up and become the writer he wanted to be. I would have tailored some mesmerizing novels, screenplays, even a rock opera, and much more. I would've finally received the critical acclaim and acceptance in the esteemed writers community I had always dreamed of. More so, I would've met a beautiful Angel I could give my soul to, not the bits and pieces like the many who came before her. She would've gotten all of me and nothing would be held back, because with her, my soul would be on fire and I would not be able to hide my feelings at any given time. She will still receive my soul, if she will have me.

We would've had two children, a dog and a few beautiful homes. I never had a home, but once I would've met her, I would want to give her one because she would be my home in the deepest sense. Our kids would also need a home, and they would want for nothing, most of all, love and understanding. I would be a faithful husband. I would've met her when I was older, and I would have sowed my wild oats, and then some, and be more than ready to settle down. I would be possessive with her and jealous at times, but I would not stray from my Angel. I would be too hopelessly in love with her and our life together. As I speak, she is still on Earth, this is only the beginning...

After I crossed over, left my body, saw the aftermath of my untimely death and did a life review, which was rather difficult, very sad and in some ways, pathetic, I was able to see what would've occurred if I had lived, and a greater understanding of my destiny was revealed. Meeting Ray Manzarek was my fate, my destiny. It was not a coincidence I stayed in California after graduating from U.C.L.A., heard a concert in my head, and ran into Ray on the beach. My fame was gained as a doorway, I was to open it and bring some of my fans along on a journey that as I got older and the times changed would have culminated in tremendous spiritual growth for a large number of people.

I was not to do this alone but with an eternal soul mate, my true love, who I had not yet met and was incapable of truly connecting with during the 27 and a half years I was on Earth. My true eternal soul mate, my one true love, was not to come into the world until I had already been on my journey. She was a young child, a baby, when I crossed over. I was to meet this beautiful, amazing woman later in my life after I had learned the lessons and dealt with much of the karma. Those I met in those 27 plus years were not, for the most part, long lasting or life-long friends. The other members of The Doors and I would have had an on again, off again relationship over the years, and some of those who worked with us in the music industry, such as Bill Siddons, Bruce Botnick and even Jac Holzman, would've stayed in touch with me.

But I, like a great reptile, would've shed my skin and gone onto a completely different existence after a time.

I would've been in a few relationships over the years, a couple of them long term and somewhat serious, but it would not be until I met this one, very special, very alluring woman that I would've wanted to truly give my soul to her. It would've been a rather instant attraction, and I would've become quite attached, addicted, dependent and rather obsessed with her. It would've been a truly passionate love affair that would've lasted the rest of my life and then carried on when we both crossed over.

We would've had children, and when I saw my life with her, what I never got to have, what I never gave to her, I became isolated on this side, deeply saddened and angered. I was mourning the loss and mourning what I never gave her and now, would never be able to. She would never know she would've had this great love and beautiful life, and I watched her and came to her while she slept and even from this side, fell deeply in love with her. It was difficult and frustrating, since she couldn't hear me, she didn't know I was there when she had a bad day, when she had tears streaming down her face. I love her still and always will and cannot wait until she comes home to me. I will make up to her, the Earth life I did not give her for as long as she will allow me to. She will not meet a great love on Earth, I was the one. She was the one for me, the only one. She would've filled all my voids, much like alcohol did but this time, she would've freed my soul as alcohol could never do. She would've freed my soul as only true, passionate, never-ending love can possibly do.

This is the letter for my eternal soul mate, the one I left behind, the one I had to find to see how my life would have gone, see the love I have found, the kids, the dog, the white picket fence, I have been in mourning ever since.

My Dearest Rebecca,
I can only begin this by saying, I'm sorry I left you honey. So, so sorry. I did not know of you until the very end of my life while crossing over, I must say I truly knew it was too late. I left you baby, and you needed me and need me still. Love does not die, just as I did not truly die.

Jim Morrison & Michael Hutchence

I am more alive on this side than I could've been walking through the haze I lived on Earth. I can see you, and I have stood next to you many, many times. Sometimes you feel something touching you, it's not something honey, it's me. I am with you, I so long to hold your hand, kiss your lips and just whisper my feelings for you in your ear. I have caressed your cheek and at night when you sleep, kiss your eyelids.

I mourn the death of what would've been. I was the one who caused this pain and if you can never forgive me, I understand. I have changed the course of your life by carelessly allowing mine to end. But my love, if you give me another chance, I will be here, hoping, praying and waiting only for you until you come home. Beautiful woman, please allow me to make up what I was not able to give you, not able to show you, and you will see, I will give you my soul, which is all I have, take all of me my love for without you, I am nothing.

I'm listening

I came back to let you know
I'd never leave you if I had known
You were there waiting
It broke me in half as I saw
You on the beach, anticipating

The life you would have
The husband, the love
The dream of a family

That was supposed to be me
That was supposed to be us
It's hard to let this be my Angel
Yet it's hard to discuss

I have walked the desert nights alone
Wanting you, waiting for you to call my own

I can't be forgotten, I can't be ignored
You need to hold me in your heart
I am truly yours for all eternity,
So when you finish your jail sentence on Earth
The gate will swing open
I'll be there and I'll never let you go
I just thought you should know of me,
thought you should know of us
maybe there is something you wish to discuss…
I'm listening

—*channeled from Jim Morrison*

You belong to me

You can hold his hand
and whisper sweet nothings in his ear,
But what he doesn't understand
All he has is this time with you, not years.

For you belong to me,
I can't forfeit my one chance
to make things right,
have true love, true acceptance and true romance.

You are all I've focused on
Since the day I got here
Waiting for you to hear my song,
Filled with sorrow, remorse, anger and fear.

I am a secret door that is locked,
You alone hold the key
even though I realized you are shocked,
You belong to me.

No other lover can meet your needs,
No man can see how perfect you are,
No man knows how your heart bleeds
Or how deeply your psyche has been scarred.

I see you as everything you think you are not,
Perfect, beautiful, angelic.
Has he forgotten you are an Angel sent to earth
filled with light from the moment of your birth?

I cannot put you on a high enough pedestal,
You'll get used to the view.
One day, not too long from now
you'll recall, you belong to me
And I only belong to you.

—*channeled from Jim Morrison*

The Mystic Sees the Truth...
The Rose of Mysterious Union

by Kathleen Tucci

This life we endure on the earthly plane is convoluted, at best, with many options, yet destiny has its place. When we make an agreement to incarnate here, we as souls examine within our own individual soul group, which souls we will encounter and in what capacity. Of course, there is much debate on what exactly is destiny and what is free will. Consider that we continue to incarnate with the same souls over and over again in a seemingly endless cycle of incarnations interchanging roles each lifetime.

In one life you are the other, in the next you may be the father, brother or sister or even perhaps grandparent or uncle within the same framework of souls. You have agreed, each of you, to exchange experiences, passing information on to one another and even thoroughly enjoying, sometimes enduring specific, and challenging life lessons which elevate your soul.

When discussing this matrix of webbed lines of dissention and encounters on the Earth of his life, but not finding her, Jim settled for what he had. This caused him to be very empty inside and continually try to compensate for the black hole in his heart. He explains how saddened he is by the fact that he placed himself in the position of trusting Pamela with his life. Had he been with someone who he truly loved and they loved him, he would still be alive today! He was not well enough that fateful July to take care of himself. He had no one to rely on and he communicates strongly how he and Pamela were leading completely separate lives. That he was seldom with her in the weeks leading up to his passing, spending most of his days alone walking the streets soaking in the summer air and attempting to rejuvenate his tired body and mind. In studying the esoteric, there is an inherent underlying component in every fabric of example…each thought, word, deed, action, and circumstance is multi-faceted. It is never about one purpose or one reason. That is what circumvents the intricacy of how our lives are woven together.

There is a plan, if you will, or a road map and time line provided for us before we come here. We are actually involved in the fabrication of this with a higher counsel of elders, guides and angels who help us orchestrate it. On this grid are ingredients which will lead us to our karmic lessons leading up to our next step continually. Say if one of our soul lessons is to learn compassion and at the age of twelve we are in a situation of being present when someone is bullied by their locker in the hallway of our school. At that moment we have the choice to be brave, step in and come to their aid, or in turn can walk away leaving the individual in the lurch.

If we chose the latter, we have compounded a block in our karmic path and will now be challenged again, in this lifetime, with another circumstance to learn compassion and mercy. That's not to say that we can overlook our lessons and get to them when we feel like it, but that our guides, angels, and the divine understand that we "are learning" and that our free will choice comes into play. That we may need, and this is more than likely to be the case, many situations placed in our life path which will revolve around the same exact lesson before we completely conquer it. What this example shows us is that our lives truly are complicated given that we are not working alone, but rather with our entire soul group, exchanging roles, learning lessons lifetime after lifetime. Now roll this into how our soul mates fit into this enigma.

I'll start by telling you that we are a soul first and a physical body second. That being said; consider that the soul never sleeps and that your subconscious is your soul. The soul retains the record of all existence of itself. Your Akashic record or your soul's record is available to each of us. Tucked deep into the recesses of our mind, we have stored information of all our light experiences and incarnations, both those in the physical and those lives between lives in the spiritual. The soul knows all. An easy example of this is explained by the evidence of child prodigies and geniuses. As a psychic medium, I have been exposed to numerous instances where evidence that the soul knew it was going to cross is clear. One story comes to mind where a husband and wife were sitting at dinner on a Friday enjoying casual conversation. Out of the blue, the husband says to his wife; "You know if anything were to happen to me, we have no will. You would be left in quite a quandary of what to do with passing heirlooms to my next of kin."

Thinking her husband a very loving man, his wife discussed with him her wishes and he made his. They made plans to visit their attorney to begin drawing up a will that next Monday. The very next day, her husband was killed in a head-on collision accident.

This story is quite astounding, displaying that the soul truly knows on some level what it is about to experience. The lesson here is that if we work to bring out spiritual intuition and mind closer in tune with the physical attributes of our pragmatic existence, we begin to tap into the knowledge base which is our light source of higher selves. We begin to hear, feel, see and understand these nudges which the soul so amply provides us if we only know to recognize the information. As such, the soul also knows when it finds its soul mate! If you have ever met someone for the first time and without an uttered word you feel a dramatic "pull" to this individual, you may be encountering your soul mate.

The soul literally identifies and remembers other souls it has encountered in previous incarnations. Souls which follow the same vibrational pattern, when placed together as a union, are far greater than their individual existences. They can, like a well-oiled machine, accomplish miraculous events and actions. There are numerous nadirs in our auras, spinning wheel like circles of energy which act as transmitting devices picking up vibrational energy of other souls both living and deceased. These mechanisms of energies caution us when we encounter someone of a lesser energy as well as enlighten us to be in tune with knowing we've just encountered someone who will serve great importance to us in this lifetime. There are some of us, unfortunately, who never encounter this in an incarnation. Some are not patient enough and instead of tolerating the mundane until the right opportunity presents itself, become intolerant and make wrong choices when choosing their life partners. Motivated by our physical sides, driven by greed, complacency, prejudice, chauvinism, bias, fear (false evidence appearing real), or insecurity, we settle and place ourselves on a path of difficulty and strain against what our higher self knows to be in conflict with our higher purpose. We then experience a deep void. On the contrary, when we listen to those "nudges" or intuitions we are almost always guaranteed to come in contact with our soul mate as well as experience many great incidences of soul growth and happiness. Some souls are here to also be independent, and therefore, will lead fulfilling and rewarding lives making significant contributions to the planet, yet never needing a kinship with another soul on a romantic level.

Have you ever had a particular type of man or woman that you were naturally drawn to? If you answered yes, you were recognizing what your soul was telling you. Have you looked into someone's eyes for the first time and sensed you have met them before? How about discovering with a lover, that you had traveled to or lived in the same numerous places at the same times for many years yet never met until recently? The universe was trying to put you together, yet free will choices you made delayed the meeting until now. Like the convoluted intricate workings of the universe, so too are our lives and the reasons for finding, or perhaps not finding, our true soul mate.

Jim Morrison has been learning this lesson he says on the other side. The lesson of virtue and trust in his higher self, and the experiences he accepted as fate when, in fact, he possessed the power to change the outcome. How he accepted the weight of abuse and it manifested as hate, how he allowed the flow of negativity to mold his perspective of low self-worth and although fully comprehending his own intellectual properties, lowered the bar of expectation to being truly loved in his incarnation here.

Searching aimlessly for a red haired woman who would "light his fire" he fought many obstacles admittedly placed there by himself, and therefore, did not find her. His soul "knew" that she resided here. It's evidenced in numerous lyrics. Passion in the arts has long been revered a prosperous cause. Magnificent works have been the result of lost love, unrequited love, and love that has dissolved. The absence of love can be devastating and crippling to a soul who has not found his twin flame, yet "knows" their partner is out there somewhere waiting for them. It is easy to settle and I find it grand, those who pine on, searching, even through pain until they connect with someone their soul knows. When channeling Jim one afternoon he gave me these lyrics:

"There is but one love in all eternity
She is with me always and always will be
Her eyes, look deep into my soul
She uncovers all, I am told
My trust is never tested for I am loving true
I feel her in my existence and she in mine too
Never are we to part for our essence is one soul
Traveling through space and time
We merge and unify
Together we are one
Together we are one
Why waste my time looking for what is not there
I will wait for her and call to her

She will respond and meet me here
In the corners of my mind I find
She is continually with me all the time
I will fight for her, die for her
Until she once again is mine
Traveling through space and time
We merge and unify
Together we are one
Together we are one"

While Jim did not wait to find his soul mate but rather succumbed to lascivious behavior to counter the anguish he was experiencing being alone, he did pour his emotions into extraordinary music and poetry. Music and its vibrations can achieve relatively high states of elevated grace and induce the subconscious or soul to experience itself in its purest raw structure.

We unknowingly are drawn to re-experience those feelings over and over like a moth to light. Again the soul identifies what it needs and will most certainly seek out the elements it can to fulfill that need. The mystery of understanding our own soul's path and how that fits in with locating our soul mate requires us to measure all experiences with a lesson. In each occurrence of our lives we can discern by close examination what the positive and negative results consisted of, what drove our motivations, and what determined our choices. That is what soul growth is all about. Even for those of us who may find happiness in this life with a significant other, sharing love and passion, there needs to be a consideration of thought that there also may be another soul compatible with their own, even one possibly residing on the other side waiting for them to return home. Souls are built to work toward common goals and there are indeed many variables in the matrix of life existence. We act out many scenarios lifetime after lifetime searching for the soul which intermingles perfectly with our own. Wars have been fought over love, whole countries have dismantled over love, massive nations and cultures have been influenced in traditions built on love. Make no mistake that the most powerful of life force is love itself. Miracles happen daily.

Jim Morrison & Michael Hutchence

CHAPTER 25

Rebecca

"I held her close for only a short time, but after she was gone, I'd see her smile on the face of a perfect stranger and I knew she would be there with me all the rest of my days."

—*Brian Andreas*, Strange Dreams: Collected Stories & Drawings

Jim Morrison & Michael Hutchence

Rebecca and I will be joined as Geb and Nuit are in Egyptian Mythology, eternally sexually bonded. Geb and Nuit were separated by another and there will be no separation between me and Rebecca. I will not permit it to happen again.

Elvis Presley was one of my favorite singers on Earth and still is now, and he a sang a song I send to my love, called "Kentucky Rain" as my love is now in a storm on Earth and I will bring her home, as nothing can keep her from me again.

Every time she hears a song on the radio by The Doors that I sing, it's for her. She was my unidentifiable muse, so those songs really are hers. While they hear me sing all over the world, I now only sing for one.

I send her butterflies and blue jays. She has wondered where all the butterflies and blue jays have suddenly come from, and why they are always around her.

I move things around her bedroom at night, things I don't like, or things I want her to notice have been moved. I kiss her eyelids, I softly touch her lips or the nape of her neck while my beauty dreams.

Sunday Afternoon

I just got into town about an hour ago,
looking around for my woman

She's reading "Wuthering Heights"
reclining on a daybed, and
she gently doses off right before
Heathcliff returns to Cathy

Jim Morrison & Michael Hutchence

She starts to dream of a house,
a mansion that resembles
the gothic palace in the
novel she loves

She is inside the cold,
dark, dreary rooms
when she hears a knock
at the door, a man
of about 27
stands at the entranceway

His hair is long and wavy,
blackish brown, his eyes
are blue, he is clean
shaven as he bites his lower
lip

Rebecca looks like an Angel,
as she opens the door and asks
"Who are you looking for?" and
I respond "you of course, I'm not Heathcliff and this is
not Wuthering Heights but
we are where we are
supposed to be"

Rebecca ponders for a moment
and then asks "Where is that and
who are you?"

"We are in Zion" I say
with all that is in me with
my eyes closed, then I open
them, look at her and smile and

tell her "My name is James and
I am your guide"

"It's time to go Rebecca"
I say forcefully as I grab
her hand and remove her from
the dusty, eerie, lonely mansion

Rebecca holds my hand tightly
and asks "Where are you guiding
me to?" and she gives me a
pretty little smile

"It's not far from here" I tell her
reassuringly and "I have made
sure it's just as you would
like it my lady"

I am pleasantly surprised
at how compliant my Angel is
as we cross the grounds,
walk through massive gardens
and jump across streams

I point to a white house
at the top of the hill
"that's your home Sweet
Rebecca"

Her smile illuminates
the sky "That beautiful
house is for me?" she asks
in her true amazement

"yes it's your new house
and you can stay forever"

Jim Morrison & Michael Hutchence

She looks down at the ground
as tears roll down her cheeks
as we tread up the grass
covered hill

She doesn't comprehend
why she was given this
beautiful home as she turns
and inquires "Do I live there
alone?"

I respond nervously,
"I was hoping you'd ask
that Rebecca, you see um"
I continue to bite my lower
lip, "You see Rebecca
as your guide, I would like to,
well, you're new over here and
you're alone and all and maybe
I should stay close to you and
join you in the house for now
if…"
Rebecca stops and hugs me
tightly "Please stay with me
James, this is all new to me and
I'm a little scared"

I stayed with Rebecca in
the house I custom built for
her, and now I know I'll
never leave

We wed in the garden
under the moonlight,
she gave me babies

and I brought her
home a fuzzy mutt
we call Mojo

I waited for what
seemed an eternity
to knock on that door,
to claim my bride, to
find my life

It all happened
on a Sunday afternoon,
as Rebecca is my
L.A. Woman and
my own true love
of the Blue Sunday

There are no more
blue Sundays as I am
happy, drenched in joy
to the likes my soul
has never known

I no longer wonder,
the nomad has hung-up
his worn out boots as I am
happy at home
Rebecca never finished
"Wuthering Heights" that
fatal afternoon, she never
got to the part where
Heathcliff returns to see
Cathy, she didn't have to

She has left her gothic
mansion known as Earth

Jim Morrison & Michael Hutchence

with all the musty,
cobwebbed rooms
as Rebecca mysteriously
crossed over from
unknown causes
in her sleep on that
fateful Sunday afternoon

She is free,
she will always be
with me, I waited
so long for that
Sunday afternoon

—channeled from Jim Morrison

FINAL THOUGHTS
Riders on the Storm

"A poet is a man who manages, in a lifetime of standing out in thunderstorms, to be struck by lightning five or six times"

—*Randall Jarrell*, American Poet

Jim Morrison & Michael Hutchence

In closing, I would like to sum it all up with this. My life was a fast blur, over in the blink of an eye and during the last few years, one day simply ran into the next. In this book, I have discussed many of the events people seem fascinated, curious or opinionated about pertaining to my short, unfulfilled life. I have given you the naked truth, but I am sure there are some people who just won't be able to handle it. I can't waste energy on those who condemn this work.

Throughout my life, people around me have always wondered what went wrong. How did things get so out of control? How did I become this hopeless alcoholic and why did I continue to be a degenerate lush when some found the soul of a real artist within, and the potential to create not just art, but maybe even the semblance of magic?

Many people have long blamed the alcohol, or other factors surrounding me, but the truth remains, I did have an eternal soul mate, which many of you would call a twin flame, and my soul is so connected to hers on every level, I had this huge void while I wandered the Earth. This void could not be filled and so I drowned myself in one bottle after another. I buried myself in books and later buried myself in notebooks, writing down everything, because I could not fill this void, I could not stop the longing for this unknown quantity.

This unknown quantity showed up on Earth toward the end of my life, but she was just a young child and so our paths would not have crossed. I was supposed to stick it out, wait around, evolve, learn hard lessons and grow-up to become a helluva man prior to meeting her later in my life. As I look back now, it remains a great mystery to me how I would have endured all those years without her, and made it to the finish line of our life together on Earth. I didn't do well without her and despite the other women who did love me or wanted to take care of me, it never filled the void, because Jim Morrison was never in love.

People can believe what they wish about alcoholism, but it tends to be different for each person. Mine was due to a void, plain and simple. I would've conquered it, but the void would still be troublesome until the day I met her.

For many, self-love is the key to overcoming personal demons, but even that would not have been the cure for what ailed me. I should've chosen to fill my void in other, less harmful ways, but in my case, I was truly an actor out alone, and never wanted to be. I wanted to be fulfilled and loved and it turns out, only one other soul was the missing link for me. This nomad would have finally found a home when I looked into her eyes. I was a loner because I needed her to complete me, no one else would do and anyone else would turn out to be a poor substitute for true love.

I am over my life as Jim Morrison, and it would be almost as tragic as my messed up life if I hadn't moved past it. For a place that revolves around time, many on Earth can't seem to do what I have done, move on from me, move on from that sad, short life.

I ponder why people still like to discuss me or write about me. I believe there are far more interesting people to immerse yourselves in. Due to the absence of love in my past life, there was also an absence of truth, so my perception was skewed.

I have filled in all the blanks I intended to about my past life, and for me, it's a closed book. If you think about me at all, I ask for you to do so in this way. I was always about breaking through the boundaries society put around us, and I am here now to say, there are no boundaries in regards to true love. It's everything to me and all I aspire to on this side. Earth is not a boundary for true love, heaven is not a boundary for true love, in fact, no dimension is a boundary of any kind. There is no space, there is no time, there is no real containment. My soul will not be contained or held in by an artificial boundary. I have true love, I have one that completes me as no other could and in the absence of her, I made my life a complete mess. I will not be separated from her again.

When she returns to this side, we will not have to be apart ever again, and I live for it, I wait for it, I long for her, I crave her. This purgatory of its own making is difficult yet filled with the joyful hysteria of knowing she will be home and with me for eternity, and it is something I cannot describe to you in this writing.

Forget everything you thought you knew about Jim Morrison and remember my most important message, true love is all that matters, without it, you are only half of what you could be. Nothing separates a soul in love from its true eternal mate, only your perception can separate such lovers. Remember those words, as they are the most important ones I ever shared with the world.

We are Riders on the storm when we come to Earth and for me, the storm will be officially over when my woman comes home. I will no longer be a rider but I will share with the world the lessons I have learned during the storm and what life is truly like in the afterglow in future words through this channel.

Last Words...Last Words...Out

Summer winds blow the white sands
the salty wind whips across her face
She stands alone on the beach of our dreams

No one close by, to dry her tears
No one in sight to hold her hand
She has a true love, a man

who would give up heaven to look in her eyes
but he has forfeited his one chance
to be loved for all he is
He has done this by his own hand,
he will never be complete until she is near
and she is home

the candle burns in the window
only for her
I can't let go, I can't go on
for eternity without her by my side

No one else can take her place
No one else will fill the void
I want her to know, I need her to come home

—*channeled from Jim Morrison*

FEAST OF FRIENDS

Rev. Dr. Marjorie Augustine was born in Panama and is a Cuna Indian. Marjorie was blessed to be born into a family of healers, Shaman and Medicine women. She began to see and communicate with spirits at the age of 5. Marjorie is a psychic medium, teacher and lecturer. Her office is in Pittsburgh, Pennsylvania.

www.moonstonemediums.com

Judy Hevenly is one of the world's most respected psychics and spiritual counselors. As a leading intuitive, Judy was featured in the best-selling book "The 100 Top Psychics in America." Judy has been blessed with an amazing gift of prophecy which is recognized globally. Judy is based in Los Angeles, California.

www.judyhevenly.com

Rev. Francine Milano is a clairvoyant medium, intuitive and workshop facilitator as well as a psychic development mentor. She is a frequent guest psychic on many nationally syndicated radio talk shows. Francine's office is located in Lancaster County, Pennsylvania.

www.francinemilano.com

Christopher Reburn is a world renowned clairvoyant psychic medium, spiritual teacher and healer with an impressive 20-plus year track record of accuracy. He is known for his compassion and his amazing ability to provide specific details in readings for his clients. Christopher's office is located in Clearwater, Florida.

www.thepsychicspirit.com

Linda Salvin is a respected psychic, healer and channeler and has her own nationally syndicated radio show on the West Coast. Linda Salvin's office is located in Los Angeles, California.

www.lindasalvin.com

David G. Speer is a respected healer and has been teaching for 30 years in the metaphysical sciences. He has Ph.D. in Naturopathy and a Master in Reflexology. David Speer's office is located in Pittsburgh, PA.

www.pittsburghealer.com

Kathleen Tucci is an internationally recognized psychic medium and best-selling author. She uses her gifts of clairaudience and clairvoyance to receive detailed messages from the spirit world. As a teacher and lecturer, Kathleen has helped countless people connect to their loved ones on the other side. Kathleen is based in Dallas, Texas.

www.kathleentucci.com

Jim Morrison & Michael Hutchence

A TALE OF TWO BROTHERS:

Jim Morrison

and

Michael Hutchence

Volume Two:

CHILLED DIVINE

(The True Essence of Michael Hutchence)

If you are stuck in a moment you can't get out of, if you feel as if all hope is gone, this is for you, allow my words to heal your soul.

—Michael Hutchence

Jim Morrison & Michael Hutchence

FOREWORD

"I have worked in the metaphysical community as a healer and teacher for thirty years and have had the pleasure of working with Jacqueline Murray. She is a highly spiritual and gifted channel who is very devoted to embracing her gifts and using them for the betterment of this world. One would need to experience Jacquie's "love vibration," to understand what she brings to the table with her intuitive and channeling abilities. She is selfless, kind-hearted, and strives to bring people closer to their enlightenment. It's not every day that you meet someone of Jacquie's stature and inner-beauty and I am honored to know her.

Love and blessings,
David G. Speer, Ph.D.
Doctor of Naturopathy

Jim Morrison & Michael Hutchence

Table of Contents

	Forward by David G. Speer, Ph.D	469
1	Mystify Me	472
2	Falling Down The Mountain	488
3	Horizons	496
4	Just Keep Walking	506
5	Two Worlds Colliding	514
6	In The Dark Of Night	522
7	Kill The Pain	532
8	Days Of Rust	542
9	Kiss The Dirt	556
10	Make Your Peace	572
11	This Ain't The Good Life...	600
12	Listen Like Thieves	618
13	The Gift	626
14	The Messenger	632

15	*They were lying through their teeth...*	658
16	*Get on the Inside*	672
17	*All You Got Is This Moment...*	682
18	*Don't You See There is a Rhythm?*	692
19	*We All Rotate...*	704
20	*The Mystic's Mosaic: Putting the Pieces Back Together*	734
21	*Gonna Take You Over...*	762
Final Thoughts	*Slide Away*	774

Jim Morrison & Michael Hutchence

A TALE OF TWO BROTHERS

CHAPTER 1
Mystify Me

Jim Morrison & Michael Hutchence

A TALE OF TWO BROTHERS

Jac = Jacqueline Murray

Michael= Michael Hutchence

Jac: This is a little too much for me to believe. Why would you also come through and speak to me and ask me to write down your words?

Michael: We have a common link dear one. It's rather complicated but we are members of the same soul group and you are the chosen channel not just for Jim Morrison, but for me as well. You are very, very clear and furthermore, your intent is absolutely pure. You took Jim's words down perfectly.

Jac: Thank you. I am honored. But I am still trying to wrap my brain around you coming in with Jim Morrison.

Michael: This may not make sense to you angel, but you see, Jim Morrison and I were often compared in our lifetimes and I took it as a great compliment. But the truth is, we came from the same soul group on the other side. It's like a family that is very close and you learn together, and grow together, among other things. Reincarnation may be a tricky subject with you and your religious beliefs of origin instilled by your Catholic indoctrination, but regardless of whether you believe in reincarnation or not, if you think you have one life on Earth or several, each of us belongs to a soul group and Jim and I happen to be in the same one. You are also a member of our soul group.

Jac: I am? I was?

Michael: You are a member. In fact, you were our teacher and you will be again someday.

Jac: This is becoming less and less plausible.

Michael: On Earth, the truth is masked and you are not supposed to remember who you really are. In fact, think of it as a masquerade ball you are attending — a great charade. You were and are the teacher in our soul group and that is precisely why we feel such a great connection to you and trust you implicitly with our memoirs.

Jac: This is pretty amazing and humbling. So, I was a teacher for both you and Jim?

Michael: Not just for us. You have other students. Of course, I was more focused than Jim, but he had his own bravado. Jim and I used to be with you in this place on the other side that is a big glorified library, because you were — and still are — a reader of the records. But I couldn't read them and Jim couldn't either. We call them Akashic records, dear one. I am inclined to tell you this is where Jim developed his great love of libraries and bookstores, and I became extremely well read in my adult years on Earth, because of our fondness of learning from you in this grand place.

Jac: In this soul group that we all come from, were most of you singers?

Michael: Not at all. However, it's a creative group, but it doesn't mean we were all famous.

Jac: Why did you and Jim have lives in a similar fashion, meaning the fame?

Michael: We charted our lives in a parallel way, Jacquie. Jim has been sulking that you didn't recognize him when he first came through to you. Although you really weren't supposed to, we felt you should've already known us, Jacquie.

Jac: Sorry, I really didn't understand what was going on — and I still don't to some extent.

Michael: Someone you know, Beth Daudet, has met me in person and she will tell you this soon. It was in the '80s. What you don't know about her yet, is that she's a big INXS fan and she has a picture she took of me. Eventually she will find it and give it to you as a gift, Jacquie.

Jac: Beth met you? WOW!

Michael: Yes, you will find that the reformulated version of INXS will show up in your town. As of right now, they are not even scheduled to do so. It will be very last minute and Beth will be attending. She will mention it to you the next time you see her.* She has some psychic gifts also, Jacquie, as do many around you that you are unaware of, and quite frankly, they are unaware of. You attract other gifted ones to you. Speaking of psychics, have I not done a great job showing up at readings? Of course, Jim is such a big time hog, Jacquie, that I have to work hard to get a few minutes in as he loves to pontificate during your readings.

Jac: I am always nervous when I get readings, Michael, and yes, you've done more than a great job giving specifics.

Michael: Did you see how clearly Christopher Reburn brought me in and revealed my hidden secret?

Jac: Yes, he revealed it in the first five minutes of the reading.

Michael: Christopher Reburn is your spiritual guru on Earth. While you will have many teachers and teach many yourself, Christopher can go deeper than many other psychics. He has been going to this side, literally traveling here since he was a young child.

He is very unique and will be very recognized in the future, as he is still a young man, but we are very fortunate to have connected to him, dear one.

Jac: I agree, he's amazing.

Michael: Judy Hevenly also picked me up quite well, and she has a great love for me and Jim. She really has a great understanding of what we are doing here. I will come through to psychic after psychic for you, and I send you a good many validations, Angel, because when I was on Earth, I would've also had a difficult time accepting this. I swayed back and forth between being an atheist and having some belief and excitement about Buddhism.

Jac: I know you have important messages to share, Michael, but I have wondered who in the world is going to believe this.

Michael: At this stage, Angel, I have come to believe it's absolutely not important to be concerned with how this information is perceived by anyone, even though I wish my family, friends and fans would embrace it wholeheartedly. We are here to tell the truth and you are the messenger, my dear. You are not here to prove anything to anyone, because not everyone will be open to this sort of communication to start with. All you can do is take our words down clearly, put it out to the public, and allow each individual to sort it out. I took several wrong turns on Earth, Jacquie, and I would do whatever I could to prevent another from going down the paths I chose.

Jac: I feel this is a huge gift from God, and if I don't use it, Michael, it's pretty much like slapping God in the face — and you and Jim, who are putting your faith in me. I will probably end up being burned at the stake at some point. What do I say to those who feel the Bible claims spirit communication or even fortunetelling is the work of the devil?

Michael: I certainly wasn't a Bible reader in my past life, Jacquie, however, I have come to know it and understand with some of the great teachers on this side. It's hypocritical; would those same know-it-alls condemn the Archangel Gabriel for communicating to the Virgin Mary or the young men who received visions in Corinthians?

Or what about Isaiah?

Jac: I honestly haven't done much Bible reading lately, Michael. My favorite book was actually the Book of Revelations.

Michael: Another channeled book, Jacquie. Most of the bible was channeled from this side. Ask the Bible study crowd if Ezekiel saw the wheel or not? Also ask them about Deuteronomy and Hosea, and if it was fine for those in the Bible to speak to this side but not fine for you?

Jac: I don't think I would want to debate people with those beliefs. Live and let live.

Michael: Agreed.

Jac: I do wonder why you did not go to a professional psychic or writer with your story as opposed to me? Writing is not something I actually enjoy, Michael.

Michael: The soul group connection would be the primary answer, and of course, people believe some of the absolutely most ridiculous psychics on TV. I find you to be much more believable as you are not doing this for fame or money. You won't become jaded, which seems to be a growing problem in the psychic industry.

Jac: Thank you for the confidence, but I want to make sure these messages are yours and yours alone. I don't want to project any of my own ideas or thoughts or do any embellishing on what is given to me.

Michael: You can hear me clearly. You can hear my voice, and you damn well know these are not your thoughts. Would you have played the song "Mystify" over and over in your head fifty times or so in the last two weeks?

Jac: No, but it's been there.

Michael: It takes a great deal of energy and work to pierce the veil and come through to you Jacquie. It's an investment, and obviously, we must trust you tremendously. Please do not let us down because you are worried about what the neighbors may think or some geek who knew you in high school. I could appear in front of family and friends and they could still not actually believe it's me. Not everyone is going to be receptive to this, but we are only asking for people to be receptive to the possibility this communication is real.

Jim Morrison & Michael Hutchence

Jac: I understand, but it's funny. I wasn't a fan of Jim's or of yours, Michael, but it now turns out I sure knew more INXS songs than I did Doors songs.

Michael: Well, you always had good taste. I will begin to channel my thoughts for you on my former life as the hedonistic rock star I once was now that you have finished Jim's book, a.k.a., his police blotter.

Jac: Michael, are you close to Jim?

Michael: We are brothers in arms, dear one. We have long known each other and at times would prefer to beat each other to a pulp, but we certainly have a great love and respect for each other. Jim simply believes [that] no one ever understood him, and to an extent, he's right. But I believe people can and will identify with our stories, our pain, our self-doubt and so forth. I certainly know many out there suffer with the same thing I did, known as manic depression, which is termed bipolar. Interestingly enough, many suspected Jim Morrison had that condition, but he didn't. Jim had anger issues which he turned inward and that spurred a rather steady depression, not a manic one.

Jac: Jim has channeled to others Michael, what about you?

Michael: I would correct that. Jim has channeled very little to others, though there are many false claims that have been made about that. He was also practicing a bit in order to channel an entire book to you. It's an incredible amount of work and energy for us. I have only had small and somewhat limited amounts of communications with other channels, and that was mainly due to the fact that I had a family member and a dear friend trying to make contact with me through some mediums, mostly pertaining to my death. (Well, there is no "death.") But anyway, some of those communications were alright but brief, and some of the information got rather jumbled at times.

It was not the most pleasant experience for me, dear one. It's almost a complete waste of our energy to come through to someone who isn't clear, pure of intention, who suffers from mental illness, or who is in a fog due to the consumption of drugs or alcohol. In other words, I would never come through to myself if I were still on Earth.

Jac: (Laughs). Michael, maybe I was naïve, but I always thought that when you get to the other side, you leave all your earthly concerns and cares behind and the rest of us are left behind to fend for ourselves, meaning you are in your own dimension and we are in ours. You had your time on Earth. It's done. And now we are living out our time. I never thought the dimensions should clash or overlap, so this is a new concept for me.

Michael: While I can obviously see where your point of view originates, I think it's an incredible myth the dimensions were created to remain separate. You don't stop loving when you get to this side Jacquie. In fact, your eyes open wider than they did on earth. You can see things and understand them in ways you could not possibly have on earth. Many of us are not only left without saying goodbye but really being able to show any appreciation. By the way, there truly is no goodbye. It's all meant to be continued at a later time. Life goes on, loves goes on. It never dies. You never die. I know this is a new concept to you Jacquie, but what about this one? Instead of someone writing a biography of what they think I was like, of how they think I crossed over, you are allowing me to tell you my own story. There is a significant, unknown element, involving what happened to me on the morning of 22nd November, 1997 in room 524 of the Ritz Carlton Hotel in Double Bay, Sydney, Australia.

I am utterly surprised members of the press never uncovered this missing piece of the puzzle which for the most part, explains everything on top of what is already known to be factual. I will be making this huge revelation to you, Jacquie, during the course of our channeling. And it will not be easy for you, dearest. I suspect, at times, it will become quite emotional for you, but I assure you, we will get through it.

Jac: I had to stop channeling Jim for awhile when we were working on his childhood and his death. It was very intense.

Jim Morrison & Michael Hutchence

Michael: There is an emotional toll to this work, as you are such a sensitive, caring soul. In Jim's case, he never really related to his fans while he was on Earth. So over here, he sees them and cringes. He did not believe he deserved accolades of any sort, really, and in his own words, he just went out and "did his thing." He feels quite cheated because his life was cut so short, but of course, like me, he cheated himself. This is a lesson for you Jacquie. You can be in paradise and hell, simultaneously.

Jim never found true love in his life but I, on the other hand, was rather fortunate to have found real love...true love, a few times on Earth and to be much more connected to my fans whom I had a great love for, and still do. On this side, I see them and adore them as their love is still so bright and overwhelming. However, when I first came to this side, Jacquie, I must tell you, I was not in a good place for a while.

I felt rather stuck. I had so many regrets and could not seem to come to terms with leaving Earth when I did. I loved my life, my family, my friends and above all, my daughter so much, I could hardly stand to be separated by the dimensions from my sweet Tiger Lily. I really can't forgive myself, but I have been through quite a cleansing and healing process. I am still not 100% purified, but I am much better off than I was when I came here. I will be extremely happy to come face to face with the loved ones I recklessly left behind. But for now, I want them to lead full and happy lives and deal with the things I didn't seem to know how to — the depression, the fears, the manipulations. They need to seek the truth in every given situation in their lives. Look at Jim Morrison, Jacquie. He's here on this side moping around, has been since I came here, and chooses to do so until his true love returns. He can't be fulfilled without her, and it's rather sad, actually. I cannot be fulfilled until I come face to face with the closest ones to me and ask for forgiveness.

Jac: That's very beautiful Michael, but I would think they have already forgiven you on earth.

Michael: Yes, but I need to say my apologies directly to each one. Jim and I were actually hoping you would recognize us, as you are our teacher, our soul group teacher, Angel.

Jac: I am sorry Michael. I didn't make the connection.

Michael: People will wonder why I didn't talk to you about this person or some incident, but really, it's about what is important for me and for Jim to discuss and make our peace with. It's a karmic cleansing of sorts. I was terrible with dates on Earth, a fact you couldn't have known, Jacquie, so I won't be terribly worried about dates in this book. But I will be about the things that stood out in my life and what I hope others can gain from my experiences and bad choices. I need you to understand — this is a really big thing for me, Jacquie. I have never revealed the things that will be said to you now. But I do believe, it's time, so let me present to you the good, the bad and the ugly parts of the life of Michael Hutchence.

AUTHOR'S NOTE: As Michael Hutchence predicted, Beth revealed to me she was an INXS fan and was attending their Pittsburgh concert featuring J.D. Fortune. Months later, she gave me beautiful framed picture she took of Michael Hutchence on stage.

Awareness

Who's aware of your awareness?

Do you think you're not connected to anything?
To anyone but your so-called family?

Where do your thoughts come from?
How do your dreams arise?
Is your loved one gone for good
because he's on the other side?

Jim Morrison & Michael Hutchence

What is the other side? Better yet,
where are you? Where is Earth?
Do you think it's the only planet that matters?
That those that have gone before you or after you
or who exist on other planes are not substantial
and figurative at the same time?

Do you think the maniac psycho
in the papers is the real killer
or is the disease that rips through your veins,
arteries, and blood cells that is the most dangerous?

Because it went undetected for so long,
does that mean it's not your murderer?
The body cannot corrupt the soul
unless you place your poison guillotine
over all that is sacred and sever the divine connection

You live in a mansion full of secret doors
They are everywhere, but cannot be seen
with the naked eye, you must search for them
carefully, with great discernment

Who's aware of your awareness?
Who's aware of my awareness?
Because you cannot hear my voice,
does that mean I am not speaking?

If you throw a pebble in a still pond and turn your back, were there
no ripples because you didn't see them?
If a tree falls in a forest and no one is around,
do you contend it didn't make a sound?

You sat in front of your Buddha statue and
asked for blessings in abundance but got no money,
Were you not heard?

A TALE OF TWO BROTHERS

You entered a Catholic Church
and prayed with all your heart to the Virgin Mary
to cure the disease that ravages your body,
but the diagnosis has gotten worse,
Were you not heard?

Perhaps you were given abundance
and a cure in ways you can hardly perceive

Who's aware of your awareness?

When you dream, who else sees what you see?
How can it be that so many experience
almost the same dreams?

Are you the only one who hears your thoughts?
Who's aware of what is going on inside your head,
your conscious and subconscious at all times?

Only in a forensic lab or at a crime scene you are told
that the dead can speak,
What if I told you, there is no death and
we are more alive here than we ever were on earth?

What if I told you, there are several other
dimensions around you, because you can't see
them do you insist they don't exist?

—channeled from Michael Hutchence

"If we could see the miracle of a single flower clearly,
our whole life would change."

—Buddha

Jim Morrison & Michael Hutchence

CHAPTER 2
Falling Down The Mountain

"I am here for a purpose and that purpose is to grow into a mountain, not to shrink to a grain of sand. Henceforth will I apply ALL my efforts to become the highest mountain of all and I will strain my potential until it cries for mercy."

—*Og Mandino, American Essayist, and Psychologist*

Jim Morrison & Michael Hutchence

A TALE OF TWO BROTHERS

So why are you here? Do you want to know what actually occurred on the morning of the 22nd of November, 1997 in Room 524 of the Ritz Carlton Hotel in Double Bay in Sydney, Australia? The coroner who handled my case, Mr. Derrick Hand, has told the world in his publicly released report, that I took my own life, no one else was involved and that auto-erotic asphyxiation was not the cause of death. Why then do so many of you not believe it?

Was it so hard to believe an international aging rock star, who had been through a bevy of beauties and a bevy of designer drugs and whose career was on a down swing, would one day, just end it? People saw me at dinner the night before, with my Father and Stepmother, laughing and practically jumping off of the walls. Well I was a manic-depressive, which you may refer to as bipolar. I would be dancing on the ceiling one night and the next morning, so low I had to peel myself off the floor. Is that what happened, dancing one night, ending it the next morning?

Has anyone bothered to ask why the coroner's report surrounding my death has been made public but the autopsy was sealed? The coroner's report ruled it a suicide and revealed a cocktail of drugs and alcohol were in my system. So what was the secret withheld in my sealed autopsy?

Perhaps something too detrimental to my image to be made known? Better for people to believe I was this self-indulgent, idiotic, shallow rock star who took his own life rather than age gracefully (or not so gracefully in the cases of many of my colleagues). Or perhaps it's better for people to speculate I may have been involved in a sex orgy my final night on earth with women, men, midgets and God knows what else…maybe a few sheep or wild boars were in the room. It's not better for me, or for those who loved me. As you see, there is one unknown element that pushed me over the edge and I could not possibly handle this factor in addition to the mounting problems closing in on me. I will reveal this factor because I want the world to know my death was not poetic, and I am sorry, truly sorry, I left my daughter, my family, my friends and my life. I am in a good place now, though many would presume I was, in fact, in hell. You can certainly and easily make your own hell on this side, but I am not in hell, I am filled with light and love beyond anything I have ever received or experienced on Earth. Holding Tiger was the closest I had ever come to this feeling. I am evolving and much clearer now, and truly living as my soul was meant to live. I was blessed to come to the Earth with all this light, but I, through my own means, dulled it many times. My light is shining through now, but I won't be totally at peace until my story is told. I have waited for this.

Time as you know it does not exist on this side. Therefore, the 10 years I have been gone from the Earth are basically equivalent to about a year and a half. That would be close to your linear time scale. It hasn't been all that long and I need to be able to come down in vibration to communicate clearly. I want every word, every nuance to come through. I would never engage in communicating with a "Hollywood" psychic. I have tried to come through to some famous psychics because a family member or a dear friend had visited them to see if they could uncover the truth about my death. I want to say, categorically, I have barely come through to those psychics. Sometimes they didn't even pick me or my energy up, but they lied and faked the reading to show how good they were. Some picked up small pieces of things I was trying to communicate, and then would simply embellish information. They did have to fill in the blanks, so to speak, so my loved ones got some confusing information.

I wasn't a fan of the tabloid press on Earth, and I am even more so disgusted and distrustful of them on this side, now that I can see their true intentions. Therefore, I will not come through to a tabloid sort of psychic. I will not go to one who just wants his or her name in a paper, or to write a memoir of how popular they are or how they have traveled doing readings or how good their skills are. Why write a book tooting your own horn? There are better things to toot if you are truly enlightened and as spiritual as some of them claim to be. They have been blessed with a gift to pierce the veil and learn from other dimensions things they cannot possibly fathom on Earth. While the veil is thin and getting thinner, not everyone is capable at this time of raising their vibration to communicate with us, or, more importantly, communicate clearly. Not everyone can tune in beyond what they see. Those that can should realize ego does not belong in this work at all. Besides ego, there is no room for opinion. I have chosen this channel because she will not mince my words. She will put it all out there, and it's up to you to sort it all out, embrace it or leave it behind. Before we began channeling for the book, I was simply conversing with my channel, and she told me she believes I am angry and rather bitter about my time on Earth. And I must admit, she is right. Before we started this karmic cleansing of sorts, she asked me why I was resonating with these lower human emotions. I am first and foremost bitter with myself for getting in the incredibly ridiculous downward spiral that took me to a place where I left my precious daughter. I am rather bitter with the unconscionable actions taken by some following my death. The bitterness will flow out, it must flow out, it's truth.

While there are no appropriate words to describe the beauty on this side, which cannot be seen with human eyes, your emotional DNA is still very much encoded. I am distressed and disgusted on many levels and very, very sorry. This will all come out, and hopefully, those of you still engaged in your Earth lives can learn from this as this is what it's all for. I am here presenting this to you in the hope that my truth, my pain, my joy, my suffering and my essence will set off a dynamic spotlight over your own life and show you the road you may go down if your existence is not challenged and you do not take appropriate actions.

Believe this information being channeled to you, don't believe it, it's your choice, always your choice, but some of the greatest books on Earth were essentially channeled. The authors often didn't know where their words came from. This one originates from the consummate rock star, and it will be raw, graphic, and at times, downright deplorable. Are you ready for that? Can you handle the truth?

Jim Morrison & Michael Hutchence

CHAPTER 3

Horizons

"The horizon leans forward, offering you space to place new steps of change."

—*Maya Angelou*

Jim Morrison & Michael Hutchence

A TALE OF TWO BROTHERS

My childhood was very expansive. I was fortunate in that I got to see parts of the world and became both cultured and worldly instead of just growing up in a small town with a white picket fence. But despite the wondrous riches I was given being raised in Hong Kong and parts of Australia, and even in California as a teenager, perhaps a white picket fence and a very happy, loving family would've been far better. I love my parents and my sister and brother. My dear sister, Tina, has been described as a stepsister, but yet we share the same Mum, so we are technically half siblings, but I always considered her my full sister. She was much older than me and my younger brother, Rhett, therefore, she was more or less the built-in babysitter, but she did show us much love.

My parents very simply had a turbulent marriage, and as a child, I was unaware of the pressures, but could feel the anxiety in the emotional energy around me. We seemed to live a rather lavish lifestyle, but it was rather nomadic and that became a habit I continued for the rest of my days. A restless feeling seemed to engulf my parents and it haunted me all the days of my adult life.

My Father, Kell, is with me on this side and we are very much at peace with each other. Kell was gone most of the time I was a child. He was an international businessman, always on the go, who found great comfort inside a bottle of Scotch and the prescription drugs he was given. When a doctor prescribes medicine, and most especially at that time, the '60s and '70s, it was thought not to be dangerous or categorically as addictive as a street drug. Kell certainly abused prescription drugs while I was growing up.

There were always financial strains on the family, along with the pressures of moving (and not just city to city but to different homes, apartments or even to a hotel within a given city), so eventually, the marriage between my dear parents fell apart. When I was 15 years old, my Mum hatched a secret plan to leave my Father. She took a job offer in the United States, in California actually, and she decided she could not take both myself and my younger brother, Rhett. In all fairness to my Mother, Rhett was quite a handful from the day he was born. He had many allergies and this made him quite irritable all the time. But the main thing no one could handle about my younger brother is that he was constantly crying out for attention. He was only a boy of 12 when my Mum and I left him behind in Australia with my Father, but Rhett was already getting into constant trouble.

Both my parents subsequently seemed to find Rhett too much to deal with, and my Mother felt she could not possibly handle both of us as she secretly left my Father and moved across the world. This is a very hard thing to speak of, even now, from where I am. I know my Mother, Pat, was torn, scared, frightened and anxious when we went to the airport and got to the gate to make our escape. Rhett begged us to take him along. He was in shock, in total disbelief his Mother was leaving him behind, and that I was a party to this and would not permit him to go with us or even plead his case. This event, I believe, shaped the rest of our lives, at least until the day I left the Earth. I am certain it has stayed with my Mother, and most of all, with Rhett.

The pain of seeing my brother beg to come along and my Mother leaving him was overwhelming for me. I could feel the pain both my Mother and Rhett felt, but decided I had to stand strong and internalize it. I couldn't understand it and thought it was only because Rhett was so difficult and being punished. Rhett simply wanted attention any way he could get it and felt most of the attention was on me at times since I was the oldest boy. By the time Rhett came along, the marriage between my Father and Mother was already beginning to show signs of becoming fractured. My Father was hardly around in those days. I could not figure out why Rhett was being left behind. My family growing up became, without a doubt, a blueprint for my adult relationships without me even realizing it. For my entire adult life, I was completely unable to deal with emotional confrontation, and this is actually the result of the incident of leaving my brother in Australia while I jetted off to California with Mum when I was 15. After that, I could never deal with emotional dramas being played out with me involved. I felt a great deal of guilt about going with Mum while Rhett was forced to stay behind. I also felt responsible for my Mum and her well-being and I was only 15 years old.

A TALE OF TWO BROTHERS

During my childhood, we had servants and cooks. I was never very responsible prior to this point in my life, for I never had to be.

When we reached California, my Mother became frightfully ill, hyperventilating. Of course, it was just the two of us and I had to take care of her in a strange country. I could hardly take care of myself, but fortunately, my sister, Tina, was not living far. It turned out to be some sort of a panic attack my Mum was suffering from. This was something I didn't quite understand; it was a really traumatic experience for me. I became an emotional mess on the inside, in a country I knew nothing of, moving again, with only my Mum. It was almost as if I had to be the man of the house now and take on my Father's role, but since he wasn't around very much while I was growing up, I felt less than capable of doing such things. This is not to say I was not somewhat entranced with California. Before my untimely exit from Earth, I certainly planned to live there at least half of the year.

I love my parents deeply, and I am well aware they did the best they could. On the inside, I was already becoming an emotional mess, and I tried to embrace life and always enjoy it. But that was because I was running, running and running hard from the pain I had been subjected to. It's not uncommon to seek great pleasure when you are in deep emotional pain.

I was on my way to something known as manic depression, even as a teenager. Through my life, I could find a wonderful, beautiful woman who would live to make me happy, but I would not be able to stay in that relationship because my depression would get the best of me. I would find more pleasure in dangerous sexual activities with women I was not emotionally invested in than with the true loves I had in my life.

As I look back now, I realize the difficult marriage my parents had, the terrible relationship they had following the divorce, the nomadic lifestyle, my younger brother's constant problems and his love for me — combined at times with his envy of me — was all too much. Instead of seeking true counseling, therapy or sorting it out over time in a rational and reasonable way, I took the other route that so many take. My life became one big party. *How high could I get? How many times could I have relations with a woman in one night? How many daredevil stunts could I do in a car or on my favorite pastime, a motorcycle? How close to the edge could I come? How much was too much? How much of an adrenaline rush could I find?* (The answer was, it was *never too much* until the early morning hours of the 22nd of November, 1997). Life was one big party. It was certainly better than thinking about how much my parents hated each other, or about my younger brother and how guilty I felt because I was seemingly the favorite. It was better than thinking about the pain, hiding the pain, running from the pain, burying the pain and the best way to do that was to get high, get off and I could never get high enough or get off enough.

I should've sought treatment for depression when I was just a teenager, but I was not aware of it. Everyone has secrets and inner pain, and you must speak of it, tell someone and deal with the pain head on and work it out over time. I am not necessarily suggesting treatment in the form of prescription medication, but the treatment of the soul, in terms of a spiritual approach.

I suggest Buddhism. There are many paths to take but even for a teenager, Buddhism can be tremendously healing. The true path to enlightenment is finding a way of conquering your demons and removing yourself from the limited mind set you have found yourself framed in.

I am not here to give parenting advice per se, how can I? I left my precious baby daughter on Earth. I am speaking of my own childhood and what I have learned from this side. Kell and I are very close. We had done much of our reconciling before I left the Earth, and we were extremely close when I was an adult male. Kell has asked me to forgive his mistakes and I have.

I truly love my Mother, Pat, so dearly, and I do understand everything much better from here. She has come home, we have had a nice reunion and are sorting things out between us which will take more time. I am so sorry I put her through this, because the worst thing for a parent is to bury their child. I never wanted to cause them a second of pain. I left my parents with the terrible burden of having to bury me and trying to understand what had gone horribly wrong.

Kell now understands my dear Mum understands as well. I am grateful to both of my parents for giving me life on earth and forging new relationships with me on this side, and it's the closest the three of us have ever been.

CHAPTER 4
Just Keep Walking

If you look for the truth outside yourself,
It gets farther and farther away.
Today walking alone, I meet it everywhere I step.
It is the same as me, yet I am not it.
Only if you understand it in this way
Will you merge with the way things are.

—*Tung-Shan*

Jim Morrison & Michael Hutchence

A TALE OF TWO BROTHERS

INXS was the most stable family I ever had, unquestionably. They not only put up with a great deal of shit from me, but we all put up with a great deal of shit from each other. I want to make it known, Tim, Andy, Jon, Garry and Kirk have felt many emotions since I left the Earth. *Guilt* should not be one of them, anger at me perhaps, sadness at what once was and what could have been, but guilt is not an emotion that should've entered into the realms of their reactions. They couldn't have saved me. Nothing could've been done or said that would've prevented what happened to me in those morning hours of the 22nd of November, 1997.

I know that my former band mates and brothers have done an enormous amount of soul searching. I know that I left them in a bit of a lurch by my untimely exit, however, it should've been a launching point or a new beginning for each of them. Contrary to what has been said, I was not a cheerleader for a replacement selected via the show "Rock Star." I didn't care who won, and truthfully, hated to see the whole thing happen. I didn't send a sign from the heavens to endorse the new singer for INXS. It had nothing to do with me begrudging my former band mates from making a living. It had much more to do with what I understand from being on this side.

Everything in the universe is composed of energy and the energy that formulated INXS was, indeed, the six of us. It was not just about the three Farriss brothers or more about me, although, it became too much about me and I was too highly defined by INXS. There was this unique history that only the six of us could share since we started out together as young boys basically and worked our way out of small, very rough places and worked our arses off. We built this legacy. We had an energy dynamic, more or less a formula, that could only be comprised of the six of us. I am not suggesting the formula can't be changed or perhaps even improved upon. But it's a different energy, and therefore, it's not truly INXS.

When there was an attempt to change the formulation of a popular soda, it certainly changed the whole dynamics. You have the "real thing" and then you say, "Well, let's make this change because the old formula is not exciting anymore." It's been around for a long time, but we must bring something new to the table.

The old formula of INXS could not be exciting anymore if the lead singer was, in fact, dead. But just like the traditional formulation of the popular soda, the old formula is the true formula. INXS (the traditional version of the six of us) has many layers and is rich in such artistic depth that it should be, in fact, what is preserved, listened to, cherished, and most of all, enjoyed. I guess I no longer have a vote, but I was opposed and still am to INXS continuing, because anyone who was chosen as lead singer would inevitably be compared to me and not really taken as much for their own merit or talent. I suppose if I had to select anyone, I would've liked to have seen a female singer chosen, as this would change the entire dynamics of the group and put the songs in a completely different perspective.

INXS was, and always will be, the six of us. And while my former band mates have done their own projects, they should've continued to spread their wings. They certainly all have the talent and wisdom to go on to new and incredible endeavors that would enable their growth as artists and men. While I did engage in some side projects during my time with INXS, I should've engaged in many others…but it becomes rather safe to stay in a mostly successful group and to not stand on your own.

I would like to point out Bono from U2, and how, of course, he is identified with the group. But he has done extremely important work separately and he has his own identity that does not damage U2 but enhances it.

I did not consider myself to be INXS. INXS was equally the six of us, and I resent anyone suggesting it to be any other way. My former brothers and I became rather estranged in the '90s at times, but there are always growing pains in any family situation. I wish, completely, we had all been closer in the last years of my life, but I was truly rather isolated from almost everyone who was significant to me, other than Paula Yates. I was like a hamster

A TALE OF TWO BROTHERS

running on a wheel of confusion, pain and frustration, and it seemed I could not leave the wheel. My band mates overall simply could not relate to me and gave up trying.

I want Kirk, Jon, Andy, Tim and Garry to know, I love them deeply. I will be here when they each return to this side to hug them and to tell them how much they meant to me and how deeply sorry I am for causing them such pain. I am the one asking for forgiveness.

I feel it necessary to comment on the official autobiography of INXS. I know this may come off as sour grapes, but I am here to speak the truth. We all had dirty laundry, and maybe mine was just more interesting, but I think to run down my laundry list and kick dirt in the face of my Mum, Pat, was completely inappropriate. Pat and I had a complex relationship, and I am sure I bitched about her as I did almost everyone I knew at one time or another. While I considered it an intrusion for her to vocalize her thoughts at times, she was right more than she was wrong about what was going on with me. Sometimes the truth hurts. I love my Mother, Patricia, very, very much. She will never recover from her loss, and she will never be healed until we meet again on this side. To speak disparagingly against her is deeply upsetting and certainly wasn't necessary in an INXS biography. She was, and is, a grieving mother who has felt more guilt over my death than the members of INXS.

Jill Farriss, the wonderful and beautiful Mother of three of my former band mates and I have seen each other on this side. She watches over her children and is constantly around all of you and her grandchildren. She told me she is glad she left before any of her sons, because the pain of a mother losing a child is not measurable. I realize I left the lives of others in shambles, but each of you has grown from this and learned new lessons as it was not all for nothing. Our joys, our pains, our triumphs, our laughter, our anger, our frustrations, all of it was shared by the six of us and it was, what it was. Moving on is simply a part of life, and perhaps in some personal relationships, I did so too easily. But I stood by INXS and remained loyal to it no matter what. It was the most stable family I ever had, and I ask very simply, how do you honor my memory? How do you honor my loyalty, my friendship, my life?

Jim Morrison & Michael Hutchence

CHAPTER 5

Two Worlds Colliding

"Captain James Cook's ship, The Endeavour, hit a coral outcrop in the Great Barrier Reef in 1770. Cook and his crew camped in what is now called Cooktown for nearly two months while making repairs. Then they sailed south, where Cook claimed the east coast of Australia as British territory."

—*Julie Murphy* (Great Barrier Reef Under Threat)

Jim Morrison & Michael Hutchence

TO ALL MY FANS:

I love my fans. I never knew I was so loved. I never felt so much love as I have on this side from you, my fans on Earth. I was walking around the last few years in true oblivion and now I see from here all the lives I have touched, and I'm so grateful and filled with both appreciation and true love for all of you. You make me feel as if my life had meaning and it all wasn't just a waste of time. You are very precious to me and I never looked down on any of you in any kind of a condescending way. The fans made INXS and gave me a chance to perform all over the world and to experience things I could've only dreamed of, if my imagination had been that spectacular.

I appreciate all types of my fans, those who were only into INXS in the '80s and those who stayed with us for the long haul whether the music was popular or not. I appreciate those who have actually gone and listened to my solo album (which meant the world to me that it was still put out for the public to hear), as it was absolutely where I was and what was going on with me internally for the last few years, and it was pure Michael Hutchence. I appreciate each of you who came to see INXS in concert once, a few times or several times. I truly am honored and eternally grateful that you allowed me to be some small part of your life and your precious time on Earth.

I want to say to my fans, you are aware the music did change in INXS, and I was not always pleased with our direction. This is why I can completely understand why some of you left our camp. If you are a fan of a certain singer and they come out with a new style and go country or techno or whatever, you may take a pass on it and that's understandable. The world is about individuality

Jim Morrison & Michael Hutchence

(though I know some spiritualists will jump all over me for that statement and say we are all a part of one), and while that is true, you must be yourself first, learn who you are and what you are on Earth for, before you go and throw yourself into the big melting pot. After all, you need to learn what you can contribute and what the point of it all is.

I would like to take this special opportunity to communicate to my fans, I may have not always loved what the critics had to say about INXS or about me, but I certainly never dismissed any of you. Your thoughts and opinions did matter and still do, because you gave me twenty of the most memorable and magical years anyone could have asked for on Earth. No matter where I was in my life or what was going on, you were there for me, and I am so glad to have left you many years of music. I also do not wish to suggest you should not be listening to or enjoying the new version of INXS minus me. I have a certain perspective from this side about the dynamics and structure of things on Earth that is not necessarily going to be savored by your palates.

I believe, as I have stated, the notion that things should continue on once one of the members has left the Earth, does not gel with a more spiritual perception of things. Certain doors must close for others to open. When you change the energy, I want to be clear, it's not a matter of saying it's better or worse, it's a matter of continuing something in a manner it was not destined to be.

Although this is quite hard to comprehend from Earth, the destiny and history of INXS was pretty much written out ahead of time, and I am sorry it all came to an abrupt end. But you see, I had said the anniversary tour we were on would be my last with INXS…and I wasn't kidding. Have you ever read a great book and then seen the film version? The screenwriter's vision of that book is not the same as the book itself, so of course, it will be different. INXS's 20-year history is like a great book with some strong points and some weaker ones, but it was taken and made into something it was not meant to be or should not become.

You, as a fan, have a right to decide what you like and don't like. I respect that many of you truly like or love the newer version of INXS. It's not for me to say what you should listen to, but I love you, I treasure you, I thank you, and I am so terribly sorry I was in such a state at the end that I could not fully see your love and your light that surrounded me for 20 years. I will always have a place in my soul for each and every one of you.

I realize some of my fans have gone to my memorial site. I think it's beautiful. I have seen the things you left in tribute to me, and I have heard your comments. I cannot say how much this means to me. I am not there very much because clinging to my past life causes me to regress, to regret and to feel a great deal of pain, but your love embraces and holds me. Please never doubt that while there are no "celebrities" on this side, you make me feel as if I am the most loved man who ever lived! I have some fans I am concerned about, and I view them as overzealous. I think sometimes they need some sort of help to cope — God knows I did. They have problems and situations in their lives that are very difficult and they turn to me and become rather obsessive. A few of them believe they are channeling me or have channeled me, and some will even try to channel me very soon. I must tell all of you, that's not the case and it never will be. It's not because I don't want to reach out and touch all of you from this side and help you realize life never ends, it's simply not possible. Energetically, I couldn't do it if I wanted to and I have things to do here that are rather important for my own growth and the growth of others. I am not idle here, and it takes a great deal of energy to come through to those on Earth, so it's rather limited for me. I do visit my family, of course my daughter and her sisters whom I truly love, my Mother and Stepfather, my nieces and nephews, and my sister, brother and grandnephew. I visit my close friends occasionally, as well, and some of them are very much aware of this. For the rest of you, this is my way of coming through, having someone who can hear me clearly and record exactly what I wish to say and not question it or change a word.

While all of you are very precious to me, if you have tried to contact me on this side, I am sorry because it's not at all likely you are speaking with me, so please be very careful. I would have no reason, no energy and am simply too busy working through the damage I did to my past life to be channeling to any of you. You must know, I am highly flattered you wish to speak to me on this side, but it must be enough for you to listen to my music and read these words I am sending you in this book, and to know, your love and light sustains me.

Jim Morrison & Michael Hutchence

Barrier Reef

In order to understand who you really are,
you must dive into the ocean. You'll only
be this small particle enveloped in a vast
mass and your ego will be lost.

The beauty will captivate you, but there are
also things to fear as you learn you do not
understand the first thing about nature after all.

You will become thirsty, yet you cannot
drink the water you are surrounded with.
To swim with the dolphins, to sail on the
sea were the things I treasured most on Earth.

I long to swim to the Great Barrier Reef with
you where all the pieces of your existence
will come together and you will never be
the same…eternally changed by the
essence of who you really are.

—*channeled from Michael Hutchence to each of his fans*

CHAPTER 6
In The Dark Of Night

"A dreamer is one who can only find his way by moonlight, and his punishment is that he sees the dawn before the rest of the world."

—*Oscar Wilde*

Jim Morrison & Michael Hutchence

A TALE OF TWO BROTHERS

Commercial success is a false high. I did consider myself an artist in my past lifetime and yet, art should be determined on many factors, excluding where you are on the charts, as art has nothing to do with either popularity or a marketing contest. It's rather difficult when you have great commercial success and you are performing in front of 80,000 fans to be reduced to playing in smaller venues. You begin to lose your confidence, but the commercial success should have never given you any sense of confidence, as it is not true confidence, it's ego. Feed the art, not the ego. Feeding the ego is not going to bring true self-fulfillment, on the contrary, it brings anything but true self-fulfillment.

When INXS was on the top in the late '80s and early '90s, I wasn't anticipating the ride would end anytime soon, and it was a terrible ego bruise when we were no longer as hot as we once were. I smiled and acted as if it was acceptable, yet it was barely tolerable for a man who was already sinking in his own misery and depression. It was easy for us to say we were not being marketed properly in the United States or other parts of the world. What we were putting out for the public was not trendy, but worse, it wasn't even us in my opinion. It was more of a forced, or perhaps coerced, effort to have something to distribute to the public.

Art should not depend on commercial success, and I contend, true art, never has. When you get to a level where you are living a jet-set or high expenditure lifestyle, you are pressured to keep going in a direction which only feeds (and then depletes) the ego, not the art.

My solo album was where I was and who I was in the last years of my life, more so than the music I created with INXS in the last years. I was ready to move on from INXS, and they knew it. This was not due to a lack of gratitude; it was truly time for a renewal for me and to find myself as an artist minus the five men I had more or less grown-up with. I had wished I would always be welcome in the INXS family, but it was also quite strained at the end, even in the years prior to my exit.

If I had to go down this path again, I would not seek commercial success. I would not feed the ego, which had to be one of my worst mistakes, but I would absolutely create and feed the art. If you never have all the money and trappings that go with it, you don't miss it when you are not making millions. When art is truthful and not for marketing purposes, its purity is recognized and it will find its own audience.

I am not unappreciative for the fame, for selling tens of thousands of records and touching so many thousands with the music. I would simply say, for someone like me struggling with manic depression, fame was more harmful than helpful. Some artists can go through the transformation and create wonderful things due to their fame, but many can't handle the ego trip and it ultimately contributes to their downfall. You cannot determine your personal value by fame or fortune, and it's a trap, I tell you, it's a trap you need to get out of immediately. On this side, there are no celebrities, and it's so much better than what you have on Earth.

I realize now there were so many people who wanted to be with me, and as difficult as this is to imagine, who wanted to be me. While this is extremely flattering in a number of ways, I was not one to worship, or even more so, envy. I was pretty much a mess in the last few years of my life. I felt impending doom and I created this monster within. Envy is a strange thing, and if you saw the total picture of who I was and what was going on inside my head, you wouldn't envy me. To take it a step further, if you were really able to step in the shoes of most rich and famous people, you wouldn't envy them either. Many were doing and still are doing as many drugs as I was and that's an enormous amount of drugs. Many were and are still drinking as heavily as I was and measuring their worth by their ego, and their ego is often determined by how successful their latest project was, so it tends to fluctuate. What do you think about that? What is there to actually envy? I was never one to tote a Bible, and everyone who knew me is very much aware of this. But there is this very interesting commandment about coveting your neighbor's goods. I am not here to preach or suggest you are this horrible person if you are not following the commandments, but I would like to suggest you consider that to covet, to envy, to want something someone else has, is detrimental to the very essence of who you are. Not everyone's path includes the materialistic lifestyle, and while you have surely heard this before, you can't take it with you.

I was a true art lover and was fortunate to obtain some of the most beautiful paintings and works of art the eyes could take in. They were left behind, and while I got to hang some of them, most of them ended up in a storage area because I was such a nomad. I never got to hang all my beautiful paintings, just some, and I rarely got the chance to savor them. I owned many things, many things I rarely if ever used or saw. How much is too much? My point being, enjoy your earthly things, but appreciate them with love and respect. Beautiful art should be displayed, not stored, and all beautiful earthly things were built for enjoyment while you are on Earth, which is simply a drop in the bucket of eternity. Objects should be cherished, used, displayed and appreciated. Why acquire so many material things like a glutton, unless you truly have the time to use them and appreciate them?

What good is your prized car if it sits in your garage and is only taken out on Sundays? No one has a written guarantee that you will be given another day, so enjoy what you have. A dear friend of mine, named Bono, has a song I happen to love called "Beautiful Day." Here is my favorite line, "What you don't have you don't need it now." I would suggest to you, that line is very accurate. What you have in your possession is what you need at this time and in the place you are in, beyond the necessary types of things like food and water. I am speaking of material goods. The things you envy and have dreamt of are truly not needed, are they? When you learn to be happy with what you have now, you will find peace and keep your ego in check. There is only so much time. Do you have enough time to enjoy all the stuff you busted your hump to own?

I had all these cars and really could've been happy with a jeep and a bike, meaning my prized Harley motorcycle. I had owned such beautiful and lavish things but hardly got the time to enjoy them. I even owned a handwritten poem by John Lennon. How do you put a price on that?

I owned beautiful paintings and loved all sorts of art, but sometimes the impressionist paintings really took me off the planet, to my own world. I was fortunate enough to visit the greatest art museums in the world and got very emotional in each and every one of them. I had no idea at the time, or throughout my life, I was connecting to these great artists through the use of the psychic gift of being what some call an "empath," and it allowed me to pick up the feelings the artist had when creating his masterpiece. Some of the greatest artists were truly touched in the head and also suffered from manic depression, so connecting to them emotionally was quite overwhelming for me at times.

I wished while I was on Earth as Michael Hutchence, I could've been a painter, a true artist who painted great but rather interesting landscapes. But I didn't believe I had the talent for such things and didn't spend enough time trying. On this side, I paint and I create. Earth is so abundantly beautiful and the interpretations of Earth and people on the planet are just so amazing. You can look at the "Mona Lisa" and wonder how it was done, where are the brush strokes? We all leave behind brush strokes, those seen and unseen, our own signature strokes. We are creators, artists and navigators of our own destiny, and I am still very much a creator, artist and navigator on this side, working to heal and evolve.

I would tell anyone I could on Earth to visit your nearest art museums even if you are a complete novice and don't know the difference between perception, contrast or still life. All you need are your eyes and your heart; see the work with your heart and let it speak to you. So much of it is divinely inspired, so when you see much of the art, you are moving closer to the divine. One can only look at the inside of the Sistine Chapel and be in awe, and you don't have to be religious to appreciate such a wondrous thing.

One of my fondest memories on Earth, believe it or not, was seeing the brilliant and stunning art and feeling the emotions within. I also quite enjoyed creating in the kitchen of all places. I was, in fact, quite a decent and adequate cook, and made a few things quite well, such as Bouillabaisse and omelets. I should've spent more time cooking because I truly enjoyed it, and it truly is an art. Even the barbeque — while I thought anyone could throw something on the "Barbie," truth be told, that can still be art as well. When you create on paper, in the kitchen, or on a canvas, you are moving closer to the creator by celebrating the creator within. I miss seeing the great works of art I viewed in my past life for the first time or something as simple as cooking an omelet. Of course, most of all, I miss my greatest single creation, my baby girl, Heavenly Hiraani Tiger Lily. I watch over her like any doting father would, and even more so. She is the most beautiful girl in the world, and I know that's a very biased thing to say, but she is more precious than the stars in the sky are to me and she will someday know how much I truly love her. Many people look at my daughter's life as so tragic because Paula and I are gone, but truth be told, when it comes to our daughter, we are never gone from her and never will be. I wish she could hear us or see us and/or feel the numerous hugs we want to give her. But the love I am sending Tiger Lily is more than I held in my heart in my entire lifetime. And that says something, because I was full of love, just didn't have enough of it for myself.

They do not love that do not show their love.
The course of true love never did run smooth.
Love is a familiar. Love is a devil.
There is no evil angel but Love.

—*William Shakespeare*

Jim Morrison & Michael Hutchence

You're One of My Kind...

You have chosen someone else to spend eternity with,
I am like your brother so I am happy and yet,
I must reveal I love you more than anyone,
our energy is aligned.

We have so much history, I'm sad you are not mine.
But my Angel, I'll always be here, you'll never be alone,
I'll never leave you, for my soul you truly own.

The love you have needs you desperately, but don't believe he
loves you more than I,
For my love can move mountains, part oceans.
You alone are the Goddess I worshipped and loved.
I'll be your brother if that's is what you need,
But my soul is yours eternally.

XoXo

Michael

—*channeled from Michael Hutchence*

"That is the true season of love, when we believe that
we alone can love, that no one could ever have loved
so before us, and that no one will love in the same way
after us."

—*Johann Wolfgang von Goethe* (1749-1832)
German dramatist, novelist, poet, & scientist

CHAPTER 7

Kill The Pain

"People are afraid of themselves, of their own reality; their feelings most of all. People talk about how great love is, but that's bullshit. Love hurts. Feelings are disturbing. People are taught that pain is evil and dangerous. How can they deal with love if they're afraid to feel? Pain is meant to wake us up. People try to hide their pain. But they're wrong. Pain is something to carry, like a radio. You feel your strength in the experience of pain. It's all in how you carry it. That's what matters. Pain is a feeling. Your feelings are a part of you. Your own reality. If you feel ashamed of them, and hide them, you're letting society destroy your reality. You should stand up for your right to feel your pain."

—*Jim Morrison*

Jim Morrison & Michael Hutchence

A TALE OF TWO BROTHERS

Here I was, a happy-go-lucky, hedonistic man, living life to the fullest, loving every minute of it. So what happened? Where did it all go wrong?

An incident happened in 1992 that changed everything and took me into a cyclone I never could pull myself out of. It was incredibly life changing and more so than I ever let on to most of the people I knew. Throughout my entire life, I wanted to make everyone around me feel happy and comfortable so unless I was hideously drunk, the truth never came out. In 1992, I was with my beautiful love, Helena Christensen and we were on our way back to her apartment in Copenhagen. We stopped at a stand for some take-out food as we were on pedal bikes. (I liked anything with wheels ever since I was a young boy.) I didn't move out of the street quickly enough for a hurried cabdriver and he was yelling at me, so I gave him the universal sign, otherwise known as "the finger."

Words ensued, tempers flared, and without going into who was wrong or right, the angered driver jumped from the cab, and I didn't see it coming...the way my head hit the pavement, that is. My eyesight was not very good to start with, so this made it even more unexpected, I suppose. I took an incredibly hard and unexpected hit to the head and had no idea where I was at the time. I did not seek medical attention right away, and soon I suffered the most incredible, unbearable headaches and terrible nightmares to the likes I had never experienced. Meanwhile, my waking nightmare was just beginning.

After consulting with a neurosurgeon, I learned I literally had some brain damage and that my sense of taste and smell would be hampered and should return, but there were no guarantees.

My brain was actually bruised. I was a man who lived by my five senses. To suddenly not have two of them — and no real guarantee they would return — was incredibly shocking! I could not taste my food or smell anything — pleasant, disgusting or otherwise. I could afford to dine in the finest restaurants in the world, but I could not taste the expensive cuisine or smell a fine bouquet of wine before sipping it. I could afford to have my own cologne custom made, and I did, but could no longer smell it or smell my beautiful girlfriend.

This particular incident sent me into the greatest depression of my life, but I downplayed it to everyone and it was truly the beginning of the dark journey which lay ahead. With this brain injury, I also suffered from severe mood swings, the likes of which I could not conceal. I already had manic depression, which many doctors now term as "bipolar." And while I had bouts of my manic illness, they were few and rarely seen, and if someone caught a glimpse, it was rather short lived. After the attack of the cabdriver, I could no longer contain my temper - it would be short and I would have outbursts that were unquestionably out of my character until this point. The headaches continued for some time and my senses of smell and taste never fully returned up until the day I crossed over. While I did regain some of my two lost senses, they were not even half of what they had been before the nightmare began.

I want to explain something that to some people will seem quite foreign. The 1992 incident of the head injury was a divine signal from the universe that I actually brought to myself without consciously being aware of it. I was quite pampered and leading a very indulgent, hedonistic lifestyle. I am not here to pass judgments on anyone leading a similar lifestyle, because I won't be hypocritical. However, I need to be clear, I was given this head injury where two of my senses were literally and suddenly removed so that I may begin to appreciate even half of what I had.

I had led a very charmed and abundant life that others could only dream of. And while I truly loved life and truly lived life, there were times I would get bored and feel a bit too pampered and take monumental risks. I now realize, without a doubt, I was often protected from the side I am now on while I was running around playing the daredevil from hell on Earth. I never gave a second thought to the others I may be putting at risk. I could be quite irresponsible and dangerous while driving a car or a motorcycle, and while I was a skilled driver, at the speeds I went and with the chemicals in my body I drove under the influence of, I should've been killed at least a few times if not several. It's amazing how long I lived when I look back on all of this. I began to get this oversized ego...*I was invincible, I was Michael Hutchence the rock superstar, selling out Wimbley Stadium, and look who was on my arm, one of the most beautiful women on Earth, the Danish supermodel, Helena Christensen.* I began to become shallow after the success we, as INXS, enjoyed in 1991. I began to be caught up in the celebrity.

I started to believe my own hype, because, of course, I had a "YES" crowd of men and women surrounding me, these hangers-ons that show up because they have little or nothing else to do in life.

The brain bruising was placed upon me as a way of the universe shoving me back and saying come down off your high horse, who do you think you are? It was telling me to get in check, and it's very true, the other senses that remained did increase. I should've stopped taking so much for granted, but instead, I became rather dark and moody, and that was simply never who I was up to that point. After this incident, I needed to kill the pain emotionally, physically and mentally. My drug use began to increase, which is hard to fathom.

Now it has been said, I lived my life in excess and it's very, very true. I wanted to feel good at all times and have the same for everyone around me. I would like to come to you from this side and say, my drug use has been greatly exaggerated, but it hasn't been at all. There are a few works of fiction that have been published pertaining to my lifestyle, but in all fairness, I did massive amounts of legal and illegal substances in my life. I never wanted to become addicted to any one of them, so I did them in rotation of sorts. I would binge and rest, and binge and rest some more. After a great binge, I would tend to take a couple of days where I would do without. But the coming down as I got older from these binges really became awful. I am not here to lecture anyone about the use of substances, because while I was on Earth, I wouldn't have listened. I believe you must search your own soul and figure out why your view of life is so limited, you feel you need or want to get high on drugs or alcohol. I now can see clearly from where I am, engaging in an expansive manner, that it comes from a sheltered view of who you are and what you *don't* see in yourself.

I need to state, categorically, if I had given up drugs and alcohol following my brain injury in 1992, I would be alive today on Earth and I would be raising my beautiful daughter. It was absolutely due to both drugs and alcohol that I allowed myself to get into some truly bizarre and outlandish activities with some truly bizarre and outlandish people. The drugs increased my paranoia about everything. And those around you who are also engaging in drug use, are really of no value to you because they tend to agree with everything you say, turn a blind eye to everything you do since you are the rock star, and they want to take part in your stash or get you to provide funds for more of a supply. It's hard to put into words the catastrophic effects on my central nervous system of mixing all those drugs together combined with alcohol. My judgment was not only impaired, it was completely redesigned — and not by nature — but by something synthetic and it cost me my mind, my lifestyle, my family, my friends and, of course, my life. It cost me everything, and don't allow your ego to make you believe it cannot happen to you.

I went to the doctor, I got the so-called magick pill for my depression. Those pills were not meant to be mixed with other drugs or alcohol. I will be the first one to state I was not at all taking them properly, but if you are a chemist, perhaps you understand this and if not, please investigate this for yourself.

You must be very, very careful when taking anti-depressants and playing with your serotonin levels. If you already have chemical problems in your brain, have you ever considered that a pill is not the answer? I realize many claim an anti-depressant has given them back their lives, or at least brought out a more joyful, productive manner to their everyday existence, but I must say to you, anti-depressants do more damage to those on Earth than you are currently aware of.

If you mix an anti-depressant with alcohol or other drugs, street or prescription, your brain waves are likely to go as mine did, in a zigzag. You may find yourself doing things out of character with people — or alone, and they may cause very grave consequences.

A TALE OF TWO BROTHERS

When things are overwhelming in our lives, like mine: losing my sense of taste, losing my sense of smell in one quick moment; it's easy to recoil and fall into a hole so dark and deep and allow the dirt to pile on top of you. It takes real strength to stop and ask what is this going to teach you? What am I to learn from this awful thing that has happened to me? If I had stopped, and asked and listened, my daughter would not be fatherless today.

My parents would not have had to bury their son. My pain seemed unbearable, but now I can see, it is more unbearable watching my daughter grow-up without me or my Mother's tears or not being with my friends when they need me the most. You can't kill that kind of pain, I assure you. Pain on Earth is there to teach you, to wake you up in many instances, to change how you perceive things and what you, or possibly who, you take for granted. I, the great heathen, was becoming much too much full of myself. I, the great mess, could hardly face what had happened to me and instead of being honest with those who truly cared about me, I tried to go on and pretend it didn't matter.

Remember, I was invincible. To be human is to be fragile on many levels, at many different times during the life cycle. When you kill the pain, as I did, perhaps you kill your life force, perhaps you kill the essence of who you are. The pain is a part of you, and it's there for a reason. You must understand why it's there, and what you are to learn from it if you want to be able to co-exist with it. You can go into denial, you can pretend but then you are not giving recognition to a part of who you are.

I had three senses that were increasing, but I certainly was cursing the ones I lost, not relishing what I still had. Instead of reaching upward and outward, I became unrecognizable to myself at times with my wild mood swings and volatility. There were so many others who had been in accidents or had been abused and beaten who also had brain bruising, and losing two of their senses was the least of it. I could've extended myself to them, gone very public with my battle, and we could've helped each other cope with the headaches, nightmares, depression and mood swings. I could've spoken to younger people about the depression their older relatives were enduring, as so many of these relatives had greatly diminished abilities to taste and smell. I didn't do those things, and I would like to suggest that sometimes in sharing your most private pain, you can find more relief than any pill will give you.

When you network this support group, you realize you are not alone, that in itself is often a great help. You realize how fortunate you are as you will always find some unlucky bloke who has it worse than you. You can give others a boost and they will inevitably give it to you. I implore you to not keep your pain internalized, as I did, and just go along in denial or as if what happened didn't really matter to you. Sometimes you have to reach beyond your family and friends to connect to others in similar circumstances.

The point is, stay connected. Do not become isolated, as I was, or you will become your own worst enemy and when you have these difficult situations, an enemy is the last thing you need. *What is the universe trying to tell you?*

CHAPTER 8

Days Of Rust

"You have to die because no soul has passed
The heavenly threshold since you have opened school,
But grass grows there, and rust upon the hinge;
And they are lonely that must keep the watch."

—William Butler Yeats

Jim Morrison & Michael Hutchence

A TALE OF TWO BROTHERS

There are many things in my past life that have been "spun" by the press, and my untimely death is just one of them. Over here, small details and earthly concerns are not of great importance. You are free from the games, and being in the entertainment industry for 20 years, I was much more familiar with games than anyone should ever be. While I left the business details to others, I was still made aware of the game that is called the music industry, and how it operated, from the public relations to the marketing, to all the B.S. you must endure to make a living making your music. I wasn't the best looking cat, and yet I was quite often referred to as all looks with no substance as a singer, songwriter or performer. I never looked in the mirror and saw a beautiful man.

I thought I had something, some sort of indescribable charisma, but I certainly never believed I was handsome or gorgeous. My true dislike of my outer shell came from having some rather intense acne during my teenage years and that caused large pores on my face due to the acne scars. My teeth were not heaven, the bottom being the worst set, but I did correct the small gap in the top front ones. I thought my eyes were dark and ugly and my lips were kind of odd. I was not God's gift to women, but I did respect and cherish women for all they were. The Michael Hutchence I saw seems contrary to what others saw. I was always insecure about my looks, but I am here to say, that is a problem that arises from the inside, not the outside. If the culture believes you are not "in" or what is considered "hot," I would suggest that you be thankful, because the culture has this tendency of chewing you up and spitting you out if they believe you are "in" or "hot" at some given time. The culture does not love you, appreciate you or cherish you. It just uses you so that some people around you may gain monetarily, as well as yourself, by the mere fact you got lucky at birth.

The years I spent being insecure about my looks were an incredible waste of time. If I had developed more of the man on the inside, the artist, I would've begun to view the outside in a very different way, and believe it or not, I was trying certain therapies to accomplish this, including looking at a myriad of photos of myself over and over again and trying to accept and love what I saw. I certainly had hordes of females claiming I looked good, but when you don't feel good about yourself, I'm afraid that doesn't register in any meaningful or lasting way. I could strut on stage with the best of them, because on stage you had to have some ego to do anything. My ego was intact when I went in front of a group of people, large or small, but for my very last tour of the United States in 1997, I had strangely lost my confidence on stage and those were by far the worst performances of my career.

I did not want to be on that tour, and still, I wasn't trying to let down the fans. It was a disaster, and INXS should've canceled the rest of the tour after we completed our leg in the United States.

When the lead singer can't recall the lines of songs he had sung for many, many years, hundreds and hundreds of times over, and he is missing cues after performing on stage for 20 years, it should've been a clear and compelling indication, it was time to dim the lights and send the band home. Everyone could see the distress and despair I was in. There was no hiding it, not even from the fans...especially not from the fans. I wish I could give each and every one of those fans a better show now and better memories of me and INXS. I apologize for the poor performances, and I can only hope the fans who attended those shows in the final months of my life, can remember me in earlier times.

I realize that some of the things I am channeling may sound harsh or uncalled for, because after all, everything is supposed to be peaches and cream on this side. Isn't that what you were taught? What I would like to point out is, there are no more games on this side, and I won't mince words. I am evolving and one of the keys to any true purification is to tell the truth. I have perhaps seemed rather hard on my former band mates, but I do not feel some of their actions and words were appropriate ways to aid or help their so-called brother. This does not suggest they could've changed a damn thing that happened or the eventual outcome of my crossing over. It simply means, in 1997, the tour and the money were put *before* my mental and emotional health and that is something that should've never happened. I was very clouded, very much in a fog during those months, so my belief is, my former band mates had a duty and an obligation to stop that tour. I know it was a big deal, the 20th anniversary, but we were not giving the people what they paid for. We certainly were not celebrating INXS and its two-decade long musical legacy.

Unfortunately, I was in such a haze during those days, I was unaware how awful those performances really were, but for the one shortly after the news of the deaths of Princess Diana and Dodi Fayed. I knew I was pretty much comatose during that one, but now I see clearly, most of the performances on that tour were horrid and should've been stopped. Diana and Dodi's deaths were surreal. I had met the Princess, traveled in the circles and knew Dodi. But you see, the British press had made my life a living hell, and on the days Diana was not headline news in the London papers — believe it or not — Paula Yates and our love affair was. I had believed the press ended the lives of Princess Diana and Dodi Fayed, and it placed me in a deeper state of paranoia and depression.

The final chorus of my downward spiral, truly began in September of 1996. I had been in love with Paula Yates, and we had a torrid love affair. At this point, we had a baby girl, and I was more or less sucked into the drama of Paula's life, which was overwhelming for me. Paula and I were with Tiger in Australia, I was more content than I had been in a long time, but then the bottom simply fell out. There was a drug bust at Paula's home in England. From where I am now, this is a trivial matter. But here I was, someone who did engage in using drugs but never attempting to hurt another human being. Then one day, out of nowhere, drugs are found in Paula's home. They were not my drugs. I had no part in any of it, none of it was mine, but I must explain. Four people were involved in the set-up. Two were after the fact accessories, but Bob Geldof was absolutely not one of them. He was completely innocent and dumbfounded when he learned of what was in Paula's home. I never left drugs like that around a home, those were things I did in hotel rooms and clubs, not in a house with children. I never had the need to hide my drugs in tubes for children's candy (Smarties) or to have them sent to the house in packages. I was an international rock star for God's sake, and that meant I had access to huge amounts of drugs at all hours, 24 hours a day, every day. I would not have sent drugs to the house in packages. Think about how absurd that would be with how Paula and I were being stalked by the press during that time. Not even the children could leave the house without being photographed.

I am not here to name names of who caused this horrendous drama to take place, For various reasons and to protect others, I will simply leave it like this and you draw your own conclusions. Two of the people responsible for this scheme, did it so I could be the "knight in shining armor," and become even more committed to Paula and more determined in my fight against Bob. Two others involved were tipped off , and they were actual members of the lowdown press in England. They were aware of many of the facts and actual truth, but of course, had to stick to the fabricated version of events. They would do anything for a sensationalized story, and no one thought it was odd how quickly they learned of the events.

In 1996, Paula Yates was nearly as popular in the headlines in England as Princess Diana. She was going head to head with Sir Bob Geldof, a knighted V.I.P., and she was also a television star and author in her own right. It was very strange when this opium was found in Paula's home how people later claimed I threatened them, slashed their tires, and almost killed them. I can assure you, that just wasn't my style. I didn't want to hurt anyone, just be left alone. They were not my drugs that were found in the home of Paula Yates in September 1996.

The charges could not be pursued, that was how insufficient the proof was and how mangled the stories were about the drugs.

The officials had drugs in their hands. They had opium and could not do a thing with it because the evidence was so shaky, and that was because it was all set-up. I was bitter about it until the day I crossed over. I will not name the parties involved, but I do wish to fully clear Bob Geldof and one of the key reasons I will not name names is because it's important for those involved to confess and clear their souls. This was an abhorrent thing to do because of all the children involved, wouldn't you say?

A TALE OF TWO BROTHERS

The need for attention and to be rescued can become a twisted obsession. This event which I could never understand fully, began to take me to a destination I did not ever foresee going to. It was dreadful and in some ways terrifying to be set-up, and you don't know how or why. The peace I had in Australia with Tiger was shattered, and it was at this stage that my relationship with Paula began to hit the skids.

It began to make me so paranoid, and I was brought into it because those around me liked for me to be paranoid. It sounds a bit convoluted, but truthfully, I had some people around me who loved how I detested and blamed Bob Geldof for just about everything, short of the rain falling from the sky. This way, I would need these crooked solicitors (lawyers) even more, because I would need them to fight the enemy.

Well it turns out they were my true enemy, playing on my worst fears and weaknesses to keep themselves close to me — and more than anything — close to my money and the detestable property schemes they had in place. The more I began to question my finances, and even more so, my properties, the more I was told Bob was the enemy and I must do what the powerful lawyers and accountants said. I had to take direction or Bob would ruin me, and worse yet, take my daughter away. I was reminded continuously that Bob had drawn up legal documents to gain custody of my daughter, Tiger Lily. I believed this because the men feeding me this line of the most asinine bullshit I had ever been fed, were indeed my confidants. I was in a confused, paranoid state of mind and when my mind would start to question any of it, I was assured there was legitimate paperwork filed that Bob Geldof wanted custody of my daughter for himself.

Of course, now I can tell you, Bob had no intention, no legal grounds and did not make any attempt to remove Tiger Lily from her parents. But you see, this whole "hate Bob" campaign was a way to keep me occupied, distracted and it was an insurance policy so I would renew my financial advisor's contract, which was due up before my untimely demise. This man simply had to have his contract with me renewed, because he was mainly responsible for filtering monies and properties of mine into the hands of people they should have never been in. The thieves and connivers had me focus on Bob, so they could continue to rob me blind and worse yet, the inheritance of my daughter.

I strongly suggest you do not permit others to create your reality, you must examine the facts yourself, have direct one-on-one conversations, and determine your own truth. Otherwise, your vision will be skewed and the decisions you make may have grave consequences for yourself and others.

Tiger meant the world to me, and she still does. I hated to be away from my baby for one day, and the thought she would be taken away from me was worse than death. I know now, of course, that Tiger would not have been taken away from me or Paula. She was ours, but in irrational paranoia, I now have done exactly what I feared. I lost my daughter on Earth and she is now being graciously raised by Bob Geldof. What I feared the most, became reality. I want to publicly apologize to Bob Geldof. I believe he has forgiven my ignorance and arrogance pertaining to the situation we were all in. I thought I was defending the woman I loved and protecting my child, but of course, I was doing no such thing. I was creating mountains out of non-existent mole hills, and I was inflicting more pain because I would not take the time to sit down with Bob and talk to him, man to man and establish the facts and find some common ground for all the children involved. I did love Bob's daughters as my very own and still watch over them. I am extremely grateful, actually more than grateful, that he is raising my gorgeous girl and loving her like she is his own. I know Bob would never abandon Tiger. Bob is more of a man than I was, and I am sorry, I did not see the truth Sir Bob, but I do now and I bow before you and offer you my deepest apologies and deepest gratitude. Tiger is blessed to have you and Jeanne.

Leaving Tiger was never in my plans, or in Paula's, and I encourage everyone to search for the truth, and not the words, of anyone around you without seeing the facts for yourself. People have their own agendas and motives for distracting you, creating false enemies and unreal situations. Please do not be as gullible as I was in my own life and never assume you can't end up as I did.

Without truth and clarity, you can end up in the days of rust I walked around in and sadly, never came out of.

Free at Last

I don't have the shadows anymore
They are no longer on the wall
I don't have the battles anymore
and I don't wake-up to the fall
of my head pounding

being surrounded by sad,
sad stories
There is no glory
in living on the edge of despair

I can't see the trees for the forest
when I look back
and I don't want to join the chorus
of the reformed believers

but be a real achiever
now that I've done the devil's way
I can't live another day
in the trap you call Earth

I am in the midst of a rebirth
I can live without restrictions
never need permission
But when I answer to myself
don't need to call a pusher

they won't reward me
with anything more than mind poison
no more suicide horizons

Never to wake-up again
cause I won't be sleeping

Jim Morrison & Michael Hutchence

Never to descend
into the dark secrets I was keeping
You can believe or not
believe at all
but one day soon you'll
start to fall

Who will be around
you when you get the call?
The pushers, the groupies
your flunkies and fools
will be nowhere to be found
and neither will your jewels

The mindless games you
played to ease your pain
will prove to be time
wasted among the insane

You cannot stay around
when the rides shut down
You can't hide in the darkness
by being the clown

The tour is over and I've gone home
to the crashing waves and the ocean and the sand.
I miss my life, my family
my band but I was wasted
so much when all I needed
was the human touch.

Remember me as the poet
and friend and with your love
my life never ends.

—*song lyrics channeled from Michael Hutchence*

CHAPTER 9

Kiss The Dirt

"The whitest white dipped in clinging dirt. Another summer has thrown its corpse on my floor. The streets have given birth to even more strangers. Rivers of urine stripe the sidewalks. It rained the other day and the only thing that occurred to me was it would wash the smell away for a few days. Tonight is the first hot night. Outside my window, the human noise factor is intense. It's past midnight. They talk too much. They scream liquor-fueled idiot chatter. I pull away and close the door. I think about how it's all going to play out. How much time people spend trying to get across to each other, trying to clear their names. Trying to overturn the charges brought against them. I have decided to tell them that it's all true and not seek a fair trial. It's the only way to be free. Stop trying to matter. I could get my body tattooed with air-colored ink and walk invisibly amongst them. I have heard people say that they felt closer to their parents after they have died. Maybe if I treat people as if they were dead, I could get along with them better. I want to be able to like living people somehow. As it is now, they're I best coming through speakers or trapped between book covers. Here I go into the heat. Four months as a human anvil."

—Henry Rollins

Jim Morrison & Michael Hutchence

A TALE OF TWO BROTHERS

A Room with a View

To Murray River,

    There is a pink elephant in the room and it does no good for you not to speak of it. Maybe it's because you've been drinking so much lately and your drunken antics aren't really very funny anymore. Remember falling at the video shoot and bruising your ribs?

    It's fair to say, your life is spinning out of control but no one is going to tell you what to do, you won't stand for it. You show up for rehearsal buzzing like a bee, already wasted and not so elegantly either and you go out on stage with so many chemicals mixed in your bloodstream, higher than a kite isn't exactly the correct metaphor. You've been forgetting the lyrics you actually wrote, it's rather pathetic isn't it? You've been trying too hard on stage, at least during those times you don't miss your cues.

    You bloody fool, who have you been in these last few years? Did the bashing of your head by that jerk-off bastard taxi driver kill your common sense, not just two of your senses? A bottle of Prozac® is going to put you back on track? Who are you kidding?

    You say you want a fresh start with the girls because the British dogs are biting at your heels and nipping at areas you don't want to mention?

    Look in the mirror, your face looks puffy and that dyed black hair makes you look almost ghoulish. Have you considered, you seem to want to dress more like a man of 24 than one of 37? You fear being a has-been, don't you?

    You've become so judgmental, what happened to Mr. Greenpeace, the tree hugger? I suppose he's on holiday, because the coke, the booze and Valium® seem to be making you a little edgy. So maybe you'll go get some "ex" to smooth things out. Did you just make a call to ask someone if they could locate some heroin for you? Have you gone completely mad? You have been spending some time you can't quite remember in some unusual places with some very bizarre strangers, bizarre even for you, Mr. River. You don't seem to want to be around your close friends anymore, because they don't quite see it your way, but then again, they're not under the influence of so many drugs and so much propaganda 24 hours a day, are they?

Does it really matter anymore? Who the hell are you? Is your bitter enemy really Sir Bob or is it really you? Perhaps you're a self-defeating, sniveling jerk who ran into a Kitchen hotter than hell in the middle of summer, but then you decided you can't take the heat, so you want to find an easy way out. There isn't one, Mr. River!!!

I can see you there in Room 524, living in the land of delusions and not knowing what to do, let alone who to turn to. I wish you'd take a good, hard look at yourself before you lose everything. Mr. River won't be going to rehearsal today? Why not?

Best Wishes mate,
Michael

—*channeled from Michael Hutchence*

When it comes to my untimely demise, many have written it off as some has-been, self-absorbed rock star was partaking in some sick, demented sex orgy, he got what he deserved, the dumb motherfucker! Or that some piece of shit rock star took his own life, who the hell cares?

Actually, maybe I was a has-been, but I could have and would have reinvented myself and my career. Maybe I was too self-absorbed, but I tried to be consciously aware of other's feelings and never desired to hurt or harm anyone. Maybe the words "sick" and "demented" could have applied to me, but in truth, the combination of the anti-depressant known as "Prozac®," along with the alcohol and cocaine in my system made me completely out of my mind. This was in combination with the thoughts of losing my daughter, who I loved more than anyone. I felt a complete state of panic, and I realized I would have to cancel the INXS tour and let the band down after 20 years together, to go and be with Paula and the girls, because Paula was not going to be able to join me on the tour with Peaches, Pixie, and Tiger Lily for weeks. I was seriously in bad shape, because you see, I had a deep, dark secret and had no idea how I was going to tell Paula, my family, my friends or anyone else for that matter.

It's an interesting fact that the coroner's report surrounding my death has, in fact, been made public. Everyone can now see the drugs and alcohol I consumed the night before I left the Earth.

So why then, is my autopsy sealed? What is in there that was kept from the public? Why was my body cremated? I never told anyone I wanted this done and yet my parents were informed by those controlling my estate that I did want to be cremated. It was done rather rapidly, and truthfully, it doesn't matter at all from where I am now. There were some things going on around my death that should have raised more questions, but my loved ones were in both deep grief and total disbelief.

A short time before my crossing, I had received some medical news. I had a condition that ultimately killed millions around the globe. There was no cure, but it could be managed, hopefully, and possibly prevented from becoming terminal if I went on these very expensive drugs and watched my health very closely. I want to explain here and now, my promiscuous lifestyle finally caught up with me. I saw this condition as the final straw that would cause me to lose my daughter. I expected Paula to leave me after this was revealed, and I also felt it would be a complete career killer, and my lifestyle, the only one I really knew after two decades, would be over as well. The roof was caving in on me, and I had nowhere to run to and nowhere to hide. In my mind, Bob Geldof, my arch, enemy had won. When I got the news in those early morning hours that Paula would not be joining me on the tour because she could not bring two of her others girls, I felt as if I was already dead.

As if this wasn't enough, I had many questions regarding my finances that were not being explained to me and were never truly answered, but I knew something was askew regarding the money and financial holdings I had worked to obtain in 20 years. I lived with very little cash, but I had an American Express® card that did everything for me and it began to "bounce" a few times in the years before my death. This shouldn't have happened, and then I was told some of my investments had gone south. But I never truly understood the legal maneuvers of any of it, as I was under the misconception that those who were in charge of my money were honest, trustworthy and valiant men.

I also came to believe that I had ruined the life of Paula Yates. In beginning the affair with Paula, it appeared this had lead to her complete loss of income and a messy divorce with Bob. It's no secret that Paula chased me for many, many years, but at the end I had succumbed to her absolute charms. Although Paula was truly miserable with Bob and suffered from her own emotional distresses and problems, truthfully, the whole relationship was a horrible mess...but it was not a mistake. I could never say my beautiful daughter Tiger was a mistake, because she was the greatest blessing of my lifetime.

At one point, Paula and I had a great love for each other, but we never really knew each other as people think. Paula was the trapped beauty being kept by this awful, controlling, abusive man in my mind. In her mind, I was the hero, there to rescue her and her girls, and at one point, I tried to become what she wished for, but fell painfully short of this goal. It was a complete nightmare from the start because I took the press coverage very, very personally. I could not sit back while they stalked me and Paula — and even her girls on the way to school — and not feel irate and crazed half of the time. Between the depression, the fears of losing my daughter (which were created and embellished greatly by some young solicitor around me), the men embezzling my money, and Paula's own paranoid mind, I was losing my temper and losing my way more and more each day.

During my final tour with INXS, while I was in the United States, Paula had made a suicide attempt in England. She was very lost at the time. If she had done it, I didn't know how I could've lived with myself or explained to her children (who were very

A TALE OF TWO BROTHERS

much like my own children in my mind), why she did it! I felt I was absolutely to blame for this attempt and could hardly bear it.

It seemed I was making Paula's life worse and creating sheer misery for this very intelligent, successful woman in her own right.

I was ruining her, ruining the lives of her daughters. Meanwhile, my career was tanking, my finances were quite rocky to say the least, and I was well aware it would take millions to fight Bob Geldof in a custody battle. When my blood test results came back and I learned of the condition I now had, it was a surreal moment I couldn't quite accept. I sort of went on as if it didn't happen, but you can only do that for so long. I was tired, so tired, I just wanted to sleep and sleep and make it all go away. I couldn't cope and I woke-up from a terrible dream during the short nap I was able to take on the morning of my great demise.

When I went to get out of bed, after I spoke to Bob by phone and dealing with a distraught — and I thought possibly suicidal — Paula, I tried to figure out what to do, where to turn, but I was disoriented and hit my head on the corner of the night table in the hotel room. This caused a small cut above my left eye, and I tried to blot it with a napkin and then band aids. I took a look at myself in the bathroom mirror and wasn't sure where I was, who I was, or what was going to happen next, but I felt impending doom...*What if Bob were able to take my daughter away? What if Paula did make another suicide attempt and succeeded? It would be all my fault! What if I had to tell my band mates I was leaving to be with Paula and the girls? There was already this awful tension between me and my band mates, and I knew it was my last tour with them but how would it be to just walk out on them? What if I were truly broke in the near future? What would I do for money? How could I fight Bob for Paula in her custody battle or keep my daughter safe?*

*How could I fight this medical condition I just learned I had? What if my career were truly over...*I never had a traditional job in my life. I don't count the few days I showed up to work at a factory job when INXS started, it was under a week. WHAT IF, WHAT IF, WHAT IF, compounded by enough alcohol to intoxicate a crowded bar on a Saturday night, mixed with Prozac®, cocaine, and later on, Valium® to sleep. Even with all the drugs I had done, the yo-yo effect of cocaine to keep me awake and Valium® to come down. It just all caught up with me one day, and I either had to sink or swim. I sank, for I no longer had the emotional fortitude or mental capacity to swim.

My Dad had just asked me the night before if everything was alright and said he was worried about me, Kell knew. He knew me, and I lied to him because I wanted to believe everything was going to be alright. I wanted to believe these problems I was facing would suddenly vanish. The Peter Pan approach doesn't really work well when faced with serious issues about children and diseases. Looking back, I lived half of my life in never-never land, the life of the party, let's all have a good time, get high, get drunk and forget about tomorrow. Well now I know, tomorrow may never come on Earth and when it doesn't, it's truly heartbreaking leaving your young daughter behind, and the other girls that you felt were like your own. It's hard to leave their mother who wasn't coping well to start with or your parents or your friends.

My dear Michelle, my first love, who had remained my friend through all the years and was closest to my heart, was knocking at the door and I was on the other side of the door, but I couldn't answer, because I was dead. My lifeless body was behind the door and later my sweet Michelle would have to learn that while she was knocking, coming to save me for the umpteenth time from myself,

I was there, blocking the door...dead...gone. I had taken the cowardly way out. Thank God Michelle had not gotten someone to let her in my hotel room, because it's been hard enough on her, and on me, living with myself on this side, thinking about what I did and the pain it has caused.

I had called Michelle, she was on her way, and if I had truly remembered that, I would be alive today. But the drugs were mixed with alcohol inside my body, the paranoia was mixed with fear and my brainwaves were literally zigzagging all over the place.

This was not the first time in the past months I had called Michelle and was so messed up, had forgotten I had spoken to her. I didn't remember calling her and I was stuck in a moment, but I am here to tell you, there is *no* moment on Earth you *need* to be stuck in.

Everything, every little thing has a way of working itself out and every large thing does as well, but only if you want it to. I was in a maze, and I could've found my way out and emerged a stronger man, a better man, but I needed to stay calm and think clearly. The drugs and alcohol simply didn't allow for that.

I loved life, I loved life more than almost anyone I ever met. But I was not capable of dealing with the unhappiness or pain of others around me. I felt I could not live without my darling Tiger, and now I have brought that to myself. I felt I would break the hearts of everyone I knew when they learned of my medical condition. I was breaking it all — everything I touched — but most of all, I broke myself.

I took my own life, and I am downright ashamed of my actions on the morning of November the 22nd, 1997 in Sydney, Australia. It was not premeditated, it was absolutely an impulse that occurred upon waking up completely out of my fucking mind that morning. This is why there was no note. I never intended to do it, and, indeed, after the fact, I was completely shocked I was on the other side. I had a hard time accepting I had killed myself and I had actually left Earth. There was no one else in the room, there was no sex orgy going on, and in all truthfulness, it would've been a much better way to go out. Just about any way would've been a better way to go out, because suicide causes the most immeasurable pain to those you leave behind. I am sorry I did it, I am sorry I left, I would still be with you now if I could.

Midnight Rose

Heaven came calling sooner than it should
I would be with you if I could
Nobody knows
I love my Midnight Rose
Nobody sees
What she meant to me

Jim Morrison & Michael Hutchence

Stuck in a moment
Trapped in a space
I was handed the key

I was free when I saw your face
Nobody knows (my love only grows)
I love my Midnight Rose

Nobody sees how she blooms for me
Standing and waiting
hoping she will see
She's the only real lover
meant for me

Nobody knows
My Midnight Rose
Nobody sees
what her beauty does for me

Midnight Rose
Alone in a desert
Your beauty is timeless
Your fragrant scent
travels through space

I became free when
I saw your face
Nobody knows
My Midnight Rose

Nobody sees
what she is to me

—*song lyrics channeled from Michael Hutchence for Michelle*

Nocturnal Emissions

I held the phone to my ear all night,
couldn't stand to be alone.
Now that I'm gone,
who do you talk to in those dreadful,
lonely hours?

Who is there to dry your tears
and tell you how beautiful you really are?
What would happen if one night you
suddenly got a call
and I was on the other end of the line?
Would you be happy to hear from me? Frightened?
Or would you dismiss it as a dream?

Perhaps I called to dry your tears and tell you how
beautiful you really are.
Perhaps I called to tell you there is no death, I'm just
living in a different neighborhood now.

Would it be the same, as if time hasn't passed?
But it has passed, hasn't it?
You are not the same and I am not the same.

We have both been through such painful things,
almost too difficult to speak of, but we've come out
stronger for it, haven't we?

Maybe your phone will ring in the middle of the night and
no one will be on
the other end when you say hello,
or will they?

Jim Morrison & Michael Hutchence

Maybe you'll hear someone talking through the television,
but you'll think you were just hearing things, or were you?

Maybe a photo won't be in the same place in the morning
it was before you went to sleep;
I'm still talking to you at night and by the way, you're still
beautiful.

—channeled from Michael Hutchence

CHAPTER 10

Make Your Peace

"Everything is changeable, everything appears and disappears; there is no blissful peace until one passes beyond the agony of life and death."

—*Buddha*

SECTION:

Flesh and Blood...Paula and her girls...

Her Eyes Like A Winter Sky...

by Christopher Reburn

Jim Morrison & Michael Hutchence

A TALE OF TWO BROTHERS

On this side, I am hopeful to make my peace with each and every one I left behind among my family, friends and even those I called my enemies. Rumors are hardly worth addressing, but for the fact, I want the record clear on everything as it is part of my own karmic cleansing from this side. I was absolutely probably one of the most sexually active men you will ever find on Earth, and I was into what many would consider kinkier sex, which seemed to get kinkier and kinkier as I got older. I was not above trying almost anything, and I am not here to pass judgment on anyone who is as sexually active or is not very sexually active. I am also not bragging, as rock stars and athletes do, as this is not about my ego, that was pretty much destroyed before I crossed over.

I want to say I was familiar with auto-erotic asphyxiation, because I knew what it was and I had discussed it with others, including some who tried it. But very frankly put, it scared me and I realize that is hard to believe, because for over one year before my passing, I was, in fact, participating heavily into S & M (sadomasochism). I don't really want to discuss kinky sex practices, you can discover those at your own speed and at your own time, but I am here to say I never once participated in autoerotic asphyxiation. It was not past my realm of proclivities; I simply never chose to do it. I had a manager and friend who had seen some things and she thought I may have been participating in what is termed "AEA." She got this idea because, without going into too much detail, the bondage practices I engaged in involved being tied up or tying others up, so gadgets, hooks, screws or rope and things of that nature may have turned up around me.

Mundane sexual acts ceased to turn me on for quite some time before I departed. I had seen it all, done it all, and it was no longer a thrill. As with anything else in my life, I had to take it to the next level to truly enjoy it. "AEA" was not a part of my life prior to and including November 22nd, 1997, and was not the cause of my death, so to speak. There have been very, very ugly rumors circulating that truly hurt my family and friends and perhaps some of them just felt it was more realistic that I had ended it during a failed attempt to reach sexual climax instead of taking my own life. This rumor did not start with a friend or family member, instead it began by a member of the press who despised me. It was immediately believed because, well…you know, how could someone from the press lie? I was seen as this sick hedonistic rock star, it just fit too perfectly, didn't it?

    I was very sensitive to other people's energy, some would call me an empath, and I didn't quite realize the abilities I had. I could feel someone else's moods to the point it would alter my mood so much, it was vital I kept everyone around me happy and smiling. I never meant to hurt any other single, living person or cause anyone the smallest amount of pain. I was not the self-centered, narcissistic jerk I have been portrayed as while I was on Earth.

    At the end, I felt so isolated by my many problems and fears, and it wasn't because I didn't care about others. I was so completely out of my mind, so completely void of any semblance of hope or reality, I was not as aware of how others felt as I may have been in the past. There is much to be said about being grounded. I can't speak to you enough about the need to be in touch with truth and fact, versus paranoia, confusion and fear. At the end of my days, fear was the driver of my car, and if I had truly stopped and got the "YES" people out from around me who just kiss your ass to continue to remain on your payroll, and looked at some cold, hard facts, I could've gotten a grip on my worst problems.

    The money and fame tends to attract the most envious people to you who simply want to be attached to something, as they do not feel fulfilled, whole or worthy on the inside. The bigger your life becomes, the more daunting the task of cleaning it up, because the mess can become so huge after the indulgent party you allowed those around you to enter as your invited and uninvited guests.

    The "AEA" rumors since my death have greatly distressed me. They are a disgusting lie started by someone who simply had no use for me. I am absolutely dismayed they have been paraded around by so-called mainstream media sources. I am also quite dumbfounded someone would publish a so-called "official" autobiography of a group after one of its members is not there to take part. WHERE IS MY STORY IN THE INXS AUTOBIOGRAPHY? Here it is, and it may not be accepted, because it's not all wine and roses — far from it.

There are many things in the "official" INXS autobiography that should be researched and then corrected. For example, it is suggested there was a book on auto-erotic asphyxiation found in my hotel room the morning I took my life. The police reports, which inventory everything in the room, as they must explore various possibilities when they discover a dead body, prove this to be incorrect. No such book was with me. I know I left my former band mates in a bad, bad state, however, they should get their facts straight. I know I took the spotlight for many years as the lead singer, and I realize the very talented other members of INXS were not given the recognition they deserved, but maybe one should do their art for love, not for money or fame. Their soul searching led them all back to the group, so they could continue to make money. I certainly know they need to support their families, but when writing an official autobiography, the word "candor" should coincide.

I actually consider performing the songs we wrote and sang together for 20 years quite morbid with a new lead singer *and* in an exploitive reality contest. The greatest groups on Earth, do not try to reformulate. Once the four Beatles were in place, after they switched drummers early on, and they made their timeless music together, would it be appropriate to recast the group? It would be considered sacrilege by many of their adoring fans.

The great Motown groups are not of the same formulation now that others are touring in place of the originals, and it's completely disdainful. These people did not help to mold the Motown sound, but they are profiting from the work of others.

I will relish the day I can sit with my former band mates on this side and make our peace. I have so much to say to each of them, and I wait to see Garry and really apologize to him. I wish to see Andrew, though I can see him now, and I hope he thinks of me when he is looking at that beer stein. I left things undone with each of them, with everybody really, especially myself. The only member of INXS I was on good terms with was actually Kirk, but I do look forward to making amends with each of them.

Jim Morrison & Michael Hutchence

There was no one with me in the room when I took my life. I wasn't sure what room I was in or what was going on. I had woken up nauseated, my equilibrium was extremely out of balance, and it was like being extremely sea sick. I wasn't participating in a sex orgy and if I was, I would be truthful about it from this side. The way I went out wasn't painful, only because I was unaware consciously of what I was doing, and so out of it, I felt no pain physically, so I am very thankful for that.

There was no suicide note because I never thought about this ahead of time or planned it. There were unfinished lyrics in the room, not a suicide note. I had started these lyrics on November 20th, 1997. If I had truly thought about it on a conscious level, I would not have done it. If I had remembered my dear Michelle was on her way over, I would not have done it. If I could see half of what I caused, I would not have done it. If I could see for one moment that my daughter would grow-up without me, I would not have done it. People do snap — it's very, very real.

My mother and sister have written a book about me, as well as my brother. I actually love the fact my family members have written books about me. It's not cashing in, it's out of love, pain and confusion. They also were aware I was being lied about left and right by so-called journalists, and worse yet, even some so-called friends. They wanted to defend me, but also tell of their pain as other families unfortunately go through this terrible heartache. They loved my life, they loved me, and I did shut them out of my darkest struggles to spare them, but I now wish I had let each of them in more than I did, for I failed to prevent them from the worst pain I could've possibly have caused them. A mother's pain of losing her son this way and a sister who tried to speak to me on different occasions about my problems and lifestyle is hard to measure. My Mum and Sis' wrote the book as a tribute of love, and they were absolutely right about most of their thoughts…they knew me better than I ever thought. My brother, Rhett, wrote his own book, and I am extremely proud of him.

I love Rhett dearly and always felt my own spotlight dimmed his self-esteem. Rhett was honest about his life as an addict, he didn't glamorize it. He has also searched endlessly for answers to what happened in Room 524 of the Ritz-Carlton in those morning hours of November 22nd, 1997. My family has always had some tumultuous relationships with each other, and my untimely demise has only added fuel to the fire. It was hard at times, doing the juggling act, as they could not seem to get along, and I tried to maintain relationships with each of them. Kell is over here now with me, and we both wish to say that you have no idea how you will feel if you leave the Earth with regrets and if you haven't made-up with each other and expressed love. You don't necessarily have to like another person's actions to appreciate them, and it's far better to let things go, because no matter how trite this may sound, life is short, it's over in the blink of an eye in many cases. Above anything else, make your peace.

One of the hardest situations I have had to make my peace with involves my former partner, Paula Yates. It is true, Paula believed I died from AEA, because she knew I was quite kinky and would put nothing past me. But mainly it was too difficult for her to comprehend for one second I would leave her or Tiger. She could not fathom that I would abandon her, let alone my daughter, who she knew I loved more than anyone. I do not blame Paula for her actions after I left. She was in a huge mess, much of it was her own making, but she simply could not find her way out.

I did love Paula very, very much, and she gave me the greatest gift anyone has ever given me, obviously my daughter. I loved Paula's girls as if they were my own. Unfortunately, Paula and I got together romantically at a time when both of us were going through so much and the stresses continually built-up. I doubted I could be a good father to Tiger or the other girls though I told myself and anyone who would listen, I was the father of *all* of Paula's wonderful daughters and I loved them — and still do.

I am not here to speak for Paula, but I am clear now on the fact she was always fearful of becoming mentally ill because of her heredity. I feel I further spun her life out of control because her love for me made her sacrifice so much of who she was. She became hated, lost her job and pretty much her sense of self along the way. We both began to lose ourselves at a time when we should've flourished, and the substance abuse, on both our parts, was by far the biggest blunder we could've made.

Paula Yates was a very intelligent, grown woman, and I didn't force drugs, alcohol or anything on her, but I think at times she wanted to be my fantasy woman and be someone who could keep up with me. I could hardly keep up with me. Paula never needed to keep up with me. She was very, very loved and cherished as she was. Many wrote nasty things about how I could leave a super model for Paula. Paula Yates was arguably one of the most beautiful, intelligent, caring women that ever lived. If both of us had stayed away from the alcohol and drugs, I am quite certain we would've made it through and still be on the Earth at this time.

I cannot tell the world that Paula and I would've stayed together as a couple or as a family unit. We had so many pressures, and it's possible we would've sorted everything out and gone onto a better life, but that is not how it appeared to be going at the time I crossed over. Paula had a TV job lined up in Australia, and there, we felt we could've gotten away from the smothering, low crawling, sniveling rat bastard press in London. I regret we never got the chance to see how things would've played out. We could've gotten away from the press, but we could not have gotten away from ourselves. Regardless, we would've been parents to Tiger and friends forever.

Interestingly enough, in attempting to make my peace on this side, my brother in arms, Jim Morrison and I are sharing the same channel. It so happens, I was quite a Doors fan and, in fact, a huge fan of Jim personally. Some suggested I should've played him in the Oliver Stone flick, and I am so glad at this stage, that part went to someone else. I do understand how it feels to be lied about, and while you are no longer concerned with fame or the trappings that accompany it, it's very unpleasant — even on this side — to be continually trashed and have people fabricate things about you for sensationalism so they may sell their filthy papers and books as they are too self-indulgent or perhaps stupid to research or care about the truth.

Do they realize, when we ascend to this side, we leave loved ones behind? But who really cares how my daughter feels about things as she grows up or how my grieving parents feel? My Father, Kell, was deeply hurt following my death in regards to the things written about me. The poor man was suffering with cancer, but they continually trashed me and claimed I died in a sex orgy with midgets or animals or some nonsense. Forget about the Mother I left behind, who has had her own share of health problems over the years, just trash her deceased son because it will help sell a trashy London paper or disgusting tabloid book.

Jim Morrison and I are, in fact, victims, somewhat, on this side of lies perpetrated by what you call "mainstream media." Our personalities could not be more different, and yet we have some common links. Our deaths have been greatly lied about and continue to be. Lies upon lies are put out, and then revised and repeated, and people are gullible enough to believe and swallow it, hook, line and sinker.

The major difference about the demise of Jim Morrison versus my own simply put is, Jim did not take his own life, nor did he intend to. While we were both depressed, Jim was finally about to take action about his own life and make necessary changes by eliminating poisons, so he could go on and be productive. The two main toxins he was aiming to free himself of were alcohol and his companion, Pamela Courson. He was ready to go on and write the next chapters in his life. He did not have to die in Paris and certainly was without a doubt, accidentally murdered.

It's interesting, since I will openly admit I engaged in some heroin use, but Jim Morrison who was vehemently against it is the one accused of dying from it! I have to say, Jim admits to doing lots of coke and grass and other things, but mostly he was more than happy with his alcohol, and compared to my lifestyle, Jim Morrison was practically a Boy Scout.

I realize the fans of Jim Morrison do not take pleasure in hearing how slow and difficult his death was, but unfortunately, it's the truth. His death ended approximately five hours of suffering, while mine was painless, because I was so messed up and out of it. Mine ended close to 38 years of suffering.

Jim and I both died alone, there were no eyewitnesses, and this is why I'm completely amazed at the absurdity of the stories that have been passed around. I realize Jim Morrison had no autopsy which would've cleared up the thousands of hours of speculation about his death. Or would it? Is it too hard to believe Jim Morrison did not die from suicide or a self-inflicted drug overdose? After all, he was a rock star, and he was so over the top. Are Jim's medical records fictional about his final months in Paris and his doctor's visits? Clearly, he was not well. There was no evidence or eyewitnesses who saw Jim die, and I think it's positively absurd someone would show-up 36 years after the fact and try to say Jim died in the restroom of a Parisian nightclub. It's interesting what people will say and write when they need cash, isn't it? Paula was in England when I took my final curtain call. Paula had no idea of the secrets I was keeping from her, but there are reasons she supported the AEA theory which I have forgiven her for. But I did have an autopsy and the coroner investigated my death, searching for anything bizarre, after all I was a weird rock star, so anything was possible right? There was absolutely no evidence of AEA (because it didn't happen) or of foul play. I was in such a depressed state, so completely whacked out of my mind, sex was not on my agenda, and knowing how sexually active I was in my lifetime, that is really saying something for how far gone mentally and emotionally I was. Besides, why would I do a solo sex act knowing Michelle was on her way over? That makes no sense, I would have always preferred sex with a partner.

Jim Morrison and I had highly controversial deaths, and it is rather unfortunate that more time and energy is spent on how we died as opposed to the work we left behind to cherish. Our lives should've mattered more than how we bit the dust. Have you ever heard another song like "L.A. Woman?" The lyrics are incredible!

I would do whatever is possible to discourage anyone from going the way I did, but while that is so, our deaths have been made a mockery of and I want to be remembered by my music, twenty years in INXS and my solo projects also. I want to be remembered by the sacred, personal relationships I had and the time I shared with friends and family. I don't want to be remembered as the has-been joke trying to get himself off one day and it went awry.

As for Jim Morrison and I, there is great energy in our work, absolute great light. It will never die, and our souls won't either. The vulgar crap printed about us should not be believed or given credence to. I know you have to think for yourself but at least search for facts and base your opinion on something other than repeated rumors, innuendos and lies printed about us over and over again.

Now here is something the press doesn't know. Jim Morrison and I were at the same hotel in L.A. many years apart, and at this hotel, I contracted an illness from a woman I had been involved with. I was visiting her room there. This was, of course, a sexually transmitted, potentially fatal disease and I know many will question this information. Only a few living people can confirm this and it would surprise me if they chose to do so, but that is up to them. They have to live with themselves. This is how I wish to make my peace with everyone: to tell the truth and to speak of one of the major factors that caused me to end my life and bow out, not so gracefully. There was an American woman, and she had a friend. They were, in fact, rather high priced call girls, and I was around them because they liked rather kinky sexual practices. I was not a paying customer, as I didn't have to be. Some close friends and associates actually saw me with these women. One of these females had a potentially fatal disease, and it was passed onto me through sexual contact. It was extremely careless and an incredibly stupid move on my part, considering I had a baby at home. Tiger was born by this time, and I am very thankful that Paula and Tiger were not affected by this.

But you see, I had taken some rather incredible chances for several years of my life, two decades actually, so of course, the invincible nature of who I thought I was played a part. I learned of this illness only weeks before my demise. I actually could not believe it at first, or accept it, and by the time it set in, I was ending my life.

The hotel at which I contracted the illness, is the same one where Jim Morrison fell, attempting one of his superman stunts in February, 1971. Jim began to cough up blood, and this injury was a contributor to his unfortunate passing approximately five months later. The disease I contracted at this same hotel, was a direct contributor to my passing months later, because I could not face it combined with all the other problems I had on my plate. Just think, Jim could've fallen anywhere and damaged his body, and I could've contracted the disease I had almost anywhere in the world, but the fact it was at the same hotel is not a coincidence. Because there are no coincidences. A contributing factor to our deaths occurred in the same place.

Jim and I both had absentee fathers growing up. We also relocated quite a bit during our childhoods. We both wrote poetry and never dreamt of becoming singers as children. I recorded a Christmas song as a young boy but never thought I would be a singer as an adult. We were both avid readers in our lifetimes. We were both very, very good swimmers. We both shared a love for Paris. We both had two siblings.

Jim and I, however, are quite different personality wise. He liked to be alone, and I couldn't stand to be alone. He liked solitude, and I detested it. Jim didn't like worldly possessions or to walk around showing off money for the most part, while I loved material possessions. Jim was not a fan of Oscar Wilde, and I certainly was, but Jim's remains ended up in the same cemetery as Oscar. Go figure!

So the question may arise, did Jim and I share lives together? Hmm, I think it's safe to say, we are truly brothers and our lives would've intersected the last time around but Jim took an early exit. I remain his fan though we are not celebrities on this side. I admire Jim and always will and he and I will always be brothers. Both of us pretty much walked into our careers as singers one day. Jim was and remains a genius. He is now an esoteric spiritual genius, and I love the friendship we now possess as we are both free of the considerable pain we experienced on Earth.

Jim and I interestingly enough, were both with women at the end who were great learning lessons for us. Both of these women, Pamela and Paula had names that start with the letter "P" and include two "As." It's safe to say Jim would not have remained with Pamela and I am quite doubtful Paula and I would have endured. Pamela and Paula both died tragically just about two months prior to the third anniversary of both of our deaths from accidental heroin overdoses. Coincidence? I think not.

The fairy tales of our romances with these women are far from true or beautiful, and the stark realities are somewhat shocking and disturbing. We had truly turbulent relationships with these women. Jim and I ended up quite lonely, quite depressed and really our lives were both disaster areas at the end. Men who are truly in love don't often end up like that, do they? Jim had the fortitude to decide to make changes, I just threw in the towel in a moment of temporary insanity.

I come here now and take part in this book to make my peace. I do so by telling the truth, but I'm hoping my truth sheds a spotlight on yours and you will understand where you are and what you are doing. You will grasp how precious life is, and what you have in your hands instead of taking it for granted and believing a month from now — or even a week from now — you are guaranteed to be on Earth. A moment of temporary insanity is not as hard of a place to get to as you may now believe. It can happen to you and that is why I come to you, to offer the lessons I have learned in my short, exciting, painful yet precious life. I have been trashed through the media since my demise. Peace comes from within, and no one outside of you can bring it to you or find it for you. Make your peace, my friend, while you wander the Earth, for once you leave it, you will be in the eternal waiting room until others can come to you. It's so much easier to do while you are there. Without peace, you could very well end up as I did, and that would be nothing short of a huge tragedy. I wish you peace, I wish you well, and I am trying to save you from the regrets, the pain, the confusion and the hell I have caused by my own hand.

Never Meant

The streets were paved with four-leaf clovers
Then why is it I have nothing but bad luck?
I used to just run to new adventures
now I am feeling tired and stuck

A good luck charm is what I need
but my charm seems to have run amuck
I am not who I once was
where the gods bowed down before me

and everyone in my midst adored me
The stars are no longer aligned in the sky
I no longer like this party
I don't feel at home, in fact,
in the midst of this crowd, I feel quite alone

Jim Morrison & Michael Hutchence

I no longer belong here, in this world
I can't seem to find my space
I can't seem to find my place
the clock races all about
I fear my time has run out
That's it, my time has run out

what I have come to do
has not been done
what I have come to say—
what was it I came to say?
I don't know…but anyway

Oh my God, Oh my God
I am on the ceiling,
I feel weightless, I love this feeling
the shock comes, I see myself
laying near the door
Medics have arrived, what is this for?

What the hell, what did I do?
why can't I go back?
I'm not done, I'm not done
I was just so…tired, so tired
I want to scream, I want to run

I am speaking, no one hears me
I am standing in front of you
why can't you see me?
Is this a joke, or a nightmare?
My body is on the floor, but I am right here,
do you care? Does anyone care?

Once they said, I had it all
They were just preparing me

A TALE OF TWO BROTHERS

for the inevitable fall
but I wasn't prepared, so I crashed
and burned

I now ask what is it
Have I learned?
I was running not away
but toward the next trap door
to find a new woman, a new Euphoria
another score

I didn't need to run
because I am Michael Hutchence
I am pure love and light
and for all intents and purposes
that was the only peace I needed to
get me through the night

I was on the phone
and talking for hours
but was I really ever connected?
Did I hear what was coming
through the receiver?

What was I saying,
Was I ever really a believer
in anything other than
the next trap door
the next escape,
I've done it now, my Houdini act
gone and disappeared
forever more

or Have I?
I never belonged there
I was never of Earth

Jim Morrison & Michael Hutchence

I was always of heaven
but I tried to assimilate at birth

The only way I could get through
was to be high as a kite
taking a ride
but hiding my divine light

The ride is over
my driver has gone home
the trap doors were illusions as was being
the quintessential rock star
But I earned my scars

I couldn't stay on the Earth plane
I did not belong there for another moment
I am sorry it went this way
I had a life, I had light but I couldn't own it

There are no more illusions
I've broken through the veil
There are no more ungodly intrusions
I've gone back to where I belong, I was never meant to be there long

—*channeled from Michael Hutchence*

Jim Morrison

Who is this girl
who searches
for you?
She thinks she is dreaming
but she has in fact

A TALE OF TWO BROTHERS

crossed the dimensions
and she asks me,
"Do you know where I can
find Jim? I was told
he was with you."

I told her I would take her
to you, but she must be strong,
once you see each other
She will not want to return
to Earth or live out
her days in her golden playpen

She became scared and nervous
and she told me to wait,
so I took her hand and
told her that you are waiting
for her, living for her
and cannot survive
without her

She knew that once she
saw you, her life on
Earth is over, for she will
hardly be able to make it
through the day

For she is your better half
and you are her other half

I gently stroke her face
and brush a tear from
her cheek, I send her back
to her dream but it won't be
long now before your lovely
Rebecca is home and she

Jim Morrison & Michael Hutchence

is with you Jim for all
eternity

The course of love
is never easy, but
it's always worth it

For Jim you have waited
since your birth in 1943
for her and when she finds
you, nothing the cosmos
can throw at you
can tear the two of
you apart

I am your best man,
your witness, for a love
more beautiful than the
sunrise has ever been,
for you will move
heaven and Earth to
be with her eternally
and I shall of course,
be happy to assist,

as I, the hopeless
romantic am privy
to witnessing one of the
greatest love stories in
history.

—channeled from Michael Hutchence

Flesh and Blood...Paula and her girls...

Her Eyes Like Winter Sky...

by Christopher Reburn...Channel for Paula Yates

The time that I connected with Paul Yates on The Other Side, I've conversed with a very spiritual feminine being who is caring and very obedient to questions being asked of her. She is a great listener, and an even greater talker. She speaks very candidly about her life on This Side but she still has a lot of trouble making sense of most of it as when I ask her about her earthbound life, she normally shakes her head, or rambles on about something else and she is unable to maintain eye contact with me.

I do sense from her that she knows of her many mistakes that she made on This Side and while she is not asking anyone for forgiveness, she is quite sorry to many of the people who became enraptured in her dilemmas and dramatic problems she had while on This Side. She mentions a male by the name of Ian, shows she sees that the two of them were too much alike to ever get along, and that she felt he wronged her, but that she has sent him amends now and that everything is alright with them. She says she is still trying to work on forgiving her estranged mother as well as someone by the name of Gary, who she feels tried (and succeeded) in cashing in on her name.

She wants people to stop making fun of her for her acquaints with Michael Hutchence and she wants people to stop saying that she was only a "star" because of her relationship with Michael. She does mention that the truest and greatest love of her life was someone by the name of Robert, and that her time with Michael Hutchence was more of a sexual connection than anything else, and their main charted goal together was to bring the beautiful Tiger Lily into the world. She wants Tiger Lily to know how much her "momma" loves her and that she will be a strong-willed, independent young lady and will learn many great things that Paula never fully understood or learned.

Despite having being coached and healed by the elders and regularly communing with Michael Hutchence, Paula still seems to have a very low opinion of herself, and while doesn't seem to be too concerned with anyone who feels she let them down on This Side, she is a lot more upset with herself, as she feels that she's let herself down, and her beloved children.

She watches over them and ironically, she says that she always put lilies around Tiger Lily and she also says she safeguards all her children with the White Light of Spirituality. She says that she wants to come to her children and she wants them to be open to what she has to say. She wants to help each of them in individual ways and she wants them to listen to her. She says that she will be coming to each of them in dreams as well as in apparition form, and she wants them all not to second guess the signs that she has been, is, and will be sending them.

She says that she wrote a lot about them in journals of hers, and also in a number of writings that she published. Paula wants her daughters to know that she is getting stronger now, and will soon be making more fruitful attempts at contacting them individually as she says a lot of the information she wants to give them is private and personal and she doesn't want them reading about it in the tabloids before she can at least get them to first and be the first to them.

—*Christopher Reburn,* The Chosen Channel for Paula Yates

12/17/07

CHAPTER 11
This Ain't The Good Life...

"When you are content to be simply yourself and don't compare or compete, everybody will respect you."

—*Lao Tzu*

Jim Morrison & Michael Hutchence

A TALE OF TWO BROTHERS

One thing about my past life I need to speak openly about was my drug use. It's no secret I tried any kind of substance I got my hands on and always believed you could never become an addict if you switched up and didn't continually use the same illegal substance. Was it because I was a spoiled, self-indulgent rock star? Absolutely, but there was also another part to these extreme indulgences. I was doing what so many with constant depression and nagging anxiety do, I was self-medicating and I had to create a euphoric feeling from drugs as opposed to experiencing it within myself.

I abused a wide variety of drugs (just the details of my usage could be an entirely separate book). I was only what would be termed, "clinically addicted" to one, and I will reveal that later on in this writing. But first, I am here to heavily caution against what you may call "recreational drug use," because your choice of recreation will greatly impact your life, and take it from one who knows, there is no free lunch. There is a large myth created that recreational drug users can function in their daily lives and hold down jobs, therefore, they are not truly doing themselves harm.

I was a person who would take 11 or 12 Ecstasy tablets before performing on stage and got rave reviews after many of those concerts. I do feel qualified to speak about recreational drug use. You simply are not aware of what those drugs do to your central nervous system, let alone the chemicals in your brain. I took a vast amount of Ecstasy over the years, and it did, without a doubt, contribute to my great demise. Ecstasy, for those of you who don't understand this substance, makes you feel on top of the world and you feel everything at a much more turned up level. I took so many Ecstasy tablets because I was of the belief, if one or two make you feel pretty good, imagine what four or five will do, and so on. You then take more because you are not getting the same effects from the drug use you originally got, so you must increase your dosage.

Ecstasy is frightening because kids are buying it in clubs, and they have no real idea how it is made or what is in it. The mixing of synthetic drugs is so common and, of course, it has lead to horrible consequences for the user but let me tell you where it lead me. It didn't kill me, but it was a contributor to things going completely awry for me. Ecstasy lowers your serotonin levels, which play a rather large role in depression. So if you are someone who is already suffering from manic depression (which you now refer to as bipolar) as I was, this is a terribly dangerous drug. A person with normal serotonin levels will more than likely encounter mood disturbances by partaking in this drug, but to a person like me, who had already had mood swings, this drug could lead to such things as suicide and other assorted topics no one likes to discuss, let alone think about. I was not a chemist or a pharmacist and preferred to believe what my friends or the dealers I knew told me about the pills. If it feels good, then do it, but no one ever told me of the terrible price you pay, and the check always seems to show-up at your table even if you think you have avoided it.

I was careful — or so I thought — in the context of only getting pills from the people I knew or friends of friends, but with this sort of thing, how can you really be sure what you are given? No one ever really said to me in a serious tone that I was going too far, because they would share my drugs with me or do their own. It was a party that went on for over 20 years really, but the party does eventually end and the damage is irrevocably done.

I was also involved with cocaine as it is the choice of artists, the whole "in" crowd thing. It keeps you moving and you don't have to sleep or eat for days. Another taste of euphoria, but the one thing I never realized I got from cocaine was the terrible, increasing paranoia. Cocaine, and I say this is undisputable, makes you paranoid, and this is a side effect even short term users may well experience. The paranoia is often completely misdirected. I should have been paranoid of my financial state, and where my money was going, who was occupying the homes I thought I owned or driving the cars my money paid for, but instead, my paranoia was focused on Bob Geldof, and it's nothing short of amazing how out of touch I was. Bob and I spoke not even 10 times during the years I was with Paula. Our conversations never reached the double digits! If I had directly communicated with Bob on a more regular and open basis, I am quite certain some of the custody situations could have been diffused.

I am not here to speak for Paula Yates, but I want to say, I will not say anything detrimental about her on this side or any of my former loves. I was truly honored to bask in their beauty and grace for the time I did, my dear Michelle, my wonderful Rosanna, my sweet Kylie, my sensational Helena, and my lovely Erin whom I had such a short time with. What went wrong in each and every one of these relationships was due to me, not to any of these incredible women. I was proud they were all very intelligent and successful women in their own right, none of them had to leach off a man for money or a name. These dynamic women I had a chance to spend parts of my life with are sacred to me along with the memories we share. They were the good life, each of them in their own way. I was the one who blew it!

Paula Yates, I will say, is healing on this side and evolving as I am. She is always with and watching over her girls, her love for them will never die. I have been given permission by Paula to report her parting was not intentional. It was purely accidental, and she has gone through tremendous grief in regards to leaving her girls. She knows she was not perfect, and made quite a few mistakes on Earth as we all have, but her love for all four of her daughters is immense and hardly describable in words.

It is not for me to speak of Paula's mistakes or anyone else's, for that matter, but to speak of my own. I placed myself smack in the middle of Paula's divorce drama, and I did not belong there.

I have found you can aid someone without engrossing yourself in their situation. Bob and Paula had a long history together, of which, I was not a part. They shared three beautiful daughters, and no one could truly understand their situation or scrutinize their relationship other than the two of them. In other words, I should've stayed the hell out of their drama while supporting Paula. The energy of it all was so intense, and Paula's depression over the entire ordeal was so extreme, I was simply not strong enough to cope with all of it…though I wanted to be. It really wasn't so much about coming into a pre-made family. I

Jim Morrison & Michael Hutchence

handled that fairly well, and it gave me a happiness and serenity I had not found in other aspects of my life. It was the drama that ensued and the intrusion in our lives by the English press that broke me in half at times. It's very taxing to see someone you love ripped apart on a constant basis by the press. It was very hard to see how I was also portrayed in the press, because, perhaps, I was used to being a darling of the media and not having much negativity in print.

There are people who love drama and must invent it and relish in it to feel alive. I was not one of those people. I was never the drama king, and therefore, it was difficult for me at times to be with someone who seemed to bask in a whole episodic soap opera of sorts. When your self-esteem is low, sometimes attention, any sort of attention, negative or positive, makes you feel of value in some twisted way. I had nothing but disdain for the attention and intrusion. It was more than I could handle, and at times, I wrongfully blamed Bob Geldof for this mess. But I have since learned I was the creator and author of my own course of action and my own unmitigated disaster.

I would do drugs, drink lots and lots of alcohol to find euphoria because, God knows, I surely could not find it on Earth. I think at this time it's important to state, I was an occasional heroin user, once again, to find the sham of euphoria. I never understood how one could be an addict of such a drug, because I thought you could never be productive with regular usage. Now keeping in mind that heroin causes neurochemical and molecular changes in the brain and is a downer and I was already a manic depressive, do I need to spell it out for you? My brain waves were in a complete tailspin because of my manic depression, the brain bruising in 1992, and I was mixing alcohol and drugs, including prescription drugs. Is it any wonder I ended up where I did? I created a biochemical disaster in my brain!

You don't have to be a rocket scientist to figure this one out. I am not here to tell you not to use drugs or have your martini tonight. Your free will is very important to me and to the universe, and I will not be a hypocrite. God forbid if anyone tried to tell me what to do in my life. But I must make this ostensibly clear, if you play with the chemicals in your brain by using drugs or alcohol, you may not be able to control the outcome. You are actually clouding your connection to the truth, the divine and the rest of the universe. To put it bluntly, you are "f'ing" yourself up mate. And there may not be a way back because you will not be able to think rationally or reasonably, and if you want to become a victim of anyone or anything, recreational drug use is a great invitation.

If I was not partaking in so many drugs on a regular basis, looking for the next party constantly, I may have been able to have been more involved with the business aspects of my career and not helping many people I never knew of sustain a lifestyle that I would've not sanctioned with my wealth. The world is obviously vast and beautiful, but society is a jungle. You must stay clear and on your feet in the jungle to survive. I was too busy smoking and ingesting plants in the jungle to really understand where I was or what was going on. The beast I feared in the dark of night in the jungle was not the danger I thought he was, for the danger was within me, Michael Hutchence.

The story of INXS, simply put was of drugs, sex, and, even more than rock 'n' roll, I would have to say funk music. The stories that have been written about our episodes on the road are rather similar in some ways to the outrageous stories of other bands. There were things that happened, such wild indulgences that have not been documented, and they won't be now. There is an expression, some things are meant to be taken to the grave, and that is exactly what I have done.

We were brothers, and as I said before, the closest family I ever had. The '90s were an incredibly difficult time for INXS and we grew apart. I will take my share of the responsibility as I was truly not a grounded soul. Other members of the band were simply more grounded when we were not touring than I was. I have been described as a bohemian, and I can accept that, and say that perhaps I should've come into my prime at the time Jim Morrison came into his. I fit into the culture of that time period better than I did later on.

By the time I got into my 30's, I tried to ground myself with my beautiful Danish supermodel in France for several years, but that was like caging a saber tooth tiger. The animal will become accustomed to the cage but never wholly accept his surroundings.

By not being a grounded soul, you end up nomadically searching for things you aren't even sure exist. For someone who was an expansive world traveler, I led a very sheltered existence in INXS. You may ask how, but you see, you don't have the "real life" or normal experiences that the average Joe has. I was in my thirties before I ordered my own meal for the first time at a McDonald's drive-thru. I don't want this to be misinterpreted because as a band we worked in some places early on most people would never want to walk through let alone hang out in. We were not catered to as kids when we started, but it was rather thrilling for us.

But, of course, I did become pampered, isolated and would have had no idea how to earn my own money if I were not a successful singer. It would have been rather difficult if not impossible for me to have worked a 9-to-5 job of any sort. I did not have a post-high school education and was not the best student, especially in science courses. My mind was never on what one would consider real world things, and the indulgences and pampering became such that it never got any better. Once I became famous, largely due to MTV, the grounding of my soul or even any insight into true human everyday struggles, was never to be achieved.

Most people would readily believe I was a drug addict, and probably even a sex addict. But I will tell you, categorically, my true single addiction was to alcohol. You've never heard that Michael Hutchence was, in fact, an alcoholic, but interestingly enough, I would rotate drugs, even the most addictive ones and do without for a few days or do a different one. Sex was a huge part of who I was, but I can't say I buy into sexual addiction. The one true thing I always had in my hand was some sort of alcoholic beverage, even in the afternoon when I got up. I drank some very sophisticated kinds of alcohol like aperitifs, or some very snobby mixed drinks and expensive wines, so it was all quite socially acceptable.

I wasn't aware while I was on Earth that I was addicted to alcohol, but without question, I was. I generally had it in some quantity almost daily. To be an alcoholic does not mean you have to be falling down drunk, on the contrary. You could have two drinks a day and be a full-blown alcoholic; it's not the quantity but the dependency. Alcohol is, of course, a depressant, and it was the last thing I needed or should have been doing. I loved my alcohol, and if my friends think back, how often did they see me without an alcoholic drink when we were out and about or sitting back lounging. I was actually trying to quit cigarette smoking at the end of my life by using nicotine patches. For what? I needed to be completely detoxed from all the abusive substances and from the drugs and alcohol I put inside of me to make it through the night, since to a rock star, night is day and day is night.

I loved my INXS brothers, so if you want to know what went wrong, it was our musical direction. When we got into the '90s, as an artist, I needed to take risks. After all, that was what we were about to start with: the white Australian boys singing funk music when heavy metal was in. In the '90s, I wanted to find new sounds and when the world was listening to Nirvana and grunge music, I found myself compelled to share it with my writing partner, Andrew. I was not suggesting we copy the sounds of Seattle, but I was suggesting we take a huge risk and try new things. I was quickly shot down and dismissed, and I believed at the time, if my band mates had any faith in me at all, they should've given me a creative license to try and work with what I had in mind. I was rather worldly, so I wanted to put it on the drawing board and see how it played out. This was not done. I was told I went to clubs too much or was trying to duplicate what was already out there. I wasn't trying to duplicate anything, but I was trying to gain inspiration, and that's a big difference.

There was always this insentient paranoia that existed in INXS that others were trying to sound like us, or we, on the other hand, needed to be careful in trying not to sound like anyone else. We just couldn't sound like anyone else, that was already established, or so I thought. There were thoughts Bono was trying to sound like us on "Zooropia," and other things, and I was told to be careful what I shared with him pertaining to our new projects. This is completely laughable, as Bono and U2 never needed help from us, and furthermore, if I inspired — or we as INXS — inspired Bono even in some small, miniscule way, I would think we should be honored.

I wanted to branch out in the '90s and experiment and my band mates were not feeling as adventurous, so I don't believe the projects were nearly as good as they could've been. "Full Moon, Dirty Hearts" was a major mess and it was clear to everybody far and wide, we had lost all musical direction. My band mates were busy running from my suggestions, they were simply all over the place so I placated them, as I couldn't take it anymore. I started to feel as if I could not voice a creative opinion on which way to go or what to try. I was looked at as a mental case after having the unfortunate brain bruising incident in 1992, because my moods swung and it was noticeable. I was uncontrollably temperamental, but this was my family, my brothers, and yet they did not understand. I felt we were all going our own way and the closeness was dissipating, at least between me and the other members of the band. When we toured South Africa, it was a turning point for me. I felt completely emotionally split for the first time from my band mates, I mean completely. Only one of them became close to me again before my passing, which is rather unfortunate.

At times, I want to be clear, I felt they were siding with my enemy, Bob Geldof, and of course, in some ways, they were just trying to talk some sense into me regarding the custody situation. If you told me anything other than I wanted to hear pertaining to Bob, I felt you were betraying me. I didn't want to hear Bob's side or know his side, which of course, was completely wrong. I was in a deep state of paranoia from all the drug use, bad press, and other pressures falling down around me. Mixing heroin, cocaine, Ecstasy, Prozac® and Valium® on different days, but almost always with alcohol and being under the pressure I was under, made me quite a mess. I wish I had opened up to my band mates more, and I wish I had gone to two male friends I could count on. Richard Lowenstein tried to get through to me — I shut him off, and I wish I had been closer to him in the final months of my life. I should've consulted my friend Bono more. Both Richard and Bono would've gladly helped me, but it was entirely up to me to "open" up and be able to receive some advice without feeling betrayed.

What people saw on the outside, was far from the good life for many, many years. Euphoria does not come from the synthetic; euphoria does not come from being out of touch. Euphoria comes from within, the truth inside yourself. Knowing one's self and the truth within and around you, really is the good life.

Surrender

Where have you gone to?
Alice went to wonderland,
what did she say it was like?

What mystical voyage
have you undertaken?
You're off to see the wizard?
Well then, who is he?

If you pull back the curtain,
will you accept what you see?
I don't think tapping your heels together
will make a difference,
do you?

What if Alice breaks the looking glass
and the wizard doesn't exist?
Would all your illusions be torn apart?
what happens next?

Do you retreat to your bed?
Hoping to dream of something more?
Are your dreams so interesting
Because your life is so mundane?

Starlight, Star bright,
I can't see the stars tonight,
The clouds hide the light

Maybe you should leave a trail
of breadcrumbs or something,
Because no one can find you

Jim Morrison & Michael Hutchence

You can't be rescued,
if you can't be found,
surrender and we will help you

There's no glass slipper,
if you don't make it to the ball

I won't convert, I'll never surrender,
I'll live in my world, not yours

—*channeled from Michael Hutchence*

Tunnel Vision

Before you blow out the candles,
make a wish once again.
When you were a little girl,
you wished for a pony
but you don't want a horse
anymore.

You are older,
disillusioned, where
did that little girl go?

Did you run away
from your innocence and
your make believe world?

hmm, Father Christmas (Santa Claus)
didn't get your letter, and you
are certain the Easter Bunny
cannot be real.

A TALE OF TWO BROTHERS

The things you once
believed in are removed
from your dreams, there is
no Prince waiting for you
so cry your eyes out
because what is it all for?

You are embarking on a
timeless journey, through a long
tunnel that you've only just begun.
But when you get to the
end of the tunnel, I'll be there,
waiting for you.

I'll be holding a bouquet
of radiant red roses and
I'll hold you for a very
long time. Your journey
hasn't been easy, and when
you get to the end — the
rainbow will shine upon you
and I'll be there to hold
your hand.

—*channeled from Michael Hutchence*

Jim Morrison & Michael Hutchence

CHAPTER 12

Listen Like Thieves

"We should never pretend to know what we don't know, we should not feel ashamed to ask and learn from people below, and we should listen carefully to the views of the cadres at the lowest levels. Be a pupil before you become a teacher; learn from the cadres at the lower levels before you issue orders."

—*Mao Tse-tung*

Jim Morrison & Michael Hutchence

A TALE OF TWO BROTHERS

In 1994, I was mesmerized with the coverage of the death of Kurt Cobain. I had been listening to Nirvana feverishly for months and really believed Kurt to be the poet of his generation. He seemed to have encapsulated the feelings of many young people worldwide. I was in my early thirties and related to Kurt's lyrics.

I was in shock when I learned he had taken his own life. I couldn't understand how he could've done it, let alone why. I could not possibly contend with the selfishness he had just shown the world and how could he possibly have left his young daughter behind? I was also pondering some of his obsessive fans, and wondering if there was a chance of a copycat death, and it concerned me. I thought this was the most spineless act of one of the most influential people of his time.

I said publicly, I never wanted to be a page one story like that. Little did I know, that in just over four years, I would find myself in the same sort of agony and pain Kurt was in. There is an old saying, there but for the Grace of God go I, have you ever heard of it? You cannot judge me or Kurt without walking in our shoes, and our lives were so unique and so blessed but our brains became completely unraveled. We certainly both had more complicated situations than any book, newspaper or magazine story has been able to explain. We were both whirlwinds of pain and emotion, yet we both desperately loved our daughters. It is easy to stand in judgment of Kurt, or of me for that matter, but while Kurt's life was very difficult from the beginning, mine was charmed but became a complete nightmare. The nightmare was heavily designed by my own hand.

I could not understand Kurt's death or pain, and in my lack of understanding, a true lesson came to me as I went through some similar things. What you do not understand, what you judge in another, will often come to you in one form or another and the universe will grant you ways of understanding complex lessons. I would suggest to be careful in who you judge and demean based on their actions. Internally, few people can begin to understand themselves, let alone anyone else. You do not walk in their shoes, even if you have had similar experiences. Many assume their grass is always greener, yet eventually, the weeds will begin to show. Anything closely examined, microscopically, has deep and very profound flaws. Perfection is in the divine, and unless you connect directly to the divine in God, those flaws will undoubtedly come seeping through the cracks. In humanness, everyone is quite flawed.

What I could not understand in the actions of Kurt Cobain, I became myself. It's a principle of transference. It's a common thing to see, a politician or man of the cloth, so to speak, find themselves in the center of controversy because of their so-called principles. They were quick to judge, condemn and point a finger at the actions of others, and now they have become what they condemned. I believe you call that a hypocrite. Of course, public figures try to hide their transgressions so the world never knows how phony or disingenuous they truly are. There is a wonderful song the late Johnny Cash sang and I wish to quote a line from it, "What's done in the dark will be brought to the light." The more time, thought and energy you spend trying to hide something or bury it, the more it will cause great destruction to you internally.

Empathy and compassion to others, in place of judgment, will boomerang and come back to you as empathy and compassion for yourself. Everything in life works on the boomerang principle, it just takes the mechanism more time in some cases to come back and hit you in the face. Your boomerang will return, and you will have to deal with the consequences. At some point, I began to send out fear and judgment as opposed to love and light. I got back what I put out, and granted, I am oversimplifying this, if you determine every thought you have comes from either love or fear, you can dispel the boomerangs that come back based on fear.

We do things out of love for others and ourselves, and sometimes perhaps out of love for the Universe and even God, or we do them out of fear. Things we do often stem from fear of loss, fear of being left alone, fear of no one loving us, fear of someone seeing who we truly are, fear of no one loving our true selves, fear of someone uncovering our dirty little secrets, fear of becoming ill, fear of someone laughing at us, etc., etc., etc.

Once we come from a place of fear, all that we fear and wish to keep at bay will swing back to us, like a boomerang, our boomerang.

"Don't expect me to cry for all the reasons you had to die."

—*Kurt Cobain*

Mirror of Fate

Say no more unless you can speak the truth
Run no more, there's nowhere to go
The mirror of fate awaits you
Do you know what it will show?

You can't lie to it
You can't hide anymore
You can cry your eyes out
Your tears can cover the floor

But it sees who you are
Who you were
but not who you will be

Only you can determine
which way it will go
for the world cannot see
the choices you make
your life is at stake

Jim Morrison & Michael Hutchence

The mirror of fate is staring down at you
Don't look unless you are ready
For once you look, you can't deny
the truth anymore
Will it set you free or rock you to your core?

There will be no more mask
Your days of hiding have ended
and what you become
may be what you always dreaded

LIFE IS A DREAM, ONLY A DELUSION,
WHERE AS DEATH IS TRUE, NAKED REALITY…

—*channeled from Michael Hutchence*

CHAPTER 13

The Gift

"In nature we never see anything isolated, but everything in connection with something else which is before it, beside it, under it and over it."

—*Johann Wolfgang Von Goethe*

Jim Morrison & Michael Hutchence

A TALE OF TWO BROTHERS

If I had to do it all over again, I would've done it without substance, drugs, alcohol or cigarettes following the brain bruising in 1992. I would've used substances to a point, as I was on Earth to experience earthly indulgences to some extent, but I wish I would've cleaned up my act. I felt manic depression was a curse when I would admit I had such a thing. The mood swings were horrendous, and I felt like I was in hell going through them.

I was prescribed Prozac® and I was on this drug when I took my life. I am not here to condemn it specifically or any other antidepressant since I was mixing it with a variety of other drugs and alcohol. That is certainly not how it is meant to be taken. I took more than I was supposed to take as well at times, going back to the old hedonistic philosophy, if one works, imagine what two will do!

I am here to say, whether you consider me an artist or not is, of course, debatable. I considered myself an artist and still do. I have found that in many instances, artists who have suffered the worst bouts of depression have created some of the most beautiful, lasting art that the world has ever known.

Handel composed his majestic and magical "Messiah" Oratoria while he was experiencing symptoms of great manic depression. If he had lived in current times, he would be highly medicated, and it is somewhat doubtful he would have composed as he did.

Out of chaos, comes some of the greatest art known to mankind. Look at the works of Van Gogh for example and his battle with manic depression.

Listen to Beethoven, thank goodness he didn't listen to those around him who thought he was a bit crazed. At one point, he even attempted suicide. His moods were known to swing, and today, it's safe to say, he would be on a sizeable amount of medication.

Jim Morrison & Michael Hutchence

Tchaikovsky was also manically depressed. Did he commit suicide? The answer is yes, but he was the only one who could've saved himself. I can assure you, a pill would not have done it.

Rachmaninoff was another great composer who was severely depressed. Is it a coincidence some of the greatest composers and artists suffered from manic depression and mood swings?

A German psychiatrist named Kraepelin introduced manic depression, at least that is what he termed it in 1896. Because you are different, your moods swing and you are not like a robot just walking through your life pre-programmed, and you feel things so intensely in terms of what is going on in your life and what is going on in the world, you are called manic. Why not passionate or intense?

It's a very fine line to be medicated or not, and I can't say everyone should not be medicated or walk around in danger to others or to themselves. But I am here to make people think that some of the greatest and most noted artists in history were deeply feeling people, and if they weren't, could they have composed or painted such great art?

It is a proven fact that physically, anti-depressants alter your cardiovascular system, your sexual organs and your digestive system, which is more controlling of your overall health than most people realize. You are creating very dangerous physical changes, because it's easier to numb yourself and not see the world for how it truly is or question the meaning of your existence.

When you come into your human existence, you were not guaranteed unending joy and happiness for you cannot learn very much without experiencing an array of emotions. Human life is hard, it's so hard for someone as sensitive as I was, and most of us artists are true misfits. Therefore, I took things to heart that most people I knew would simply allow to roll off their backs. But the drugs that I am now speaking of are prescription drugs, even taken properly, do not make it better, they simply numb you from things you are not truly meant to be made numb from.

While manic depression (now termed as bipolar depression) is otherwise considered a serious psychiatric condition, a true difficulty in life, I would say in terms of creativity in an artist, it is most certainly a gift.

A TALE OF TWO BROTHERS

Broken Mirror

If your pain is taken away, what will you have left?
If the night turns into day, what was the night for?
Do you think you're the only one who feels unloved?
Disconnected? Unrecognized? Misdirected?

How can anyone feel connected to you?
Who are you, where is your light?
How can anyone get through?
You're shut down, You're turned off

You carry a bag with money, photos
and a broken mirror
Look into the fragmented glass
at the prism of your heart
Let it go, let it go, throw it away
That's where you must start

Close your eyes
Can't feel your body anymore
You're alright, just closer to the divine
Your feet won't touch the floor

Look, Look, Look
See God, See truth, See light.
This is the reflection
No mirror can show
You are God, he is you
that's all you really need to know

—*channeled from Michael Hutchence*

Jim Morrison & Michael Hutchence

CHAPTER 14
The Messenger

"None are more hopelessly enslaved as those who falsely believe they are free."

—*Johann Wolfgang Von Goethe*

Jim Morrison & Michael Hutchence

A TALE OF TWO BROTHERS

I want to say, unequivocally, do not buy into what you have been told about reaching the other side if you are a suicide. I will not say there is no hell over here, per se, for you can create your own personal hell with the regrets, remorse and the shame you feel for wasting your life or bowing out in the most cowardly way and leaving a trail of nothing but pain, suffering and confusion in your midst. I cannot say I was in a good place when I crossed over, but that was not because I was baking in an oven with flames surrounding me and pitchforks stuck in my hiney.

What I need to reiterate to alleviate the confusion is simply, I did not premeditate my death. I did not plan it out at all, because I was so intoxicated, confused and my brain waves were going in a "Z" pattern. I did not realize I had done it. Now I know what is going to be asked at this juncture: What kind of a bloody fool are you to not know you tied a belt around your neck and hung yourself? I was really so completely out of my mind, so stark raving mad at the time, I was not consciously aware of my actions.

When I got to this side, I was one of those who wasn't quite sure he was what you would call "dead." I was basically wandering around in a fog, very unsure about what had taken place and second guessing it, and truly not believing I had done it. Of course, I didn't stay confused very long, as everything was put under a big spotlight in a sense, and certainly, I truly wished — beyond what you can imagine — that it never happened. It was too late and this is why there was no note, because I never set out to do it. If you want to term it as "temporary insanity," that may well be the best possible way to explain it.

It's a very strange phenomenon as I was now a disembodied being, floating away from the scene of my death, yet I was not immediately aware of what I had done and it was all a bit of a shock. I was brought gently into an awareness, and I spent a great deal of time (referring to "time" as you know it) on this side healing, not channeling to anyone, but healing. When you end in such a way, you damage your soul, not irreversibly, but I have been in a place of restoration and channeling this, providing you with the truth, is very much a spiritual cleansing and karmic release for me. The illumination of the facts surrounding my life and death are being given to you, so that you may realize, all the fame, looks, money, sex, drugs and rock 'n' roll in the world will leave you empty if your soul is not in good shape and evolving while you are on Earth. I was meant to experience earthly indulgences but to also realize there was so much more and to find my true solace on the inside, not the outside. I began to slowly recognize this truth when I was with a great love of mine, Helena Christensen, because the fashion world she was a part of was so shallow and even worse in many ways than the music industry.

The fashion world is a playground for the decay of the soul. There is no better way I can word this. You are made to feel you must be young, beautiful and starving, or at least willing to vomit your food up after almost every meal. And if you weren't born with a certain set of genes to begin with, you won't be fortunate enough to starve, toot cocaine until you are half crazed and lead the jet-set lifestyle that at the end of the day, makes you racked with depression. Because, well, you know, after a certain age, you are not "hot" anymore and you will probably need to visit a rehab or two, or three, just to get your feet semi back on the ground. I was around that world for several years, and there was a plethora of emotional illness and soul dementia that was unlike any other.

I realize I wore designer clothes and had someone's name tag attached to my back side quite often, but the questions must arise: What is this doing to the women in society? So many of them are trying to live up to unrealistic, unnatural and potentially harmful standards. You can nurture your looks for a lifetime, do very unhealthy things and try to maintain a beautiful youthful appearance, but your eternity is on this side, not on Earth so it would only make sense your concern should be with your soul and spiritual connections. Those who viewed my corpse said that I was very good looking or even a beautiful dead body. Do you believe that has any significance or bearing to my life on this side? If you are to receive such a compliment upon your passing, it will be a reflection on the time and effort you wasted to suit the culture and have others think you were "hot." What good did it do me? What good will it do you? Did being this good looking corpse make my transition any easier? Did it ease the pain for those I left behind or dry my tears on this side? While it is much more beautiful here, and there are colors you cannot see and music you cannot hear on Earth, there are tears in heaven.

When you attempt to make yourself something you are not naturally, keep in mind, you will always have somewhat of an awareness that you are not organically of that state. What is not natural, will not be accepted completely or ever feel completely right. Your pursuits on Earth are determined by multi-million and multi-billion-dollar conglomerates who want you to want to be someone else other than who you really are, so you will buy things you really don't need to try to achieve the unnatural state. This is obviously not the pursuit everywhere. In countries on certain continents, they are more concerned with having enough food for that day or clean drinking water. I can assure you, the others living for survival who enjoy basic and simple pleasures and not take them for granted are more in tune with the soul than those riding around in "hot" cars and shopping at over-priced stores and providing the wear on their backs with the abomination of slave labor. You may want to stop and consider: what designer clothes you now wear, what expensive car you drive and how nice your abs are kept, won't mean squat when you do the inevitable, cross to this side. I certainly wish I had considered that while I was on Earth.

You don't lay around on clouds over here and eat bonbons while an angel strums on a harp. Most of us work and also go to school. When you come here like I did, in a damaged and very delicate state, the work is rather intense at times. You are not working for money anymore — to buy a mansion, or a yacht — you are working to become of the light. It is in the light you are in your true state, and you can experience sheer joy like you have never experienced on Earth. The darkness in your soul leads to anger, sadness, and a state of unbearable loneliness. When you come here, you must reconcile who you were, what you did with the gift of your life, and those you hurt with the true light, otherwise known as God. Or you can choose to sit and waffle in all the pain you caused and the pain you had within.

Jim Morrison & Michael Hutchence

Of all the things I have come here to share with you, please hold onto this one above any others. Work to repair your soul and your relationship with the Source (God) before you exit your life on Earth. The better shape your soul returns to this side in, the easier time you will have. All the aerobics, Pilates, and liposucking in the world will not matter the day you cross over.

The time you spent in the workplace won't matter either, unless your occupation was that of a healer, or artist perhaps, creating something beautiful. Your stocks and bonds and mutual funds will not add up to zilch, because what you value most, has no value in this, the real world. Your body was not built to last. I am not suggesting you should not take care of it, but not for vanity reasons, but rather so it may function to its full potential. Your soul is here for eternity, it's who you really are. Many of you are investing in the short term, and God knows I did that for close to 38 years on Earth. I suggest you turn your attention to the long term and the investments that really pay off.

There are many spiritualists, church goers, ministers, psychics, and so on, who believe many things about a soul if they were a suicide. It angers us on this side that anyone on Earth can be so presumptuous about such important, spiritual truths. I am not at all proud of the fact I took my own life, and I make no excuses. I have simply chosen to explain what went wrong. It's imperative I make this clear, people who claim, if you are a suicide, you are trapped on Earth and will not go to the light, are not playing with a full deck. They are missing a few cards and need to know, there is no way to predict or to know from Earth what happens to each and every soul upon their crossing to the next transition of life.

Do you honestly believe that on Earth, you have inherit, complete knowledge of this side? You can only obtain so much information on Earth, and suicides do go to the so-called light and they do heal if they so choose. I am not suggesting it's an easy road or a road that is the preferred choice, because there is so much work to be done and you must deal with such heavy remorse, regrets and sorrow. But each soul does in fact travel their own, unique journey. There are some souls who remain closer to the Earth and do not wish to be on this side due to their fear and confusion and those are spirits you call "GHOSTS." I want to categorically state, few of them are actually suicides, because suicide requires some action on your own part for it to occur. Many of those who are not transcending to this side were involved in sudden deaths. This is not to suggest that all souls involved in sudden deaths are not on this side, healing and thriving, on the contrary, this is a very small group in all actuality who remain earthbound. There are other reasons people see ghosts. It is often due to certain energy imprints and other things I am not here to go into this, as I am not going to offer a lesson on the paranormal. But I am here, in fact, to speak of suicides. We do not go to hell, though we can create our own. We are able to go to the light, as you call it, and are fully capable of healing and being filled with the light.

Please realize, your prayers and thoughts do help. It helps us very much when you forgive us and we do hear you. It helps us very much when you pray for our souls to whomever you wish. It does not help us when so-called enlightened, wise people continually fill the shelves of major bookstores with such propaganda about suicides, as if God does not know you and what is in your heart and mind at the time of your passing. God does know, or as we call God on this side, the Source, knows all. You should have no fear of coming to God and speaking directly to him, because he already knows all there is to know about you.

You are more loved than you know or can even imagine. You are more accepted and wanted than you have ever dreamed. God will not abandon you or your soul regardless of the peril you allow yourself to become a part of. You will not be left and disregarded unless you choose to be left and disregarded, and there will still be attempts to bring you home. Each person who commits suicide is an individual case, and therefore, why would such a blanket statement be provided? We are talking about the supreme source of knowledge, wisdom, and enlightenment when we speak of God. What ego must exist to believe you can speak for God on Earth. I do not believe any human being can speak for God in terms of what occurs to the soul who crosses over by his or her own hand.

Life is the most precious gift and to squander it is one of the saddest, most horrific things I have ever witnessed. But it also may be prolific in the life changing events that occur to those left behind. It can open the way for important dialogue to take place between loved ones, cut through the superficial masks that are

Jim Morrison & Michael Hutchence

worn, and basically cause those left behind to ask themselves: How did he or she end up taking their own life? How did they get to the end of the road?

There is usually an incredible amount of guilt in those who are still on Earth. This may not be a terribly negative thing. Guilt has its place too, but of course, most of the time it's misplaced and highly inappropriate. If your guilt causes you to intervene more in the lives of your loved ones, try to really speak to them in such a manner they want to open up to you, then it has contributed to something more meaningful and constructive than what was initially thought. There comes a time for us all when we have to turn on the lights, but it's most important not to flip the switch until we are willing to see things as they truly are. When someone you know takes their own life, it's such a hard thing to believe or accept. In your shock and grief, you may choose not to believe it and think something else must have happened, because it's hard to admit that someone you cared for could be that selfish. It's hard to come to terms with the fact that someone could leave you behind. Or, perhaps, you turned a blind eye because of your own guilt. Maybe you don't believe you were there for them or you didn't spend time with them prior to the unspeakable act. Sometimes it's just too much to bear.

I lived in the dark for most of my last lifetime, and I did so because of the fear over what I might see. If you are brave enough to turn on the lights, be prepared to see it all. You may have to view someone you love who is making a terrible mess of their life or see how those you think have it all, are really not so happy or capable of surviving in the world. While it has been said the truth sets you free, are you ready for that freedom? I am now, but obviously it took a long, long time, and I had to leave many [that] I love behind. But I am here now, clear and filled with light.

I did not go to hell or end up in limbo (whatever that is). I am not stuck on the Earth as a ghost or rattling around in your attic or under your bed. There is a presumption it is much like a factory over here: car accidents will go this way, cancer victims go over there and suicides will go off somewhere else. There is no factory and each and every soul is rather complex. You have heard the expression "simple soul"? Well when you come to this side, you will see, there is no such thing. Each soul is truly complicated in

A TALE OF TWO BROTHERS

their own way, and there is no one standard place to go or thing to happen depending on how and why you crossed over. Suicides, as with all other souls on this side, are dealt with on an individual basis.

There are some suicides, like my own, that could not be stopped, unfortunately. There are others that can clearly have some sort of intervention. Many on Earth simply need someone to listen to them and really hear them. That sounds rather absurd and trite I must admit, and it's hard to sustain a conversation with someone who is constantly melancholy, full of self-pity or just plain depressed. Who wants to be around *that* all the time? But they need you and they need you to really listen, to really hear them as you may be the only one who does. To say something along the lines of "you're not trained" to help them and they need a psychiatrist or a magic pill to help them, is not what most potential suicides need. They need you, their family member or friend. They need to hear your voice, your words and your heart, not what a psychiatrist has to say. You never know. Perhaps you are the true joy in that person's life and maybe other family members or friends do not reach or lend themselves to the same aspects of their heart as you do. In many instances, you do have the power and ability to save another's life at a given time and place. But if you get too caught up in your own personal existence, too busy to be bothered, they may go and take their own life when you could've helped prevent it. As I have stated, this is not always possible, but there are many cases — too many — where a simple set of words, a phone call, the receipt of a letter, or a visit, may have stopped the train wreck.

There are some spiritualists and mediums who do very important work explaining the truth of suicides. One is a woman named Lysa Mateu who wrote a very informative book about suicides called "Conversations with the Spirit World." There are other good books on this controversial topic, but when an author tries to give you absolutes of what takes place on this side, instead of just presenting the information they were given, I would have to suggest to you someone on Earth is not going to be given all the answers, knowledge or wisdom that exists on this side. You simply could not download or process it all and live your day to day earthly existence. You are on Earth to have the life you are in

Jim Morrison & Michael Hutchence

now and live it to the fullest, but it's certainly alright to question and wonder what goes on after your time in the body you now occupy is over and to invest a considerable amount of time in the soul, and in meditation.

Meditation can bring great clarity to your life and all you need is five or 10 free minutes at a time. You don't have to be in the lotus position, chanting or burning incense. Many do pray and feel that is adequate, because in praying you are talking to God. I am not here to condemn this by any means but what sort of relationship can it be when you do all the talking? If you had a friend who called you when they felt like it, just rattled on about their problems and asked you for favors left and right, and never once wanted to hear what you have to say, you would hardly call that a friend, more of a nuisance. Now you say that you are not a nuisance to God, that may be true since he loves you beyond your comprehension, but why is it you believe he doesn't want to have a two-way conversation with you? Did you ever contemplate he may want to speak to you directly? He can do so in meditation.

The human being is so wired with caffeine, nicotine, sugar, adrenaline, and sometimes testosterone, that meditation may be difficult at first. It's hard for people to find that quiet 10 minutes of peace and isolation in their day, but here I urge you to search for it. You need that time to hear the voice of God, and if you don't believe in God, then hear your own inner voice, your intuition or conscience. The noise of the world shuts out the voice of God, and all human beings need to become better listeners. I wish I had been a much better listener in my last life.

If you want to have a two-way conversation with God, you will. It may come to you in the most interesting and strange ways, but ask him and you shall be in direct communication with the one who created you and cares for you more than anything you have been told or have seen in your earthly existence. God does not force himself on you, he is too loving for that. If it is the connection with him you are seeking: acceptance, true love, truth and fulfillment, I would hope you will try conversing with God through meditation. He will help you open a large treasure chest that is contained right within your soul, and it's such a thing that I am doubtful many on Earth have seen. Most on Earth don't have the time, after all, it's not an IPOD, an MP3 player or the newest cell phone that does everything but style your hair. It *is* the kind of love you have never seen or felt, or even understand, but the feelings it will give you and the places it will take you, are worth the price of admission...and that price is only time and your willingness to ask to speak to the Source of all there is.

I realize that most of the fundamentalists and others who consider themselves "Christians" will condemn the work we are doing here and that deeply saddens me. I am not here to debate the Bible, especially since in my last life, I was not a reader, so I must tread lightly here. I would offer this suggestion, however, to Bible readers. Search through your Bible for "divination" and you will find it is used all through the good book. You can of course, take out selective scriptures to condemn what I will call the intuitive arts, but isn't the Bible a channeled work? St. Paul called it "the gift of prophecy" to describe how the human authors channeled the Bible. When God speaks through the prophets in the Bible, is that not channeling?

There are plenty of passages in Isaiah, Hosea, Deuteronomy, and Numbers, to name a few, that support divination. I am not here to upset the apple cart. After all, many believe channeling is a sin or it's Satan's work, but I am doubtful those who are not open minded are even reading this. But for those of you who are, even western religions acknowledge the soul as being the very essence of who you are and contend the soul goes on after it exits the human body. If the soul is who you really are, and you are to go onto heaven, hell, purgatory, limbo or haunt someone in their attic, it only stands to reason that you are alive and you are a creation of God. So should you not be honored or acknowledged, instead of being considered something horrifying or something that is sinful to communicate with?

Do you assume when you leave your human body that you no longer love your family, friends, pets or certain parts of your previous life? What do you think happens, that you forget about your children, parents, sisters, brothers, husband, wife, lovers or close friends? There are terrible superstitions about communicating with those who are no longer in a human body, and we are called the "dead." I assure you, there is nothing "dead" about us, for we are more alive than we ever were on Earth. We are in a pure energy form, as you will be when you leave your human body. So we can't mow the lawn for you anymore or take out the trash, is that all it's about? I didn't really do those things while I was on Earth anyway. When we cross over, our regrets, remorse and sadness are with us, it's not all peaches and cream on this side. So, it's a beautiful thing when we can communicate to those we left behind and let them know we are alright and we love them. For a grieving parent, or a grieving husband, wife or lover, to make contact with their loved one, or even a child to make contact with their parent on the other side, can be one of the most healing experiences imaginable.

Most in human bodies do not live as if it *is* possibly their last day on Earth and many things are left unsaid and unexpressed. There is a very popular thing circulating around that has actually been around for a long time known as the "Universal Law of Attraction." I am here to tell you, "The Secret" *is* to live each day as if it is, indeed, your last on Earth. Remember to tell those you care about how much they mean to you, and to give them a hug or a kiss when you leave their presence. You never know when it will be the final time you have this chance. Remember to notice the sunset, just take a moment and take a good look at the beautiful stars in the sky or the sounds of the birds and the beauty of the world you are so fortunate to be a part of, for it will not last. You are in a temporary state in your human body and all the medical science in the world cannot prevent a car accident or other such things that occur that can end it all in a flash.

Why is it only appropriate for you to communicate with others in human bodies and considered evil to speak to us who are now free from the trap of human flesh? Evil is indeed housed and quite active in certain individuals walking around you on Earth in human form each and every day, and I would truly fear others on Earth before I would fear those of us on this side. We don't have child molesters or murderers here, only former ones who walked the Earth. This does not mean that all souls are evolved, healed or even good for those on Earth to communicate with, but in comparison to the inherent evil that many walk around with on Earth, it's very simply night and day. This side is the daylight and many on Earth, are the dark, dark night. Is your mother now evil or not want to be around you and watch over you now that she is on this side and free from her sickly human body? I am surprised that someone who believes the soul goes on after the human body stops working, will suggest this communication is somehow inappropriate, sinful or perhaps even Satanic. I suggest you examine where and when these concepts came into being? You may be quite surprised. For these concepts are not of God, but they are of man.

Those who knew me will attest to the fact I was not much of a believer in the "life after death" stuff . Most of the time, I was quite the skeptic. Skepticism is healthy. There were other areas of my life in which I was so much more easily influenced, so I encourage healthy skepticism throughout your entire existence. If it keeps you from being duped, as I was in some areas, it's a very righteous thing. The psychic world unfortunately, is not full of ethical or caring people — far from it. Many of us on this side are simply disgusted by the charlatans, but not all of them are fakes. Some actually have some sort of gift, but either don't work at it or care at all about its purity or clarity. When the ego enters any type of spiritual work, the ceases to be spiritual, as the purity is removed. The psychic arena, and I use the word arena because a good portion of it is as fake as a wrestling show, is full of complete low-life frauds who are in it for their own ego, fame and greed. I can assure you, the intention of the person with the spiritual gifts is as important as the gift itself. I would hope that those people who are open to trying to communicate with a loved one, by means of a channel or medium, ask for specific validations. Do not accept that your lovely Grandmother is standing behind you or that you had a relative once with a name that started with a "J" who is holding their chest to your right side. Do be somewhat skeptical while maintaining an openness to the possibility without being duped. I know that sounds rather confusing and some readings are rather contrived that you see on television, therefore, be cautious. I suggest you go to a medium or channel without expectations, but if you are fortunate enough to get some rather specific form of validation, then consider the possibility that your loved ones continue on as does their love for you. The veil between the two worlds is getting thinner and thinner, and I am not at all encouraging someone to hold a séance to try and bring one of us in or any other entity or spirit from this side. I suggest great caution because many, many on this side want to communicate with someone. Some will seize the opportunity to be heard or seen, and unfortunately, it may not be who you requested. Channeling is a fine art, and it has to be done with the right intention and in a clear and pure way to be effective. A group of college students pulling out the old Ouija board and wishing to speak to Kurt Cobain or someone like that, is not the best idea. Kurt will not waste his energy coming in, and this is not to put a damper on your party, but he has better things to do. You may actually pick up a ghost instead, a spirit that is less than evolved and stuck, if you will, clinging to the Earth out of confusion and fear. You must be careful and most of all, sincere.

I wish to now dispel the notion that we are far, far away from Earth. We are in a dimension and vibration very close to where you are, and you can call it heaven if you wish, but it's not up in the clouds. With the thinning veil, more and more people on Earth are hearing us, seeing us and sensing us. Do you think everyone is mentally ill who has claimed to have had contact with spirits? Of course not. We are involved in your lives, as we were when we were on Earth and maybe even more so, because now we don't have day to day concerns which formerly occupied us. Of course, we can see things more clearly. "Involved" does not mean we will interfere. There are certain laws that prohibit that, and you are on Earth to have your experiences, learn your lessons and use your free will. We won't tamper with that, but we are still your friends, your loved ones, your brother, your father, your son...

There are many untruths that have been put out there who are supposedly from the spirit world. One of these myths I wish to address is that we are all present at our funerals and cannot leave the Earth until this has been done. It's complete nonsense, and, in fact, some spirits choose to watch their funerals and others simply do not, as they cannot handle the heaviness of the event.

I personally witnessed only part of my own farewell because it was a bit too much for me and my regrets were so huge, and I could not sustain the energy to watch my funeral in its entirety. The funeral is a lovely thing, all the prayers and tributes and so on, but other than the prayers, it's not held for the spirit who has ascended. It's for those who are left behind to accept the hardship and to help them cope. The funeral my parents had to unfortunately hold for me was highly criticized because it was quite religious, and those who knew me, simply didn't feel it was my cup of tea. Well truthfully, it was to comfort the family I left behind, so what I saw of it was quite beautiful and nothing is inappropriate in what a family wishes as a send-off.

The energy in a funeral home or cemetery is not that of the deceased, but often of the heavy sadness and sickness of the heart of the mourners still on Earth. All that energy in those places, seven days a week, is very intense, so what do you think you are going to feel when you visit such a place? Unless you are truly one who can seal in your energy, you will more than likely be affected beyond your own grief for your loved one.

We hurt on this side when you sit and cry and tell us you miss us. It really is difficult as we are powerless to do anything about it, but it means a great deal when you tell us you love us and that we are not forgotten. This does not mean I suggest sitting around and staring at our pictures and pining for us to the point it interrupts or shuts down your earthly existence. Compared to eternity, your Earth life is short, very short, so live each moment with the zest of your soul. When you send us energy, light and love on this side, it helps us heal as we basically collect the light within. Your condition on this side can be greatly improved, as many of us ascend in substantial turmoil due to the condition of our soul at the time we exit our bodies, due to how we left things on Earth and the regrets, and the sadness that plagues us involving those we left behind. As beautiful as it is to come to a realm that if you remembered being on this side, you would simply never want to come back to Earth.

We all ascend to this side in various conditions of the soul and will require some form, from minimal to vast amounts of healing. Pray for the healing of those you love on this side, and remember, there is no *time* here. As hard as that is for you to imagine, do not feel as though so many years have gone by that you don't need to pray for anyone anymore. Your prayers will help the souls of the so-called departed at any time, and sending your love and light is the most beautiful gift. Perhaps one day when you are here, others on Earth will do the same for you.

A question many wonder is: Who's right? Jesus? Buddha? Mohammed? Atheists? Agnostics? Well, if I answer, there is no absolute right or wrong, I may very well be condemned here. But

Jim Morrison & Michael Hutchence

in truth, there are just many different paths that lead to the same thing. The Source you call God and the true path is that of enlightenment, and fortunately, you can pick up that path from many different roads. It's all what works for you, not for your friend or neighbor, but what rings true and resonates in your own heart and soul. If you seek, you will find, as with anything in life. So if you seek spiritual wisdom and enlightenment, I am assured you will be guided to it.

An interesting phenomenon on Earth has been occurring throughout time. It's about those who are clearly mislead from enlightenment, and yet hide behind a religion of a holy book of sorts, claim they have found the way, and seem quite dedicated to the system they have learned which they believe involves the true God, or the real Source. God did not inspire anyone to fly a plane into the World Trade Center in New York City on the 11th day of September, in the linear year of 2001. God does not take the lives of children from diseases, cause your child to be molested, or cause any of the bad things you mention out loud to occur. You are living on a planet with complete and total free will, and you must find your own path. The horrid experiences of life that seem to break you, truly do make you a better, stronger man or woman.

I should know something about this because I would've emerged from my temporary insanity with amazing strength and gratitude for my life. I think the point is to stay clear in the mind, even at times of very wavering faith and hope. Strength is an up and down thing in life, no one can always be strong. But true strength is really a learned attribute, and the trials and tribulations you must go through will pave the way for inner fortitude and enable you to grasp — wisdom, meaning God's wisdom, which is not describable in a book. You are making your way in a world full of millions of others with free will, so what shall you do with it — your life, that is? Will you stay clear and focused and live each day as if it is your last chance to see the world in your human body? Or will you waste it, get wasted and try to shut the world out because it's all too hard? Will you lose your mind like I did or will you recognize who you really are, before it's too late?

Planetary Illusions

Walking through the sands of time
over decaying beaches
This was paradise once before
but man is a good user, not healer anymore

Making my peace in a
place I no longer recognize
Hong Kong looks like every place else,
it's all commercialized

Progress they call it,
when it's really the homogenization
of the world, it's more of the same,
and less of true nature, the conglomeration game

The path of least resistance
is the one you travel down
You've allowed your natural habitat
to lose character and tranquility, What ever happened to sacred ground?

It all runs the same, the traffic,
the same stores, the same coffee,
Your debit card works almost everywhere
How could you live without your cell phone,
Would you even dare?

You feel the need to be wireless in a world
where you have so many chords,
The energy vampires drain you
and your run of the mill money whores

Jim Morrison & Michael Hutchence

It's game day, you're ready to tailgate
with your beer and your friends?
But it's not really your team,
you didn't pick them,
a corporation owns them,
The brainwashing never ends

The soldiers are across the world,
eating bugs and dirt,
But you seem much more
concerned with how much your eBay stuff is worth.

For living in such a big planet,
You seem locked in your own little bubble
You'd rather send an email
because interpersonal communication skills are too much
trouble

You're stressed, better get a script for sleeping pills
and wake-up and grab your double shot of
espresso, you've overpaid for, have you had your fill?
Is this all becoming a dreadful bore?
Why watch a reality show on the tellie?
Shouldn't you be living it instead?
Starve on an island or lock yourself
in a house of strangers, there is
no real danger, you'll become
a celebrity, that's where all your problems
will really start, make sure above all,
the plastic life you live doesn't break your
heart, for you may never be able
to mend it, and like me, you may
even end it!

—*channeled from Michael Hutchence*

CHAPTER 15
They were lying through their teeth...

Man's mind is so formed that it is far more susceptible to falsehood than to truth.

—*Desiderius Erasmus* (1466-1536) Dutch humanist

Jim Morrison & Michael Hutchence

A TALE OF TWO BROTHERS

The last song I ever recorded was called "Possibilities," and it is featured on my solo album released a few years after my death. It's the song I most want to leave the world with, because lyrically, it says it all and captures my essence. I did sing other songs before I crossed over in rehearsal but "Possibilities" was the last song I recorded, and I believe that was how it was meant to be. Listen to my last song, my final words are left behind for you.

You may have heard, the famous magician known as Harry Houdini lost his Mother, whom he was extremely close to, and engaged in a search to contact her on the other side. Keep in mind, Houdini believed wholeheartedly such communication was, in fact, possible. Unfortunately, Houdini found out the truth, that many of the so-called spiritualists or mediums were using old carnival tricks or playing parlor games and were not connecting to the other side. He exposed many fraudulent psychics of his time, and of course, grew very pessimistic about psychic work and rightfully so.

Harry Houdini actually did a great service to the world and to those in grief wanting desperately to connect to their loved ones on this side. I, however, would like to say, the communication is not impossible or even improbable. Your loved ones may be communicating to you with certain signs or symbols, and they do try to come through. It's not always easy, and they do not come to you to interfere with your free will or life decisions.

You may notice more interesting things occurring around a birthday, an anniversary, or a holiday of some sort, because many times, loved ones will continue to come around you during these events. You may find things move in your house, seemingly small objects you are sure you put in one place, which turn up somewhere else entirely. They are not haunting you. Don't worry. They are, in fact, using their energy and doing what they can to

Jim Morrison & Michael Hutchence

communicate with you. Loose change laying around out of nowhere is often the sign that a loved one has shown up.

Our energy works very well via electricity, so when strange and unexplainable electrical occurrences happen where you live, even something like the lights flickering on and off a few times, you may be encountering a loved one from the other side. Fragrances are ways loved ones also show-up. You may smell a fragrance out of the blue and it may be one you identify with your dearly departed.

Most of us on this side are not here to haunt you or anybody else. We stay around our loved ones, as I stay around my daughter and visit other relatives from time to time. Love never dies, we never die, and parents do not abandon their children on Earth.

I realize there are those who are actively seeking communication from a loved one and can't seem to receive it. I want to say, it's an individual choice whether or not to communicate with those on Earth, and I can't explain why some make the choice to do so and others do not. Many are involved in extreme methods of healing on this side and energetically, the communication can be very, very hard. Many make the transition to this side slower than others. When one is in transition, of course, the communication is harder to achieve.

Many times, your loved ones are around you sending us subtle signs and symbols, and yet, you fail to recognize them. Energetically, it takes quite a bit just to do that, so when you feel you receive a sign from a loved one, please acknowledge it and thank them. We like to feel we are not being ignored.

We do come back to help you in your grieving state, and it's hard for me to tell you how many times I have come across someone on this side looking in on their loved one who is screaming and crying in pain. It's very hard to reach you when you are so emotional. It seems your intuitive mind really does cut off, but please do not believe you have been abandoned, because you haven't. Many on this side would love for you to find a good psychic or medium and connect to them, but I have to say, unfortunately, just as during the time of Harry Houdini, there are more charlatans than genuine mediums walking the Earth.

Those who are gifted should be very grateful for the gifts they have been blessed with and work very, very hard to develop those gifts, because in the matters of spirituality, you never really graduate from school. You can never be at a level where you believe you can't go any further with your gifts or go deeper. The channel I am using will not be hanging a shingle out to give readings, because she has no real interest in it. She could do it if she wants to, but she has chosen to do other things with her gifts. She was born at a higher vibration but must continue to work to raise her vibration to hear us clearly. If she is having a day full of emotions, she must detach from those earthly things or else she cannot accurately channel us.

Psychics and mediums are human too. There are days or even whole sections of time when they should not give readings. If they are in a marriage or relationship that is on the rocks, if they are having a difficult time with a child, when serious problems occur, or when out of the ordinary annoyances are put on their plate, they should not be reading for you. Separating human emotions from spiritual work is very difficult for most people. When major problems or tragedies befall even the most gifted, they should not attempt to channel or do their spiritual work, and should, in fact, take a time out.

A psychic or medium must also work off your energy as they bring the loved one in, because the loved one is showing up for you and even *in* your aura to some extent. So if your energy is very low or scattered, achieving a good connection with a loved one through a psychic medium can be very tricky.

Communicating to you from here is a delicate process. Each psychic and medium receives his or her information in different ways. My channel can hear me speak to her in the same speaking voice I employed on Earth, but of course, not everyone hears me like that. They often hear me in their own voice. My channel has this gift because she can go so deep into a trance. Not everyone can achieve this, but others who can, simply don't try in many cases. I call them surface psychics or those who scratch just below the surface. The deeper you go in spiritual work, the more you will receive. Look at Edgar Cayce and the absolutely astonishing information he received deep in trance. He could've used his gifts for surface work or to scratch the surface, but he chose to go into this deep, deep state, and in doing so, he opened himself up to some of the most incredible information from the other side ever made available to the public.

When my channel first heard my voice and saw me, she did not believe for one second she was genuinely communicating with me, because she had never heard me speak, she had only heard me sing. She said she thought I was Australian. Well then, why did I sound like I had a British accent gone bad? That is what she asked, and I told her to listen to an interview I had given. Of course, when she heard my voice on it, the poor girl almost collapsed, as the voice was the same. I have demonstrated to her in numerous ways that this communication is genuine and anyone who is really who they say they are around you, will have no problems whatsoever continually giving you various sorts of validations. Some of us are better at it than others, but you will receive confirmations that will be hard for you to dispute. I also appeared to this channel with a small gap in between my front teeth, and she certainly did not believe she really had me, Michael Hutchence coming through to her until I had her watch early videos of INXS and she saw the gap there. I also came through to her with long, blonde streaked hair, and she noticed at the end of my life, my hair was quite dark actually. I have informed her we will often appear to those on Earth, as we were in our prime. I did not like the person I was with the dark hair that you can clearly see in the "Elegantly Wasted" video. I was not the same person I had been years earlier and there is one particular picture of myself taken on a balcony in Paris, I truly dislike, as I can look into the eyes of *that* man and see absolutely no soul spark whatsoever.

Do not be surprised if you have a dream of a loved one that doesn't exactly seem like a dream and they do not appear to you as they were at the time of their crossing, but perhaps in earlier years when they were happier or healthier or what they felt was, in fact, their prime. Loved ones can work better with you in the dream state than when you are awake.

You don't have to go visit the grave of your loved one to communicate with them, and I would suggest that's not a great place anyway. There is a ton of heavy, remorseful and incredibly sad energy in those places from all the mourners who are there daily. Sometimes that heavy energy lingers and the communication works from both sides — this side and your side —

A TALE OF TWO BROTHERS

so if you want true spirit communication then make it easier for your loved one to emerge.

Clutter in houses makes it even more difficult for energy to flow through the space, and therefore, more difficult for us to come through. If you want to hear from a loved one then clean house and remove the clutter.

So what about Ouija boards, tarot cards, crystal balls and so on? A true psychic or medium does not need to rely on "divination tools," as they are called. I am not suggesting everyone who uses tools is not gifted, but these tools can become crutches to the spiritually blessed ones. They are used sometimes as gimmicks, because the public wishes to have their cards read. The Ouija board is not a tool of the devil but it's not a game either along the lines of Monopoly™ or Clue™, and should not be marketed as one. Its origins come from the nineteenth century where séances were held. It was believed that codes were being given from the other side, so this talking board was developed to make it easier. You can move the pointer around the board with your own energy sometimes, but if you do not invoke protection from your spirit guides and others, such as the Archangel Michael or whomever you believe in on the other side, and specifically request that no one comes through but your deceased loved one, you could be picking up so many different entities. It is actually frightening.

I do not choose to communicate by Ouija board and Jim Morrison absolutely does not communicate by that board either. Why would we? We have a wonderfully clear channel and our communication skills have developed. We can speak to those mediums around our channel to verify things for her, as she is such a skeptic.

If I gave you a violin or a flute, would you be able to pick it up and start playing songs? Of course not. You would need practice, dedication and discipline, and that is what is required when you are one with psychic gifts or even to communicate effectively with God, Jesus or Buddha. There are people out on the street or even on the internet you would not invite into your home, so why would you want to invite in all these energies, entities and spirits? Like on Earth, there are many un-evolved souls here. I will assure you, many of you would not want around you, those we term "lower energies." I would caution you about opening the door without being very, very careful. I would also suggest that anyone seeking any kind of spirit communication, learn to communicate with God first. I mean directly with God, and be open to the divine realm that includes Jesus, Buddha and the Archangels. You should truly master that before engaging in contact with those of us who have crossed over. Protect yourself, because any lower energies are waiting for the chance to come in to those who are not very developed or protected.

If you believe you have spoken to me or to Jim Morrison via the Ouija board, I want to make this abundantly clear, you certainly have not. There is a young male spirit on this side who led a very, very troubled life, and there is a female singer on Earth who was popular in the '80s when I was, who has held a séance and tried to bring the troubled young male spirit in. The world knows this troubled soul as Sid Vicious, but on this side, he is simply John.

Sid Vicious (John) was renowned for cultivating the absolute most recognizable image in punk music (for the short time he was on Earth) as a member of the infamous "Sex Pistols." He does not choose to come through in a séance for entertainment and some have called on him. But he has, it seems, decided he will give his story to my channel and I have introduced him to her. He is still quite troubled on this side but is working toward healing. He would prefer to speak to someone who is not bringing him in as entertainment or a game, and who can hear his words clearly. He is quite fired up and has many things he would like to address. I can't say I liked this bloke very much upon meeting him on this side, but I have come to understand the torment of his soul. He was very concerned about the "Sex Pistols" being recognized in the Rock 'n' Roll Hall of Fame and, initially, the members of his former band not accepting the tribute. He certainly wants to be remembered as the one who not only personified the punk look but also lived it, as others could only look the part.

Sid, a.k.a. John is not an easy one to channel, and I think it's important to state that not all of your loved ones will be accommodating to the whole channeling process. It may, in fact, take you quite a while to hear from them, but don't give up or lose hope, because most of the time they want to see you get on with your life and thrive in the time you have left. Most of them will still wish to connect to you, but not in a harmful or disruptive way — or to scare you, but in a loving and beautiful way.

Tarot cards are actually from the Tree of Life in Kabbalah, and I have certainly wondered why so many using them are not aware of their true origins. The Tarot should be used in conjunction with Kabbalah and numerology to give more clarity. Understanding the true nature of the tarot will help the practitioner to use it more wisely.

A crystal ball can be used in the ancient art of scrying, and I want to caution that in most cases, scrying takes incredible amounts of time to develop and tremendous focus. If you can't get into a deep meditation, it's hard to develop this amazing gift. I am not here to tell people what to do or not to do, but be weary of those utilizing divination tools and ask why they are using them. Could they read for you without these crutches? How general is the information they give you? Is it just like reading a horoscope in the newspaper about your lucky number or that you will receive a letter today? If so, you have probably come across a charlatan, not someone with genuine gifts using them for the greater good.

Harry Houdini is an interesting case, because he actually had the ability to personally receive messages from his mother on the other side through automatic writing, for example. He didn't realize this, and his search to connect to her seemed futile, but she was right there with him all along. He didn't need to try and get a third party to speak to her — he could've done it himself.

There are others who say I have come to them and wanted help or some nonsense, or even that I told them I died in a sex orgy gone awry, but they are lying through their teeth. It's interesting from this side how I have been lied about so much since I left Earth, and the charlatans in the psychic industry continue to do so. Jim Morrison used to laugh about this — how one television psychic felt she connected to him and how he was about to reincarnate into a middle eastern woman. This was supposedly done at a place in which he used to spend time. Well, Jim would not come through to a television psychic, and I wouldn't either, unless it was all part of our plan to get our authentic messages out. We are not here to help someone's ratings. Why would we use our energy in such a way?

Jim Morrison & Michael Hutchence

We are here to tell the world what we did wrong in the hopes that it will help someone else and make you think before you end up like us. We are not here to show-up at our old dwellings. Jim doesn't go to California, I assure you. He has been there so little since I have known him on this side. I don't go to many places on earth unless my daughter or other loved ones are there. We are not here to show up like Our Lady of Guadalupe and convert the masses. We are doing a karmic cleansing with this channeling and attempting to show what we could not on Earth, but perhaps we should've. I can't prove to you this is the truth and others have lied about me, but it doesn't really take much to see all the possibilities and to know nothing is what is seems.

"False words are not only evil in themselves, but they infect the soul with evil."

—*Plato, Dialogues,* Phaedo

CHAPTER 16

Get on the Inside

"Are we to paint what's on the face, what's inside the face, or what's behind it?"

—*Pablo Piccaso*

Jim Morrison & Michael Hutchence

There are those of you reading this book who are actual practicing psychics or mediums. There are those who are interested in developing your own spiritual gifts, for which I applaud you, because it really does take so much patience and discipline. I am here to suggest three books each of you should consider reading, because I believe they will help to put you in touch with truth and your own spiritual experiences more than any other books will do at this time on Earth.

I am fairly surprised and shocked that more practitioners of the metaphysical arts do not chose to read these particular books or pass them along to their colleagues, friends and clients. The first one I wish to share with you was actually written in 1877. It is called "Isis Unveiled," by Madame (H.P.) Blavatsky. There simply has not been a book since this one written so long ago in Earth time, that truly explains spiritualism and how religion and science correspond in very specific and real terms. Many credit Madame Blavatsky with originating the "New Age" movement, and I would prefer to say that since "New Age" is such a broad and overly inclusive term, she was indeed before her time and was very fortunate to have been given such truths and wisdom that she shared with the world. I believe that anyone who reads these two very impressive volumes will gain so much insight and knowledge not only of spiritualism in general, but of their own personal journey. It's absolutely worth your time and energy.

There has been much written about Madame Blavatsky and much speculated as well, and regardless of what is true and what is fictional about her or her life, there is no doubt "Isis Unveiled" is a gift given to the world, more specifically to you, to enrich your life.

The second book I would like to suggest to those of you wishing to know more about the spiritual realms or as I call it, the truth, is called "Jesus and the Lost Goddess: The Secret Teachings of the Original Christians," by Timothy Freke and Peter Gandy. This book was originally published in 2001, and it's a travesty that it didn't make more of a noise than it did. Those who are fascinated with things such as "The Da Vinci Code" would be far better served reading this book, which is one of the few to truly uncover many ancient and significant truths.

I do not suggest this book to condemn any particular religion or exalt another. As Madame Blavatsky said, "There is truth in all religions." But "Jesus and the Lost Goddess: The Secret Teachings of the Original Christians," will explain many of the principles that the Earth is sorely lacking and that need to be uncovered as the world progressively gets worse in terms of its spiritual condition. We can argue about the human condition but it's truly the spiritual condition, that is in rapid and horrific decay. You would be amazed at the number of celestial beings circling the Earth trying to assist at this delicate time on your planet. These authors have really hit on many important concepts and of all the books available to you, I cannot emphasize how important it would be to one's spiritual quest to get your hands on this one. These men have written other books, but it is this one that I truly recommend.

My third book suggestion is very special to me. It's called "Secrets of a Soul: Padre Pio's Letters to his Spiritual Directors," by Elvira G. DiFabio. It has become my honor to come to know this great mystic, healer and teacher on this side — the most wonderful Padre Pio. He is a saint in the purest sense. I would like to explain to all of you that the magnificent Padre Pio is here for each of you, despite your religious backgrounds or lack thereof. He cares for all of you, and if your intention is sincere, he will aid you in the darkest times. He is wonderful to learn from at any time.

His letters allow you to come into his heart. You will see the true meaning of the word "love" in these letters, which many of you have not really yet come to understand. His letters are priceless and so very important, that I pray and hope each of you reading this embraces them. Padre is one of the greatest mystics that ever lived, and yet each of you will easily be able to relate to his dark nights and struggles. If you want to be touched by God by reading a book, it would be this one with the letters of Padre. I believe all practicing psychics and mediums should become students of this magnificent mystic, healer, ascended master, saint and teacher.

I suggest these three books to anyone ready to take the journey of spiritualism or to enrich the journey of those who have already begun. The journey never ends — not even for the most seasoned psychic or medium.

There is a great deal of material available pertaining to metaphysical and esoteric studies, but I would suggest that you are careful about what you buy into. Not everything out there is from the Divine or God. Much of it is from a place of questionable intentions.

I do realize there is a huge belief in "abundance" in the spiritual world that suggests it is desirable to work to create wealth and material goods in accordance with spiritual work. I realize I led a rather hedonistic lifestyle, so this is quite likely to come off as the pot calling the kettle black. However, I've come to realize that decadence in most cases causes the decay of the soul.

I am not suggesting that soaking in your hot tub with a nice glass of wine after a long day is not deserved, or a luxurious vacation once every few years is something of which you are not worthy. I am here to suggest that the more spiritual one becomes, the less he or she is concerned with material possessions. The greatest teachers I have come to know on this side lead very frugal and humble lives, and there is something to be said of that. Does it make you a better person to drive that expensive Italian sports car or wear those designer rags, or does it simply make you look better? If it's all about how you look, I would suggest you are in some form of soul decay. Most of you in a physical body wish to look attractive, as it makes you feel better about yourself and causes you to more readily face the world with a smile on your face, but I strive in these writings to suggest you are in a temporary state in this your life on Earth. You will spend eternity with your soul, and the work you do on it now, on the inside, will pay off better than your new designer shoes or highly anticipated nose job.

There are those cultivating wealth to aid others on the planet, and I applaud you as I wish I had done more of that. But I would like to leave this section with this thought: It is sometimes the ones who lead a simple and quiet existence who bring more to the lives of others than those who are loud, kicking and screaming to be in the public eye. When your world revolves around "me, me, me," it's very shallow and not truly big enough to accommodate caring about others. Self-centered is not God-centered. I share with you what I have learned about myself, hoping that you will wake up much sooner than I did.

Purposeful

Is each small thing that happens meaningless
or is nothing without purpose?
Are there accidents? Coincidences?
Occurrences one can hardly dismiss
or explain that are not a Godsend or a sign of some sort?

Is the dawn purposeful if you sleep through the sunrise?
Is your sleep healing, or disruptive and disturbing?
Is there a purpose when dreams are upsetting
and you awaken in fear as opposed to peacefully?

Is the work that you do hard, or semi-challenging?
Above all, is it purposeful?
Does it fill your bank account or make the world a better place?
How do you contribute to the entire scenery,
beyond a few dollars to UNICEF?
What are you giving besides dollars you don't miss?

Because the world has beauty has it ceased to need more beauty
implemented by your very hands?
Well then, what can you do, you're one person and you have bills
to pay and not enough hours in the day?
I suppose Gandhi was one person and so was

A TALE OF TWO BROTHERS

Mother Teresa, they had bills to pay
and only so many hours in the day.
Somehow they pulled out a purposeful life.
They could've chosen to live with more luxuries, but the
luxuries in the absence of others having food, shelter, clean water
and safety do not seem to be luxuries at all.

Are your silly indulgences there to compensate
for what is lacking inside of you?
So what is purposeful?
Perhaps a purposeful life is filling what lacks inside of you
by giving to others?
What you don't have amazingly
you can find to give someone else.
Isn't that the true definition of magick?

—channeled from Michael Hutchence

"Our prime purpose in this life is to help others. And if you can't help them, at least don't hurt them"

—Dalai Lama

Jim Morrison & Michael Hutchence

CHAPTER 17

All You Got Is This Moment...

"We are at a crossroads in human history. Never before has there been a moment so simultaneously perilous and promising. We are the first species to have taken evolution into our own hands."

—*Carl Sagan*

Jim Morrison & Michael Hutchence

A TALE OF TWO BROTHERS

In my last days I was not yet on the medicines that would've helped me with my newly discovered, life threatening condition. I was about to go on those drugs very shortly and hope for the best.

I was on Keflex®, which is an antibiotic, for about a month and many other drugs, painkillers, Prozac®, and something for herpes simplex. My immune system was already crashing. Mixing antibiotics, Prozac®, cocaine, Valium®, and alcohol, are a sure way to lose track of who you are, and what is really going on around you and what isn't! I can assure you here and now, I would not have taken my life minus the drugs and alcohol. Despite a truly large palette of problems and concerns, my brain waves would not have been zigzagging that day.

I wanted to see my daughter grow up. I wanted to get into film and live at least part of the year in L.A. I had dreams, I had desires, but I allowed drugs and alcohol to make it so I could not see my way past anything. I saw no way out, no happy ending, and most of all, no truth in the people in my life.

When I came to this side and figured out what had taken place, perhaps I thought I would be damned for all time. It's important I convey this now, God is absolutely merciful, loving and he knows all. I certainly wasted a very precious gift, and if you are truly connected to God (the true Source), this won't enter into your stratosphere of thinking. Drugs and alcohol numb the connection so much. I suggest you seek clarity, as it will turn on your natural compass, your own personal GPS, and you will never, ever get as lost as I did. Stay connected, you are loved and you are on Earth for a purpose, your soul's purpose. You are given this amazing opportunity to impact so many, please don't waste it as I did. You cannot live this life you have now over, and it will never be the same. Do it right now, to the best of your ability, clearly thinking while you can and you will return home, minus any regrets. A big part of my past life were the women I was fortunate enough to be involved with. I was with some of the most dazzling, beautiful women the world has known. Women gave me both my greatest joy in life and my greatest pain. They were my yin and yang.

I was very weary of marriage, and due to my family history, who could blame me? My parents' divorce and the custody of the kids were always such a mess. It scared the hell out of me, and of course, once I became involved with Paula, I had to face my fears head on. I do wish to state, categorically, Paula did desire a marriage for us, but this was not at all in my plans at any time. It was *her* fantasy, certainly not *my* reality.

I feel my relationships with my former loves are beautiful, private and sacred. I will not speak ill of any of them, because they each gave me their best and I tried in my own way to do the same. I send them each love, light and most of all my deepest gratitude for allowing me to share my life with them. They put up with so much while involved with the consummate rock star. I love them all and cherish our time together for eternity.

I was involved in one particular relationship that brought me to a low level emotionally and mentally, and therefore, spiritually. I will not name names, because the woman I was involved with was a lovely person, but the combination of the two of us was, in fact, a very draining one. I began to fall into a deep depression during this relationship.

To the outside world, I had it all, but it's not about who's a good person or a bad person. It's actually about good and bad combinations of people. Do you think you came to Earth so you could be with someone you don't enjoy being with a good deal of the time? To the contrary, I assure you God wants you to enjoy your Earth life, but you must make your free will choices.

I was a person who hated being alone, because I would become restless. I couldn't sleep, and I would become very, very depressed, so I needed to have people around me at all times. From someone who felt being alone was the end of the world, I say to you, learn to be comfortable and happy in your own company, which means, learn to love yourself. Loneliness is a complete and total illusion.

A TALE OF TWO BROTHERS

You cannot be lonely if you know and love yourself. Not everyone should constantly be in a relationship, because if you have not acquired a deep and complete love of self, you have no right to be involved with anyone. You are not coming into the relationship in the purest state you can be in, and therefore, you are offering them a person who is not fulfilled or even comfortable with who they are. What is it you expect to get back when you come into a relationship in this condition?

If you are in a relationship with a partner who is trying to control you and/or monitor you, this is so damaging. I suggest you seriously think about exiting this situation. For healing to take place of either or both parties, you have to remove yourself from the relationship. So much depression arises from bad relationships. I want to stress, I am not suggesting everyone seek a divorce or run out on their children and families, but I would suggest it generally doesn't get any better unless you remove yourself from the relationship and seek intensive, individual counseling of a spiritual nature. You can't change the other person, you can't fix them, but you can change and in many ways, fix yourself.

You must heal yourself before you can heal a relationship, and much of the time, after you truly choose to heal yourself, you will choose not to return to a relationship that is somewhat or generally unhealthy and unhappy. It will no longer serve a purpose in your life or your path.

I know when children are involved this becomes a rather sticky issue, and I want to say, my own parents should have split long before they did. They meant well and tried to keep it together, but in all truthfulness, the fighting and emotional upset is very damaging to a child. The day my Mum and I stood in an airport with my younger brother left behind screaming and crying, scarred us all for life.

My mother never intended to be in such a position. I believe if she got to do it over, she would've left earlier and avoided that painful trauma from taking place…but I love her and do not blame her. Most of you never have to get to that point. You are not doing your child any favors by allowing them to live in a home with two adult role models who are not nurturing to each other. Children generally pick up the truth, it's very difficult to hide it from them.

Kids get to an age when they realize there is no Santa Claus, they do become quite aware of when you are being honest with them.

It's easy to say this now, from where I am, but when you bring children into a healthy relationship, where both parties are individuals and are productive and contributors to society before they are actually a couple, the chances are very good, it will be incredibly beneficial to the young ones as they develop. It's almost shocking from this side at the choices people make to be the other parent of their child. Is this the best you can do for your baby, whom you are to love above all others?

Wisdom from this side can be very valuable, and I am serving it to you so you can consider it. Find yourself, learn who you are minus a man or woman, and look for a relationship to enrich your life — not be your life. At different times, each partner must be a caretaker to the other, however, both should be nurturers throughout. I am not at all suggesting that a woman who stays home to raise her children is not doing a beautiful thing, but why are so many women with a man who does not give them a choice? It's shameful.

Since I lived a life of indulgence, I suggest you keep all alcohol and drug use out of the relationship, especially during the early stages. Meeting your future mate at the bar after the two of you have had a few, is not the brightest idea. When someone is under the influence, please do not pursue the relationship until you have really met them. Drugs and alcohol pretty much alter a relationship, and eventually you have no idea what is truthful about it and what isn't.

I know this is extremely controversial, and I also know many others who have channeled from this side before have concluded the same thing, there is no "addictive gene" to anything. Addiction is a behavioral problem, and anyone can become completely recovered or cured from it. There are certain things in your DNA that can cause more of a propensity for certain behaviors, however, it can be conquered and much too much is made out of the so-called addictive gene. My condition, known as manic depression is also completely treatable without any form of drugs whatsoever, but you have to do intense work to conquer it. Being numb may help you through a surgery, but do you want to walk around like that for the rest of your life? You are here to feel and experience, and yes, pain is a warning that something is not right, so deal with what is causing the pain, don't just numb the area. Feel it, understand it and identify with it. Your feelings, and your emotions should not be denied. They are you. They don't have an IQ, but they are there for a reason.

True Love

Love is not what you think it is, not even for a moment.
Love is not out of duty or obligation, love is not given
out of guilt, love takes no prisoners and does not seek
to control or make demands from.

Love is truth and the truth is you.
Love is who you really are, already perfect,
already healed, but you just haven't accepted
the perfection of the healing.

Love is not present very much,
because you have decided that love
is everything it is not.

Love does not make you feel tired
or exasperated but rejuvenated,
giddy and free.

Love is forgiveness in all you are,
and all you are not; Can you forgive
yourself these things? Or are you
not ready to love!

You must love yourself as you are
with complete abandonment as you
are God's creation. How can you ask

Jim Morrison & Michael Hutchence

another to love you if you can't find
appreciation for your very essence?

It is easy to say I love you
in the heat of passion but it's
harder to know what love is,

but you say the words because
you want to be loved, and have
someone because it's better
than being alone.

You already have someone —
yourself, and unless you can
fall in love with all your
faults and flaws, should you
be falling in love with someone
else's faults and flaws?

Love is truth. Truth is God.
Be a seeker of truth and you will
find God.

—channeled from Michael Hutchence

CHAPTER 18

Don't You See There is a Rhythm?

"Music and rhythm find their way into the secret places of the soul"

—*Plato*

Jim Morrison & Michael Hutchence

A TALE OF TWO BROTHERS

Would you believe that before I was Michael Hutchence I was, in fact, a composer in two previous incarnations? Music is the thread that has run through everything for me since the beginning. Music affects all humans on a conscious and subconscious level. There are vibrations, frequencies and tones that affect you in much deeper ways than you fully recognize. Who can explain the emotions they feel when they hear what they consider to be a great piece of music or a tragically sad song? There is a mystical property to all music.

The sounds, vibrations, and frequencies have a direct affect on your central nervous system. The Hindus' have a great understanding of how music corresponds to the central nervous system and how it can massage many tensions away from even your tiniest nerve endings. There is much still to discover about the healing nature of music and how it corresponds with the energy centers in the body known as the chakras.

Ancient Greek philosophers touted that the human soul could be perfected by music that was composed in an awe inspiring way. The truth about music is it haunts your memory and cobwebs in your brain are often created by certain music that rings true to your soul. I believe Felix Mendelssohn got it right when he said, "Though everything else may appear shallow and repulsive, even the smallest task in music is so absorbing, and carries us so far away from town, country, Earth, and all worldly things, that it is truly a blessed gift of God."

I would highly suggest if you want to experience music that will move your soul, listen to Mendelssohn and any of the parts of his great work ,"Elijah" such as the "Song Without Words." I am quite certain you will be touched.

I am here to encourage you to create music, your own kind of music and your own song, because if there ever was a time for a

Jim Morrison & Michael Hutchence

sical renaissance, it is now on the planet Earth. If you go back o the actual Renaissance and the Bardic traditions, you will discover the absolute connection of magick to music! Music is magick and magick is most certainly in music.

Music can be a transport for you back to a certain time or place in your life, or may I suggest, in other lifetimes. You may not be able to bring-up a truly vivid memory of that time or place, but more than likely, you will get a feeling or a sense of ambience of it.

Many of us who spent time searching, were searching for the unexplainable past we had lived.

I always wished to be a part of the creative process of music, and you will find yourself in your own music. You will also find the magick of life, the true universe that you cannot see, and you may even find God.

It is important not to feel compelled to follow contemporary standards when creating your music. Let the music flow from within and not from what has a corporate stamp on it or something being marketed essentially to make money. Keep in mind the intention in music, as with anything else. If the music stems from deep inside your soul, it will have a greater impact on those listening to it, as they will feel or sense your creative energy and some will resonate with your own vibration.

While money is not the root of all evil, it is simply how some subscribe to it. It's how some people use it, and their intent. Greed absolutely needs to be separated from artistic creation. You may believe it's better to have 300,000 people listening to your song as opposed to 300, but if you move 300 listeners, your art still has left a great impression on souls. Why value a larger quantity of souls more than a few? Every soul has such a great value that cannot be calculated. To touch just one is extremely meaningful, and that soul will touch several, and so on. There are things that while on Earth the last time, I didn't quite understand. When corporations are behind your income, you are simply pressured to produce and to produce something that generates revenue and sells concert tickets. No one will mention this to you.

I have a new angle on the whole thing, as you can imagine. The true artists and musicians I have come to admire, are the ones who are starving to do their art, or perhaps can't even do it as a full-time job, as it is not monetarily beneficial enough to pay their bills. They don't sell-out concert venues or get asked for autographs, but they play their hearts out in a small club hardly anyone has ever heard of on the outskirts of town or on a street corner or by themselves in a small room minus recording equipment. They are creating. They are feeling the vibrations, and they are feeling their own souls. No one is going to tell them this won't work, you can't do this, we need your songs to sound more like this, because they are truly artists and musicians who haven't been jaded because they are not owned by a music label.

The more superficial you become in the music industry — or actually any industry — the less you will be in touch with who you are and with the vibrations and love generated by your own soul. I had, in fact, lost touch with my soul before I left the Earth, but I was still searching for it. Once you lose touch with your soul, chaos and drama will ensue in your life. You may get this awful feeling of drowning. No soul on Earth has to drown. Prison walls are an illusion to the soul. Captivity is a falsehood to the soul. What you are within is much more substantial than what you are on the outside. The outside needs to correspond with the inside, meaning, your superficial essence should indeed reflect like a smear free mirror, from your inside.

Of course, you will think I am now suggesting this because I am not in a human body. A human body, simply put, is a vehicle for the planet Earth. And just like any vehicle you have driven or rode in previously, after so many years, it breaks down, gets rusted, worn or perhaps it has been wrecked. A sharp car will get you looks and may be fun to drive, just as the human body may get you looks and may be fun to occupy. But you can't stay in it forever. There are times you want to get out of your car, right? So you go somewhere, stretch your legs or just reconnect by putting your feet on the ground. Your soul is the same way. It can't stay in the human body forever, as it is only a shell, a vehicle, and it may be a nice one, but nevertheless, serves a purpose but is not built to last. Just think about it this way, you are still you, after you get rid of the car you are driving. After your soul rids itself of the body you presently occupy, you are still you. I'm still me. At times, when you are in the car, in a bad traffic jam or when the car breaks down and you are stuck, you feel trapped. It feels good to get out of the car for awhile, doesn't it?

The human body gives a feeling of containment just like you on Earth need to feel contained in a space, a room or an enclosure to protect against the elements and perhaps other people. Imagine what it is like not to be contained anymore and truly not need to be. That is true freedom, the kind that is only discussed and hypothesized about on Earth. Your true freedom awaits you the day you leave your human body. While you are still contained, it doesn't mean your soul must be held back. You can free your soul in the creation of music, art, writing, cooking and in all creative processes. At times it seems unnatural to the soul to be contained.

Manic depressives as I was in my last lifetime, tend to get these creative bursts. It is because they long for and often times do, feel their souls. Their souls are crying out, and they agree to let their soul's words, music, feelings, drawings, etc., flow. I call it the soul flow. When the greatest pieces of music were composed, the true timeless classics by Mozart, Bach, Beethoven, Handel, the Gregorian Chants, and songs like "Amazing Grace," they were all created from a soul flow. They were not created by the composer seeking to have a huge hit with the public. When Da Vinci painted the last supper, or any other painting, he was in a soul flow.

I am fortunate enough to have become close friends with a musician who operated in his soul flow on earth. He came to this side the same year I did, about 6 months prior. His name is Jeff Buckley. We have become extraordinarily close and he is a member of my primary soul group or family on this side. Jeff was a true conduit to other worlds and wrote music, performed music and recorded music from the deepest part of the soul. This is rarely seen or done. Jeff came here tragically, in an accident, that did not involve drugs, alcohol or suicide. Jeff was at least half the time, in another world, walking with one foot on earth and one foot in another dimension almost 24/7. This is why he came home too soon, as his grace and multi-faceted talent, have been so needed on earth. Jeff had a difficult crossing, since he wasn't ready to come to this plane. He has since adapted and we are true brothers. Jeff is a true inspiration to real artists who want to get into their soul flow, as he lived it daily and exposed it all, every time he sang.

A TALE OF TWO BROTHERS

You have more beauty, more complexities, your soul than in your human brain. So as they sa must learn to unlearn what you have learned. Wh mean to say, you must open up your intuitive mind, r. ₁ogical one who has to explain each and everything that occurs. Since nothing on Earth is random and there are no real coincidences, you won't be able to explain most of what happens to you. You are moving with a certain vibration, frequency and intent in life, and that is precisely what is drawing various things, people and events to you. It's not so much as deja vu but *deja is*, meaning it's not about the fact you have been there before (perhaps in another body or a dream state), it's the fact you have attracted where you are, what you are doing and who you are with for some time.

Of course, if I could go back and relive my life as Michael Hutchence again, it's absolutely true I would've made various different choices. I do believe when I drew the 1992 mishap to me, which removed two of my five senses, I should've made some different choices. First, I would've chosen not to self-medicate any longer. Second, I would develop my other senses even stronger than they were, as they would've opened many doors for me.

The universe sends you a nice variety of wake-up calls, signs and signals. Men have a tendency of never asking for directions, and that's a true, male-centered egotistical problem. Sometimes women ask for directions and get confusing ones: two lefts here, a sharp right at the light, keep going until you see a bridge and don't turn on the bridge but you will merge on the bridge later, and so on. It's time to activate your personal GPS. Ask for directions from the creator, the universe or even within yourself about all aspects of your day to day existence, the large things, the small things and everything in between.

When you are asking another human for directions, why do you think they *should know*? Some people ask a minister, rabbi, priest, etc., for a connection to the soul or the truth. It seems so easy to get lost when given directions, doesn't it? It's not always your fault that the directions are not always right, as a turn or two can be left out. When you get your *own* directions and into your *own* soul flow, not only will you never get lost, but you will never have to ask for directions again and will always reach your destination with complete confidence.

Jim Morrison & Michael Hutchence

As Jimi Hendrix once said, "Music doesn't lie. If there is something to be changed in this world, it can only happen through music."

As Bach once said, "Music in an agreeable harmony for the honor of God and the permissible delights of the soul."

As Bono once said, "Music can change the world because it can change people."

As Beethoven once said, "Music is a higher revelation than all wisdom and philosophy."

Though the addition of anything to these quotes is both unnecessary and may seem trite, I would like to add that "Music is the true essence of your soul, it's releasing your vibration, your energy, your light to the universe. It's your greatest soul imprint. Music was and is the true essence of me, Michael Hutchence."

An Ancient Muse

An ancient muse played her harp
as I watched transfixed by the fire.
She sang her song of sorrow
with such great pain, you could
feel her soul's desire.

She went on and on
about how his ship had sailed
and she was all alone,
it brought many to tears
and I felt as if my own music
had failed — as hers could
make you feel so melancholy
and without a home.

The muse reminded me
to write your lyrics and wear
your heart on your sleeve,

otherwise it's all dramatic license
for those that are gullible and
choose to believe.

Sing of who you are,
Play with all you possess,
Be who you are that day,
and there'll be nothing for
the audience to miss.

The times of sadness, love
and pain are equally important
as when you feel mundane.
Writing of common, everyday
things works well for it's your
own personal take, a slice of
heaven, or an overwhelming
sense of hell.

Are you an actor or
do you reveal your soul?
For people to "get you"
like the ancient muse,
then share the same goal.

Get it out, feel the power
of your emotions, like being
alone on the top of a mountain,
or not being heard in the
middle of the ocean.

The ancient muse taught me
and taught me well,
I shall tell you of my time
in heaven and my own personal hell.

Jim Morrison & Michael Hutchence

You shall finally read the words
that are inside of me,
what the world has never heard,
but I will finally be, genuinely free.

—*channeled from Michael Hutchence*

A TALE OF TWO BROTHERS

CHAPTER 19

We All Rotate...

"I shall now recall to mind that the motion of the heavenly bodies is circular, since the motion appropriate to a sphere is rotation in a circle."

—*Nicolaus Copernicus*

Jim Morrison & Michael Hutchence

A TALE OF TWO BROTHERS

I previously stated in these writings that nothing in life is random and there are simply no coincidences. I subscribe to the concept of synchronicity developed by Carl Jung. In 1952, Jung published this concept, and in order for things to be in synchronicity, he states, two or more events must occur in a meaningful manner, but which are not causally related. The events have to be related in concept. For example, you are reading this book and at the same time, you turn on the radio and whatever station is already on starts to play "Listen Like Thieves" or "The One Thing" by INXS. The chance the events would occur together randomly would have very high odds. Synchronicity is the desired state to live, in because things will come together for you that previously were simply loose ends.

I am not here to give a numerology lesson, however, I am here to suggest that numbers control and form the universe. There is a number to the vibration and frequency at which everything operates and amplifies to bring you closer to the mind/body/spirit harmonic. (This has nothing to do with math class, I was pretty horrible at math in my last lifetime.) This has to do with universal tones, vibrations and messages.

The number "22" in my last life was quite important. The duality of "22" with a repeating single number represents the ideal and the real. This number represents true magick with a "k" and the vibration this number vibrates is so great, it can help you fulfill your dreams. I was born with this higher vibration to create magic, and it seems I walked into a career where that was very much possible. I did not plan on becoming a singer, a star or a sex symbol of any kind. I was interested in becoming a pilot, or perhaps, a professional swimmer. Acting caught my eye on and off, but I wasn't sure I would be any good at it.

Jim Morrison & Michael Hutchence

It's no accident I exited my magickal existence on the 22nd. It was all so unfulfilled. The number "22" has great significance in a great form of mysticism known as the Kabbalah. At various times, I was fascinated with Buddhism and should have followed it more closely, but I am quite certain I would've become engrossed in the Kabbalah as well if I remained on Earth. While it is true, the Kabbalah does not seek to take scripture at face value, perhaps it understands the deeper meanings of the sacred words. I have become a great student of the Kabbalah on this side, and I would suggest to those who are fascinated with the Da Vinci Code or the like, that the codes you are really seeking are very much contained in the Kabbalah.

When I speak of the Kabbalah, why would I have been inclined to become involved with it and why would I suggest that you reading this may wish to pursue it? Very simply put, because with the proper understanding of this form of ancient mysticism, you can unlock not only the secrets to creation but many of the secrets to the universe, literally.

According to the traditional Jewish religion and what many Christians also believe the first five books of the Old Testament (known as the Torah) are divine. When Moses received what is considered written law from God, he also received along with others, what is known as a secret oral tradition. This oral tradition is the code — or the key — that unlocks the secrets, hidden meanings and all that is divine within the Torah. This oral tradition was later written down in what is now known as the Kabbalah. Therefore, I would suggest to you, if you want to expand your thought process not only on the first five books of the Old Testament, but on creation and other truths of divinity, the Kabbalah is an essential study.

Kabbalists have long disagreed on the exact origins of the magickal Kabbalah, but I can now suggest to you, a greater study of Melchizedek would be worthwhile, as this is where I believe you can safely trace much of the original information of the Kabbalah back to. Melchizedek is mentioned in the Bible in Genesis and in Psalms. There are some very good resources to research this former King of Jerusalem (which was then known as Salem), who is a more important biblical figure than has ever been given credit. Melchizedek was the first priest truly mentioned in

A TALE OF TWO BROTHERS

the Bible, the one who gave Abraham (Abram) bread and wine, as he was the first one to make bread and wine sacred.

Melchizedek was written about in the Dead Sea Scrolls, though it's rather fragmented. He is also written about in the Gnostic Gospels, which I will delve into during this chapter.

I would also contend that if you go back and study the Emerald Tablets of Thoth, you will certainly realize the teachings and philosophies within the Kabbalah surfaced even back in Ancient Egyptian cultures.

Without the Kabbalah, I am afraid you don't have the most complete information on Earth to understand mysticism, or for that matter, authentic divinity.

It's important to understand that much of the Kabbalah was passed down by oral tradition, but I would suggest that anyone seeking to study or understand the Kabbalah research the works of the French alchemist, Nicolas Flamel. He was truly a great Kabbalist, and there is a great deal of myth surrounding his life and death. But I can assure you, he has indeed crossed to this side. His writings and drawings are much more important to understanding the Kabbalah than it has been recognized. A book was given to Nicolas which was, in fact, an original book of Abraham also known as the Codex, and Nicolas spent many, many years deciphering this great book. Nicolas did not at first feel worthy of being given this great knowledge. His humility was a key, because ego does not coincide well with spiritual work. I am not speaking of the "Harry Potter" character but the real man, who lived and did the most incredible drawings that are significant to the Kabbalah. His drawings are much more important than it has been realized, and although he did not discover an actual stone, that would be called the "Philosopher's Stone," he was given some of the most amazing knowledge of the spiritual realms and enlightenment imaginable. His image of "The Adept" is most especially significant. The codes of Nicolas Flamel are much more amazing and important at this time than that of Da Vinci.

There are of course, many works of enlightenment to read and study and too many to name. But, I am here from this side to offer a treasure chest for those searching for truth and answers. I have an important key to Flamel's work I will mention later in this section, but at this time, I would like to speak of a work that combined alchemy and the concepts of Jung and is truly one of the greatest literary works you can aspire to read. It's called "Faust," and it was written by the great Johann Wolfgang Von Goethe. It's a rather tragic play, composed in two parts, the second was written later than the first.

"Faust" takes place in two worlds, the small one which you are on now and the larger one, a different dimension you can transcend to. There is much truth in this timeless literary work. I would also suggest that Goethe's "Theory of Colours," which actually influenced Darwin, is an essential read at this time on Earth. It has to do with perception as related to color. Goethe does not ask you to believe his theories, he simply offers you some of the most incredible food for thought.

"The highest is to understand that all fact is really theory. The blue of the sky reveals to us the basic law of color. Search nothing beyond the phenomena, they themselves are the theory."
—*Goethe*

Goethe was inspired to do this work because of how he saw light work in a prism. The smallest things, can be the biggest inspirations. Sir Isaac Newton and Goethe saw things differently, yet can we honestly say either of them is right or wrong? Goethe's work on light and darkness must be considered from a soul perspective. Goethe proposed that darkness is not just the absence of light. Think of that concept from a soul perspective, are darker souls or energy absent of light? Or is the darkness its own, unique energy? To understand the world you live in, to touch the soul, I feel that Goethe is a must read.

I would also suggest you refer to Moses Mendelssohn, because when we speak of enlightenment or when seeking knowledge of the Kabbalah, I believe Moses had the answers. Moses was the grandfather of the famous composer, Felix Mendelssohn. Moses may have truly been the German "Socrates" or German "Plato." Moses Mendelssohn's interpretation of Exodus is quite important to those followers or students of the Kabbalah. Moses Mendelssohn was a great prophet of enlightenment, and I contend his writings are more important today than when he lived. There is a particular work of Moses Mendelssohn I would like to call attention to which was a brilliant paper on religious dogma. It's entitled "Jerusalem," or "On

Religious Power and Judaism." Another important work that was published is called "On Evidence of Meta-physical Sciences," which needs to be studied in great scrutiny because important spiritual information should be re-examined at this time. Moses Mendelssohn contended in a writing called "On the Main Principles of Fine Art and Sciences" that the human spirit learns to imitate beauty in works of art.

Moses Mendelssohn, in his most famous work, "Phaedon," was believed to many to have proven the immortality of the soul and won him international acclaim in the literary world. Mendelssohn's work is directly, and indirectly, related to the book of Zohar in the Kabbalah.

There were, of course, many divinely inspired and channeled paintings around at the time of Moses Mendelssohn, but some had not yet been done. Many have been examining Da Vinci's "Last Supper," and the truth is the controversy surrounding this work of art has gone on for centuries. It did not begin with a fictional book that focuses on it. Is the book, "The Da Vinci Code" fictional? Mostly it is. However, there is some truth not easily detected behind it. I suggest people study what is behind Jesus and the Apostles in the Da Vinci painting, because there was certainly more there. Due to deterioration, much of that is hard to detect at this time. The painting was inspired, without a doubt, from the Gospel of John, and it's a very safe assumption that the Apostle John is very much in the painting. The number "3" shows up all over this painting, and of course the number "3" has many meanings related to the Bible and spirituality. I would suggest, it's completely related to the divine and divine intervention, and I would also suggest it signifies the Holy Spirit. In this painting, there are things not easily seen, and these things are not at the table but behind it, that must be decoded. Those working on it have not yet completely decoded what is in the painting. It was, of course, divinely inspired.

Why has there been so much interest in "The Da Vinci Code?" Very simply put, many on Earth are sensing there is more to Jesus and his life than what they have been told or given. There is a greater story within or around what they know of Jesus and his disciples. It's not about people loving a good mystery, it's truly about how many on Earth are searching and they fall into this search through what is available — and often times in the popular culture and what their friends are reading and talking about. What "The Da Vinci Code" has sparked, is a great interest in the subjects in the book. You have people researching Sacred Geometry, the Knights of the Templar, and so on, in their search for truth, which is a very positive thing for the planet.

Other paintings that I would suggest more time is spent on, include the version of the "Last Supper" by Salvador Dali done in 1955. Da Vinci's "Last Supper" seems to contain more codes, but I would suggest, Dali's "Last Supper" was indeed a product of divine inspiration. The painting, many have noted, is done in the form of a dodecahedron which is a platonic solid composed of twelve pentagonal faces. There are twelve pentagons and twelve apostles because Dali believed that "communion must be symmetric."

Twelve is a sublime number and it's referenced in all the major spiritual teachings throughout history. Twelve is throughout the Bible, and quite notably in the Book of Revelations. Twelve is important to the Kabbalah and the tree of life, and "12" is also featured in Buddhism. I want to specify the dodecahedron is mentioned by Plato as how God placed the constellations, and I want to tell you, from this side, Plato was correct. The energy of the universe is indeed in the form of the dodecahedron, so it's absolutely amazing that Salvador Dali formed the "Last Supper" in a hollow dodecahedron. He has captured on canvas the true design of the Universal energy which brings everyone closer to God, the true Source. Many view Dali's painting and think it's rather simplistic, but is it really?

One of the most intriguing works of art with amazing spiritual symbolism happens to be a mural called "St. Peter Walking On Water" by the artist Jean Cocteau. Cocteau has been criticized for often putting his own image or that of his muse in his work, but I would suggest to you that there was indeed some divine inspiration in a few of his works. This particular mural needs to be studied and analyzed because of the many references in it. One pertains to Lazarus, and I refer to the Lazarus mentioned in the Gospel of John, not the story of Lazarus in the Gospel of Luke.

Lazarus had been physically dead for four days, the Gospel says, when Jesus caused Lazarus to rise from the dead. Jesus claimed in this Gospel to be the resurrection and the life, and those who believe in him, though dead, shall live. Now, of course, perhaps it's time to stop and ask: What is the great hedonistic rock star Michael Hutchence doing speaking of Jesus? I am here now to tell you, that I am a follower of Jesus, and became so, since the time I came back to this side. Jesus, as far as I am concerned, is the greatest teacher one can ever know. I have seen the true essence of Jesus, and I have come to realize the story of Lazarus is not about one cheating death. It's about those on Earth who are walking around like complete zombies and so disconnected from truth and their intuitive minds.

You don't think you live in The Matrix? Similar to the films Keanu Reeves starred in? Then ask yourself, hasn't the machine world come in to rule your existence? Can you get money without a machine? Can you pay for anything minus a machine? Where is your focus for hours upon hours a week or even a day? Is it on your computer screen? TV screen? iPod? Cell Phone? MP3? Portable DVD? Are you not influenced to eat or drink what you see on TV? Can you wash your clothes minus machines? Some of you can't even exercise minus machines. You are probably much more dependent and controlled by the machine world than you have come to realize. Technology can do amazing things and save lives and make time management more accessible for busy and important people. However, all this technology, all these machines that you focus your attention on, also take you away from your intuitive mind, and that is the part of you that connects directly to the creator. I am here to suggest becoming a student of Sacred Geometry, the Kabbalah and Alchemy can bring you closer to the divine and help remove you from such worldly and materialistic concerns.

I am also here to suggest, that when you don't connect to the divine — whether through Jesus, Buddha, the creator himself, your intuitive mind, the universal consciousness, the Archangels or whomever you choose, you are living like a zombie and walking around being programmed by those who have something monetarily to gain from your programming. It's a good idea to think about this. Lazarus was raised from the dead as he was raised from his "zombie" Earth state and connected to the truth and the divine. Lazarus could have gone to many and told them of this miracle he experienced at the hands of Jesus but did not. Just as the culture is currently, even at that time, when people have their own needs met and are living in a comfortable way, it (a miracle) seems to have less effect on them. When you are not a searcher, it's very hard to find.

Referring back to the Cocteau mural known as "St. Peter Walking On Water," I would suggest those searching for the "The Holy Grail" in the Da Vinci painting may find more clues in the Cocteau mural. There are important and spiritually essential messages in the mural related to King David. When viewing this mural, it would be ideal to pick up a book of channeled material from the great psychic, Edgar Cayce, and read of his visions of Atlantis. Some of those visions are also contained in this mural. Cocteau truly had no real idea of exactly what he was composing on this wall when he did this amazing work, but it has multiple spiritual messages.

There are works of art that actually contain the true and pure Christ energy. One of them is a painting called "Christ and the Disciples at Emmaus" by the artist Pascal-Adolphe Jean Dagnan-Bouveret. This painting was done in the 1890s and was divinely channeled directly from the dimension I now reside in. If you stare at this amazing painting, you may feel a bit, if not very, dizzy.

This painting may instantly raise your vibration and your emotions may flow when seeing it in person, because you are making a direct connection to the true energy of Jesus. You will see and feel his light if you allow yourself to, and while you may do this without the aid of a painting, viewing this is a rather instant and precise transport. In this incredible gift from God to you, there are three people viewing Jesus in the painting — a child, a woman, and a man. It is the child who really understands and takes in what he is seeing. The child is using his intuitive mind and making a direct connection to Jesus. The woman is simply going on faith — nothing wrong with that. After all, Mother Teresa did it for most of her life. But the woman is not allowing herself to make the direct connection, because she is docile. The man is pondering the reality of this because of science and doubt. I am not suggesting that you should not question matters of spirituality, but he is not using his intuitive mind, for he is not allowing that side of his consciousness to emerge. I find this to be a very, very important work for anyone to view.

There are many other works that simply are channeled from the divine, but I have just named for you the ones I wished to mention and encourage in-person viewing and study.

I could connect as an "empath" to the great artists of the works of art I had the honor and pleasure of viewing while on Earth. I had no real idea why paintings and other art works moved me so deeply, and as it turned out, I was picking up the emotions of the artist while they were painting their great paintings. Sometimes, I felt the emotions of the artist after he viewed the finished work. It was amazing, but I was not attuned to what was happening within me and simply got very overwhelmed with emotions when visiting the greatest art museums in the world. I wasted my spiritual gift on Earth, but I can assure each and every one of you, if you visit the paintings or the mural I have spoken about in person, you will be touched very, very deeply. But you must go with the intention of touching the divine and becoming more centered with who God really is.

The study of paintings that contain the divine will bring you closer to raising your vibration, and therefore, getting more in touch with your own intuition and closer to the divine. Reality as you know it began with sound, color and light. Souls sparked with light spiraled from the central source into grids of conscious experience. In the fictional work, "The Da Vinci Code," obviously Sacred Geometry encircles the whole thing.

Sacred Geometry enters into much of the divinely inspired works of art. Sacred Geometry is, in fact, the blueprint of all creation. It deals with both energy patterns and the energy of creation itself. It's all about timeless geometric codes, and this is not to be at all confused with Euclid's Geometry. There are symbols and codes all through Sacred Geometry, and we see some of the very best natural examples of such things in the cornea of the eye, spiral shaped nautilus sea shells, the branches of trees, a snowflake, and we actually spiral within our galaxy. In Sacred Geometry, you can make a complete and direct connection to the Universal mind and completely change your consciousness and awareness. Many of the ancients spouted that sacred geometry was essential to the education of the soul.

Jim Morrison & Michael Hutchence

There are obviously great works of architecture that were truly divinely inspired. You may have heard of one I will refer to, the Chartres Cathedral in France. Of course, it's the most perfect work of Sacred Geometry currently on Earth, and I am here to tell those who seek, you will find it in Chartres. It's what is called the Golden Sphere, or point zero, and it's another very direct transport to the source, whom you call God. You can achieve this state without ever entering this cathedral, but this is a good way if you've not done that yet in your meditation. It's fascinating that while so much has been written and researched about this cathedral, there isn't more study of it done in terms not only of the Sacred Geometry, but of the other things that intersect within this magnificent and magickal place. Those studying the Kabbalah need to visit this cathedral, as it contains some answers to this sacred work. Some of the answers are related to its two towers. The Kabbalah and Alchemy go hand in hand, and Alchemy is certainly throughout the cathedral. This sacred space also contains elements of Buddhism, and believe it or not, the Gnostic Gospels.

Can you imagine one place where all these things intersect? They do at Chartres and the builders and designers were not even aware of what they were doing in terms of this circle of the greatest spiritual teachings. It's all a circle, very much like the beautiful rose window in the Cathedral. The labyrinth will instantly take you to other dimensions if you allow it, and I have to go on record and suggest the labyrinth is really full of hidden codes — and so is the rose window. Even those who have studied both are truly not open enough not to study it in a certain context and I suggest you lose your preconceived ideas and start anew. There are more answers to the Kabbalah, Sacred Geometry, Alchemy, the Gnostic Gospels at Chartres than any other single place on Earth. Even those who believe at least partially in the Da Vinci Code will find answers.

I want to point out specific Gnostic work that coincides beautifully with Chartres. It is called "Pistis Sophia." The "Pistis Sophia" is contained in the Codex Askewianus and has been around for a couple of centuries. Who wrote it? What is it about? I am not here to divulge this, because it is for *you* to determine who you believe wrote it and what it indeed is about. I would not separate the Chartres Cathedral from the "Pistis Sophia" because they coincide more than anyone on Earth now realizes. I also would suggest it's an authentic work. Whether or not it should be placed in the Holy Bible is not for me to say, but it's not something made up or cultivated with anything but divine inspiration. All major paths to God intersect, and for whatever reason, man seems to deny that or believe that each path must be kept separate, almost like compartmentalized spirituality. The way to become whole and complete is not in compartmentalizing, as it is all part of the whole and must be recognized by the other parts.

For a very long time, suggestions have been made that Shakespeare did not compose his own works, but that several writers combined (or at least a few) were indeed "Shakespeare." My question to you is, does it really matter who wrote the works of Shakespeare? They are what they are, and the world takes them as such. The Gnostic Gospels upon reading them are what they are, and what exactly about them makes them not worthy to read and consider? Because they do not fit into the mold of a certain faith, or what a Church Doctrine has taught for a very, very long time? Do you have direct word from God or from Jesus to throw them out, or did you hear it from other human lips and you just accept it? I would highly encourage anyone — and everyone, from all faiths or having none at all, to explore the Gnostic Gospels and their concepts.

You may believe you are living in the smartest, most sophisticated society at this time, and that you are so far advanced beyond those who lived hundreds of years ago. Guess again! Those who lived hundreds of years ago didn't have the computer screen in front of them to tell them how to live their life. Or the television. Or movies. Or even recordings. In other words, they didn't have all the noise and distractions, therefore, they were much more in contact with the divine realm than you are now. They could hear their inner voice, or their intuition, much better than most on Earth do at this time. Those who built Chartres and visited it for hundreds of years were much more in touch with the divine than the culture you now reside in. You are too distracted and too tuned out to your intuitive voice, because you cannot maintain the focus to hear it with all the distractions and noise around you...not to mention how you key up your mind with caffeine and other stimulants.

Jim Morrison & Michael Hutchence

Had I not crossed over, I would be a practicing Buddhist on Earth, engrossed in the Kabbalah, as I am on this side. Simultaneously, I have come to see Jesus as the truth, the way and the light. I can still find the enlightenment in Buddha and Buddhism and realize what an amazing treasure of truth the Kabbalah is, and can still love Jesus and follow him as the greatest teacher of all time. Jesus would never ask me to choose between Buddhism and Christianity, because his concern is not that of control and fear. Do you believe Jesus does not acknowledge the Kabbalah and Buddhism? Of course he does. His wisdom is perpetual. I am not here to put down the Holy Bible in any way, shape or form, but I do believe, it's only part of the story. There is more.

It is well known, the Gospels of Mark, Matthew and Luke are the synoptic gospels because of the similar nature in which they view events regarding Jesus. The Gospel of John does not align so well with the other three, but, thank God, it was still included. It is in looking at the four Gospels together, the various aspects of Jesus as the Messiah, the miracles, and the historical context of the stories, that it becomes more of a mosaic than a single picture. It is said the Gospel of Mark was written for the Romans, and therefore, it appears the Gospels were written for different audiences. Yet, the varying perspectives add great depth to the story of Jesus. If you combine the traditional Gospels of the New Testament with the Gnostic Gospels, you will have a greater, richer mosaic that will bring great illumination to your life.

I am attempting to give you the keys and free you from the "Matrix" you live in. The Matrix only works if indeed everyone believes in it. Once you free yourself from it, you can hand others the keys. I am attempting to hand each of you reading this the keys. I can assure you, once you begin to use these keys, you will not view life on Earth, God, Jesus or anything you know, in the same way.

If you read and study the Kabbalah, along with the writings of Carl Jung, the drawings of Nicholas Flamel, and the writings of Johann Wolfgang Von Goethe and Moses Mendelssohn, you will unlock more codes than the book, "The Da Vinci Code," could ever make you imagine. While these writings have been written

A TALE OF TWO BROTHERS

about and much discussed throughout time, they have never been put together like this.

The Gnostic Gospels play a great role in truth as well. Many have long suspected there were more Gospels or works that could have been included in the Holy Bible. Around 862 A.D., two brothers known as Constantine (St. Cyril) and Methodius created a Slavic language, as they called it, and they translated the Bible to Greek. The Pope disapproved and decided later on, it should all be in Latin. There were writings left out when Constantine and Methodius undertook this work, and some things were added, and of course, things changed when it all went to Latin. Much of those early works, divinely channeled or even witnessed, have been lost in translation, and so I ask you who you that read the Bible today, how authentic is it? How genuine are the words? A few key words or phrases can change the whole thing and so to suggest what is contained in the Holy Bible currently are the *only* Holy Scriptures on Earth or the only ones with value or meaning in existence, is preposterous. But once again, you must seek to find, and not be a complacent with what you have in front of you and believe that is all the truth there is. I would highly recommend you do not become complacent with your search for God and truth in the universe. It's an easy way to stay spiritually stagnant.

Jesus is the way, the truth and the light for me. It's hard to explain the joy I have been given by experiencing the true essence of Jesus Christ. Why is it so hidden on Earth? If Jesus is the greatest teacher in the universe, as I can contend he is, why must the view of him be so limited and close minded? When I was on Earth, I did not seek to find the spiritual truth, and this is why I am attempting to set you free, before it's too late, before you end up like me. As I sat in 1993 and told a member of the press, I never wanted to end up like Kurt Cobain. I felt it was impossible for me to do so. Please do not believe for a second, you can't end up like I did. It will become more and more common on the planet Earth in the next several years. But if you seek the truth and stay connected to God, or the universal mind, I am quite certain you will not end up like I did.

One of the many things I missed the truth about in my last lifetime was the so-called mental illness I suffered from called manic depression. Manic depression often breeds chaos, and in that chaos is the creative, artistic process. The creative process is where God is! God equals passion, not fear, not control. How can anyone feel bored or tired when discussing God? God is pure energy, pure passion. So yes, I am saying that in what you term as mental illness, the highs and lows you experience like that of a rollercoaster, bring you closer to God. If you are always so even keeled and complacent, it's hard to really feel the passion that is the divine Creator on Earth. The love and light God shines is not describable, just as the love Jesus has for everyone on Earth. If you truly connect to Jesus and his love for you, I assure you that you will beg him to take you with him. You will not want to remain on Earth, no matter how many loved ones you have there. You have not experienced love like this on Earth and you are barely skimming the surface of who God really is and who Jesus, the greatest teacher the universe has ever known, is. I was not a follower of Jesus on Earth, because I equated Jesus with organized religion. How truly stupid of me, it's completely absurd.

I am offering you greater keys to unlock the ancient wisdom and knowledge that you can now imagine. I want to return to the famous story of the "The Philosopher's Stone" that Nicholas Flamel and many others searched for endlessly. This stone was supposed to be the elixir of life and bring you everything, wealth, health, eternal youth, you name it, it was said the stone could do it. The Philosopher's Stone was sought after as much as the Holy Grail, and they actually coincide with each other. I have come to learn on this side, the answers to the Philosopher's Stone are contained in the Gnostic Gospel of Thomas. The stone is esoteric. There are supposedly secret sayings of Jesus in this Gospel that should not be a secret at all. Didymos Judas Thomas recorded these sayings, so it is told, and Jesus said, "Whoever discovers the interpretation of these sayings will not taste death." This is where the answers to the Philosopher's Stone lies, in this particular Gospel. They were there all the time, they are there, and so many have searched for them.

Death obviously does not mean the death of the human body, or even eternal life, it is a reference to self-realization, meaning that if you acknowledge the possibility of reincarnation, you may achieve a state where you do not have to come back to Earth again and live a human life in the matrix. You can finally escape, and with all the lives many have had through the plague and suffering, watching their children starve and starving themselves, and on and on, it's a wonder anyone would not take this road and attempt to stay in what you call heaven. Self-realization is finding complete communion and connection of your soul to God.

I realize my views from this side contradict many of yours, but I am not here to suggest I am right or you are wrong. I am here to encourage you to become a seeker of truth, your own personal truth. This may sound like I am condemning churches and sacred religious doctrines. On the contrary, I am asking people to research it, separate fact from fiction, and never believe all you see is all there is. I do believe the Catholic Church is one thousand percent correct in the role they give the Holy Mother, Mary.

After I crossed over, someone prayed directly to the Holy Mother for me and for my soul. The Holy Mother has come to me on this side, and she has touched millions, and many of those are non-Christians. The Holy Mother wiped away my tears and helped to heal my soul. As I have said previously, your prayers are heard and do help us over here. If you go directly to the Holy Mother with pure intentions and goodness in your heart for who or what you are praying for, she will bring on a great healing with her beautiful love and light. *That* is not something I can describe to you in words for a book. Those who doubt the Holy Mother simply have not connected to her, but she is there, she is the pure Grace of God. Blessed is she among all of us on this side. She is a Queen and one that has helped to heal my soul miraculously.

I am not here to debate the story of the Holy Mother or what is true or not true, that is not my place. I am here to tell you, she is the mother of my Redeemer Jesus, and she is my Queen. She will help your loved ones on this side greatly, despite what faith you may or may not be or what faith they were when they crossed over. She has helped this hedonistic rock star, what more can be said of her love and light, other than you simply do not know it on Earth, not because you can't know it, but because you choose not to seek it in it's pure and true form.

I came to give you the keys to the kingdom within your soul. Perhaps if a saint or a great philosopher had come to you with this, it would mean more to you, but I am here to demonstrate true soul evolution does take place where I am. I am very proud of it and hopeful you will experience it before you get to this side. You can choose to believe it is me or not, you can choose to believe in this communication or not, but please believe, the truth is within your soul and don't wait until you have come to this dimension to unlock it. Free yourself from the matrix and others will follow. You will experience a joy — a completely different kind than you have ever felt. Take it from one who didn't learn it, who didn't live it, and has suffered greatly for it and caused suffering to many around him, happiness is learning the truth and living it.

I thank you with the greatest sincerity imaginable for allowing me to impart what I have learned and to tell my story, my truth. I love you all and always will. I carry your light and beauty with me, now please carry some of mine with you.

Monastery...

I could never live in a monastery,
I needed a room full of people,
to get me through the night,
to get me through the day,
I thought it would all be
alright if all of you would
stay

And tell me what I wanted to hear
tell me what I thought was true
if you disagreed with me
I would simply ostracize you

Couldn't keep you around
if you didn't see it my way
my mind was closed
I was the biggest fool
and you had the last
laugh - I have to say

A TALE OF TWO BROTHERS

But the joke will be on you
if you don't start to realize
what happened to me
was because of denial and lies
you are not above it,
you may end up snapping
one day soon, get over
yourself, before it all
balloons

What you believe is the truth
of your life, is not even close
to real, you need to find your
true purpose and another's pain
you must feel

The envy, the greed,
the self-importance
will bring you down,
What are you the King
of, where is your crown?

Do you turn away from the cries
of the starving, or the ones dying
from AIDS? Do you turn away from
the abused woman or the elderly
being treated like dirt until their
dying days?

Your little world
does not exist, you are
a part of the planet
and if you persist to deny
the plight of others and
think only of yourself,

Jim Morrison & Michael Hutchence

nothing you now have will
matter, not the cars, not the women
and certainly not the wealth

Your soul is full of dark spots
how did it get that way mate?
Turn to Buddhism, the true
teachings of Jesus or the Dali
Llama before it gets too late

Cleanse your soul,
feel the pain of those around you
comfort them the best you can
or like me, the noose around your
neck will one day, have found you

You must get out of yourself
and the monastery of your mind,
live to serve others,
true peace is what you will find

The enemy is within
that's who your true
opponent is, and remember
all the children of the world
are truly your kids

The children belong to all of you,
they are the seeds of the Earth,
what legacy do you leave them?
A planet in turmoil since their birth?

Teach them how to love, how to give,
give them the spiritual tools with which
to live, they won't have time for drama,
or jealously or greed, they will naturally

go to others and help them in their
time of need

Instead of a movie star, who gets paid to play,
Mother Teresa is a better role model,
one who's life was never
food for fodder but food to nourish
the weary soul, live as she did,
and you will finally know what it is
to be whole

—*channeled from Michael Hutchence*

For Jacqueline From Michael

I wish we could time travel
back to the history we shared,
you'd understand why I trust
you alone with my words,
you'd understand how
you've always been there

As the days go on,
you hesitate and think
why would I talk to you?
My Angel, you are the
missing link.

Our energy has always
been aligned, We've
always been close
all through time.
I sought you out

Jim Morrison & Michael Hutchence

when I returned home,
I'll be around,
you will never be alone.

I could've shared
these words with others,
as so many try and speak
to me, I can hardly
count how many but I give
them to you Jacqueline,
because I trust your soul
more than any other you see.

I've had great loves,
I have a beautiful daughter
but you my Angel
are special to me like no other.

—*channeled from Michael Hutchence*

CHAPTER 20
The Mystic's Mosaic: Putting the Pieces Back Together

by Kathleen Tucci

"There are very few human beings who receive the truth, complete and staggering, by instant illumination. Most of them acquire it fragment by fragment, on a small scale, by successive developments, cellularly, like a laborious mosaic."

—*Anais Nin*

Jim Morrison & Michael Hutchence

A TALE OF TWO BROTHERS

Michael = Michael Hutchence

Jac = Jacqueline Murray

Michael: Before we go any further, dear one, I know you are having a hard time believing in some of the material we are giving you.

Jac: Well to be honest, Michael, I am not at all familiar with the Gnostic Gospels or half of what you speak of, and I want to make sure my channeling is clear.

Michael: If it weren't, I would've stopped you by now. I don't want you to feel like I am leaving you on the edge of a cliff. If you'd like, why don't you contact Kathleen Tucci again and let's see if she can validate for you some of the things I have been channeling to you. I feel she will back you up on some of our work, and I know this would be a way to make you feel more comfortable. She's an absolutely lovely woman. I met her in person in 1983 when she was working at a tellie station in Ohio. INXS was doing a meet and greet, we were both very young. She is a very attractive woman who comes from a long line of psychically gifted family members.

Jac: I've never met her in person, but I like her very much.

Michael: Soul synchronicity does not require one to meet another one in person, and I am not speaking of someone lying on the internet about their age or looks. That is not related to anything remotely spiritual.

Jac: Yes, if we can work with Kathleen, that would be very nice. I would be really honored and humbled and I thank you for considering my feelings in all of this.

Michael: Of course, I am happy to oblige, my Angel. Kathleen will confirm that I have shown up at a few of her gallery readings in the past years, however, I did not give her a message. I just made my presence known, and she knew it was me. She assumed that since we had met while I was alive, as you earthlings call it, that was why I was around her. It was actually a preparation of sorts for you to receive confirmations from her. She was pre-selected for that, and it goes to show you, this has been in the works for a long while, my dearest. I hope you can clearly see this is a way to get you help in order to do this work.

Jac: I am trying to grasp that, Michael. Let's see what Kathleen has to say.

A TALE OF TWO BROTHERS

The Mystic's Mosaic: Putting the Pieces Back Together

by Kathleen Tucci

To think that you are getting visited by someone dead is one thing, and for a psychic medium, that's a standard daily ritual, but a famed celebrity? It has taken hefty validation and proof that only Michael Hutchence himself could have given me with regard to when I met him in 1983, that I then truly believed I was speaking with him. Sometimes he visits while I'm in a meditative state. Often times, Michael visits when I am completely lucid and sporadically while I'm in dream state. On one occasion he walks me into his hotel room. I see the room as dark at first, and there are bright light streams seeming to come in through the window like lights from the other buildings outside or cars maybe…they are non-threatening in nature. I am above, as if on the ceiling looking down into the main room. There is a woman there with medium length wavy, brownish hair wearing a mini skirt and ankle high shoe boots. She and a man are milling around in the room as if dancing. I hear music, and there is a lot of activity.

Michael says to them: "Why do they want me out of here? I have to wait three years." After a brief time, it seems as if the others have left, and Michael is there alone. There is a loud bang! I see white light, and it appears that he has fast-forwarded to the actual time of death and what he experienced in leaving his body at a very fast rate, as if thrusted. Although I know he is not shot or directly impaled by anything, I am unsure of the loud bang that I heard clairaudiently. When I ask Michael about this, I am suddenly disconnected from him. There is no direct answer. Michael comes back in with a black book or appointment book he kept records in, something he carried around with him. He also said, as much as Bob Geldof dislikes him, Bob knows, given their discussions that day of the 22nd, that he wouldn't have thought Michael would have taken his own life and that he gave Bob no indication that he was going to commit suicide. He reiterates that the appointment book will answer a lot and that the police hung on to it because he was famous, and the person who has it doesn't realize the information is in there to clear up a lot of what happened the morning he died.

I am told that jewelry is important too, but he keeps focusing on the belt buckle and what appears to be a necklace with some sort of symbols on it. I'm getting that this necklace was something the entire group shared. They literally took turns wearing it, and he had it with him the night of November 21st. He's also showing me a Claddagh ring, which is a traditional Irish ring. He says this ring is significant to someone...that they will know this when they read this portion of the book. He makes reference to his casket as being completely covered in purple irises with one solo yellow tiger lily in the corner. He wishes to pass this lily on as symbol to his daughter and the iris as a symbol of his love for a friend. To another friend, the written token placed in his casket will be remembered always, he says.

When channeling Michael one day, I felt another presence enter the room with us. It is common when channeling a spirit that they often can bring friends and loved ones who are there with them on the other side. I immediately got the sensation that it was a male, older than Michael, and above him, which means to me a father figure. I asked Michael to please let him speak, and he waved his arm, gently swooping it in front and to the side as if introducing his father to me. The dialogue went like this: "You are Michael's father, yes?" I asked.

"Yes, that'd be me," he responded, smiling. He had white hair and a full wide face. Although he wasn't wearing glasses, he gave me the impression he did need prescription lenses when he was living on Earth. His demeanor was warm, friendly and he seemed like the kind of man who got along with most people easily. I went on to ask him what he wanted to say. "I am comfortable now that I no longer have a foot problem," he said.

I mentioned to him that seemed rather trivial, and he answered me with a sharp and quick response, "If you experienced what I did, you'd understand why I said that."

I laughed and waited for what else he might say. Then he began, "The month of December is important. It relates to a

A TALE OF TWO BROTHERS

birthday and also a significant month which my wife (I am feeling he means his second wife, Suzie) will acknowledge."

When I asked in what sense, he said, "How we met and when we met is what it relates to. She'll understand. I also am sorry for the skin irritations she's experiencing, but it will pass eventually. Aside from Michael's passing, please tell her there is a birthday in the month of November I wish to mention. She'll know who's this is. I see the new baby coming...this will be a great addition to the family. I know they have tried for a very long time."

He started speaking about someone making homemade wine. When I asked who, he switched quickly to another thought and spoke of his pride in someone recently searching into the family's genealogy. He said it was long overdue and that even when he was here, he always had an interest in history and heritage. He promised to continue to try to "nudge" the right information into their path, so as to assist them in the process. He then spoke of her smelling his night clothes. This seemed like a robe or pajamas of some sort. He wanted to recognize that he has been watching over her and is still very connected to her. He also mentioned a boat connected with Michael's brother. The boat was purchased, I believe, since Michael's father crossed, and he wanted to acknowledge this as a way of letting Michael's brother know he was watching over him as well. I then felt his energy pull back from my own and could no longer hear him.

When speaking to spirits on the other side, they will mention names, dates and events to help those receiving the messages identify who it is that is coming through in a reading. When channeling Michael, he has mentioned the names Patricia, Tina, and Andrew at various times. There were more names, and I don't remember the long dialogue regarding these names. He just mentions them in passing and then he would converse on other topics and issues that emerged unrelated to those names. I say this, because I have since learned who those individuals are. He had not mentioned his brother's name to me at that point, and when he spoke of him, he referred to him simply as "my brother." I have since learned his name is Rhett.

If this isn't all strange enough, it keeps getting stranger. Michael says that he does, in fact, have a message for Richard. I was lead to believe by Michael, that this is his good friend,

Richard Lowenstein. He first gave me the name Richard in meditation. When I asked him in a lucid state who is Richard, he told me to get online on the computer. By plugging the words "Richard Michael Hutchence" into a search engine by his direction, he lead me straight to a blog on his website from April 12, 2004 where it talks about Richard. I had no prior knowledge of Richard Lowenstein, his career as a director, or his relationship to Michael. Michael says to tell him, "Don't trust the Rainbow Lady." When I asked what he meant by this, Michael showed me an old church in what appeared to be a small quaint town. In his making reference to a stained glass window depicting "Mother Mary," he says, "There are 15 colors." He and another famous singer, who shall remain nameless, spoke to each other about carefully weaving references to the Bible into their songs . He shows me an old fashioned key (similar to a skeleton key) and says this is a metaphor meaning the "secret keys to the Bible." He makes note of the Book of Thomas in the Bible and that he and his friend have discussed this.

The Gospel of Thomas was discovered in 1945 with a cache of books in Nag Hammadi, Egypt. At that time, the Christian and Gnostic books had been hidden on a hillside for 1,600 years. As book burnings spread in the Church in the late fourth century, an unknown monastic hid these scrolls for safe-keeping. The Gospel of Thomas is of immense value, because it dates from the same period as the canonical gospels, and because it is a remarkable record of what numerous scholars claim are the actual teachings of Jesus.

He is then showing me a small European town, and a light beige colored cement or stucco house with a small black wrought iron fence around it in the front. There is a window on each side of the front door. They start approximately four feet from the ground. The front door is very thick, old and wooden, very heavy appearing and approximately eight feet in height. As we enter the house there is a room on the right. The curtains seem to rarely get drawn open in there. There is a holy, priestly man in this room. He is an avid reader and seems to be duplicating information so it won't be lost, stolen or burned. When I ask Michael about this, he refers to when Emperor Constantine took away specific pieces of the Bible to ensure the powers of the church. He says this man is making certain that this information, and he as a solo, does not shed any blood. Michael reminds me of the matrix and how lives on the earthly plane and on the spiritual plane are intertwined with much accuracy in planning in a heavily convoluted web of destined and non-destined circumstances. "Time is of the essence," he says.

I sit back, take a deep breath and Michael continues. He shows me a bouquet of assorted flowers with a yellow bow. I'm not sure of the significance of this. He then makes reference to the phrase, "Yellow Brick Road," and says it is important. I am still unsure of what he means. He then says that the England stuff will escalate everything! His energy is rapid in nature and I feel he's jumping around quite a bit. Not fully comprehending the sequence of his thoughts, I continue to listen and Michael then takes me to a villa, clearly in Venice. I am now gazing out a window over a gondola and the villa has the feel of "To Catch a Thief." There is a feeling of mystery about the place…and I am uneasy being there. He then says, "Constantine's books that were removed…we are tapping into that library."

I get the distinct impression from Michael that he's suggesting there are symbols, text, and writings that have yet to be seen, which will explain many of Constantine's actions and what he was hiding, that is available to be uncovered. He then brings up a passage from Luke 1:26-38…

[26] Now in the sixth month the angel Gabriel was sent from God to a city in Galilee called Nazareth, [27] to a virgin engaged to a man whose name was Joseph, of the descendants of David; and the virgin's name was Mary. [28] and coming in, he said to her, "Greetings, favored one! The Lord is with you." [29] But she was very perplexed at this statement, and kept pondering what kind of salutation this was. [30] The angel said to her, "Do not be afraid Mary; for you have found favor with God." [31] "And behold, you will conceive in your womb and bear a son, and you shall name Him Jesus." [32] "He will be great and will be called the Son of the Most High; and the Lord God will give Him the throne of His father David; [33] and He will reign over the house of Jacob forever, and His kingdom will have no end." [34] Mary said to the angel, "How can this be, since I am a virgin?" [35] The angel answered and said to her, "The Holy Spirit will come

upon you, and the power of the Most High will overshadow you; and for that reason the holy Child shall be called the Son of God." ³⁶ "And behold, even your relative Elizabeth has also conceived a son in her old age; and she who was called barren is now in her sixth month." ³⁷ "For nothing will be impossible with God." ³⁸ And Mary said, "Behold, the bond of the Lord; may it be done to me according to your word."

In meditation 14 days later with Michael, in regard to the above passage and the extraordinary quandary in what he was saying, said to me, "Look at versus: 49-52 in the same chapter. It will hopefully shed light on the magnitude of what you are doing." These verses read:

⁴⁹ For He who is mighty has done great things for me, and holy is His name. ⁵⁰ And His mercy is on those who fear Him from generation to generation. ⁵¹ He has shown strength with His arm; He scattered the proud in the imagination of their hearts. ⁵² He has put down the mighty from their thrones, and exalted the lowly.

I know Michael is working hard to be heard. What exactly he is trying to convey is still unfolding. He keeps mentioning the Gospel of Thomas, and in looking at it, he pulls out words to me as I peruse the texts. In many transitions, there are several, but concrete, conclusions I have come to. Michael dictates that over on the other side, he has seen what Jesus refers to as "Whoever finds the interpretations of these sayings shall not taste death" and is the meaning of the crystal city. That just as light is not really light, but an interpretation of consciousness, on the other side, each reflection of color and the multitude of combining colors is the form of brilliance which resides in each of us. This light is, in fact, who we are: therefore all of us are perfect! Each soul is a ray of light, and this light begins from a divine source, which cannot and will not, be broken, bent, or cascaded in any way. Similar to the law of energy, it cannot dissipate either, only change form.

On our many journeys as a life path on the ethereal plane and in the heavenly realm, we strive for perfection, but with direct divine guidance. Whereas here on the earthly plane, we are here to elevate our souls. We choose our lessons carefully with each incarnation so as to always elevate, even if only slightly, before our return home to the other side. We CANNOT go back in soul growth. This is impossible, Michael says. He makes reference to the Book of Thomas again where Jesus said, "Let him who seek not cease seeking until he finds, and when he finds he shall be disturbed, and when he has been disturbed he shall marvel and he shall reign over the totality." Learning laws of compassion, humility, grace, and unconditional love can only be achieved on the earthly plane. When we seek, we are learning, and when we experience we "feel." And when we learn we marvel and have realization, which changes us forever. We elevate our vibrations with skilled experience.

The science of vibration dictates the laws of the universe entirely. Every molecule and every atom is energy. If every component is energy and vibration, consciously living or not, then each has a singular vibrational signature, including thoughts! Thoughts are energy and vibration. We are consciously responsible for every thought, action and deed we manufacture in the state of the senses of our true light within. In the third Gospel, Jesus said, "If your leaders say to you, 'Look, the (Father's) kingdom is in the sky,' then the birds of the sky will precede you. If they say to you, 'It is in the sea,' then the fish will precede you. Rather, the kingdom is within you and it outside you. When you know yourselves, then you will be known, and you will understand that you are children of the living Father. But if you do not know yourselves, then you live in poverty, and you are the poverty."

In understanding what we experience as beings of light when on the other side and in the ethereal realm, Michael shares something incredible that you might consider absorbing as both what he's observed and what we know as valuable information to pass on to those still living on Earth. He conveyed that as we transition to the heavenly realm, we may encounter an experience similar to this: feeling the sense of leaving your own physical body, looking up at a blue sky, you see black faceless figures moving left to right.

These figures are not frightening in any way and actually seem peaceful. You claircognizantly feel you are waiting for the light to shine on you, that you're in space and sense weightlessness. A serene feeling of peace comes over you. Your soul, and the identity of it, is revealed in this transition. As you come over a mountain, you descend upon a cathedral city. You see

..ples, castles and buildings, seeming to be constructed of light with peaks on their rooftops. Flying above, around and through this cathedral city, you land gently onto a veranda which is up high on one of these buildings. It is wide open and you are greeted by many in your soul group. They are all clapping, rejoicing that you've arrived. You're being greeted by everyone and embraced by those who have passed on before you. An elder asks what you've learned, and you respond with answers such as not to be selfish, and to love deeply.

After this warm reception, you are suddenly but gently lifted away and you find yourself lying on a four poster bed. This bed is very stately and grand and has a silk canopy which is billowing gently. You realize there is no floor beneath you, that you're just suspended in the cosmos. You throw out to the universe why this is taking place and the response you receive is that this is a time of rest and healing for your soul. There is a bright luminous white light underneath the canopy bed and it surrounds the bed and you reaching far into the heavens. As quickly as you relax, you dissipate and feel as though you are being sucked into this light, as if exploding into a thousand particles. The magnitude of the force from within you is unimaginable, but you remain totally aware of your own consciousness. You then find yourself in total darkness as if in a cave. Again, there is no sense of fear, just that you are waiting for your next step. As you look up you feel your vibrations fluttering and you see the blue sky again only this time with spirits in cloud-like appearance, rapidly moving back and forth over you.

They are faceless while you are in this cave-like dwelling, and there is a light, but you want to stay where you are. It is comfortable, peaceful and serene there. Swiftly, a single eye with wings on each side is looking right at you. When you ask what this means you get the sense it is the divine and that these spirits are passing over you — each has a different purpose as they swoop down towards you, get close, and then dissipate. You know they are helping to make you who you are. There is a crack of light and it slowly opens, gets bright and then closes back, far off in the distance.

There is a light all around it now. You are spinning, vibrating and flickering light and nearing the top of the fissure of light. You ask, "What is my purpose?" and you receive your answer, "You will be placed on earth to inspire others. You will help them touch the very vibrations you have just experienced in order that you might transcend the spark required for them to elevate to higher planes of knowledge they seek while in human form."

Michael then reminds me of the fourth Gospel, in which Jesus said, "The person old in days won't hesitate to ask a little child seven days old about the place of life, and that person will live. For many of the first will be last, and will become a single one." What Michael is saying is that we all interpret, no matter what religion or faith we follow, that we are shown mercy from the Divine. He asks, "Why do we not see that we must *ASK*, not wait, for the divine to enter our soul consciousness. Our willingness to accept in faith that we already possess the light, that which is divine in us already, is all there is. We must open our hearts and pray, and the angels, guides, and the divine will listen and help us. We must ask though. It is our free will as a soul to determine and synchronize our spiritual and physical selves to really "see" the light, that which is within us and the power we possess to elevate ourselves and others when we recognize this...young or old. We are all teachers, those that are physically old and those that are seven days old."

At this point Michael refers to feeling sucked inside himself. He begins to convey that there are so many levels in the universe. He can hardly comprehend all the levels and yet sees how they are combined both here in the physical and there in the spiritual and that there is no real definition or divide between heavenly and earthly, rather that the two always blend uniquely and consistently.

If we study Alchemy in its true sense, using all the elements available to us, we will successfully understand our true nature and power and that our life force is eternal. He makes reference to the Holy Grail and that, "All things miraculous is the Holy Grail." The science of Alchemy and the divine ability to achieve on the physical plane that which can only be described as divine or a miracle, is, in fact an example of the Holy Grail. Understanding, he says, that Alchemy, when pursued in pure form and practiced with the utmost of faith and belief in its power, is within each of us to attain these miracles, some small and some large. We have the ability to manifest that which we believe to be absolute and true. Our mind, our subconscious, or our soul, comprehends this;

our brain and our physical side does not. We can achieve fewer incarnations and attain much greater knowledge if we focus on this while on the earthly plane.

In examining soul evolutions and reincarnation, Michael refers to the Gospel of Thomas once again:
[15]: Jesus said, "When you see one who was not born of woman, fall on your faces and worship. That one is your Father." [16]: Jesus said, "Perhaps people think that I have come to cast peace upon the world. They do not know that I have come to cast conflicts upon the earth: fire, sword, war. For there will be five in a house: there'll be three against two and two against three, father against son and son against father, and they will stand alone. [17]: Jesus said, "I will give you what no eye has seen, what no ear has heard, what no hand has touched, what has not arisen in the human heart." [18]: The disciples said to Jesus, "Tell us, how will our end come?" Jesus said, "Have you found the beginning, then, that you are looking for the end? You see, the end will know the end and will not taste death." [19]: Jesus said, "Congratulations to the one who came into being before coming into being. If you become my disciples and pay attention to my sayings, these stories will serve you. For there are five trees in Paradise for you; they do not change, summer or winter, and their leaves do not fall. Whoever knows them will not taste death."

Reflections on Michael's description of what he is experiencing on the other side relates these words of Thomas as Jesus pontificates how existence permeates in the ethereal and where everything is holy. These are, Michael says, specific levels (the five trees in Paradise, yet there are no seasons) which we must experience as a light of divine, and we traverse in between these levels gaining knowledge at each step. That we evolve, is growth and escalate to higher realms as we gain more light and reduce our darkness.

When Jesus says: "Congratulations to the one who came into being before coming into being," Michael says he is telling us that the divine is rewarding those souls who have chosen to incarnate before knowing extensive knowledge. That their bravery to learn in the earthly plane, all be it through naivety is what brings their soul close to their divine purpose...learning to be in the exact likeness of the divine. Also, Michael submits that as Jesus had said, "You see, the end will be where the beginning is. Congratulations to the one who stands at the beginning: that one will know the end and will not taste death," Jesus is implying that souls who reach the realization that life does, in fact, not begin or end, and that the beginning and the end are the same, that reincarnation, lives between lives on the other side, is, in fact, the truth and the divine cannot and will not taste death, because there is no real death. The light in each of us cannot be quelled or squashed out it resides forever and is infinite.

When discussing the ethereal with Michael he seems more direct but when speaking about the physical, in what I would consider a typical reading, what transpires is rather scattered statements that I sometimes believe have meaning, yet seem somewhat symbolic and metaphoric.

In another meditation, one in which I purposely induced to speak with Michael using remote viewing, we had this exchange: He says the name Scott to me. I tell him I do not know of a Scott and ask of whom he is speaking. He then tells me, "It's a hop scotch." I tell him I am unclear of what he means, and he continues on. He begins to jump around a little bit from topic to topic. First he says he likes roller coasters, then leaps to when he hurt someone's feelings. He'll apologize, then stay silent for a while until he intuitively feels it's the right time to speak again to that person. I sometimes wonder what he is trying to say, but I keep recording what he tells me.

He says, "The walk down London street will go very fast." I then suddenly see another black iron fence with a seven-foot arched trellis opening. It looks like a two-story house with bay windows on each side and on two levels. Once inside, there is a tea cup on the table in a living area, and we continue walking towards the back of the house and approach the kitchen. We turn in the kitchen doorway and are now facing the front door. He motions to look over my left shoulder back into the kitchen. I see a cabinet or cupboard with no dishes in it. Files and papers are in the cabinet instead. There is a "For Sale" sign in the yard. He reminds me again that time is of the essence. When I look at the pantry door, there's craftsman's etchings on the door, which appear to look like a rose. When walking into the front room I see an old fireplace. There is a tall mantle, and on the mantle are several objects. One is an oval frame housing a picture of an older couple. I get the feeling from Michael that there is a map, directions, or papers of importance of some kind stuffed in between the back of the picture and the frame. There is an older, "family" Bible with one or two photos tucked inside also sitting on the mantle. He also shows me two winged back chairs in the room. I get the feeling that there was a struggle and someone died in this house. I hear the words, "Do you know what that will do to our family if you bring this out?" I also get the sense that the family wouldn't be able to protect themselves. He says I should be looking for a Bible. Michael then shows me the number "1802." I am unsure if this is an address or what it represents. Michael is unclear, and I feel his energy pull back.

A few days later, I feel Michael come in again. He tells me that there is a "Paul," who is significant to him. I say, "Who is he to you?" He simply replies that he is a good friend, that they are close, and makes a reference to black Converse™ tennis shoes and brings up the Book of Thomas again. He says he has messages for him, but that they are very personal, and then moves to talk about someone else he referred to as "Bug Eyes." He says that was his nickname for him. He says Bug Eyes was transparent and thinks he knows everything, but that he was his own boss! He then began speaking about Tiger Lily. "Tiger Lily is my precious one. She likes the flavor of mint. I appear to her in dreams. The dreams are very fairy-like, mystical. She's learning the guitar." He then shows me a red and black guitar strap, and says she, at one time, hung a necklace around the neck of the guitar as it was propped up in a corner. He says she doesn't care for school much, but that she's getting decent grades. He says, "She would have liked to have had my black boots." He shows me the leather boots, scuffed up and comfortably worn. He insinuates that she wants to put her feet in his shoes. I assume he means create music in some way.

This seems to have turned into a reminiscent discourse as he then moves to speak of his friend Nick. He says they referred to each other as a muse, and agreeably their music was very different yet they shared many mores and views of the world at large. He shows me a walk along a waterfront, which is lined with rocks. He presents this scene as a memorable one shared with Nick. I don't know why tomatoes and Nick's dislike of them are significant, but

A TALE OF TWO BROTHERS

history in readings has shown me that I am to pass on the information, not try to analyze its importance. I am assuming there is a corresponding story to this, and Nick will understand the meaning. Michael is showing me a restaurant. This restaurant seems older and maybe even worn or tattered, but none-the-less, important. I notice that the chairs do not match and the restaurant seems oblong in shape. In other words, when you walk in the front door, it goes far back rather than wide. There is a space in the back where I see music notes, and as we are walking by the bar, I notice a crack in the glass or shiny surface top. Michael says, he likes it there and that this atmosphere is pleasing to him. He makes reference to it "being real" there. As if this dwelling is a refuge of sorts, a place to hide and relax, or a destination to "get away from it all." He says, "The owners almost passed this location up, but at the last minute, the purchase went through and everything seemed to come together rather easily and quickly once they committed to buying the place." He states he wants to offer a large "thank you" to the man with a scar on his left cheek, that he is an excellent poet and musician, and that he is always remembered.

On another encounter with Michael, he appeared to me while I was sitting outside in my backyard. This was one of the few times I had purposely tried to contact him directly while writing this chapter. I had the sense that I was "missing something" and had hoped to get from him what it was. To most who are reading this, all the mention of contacting spirits and the process involved, must certainly seem surreal at best. However, those who understand the process of contacting energies in the beyond can easily discern the feelings and sense a medium would encounter when engaging in a relationship of this sort with someone who is in the ethereal. That being said, as I began to meditate in the warm sun and felt the Earth's energy around me, sure enough, Michael responded. He began by showing me the symbol which means reminiscing. He then shows me a popular footwear logo. When I ask him what the connection is, I don't seem to get a clear indicator from Michael.

He just continues showing me the logo. He then makes reference to someone, which took me by complete surprise, the actor Johnny Depp. He shows me a house and the feeling that he is there with Johnny. I am thinking, someone at Johnny's house at the time, was connected to this footwear company. Either that, or maybe they were endorsing the brand. But definitely the footwear logo was there. It seemed like Michael was trying to say he and Johnny spoke of what it would be like to be the footwear's sponsor. I know this is supposition on my part, but yet it seems important when Michael talks about the footwear company, because he makes the word larger and larger when he shows it to me. Then he mentions a Carolyn or Carol Ann or Carline, who was there or her name was mentioned, while at Johnny's house. I'm thinking it may be the poet Caroline Kleefeld, because he then makes a reference to the poet Allen Ginsberg. Michael then says, he's sorry he couldn't go to a big event. He says that Johnny went, but he didn't. He shows me Johnny wearing black slacks, a black dinner or suit jacket, and an unbuttoned white shirt to the event. Michael says that Johnny was staying at a rental house and not an owned house. There was a lot of grounds work being done at the time, renovation or construction of some type on the outside of the dwelling and/or grounds. Michael is usually there for breakfast, he says, and he left his shoes there and never cared to get them back. He also mentions that smoking is not allowed inside the house! Evidently, this was a hard and fast rule. He describes French doors that walk onto a beautiful patio or veranda. He then speaks of a woman named Erin, and states she was introduced to Michael and there is a William or Bill connection there. I didn't understand completely what he was getting at. It seemed like there was a feeling of intrigue or perhaps mystery involved when he speaks of Erin and then makes note of "secret meetings" which took place with her. I did not get the feeling from Michael that she was a bad influence, quite the contrary. It seemed like he was merely suggesting that maybe not everyone involved in his life at the time knew of the meetings they shared. He did seem to indicate that Johnny knew.

Out of the blue he says, "Johnny didn't know much French at the time." Michael continues reminiscing. He indicates they (I'm not quite sure who 'they' are, but I know he means at Johnny's house) had too much to drink or were clowning around once and someone slipped and hit their head in the kitchen. He refers to this as a funny story. He also states, there is a big deal about the bed sheets in the guest room. Michael used to tease Johnny about these, he says. He then goes on to mention that Johnny helped him name an album. Johnny came up with the name for the title of the album, yet Michael didn't mention this to his band mates. He simply told them he came up with it himself, yet Johnny knew. He then goes back to talking about Erin, and says, she was nice but had a complicated personality. He speaks of a black leather jacket which he refers to as a "gift" to Johnny from Michael, as a thank you or perhaps the other way around.

Michael begins to pull his energy back and I feel him slip away yet again. I ponder how gentle his demeanor is, how he seems to have such strength in dictating what he wants to say. He must have surely been a caring, nurturing and introspective individual when he was here on the earthly plane. I can appreciate the sincerity of his life and recognize the deep intellectualism a person such as Michael possesses. I am certain he regrets not being able to finish what he began while here, especially formulating his plan for giving back to the planet. It seems to me he would be the type of individual who would have spent a certain amount of time organizing ways to help others, whether it was those in other nations under political asylum and dictatorship, or those less fortunate in his own nation of Australia. I am lead to believe the plights of others and the realization that we must take care of those in need were feelings, as he prepared to enter his forties, just beginning to manifest with Michael. Although he had supreme personal issues he was trying to cope with at the time of his death, his consciousness was ever evolving. And he was denied the opportunity to build on another dream of inspiring others through philanthropy.

Jim Morrison & Michael Hutchence

CHAPTER 21
Gonna Take You Over...

"If...we bear in mind that the unconscious contains everything that is lacking to the consciousness, that the unconscious therefore has a compensatory tendency, then we can begin to draw conclusions, provided of course, that the dream does not come from too deep a psychic level. If it is a dream of this kind, it will as a rule contain mythological motifs, combinations of ideas or images which can be found in the myths of one's own folk or in those of other races. The dream will then have a collective meaning, a meaning which is the common property of mankind.

As individuals we are not completely unique, but are like all other men. Hence a dream with a collective meaning is valid in the first place for the dreamer, but it expresses at the same time the fact that his momentary problem is also the problem of other people. This is often of great practical importance, for there are countless people who are inwardly cut off from humanity and oppressed by the thought that nobody else has their problems. Or else there are those all-too-modest souls who, feeling themselves non-entities, have kept their claim to social recognition on too low a level. Moreover, every individual problem is somehow connected with the problem of the age, so that practically every subjective difficulty has to be viewed from the standpoint of the human situation as a whole. But this is permissible only when the dream really is a mythological one and makes use of collective symbols."

—*Carl Jung*, The Meaning of Psychology for Modern Man

A TALE OF TWO BROTHERS

Some of those that knew me on Earth have dreamt of me since I have gone on to this side. Sometimes, I have sent you dreams, but it's not always my doing when you dream of me. It can be your feelings of longing to see or talk to me again, some leftover residue of guilt, or some other intricacies of the subconscious at work. You have reasons for dreaming of me — or anyone else for that matter, but those are things not easily explored or explained. There are numerous books available about interpreting your dreams, and while some are better than others, you have dreams at very specific times in your life. To suggest because you have dreamt of falling down a mountain or losing your teeth or attending a funeral a that it has the same meaning for you as someone else who dreams of the same or similar things, is hogwash.

Your subconscious is much too complex to give a standard, general textbook answer to a particular dream. There are also visitations that you believe are dreams. These are when a loved one who has crossed over visits you at a time when you are asleep and most able to receive them. It's a fine line between what is a dream and what is a visitation.

I have sent dreams to certain loved ones in the last several years. I have a particular loved one I have been around at certain times, because she is very spiritually gifted and I have been able to communicate with her. Her name is Kylie, and I have given her messages. I was there with her throughout her health crisis not too long ago. I am not around her all the time, because she has a life to lead. I don't want to haunt her or anyone else, but certainly wanted to let her know I was alright, I made it to the light and I was with her during some difficult times.

I have sent dreams to a close male friend of mine involving black cats, and he simply has to realize these dreams are from me. I also sent him dreams of being on the water with me, sailing, and so on. Those dreams did not generate from his subconscious, they are an energy projection I sent to him. I bring this up at this point to suggest to some of you that your loved ones also will send you dreams from the other side here and there. Sometimes it's simply to make you aware of something or to send a sign or symbol. Hopefully, you will put two and two together and realize it's from them or perhaps just think about a certain person or situation in your life they wish you to look deeper into. Some of your dreams come from your own subconscious and some from your loved ones on the other side. Retention of your dreams is often difficult, but you can ask for help from your own spirit guides to retain more in your dream state if you choose.

I have sent a few loved ones dreams of fountains. I use symbolism in my dreams quite heavily. I like dreams involving water, and the flowing beauty of the water in fountains is something I like to send. I have sent only one member of INXS dreams, and there are reasons I have chosen to do this with him. His brothers may never believe this — but I have sent him dreams, and if anyone else dreamt of me from INXS, and they have, it was from their own subconscious. Sending energy projections to others in dreams is a beautiful form of communication, but once again, it takes us on this side a great deal of energy and this is why we don't do it as often as we would like. This is not easy, and if we are not careful, the dream can go awry and lose the meaning we were trying to project to you.

Another concern is with all the energy we must use to send you a dream or part of one. Will you recall it when you awake? We certainly would rather not have done all that work for nothing. Some of you are blessed with spiritual gifts that tend to show up in your dreams. Some are blessed with the gift of prophecy, and you have had vivid dreams of events that later occurred on Earth. Many with spiritual gifts had visions and dreams of the World Trade Center bombings in 2001 and other assorted natural disasters. Why did you receive this information? It wasn't specific enough and you were powerless to do anything about it, so why show it to you?

One thing I would like to suggest to anyone who has experienced a prophetic dream is that you must realize you are tapping into something far beyond your own subconscious. You are tapping into the Source, the universal mind, or the divine knowledge. When this occurs, you must remember, on Earth, the universal mind does not operate on linear time. There is no time as you know it elsewhere and certainly not on this side. We are not linear here, and we do not communicate in a linear fashion, but we must do that to communicate with you. Not all of us are as focused in that area on this side, and this is why some who do automatic writing get it in a different fashion than others. Those to whom they are communicating with are struggling to become linear again and put sentences and words together as you do on Earth.

Given the fact linear time does not exist — or really time at all for that matter, how does one receive prophetic dreams that foretell future events, since there is no future? Have you considered the event is actually occurring right now so you know of it? Or that you already had complete knowledge of the event, and you stored it and are bringing it up now, almost like pulling up a file? Or perhaps this so-called prophecy is being given to you from the other side, because you are an open channel and it demonstrates you are spiritually gifted and can receive information that is valuable this way. Perhaps, you can receive information next time, so you can do something about the situation and may work and fine tune these gifts. I want to be clear, "the gift of prophecy" works in different ways for different people. Some are truly getting communications from this side and they must be spiritually gifted to receive it, and some are obtaining prophetic dreams in a completely different fashion. They must realize linear time only operates on Earth. It's man-made, and the rest of the universe you reside on, not to mention all the other dimensions, uses no such thing.

There are some of you who have some strange and interesting experiences with time, as a matter of fact. You wake up, look at the clock, roll over and think you have spent at least several minutes with your eyes closed to look up and find the clock has only moved a minute or two. How is that possible? The answer is, in your sleepy state, you are turning off linear time and tapping into other dimensions. I know that may seem frightening or confusing, but it's a true confirmation, time does not exist but on Earth.

Many also report losing time somehow. This is another occurrence (but for that of a drug or alcohol blackout) that once again, revolves around the deeper state you are capable of getting yourself into and the fact you may indeed be communicating with the other dimensions. If you can't recall what happened, that is purposeful. In fact, it simply may be too much for your brain to deal with and may, in fact, end up placing you in a psychiatric hospital, heavily medicated. While there are a good many people on Earth walking around with psychiatric illnesses, be very aware that many who are under psychiatric care are indeed channels and are unaware they are talking to the other side or traveling to other dimensions. This doesn't mean to suggest schizophrenia is not a very real condition, it most certainly is, but not everyone diagnosed with it suffers from it. Some suffer from being very spiritually gifted and not realizing what in the world is going on.

I also wish to caution, there are those in psychiatric hospitals and doing harm to themselves and others, who are infiltrated by lower energies or dark entities. They are quite susceptible to manipulation. While I am not suggesting the devil is causing most of the serial killers or rapists on the Earth to run amuck, there are instances where these lower energies get young, impressionable children and teens to hurt themselves and others. There is some emotional disturbance that already exists within that individual, and it makes for an easy target to those walking the Earth who should be on this side, simply never evolved and don't really wish to. It's a compete fallacy all souls wish to evolve or be sent to the light. Some certainly are in fear, but others, have made their choice. There are exorcists throughout the world, priests and even Protestant ministers and others. I have come to learn this is not a crock, it's very real, and some actually need these dark, demonic entities and energies removed from being attached to them. This is not to suggest it's a common everyday occurrence, but it certainly does take place, and prayer really does help to keep those darker or lower energies away from you. It is unfortunate they remain without evolving, but it's important to realize, souls are in various conditions and some have simply never evolved and chose not to. You cannot bring all souls into the light, as all of us have free will.

I have studied very hard on this side in my effort to evolve and perhaps heal from some of the ridiculous damage I did to my soul last time around. I have access to some of divine spiritual truths. I could've channeled a [book to] you with a thousand books or more on it, instead [in this] book I have chosen some of the ones I have [deemed] incredibly truthful and powerful for the times y[ou are] currently experiencing on Earth. I have given you these suggested readings because I am quite certain you will be altered by them and some of you really will be rocked to your core. I have given you wisdom from this side that I could not have acquired while on Earth, and I feel one of the most important things I can offer to you, other than insights into my own great failings as Michael Hutchence, are some significant suggestions of the greatest written works you can get your hands on — and for that matter, your eyes on — and allow them to penetrate to your brain. You will not look at one thing on Earth in the same way when you have read these things. So in other words, they will aid you in evolving. If you get nothing more from this channeled work, at least get a list of suggested reading that hopefully you will make time (even though it doesn't exist) to do and strive toward spiritual evolvement while you are on Earth.

"Theory of Colour" by Johann Wolfgang Von Goethe and his extremely important play called "Faust," are an excellent way to become enlightened. I would highly suggest reading Goethe while simultaneously reading "Isis Unveiled" by Madam Helena Blavatsky. Reading these books alongside each other is both amazing and (could be) earth shattering. That is how important this information truly is.

I would also suggest a reading of "Jesus and the Lost Goddess: The Secret Teachings of the Original Christians" by Timothy Freke and Peter Gandy, while reading the Gnostic Gospels. Please do not separate the Gnostic Gospels from The Kabbalah or Alchemy, and certainly read Moses Mendelssohn while studying the Kabbalah.

Padre Pio's letters will bring you closer to God and the truth, and of course, I could give you so many more books to read or paintings to view than I already have, but I do believe I have given you the tools you will need at this time to seek and find enlightenment. There are many pieces to the puzzle of the universal mind. I have given you these suggestions because I have both studied hard and evolved. I would love for you to do it while

Jim Morrison & Michael Hutchence

..e on Earth, because you have this incredible opportunity I as not aware of fully, and did not, through my own ignorance, take advantage of.

A spiritual quest for truth in yourself, in God and in the universe will take you over. The more of the light you become, the more you will repel the dark that keeps you down and miserable. You can be one of these people who suggests spiritual gifts don't exist or it's the devil's work. So you just take your cue from another who is a part of a religion that is far from what it was originally conceived to be. I am doubtful that Jesus would recognize what he taught on Earth versus what organized religion has indeed become. Of course, he is very much aware of it, but is it what he originally brought to the Earth? I raise this question and ask you to study and ponder it, for I have been shown what is being marketed on Earth as organized religion, is more lacking of the true teachings, love and vision of Jesus, than it is, in fact, supporting. I wish I could suggest otherwise, for I would prefer to give people something substantial to gravitate toward. I can suggest a spiritual quest that will take you over and change your life in ways you cannot possibly fathom. I will suggest not to be taken over by believing certain things are not at all possible. You have decided due to the beliefs of others that certain things are impossible, but I assure you, the world you live in, the life you lead, and this whole universe is full of, above all else, possibilities.

"...time is not a linear flow, as we think it is, into past, present and future. Time is an indivisible whole, a great pool in which all events are eternally embodied and still have their meaningful flash of supernormal or extra-sensory perception, and glimpse of something that happened long ago in our linear time."

—*Frank Waters*, "Mountain Dialogues," 1981

FINAL THOUGHTS

Slide Away

"You are not the same people who left that station / Or who will arrive at any terminus, / While the narrowing rails slide together behind you."

—*T.S. Eliot*

Jim Morrison & Michael Hutchence

A TALE OF TWO BROTHERS

Michael's Manifesto

If you want to heal your heart,
heal the ones of those around you.
If you want to be at peace
help bring about peace in your surroundings.

If you want to stop the pain,
have empathy for another's pain and
try and give them the relief you wish you had.

If you want to find joy,
bring joy to the lives of strangers.
Be anonymous, go unnoticed
for you will be seen in the eyes of God
What else really matters?

—channeled from Michael Hutchence

    I can tell you that God loves everybody. He doesn't like you because you are gay. He doesn't love you because you are a heathen or a glutton. He doesn't want you in his "kingdom" because you have cheated on your husband. But why would you believe it? Another man or woman is telling you about what God thinks, what God wants and how you will be condemned to the fires of hell otherwise or never welcomed into the kingdom, and you believe it? How do they know any better than you do? It's pretty much like going to confession with your list of sins and

Jim Morrison & Michael Hutchence

being told to go say three "Hail Marys" and two "Our Fathers," and you are healed. You are healed why? Because these pre-written prayers absolved you?

I am not suggesting there is not beauty in these prayers — on the contrary. Healing takes place only when you remove yourself directly, and even indirectly, from the situation and ask for healing. If you are asking to be healed from abusing drugs and alcohol, you won't be asking for that while the heroin needle is sticking in your arm. If you are asking to be healed from a bad marriage or relationship, you can't be healed while living in that house with the person you are in a bad situation with. You must seek sanctuary from that which you feel you need healing. You must allow yourself to be quiet.

I always had a difficult time being alone at night, and if people weren't around me, I would call someone and talk to them most of the night. In not allowing myself to embrace being alone, to embrace the quiet and let my soul resonate with the universe, I had a hard time healing from anything in my life. Why wait to heal until you come to this side? You can heal so much, if not everything, in your life right where you are on Earth. Seek sanctuary, pray, meditate and listen to you, listen to your soul minus the noise of the world. Open up the light of God, the healing energy and become tranquil and whole. This alone could lead you to a much better, and happier, existence. Healing will stop you from feeling depressed, angry, having anxiety, from self-loathing and from the behaviors you exhibit that you heartedly dislike, such as overeating, abuse of alcohol, drugs, engaging in senseless gossip, speaking negatively about others, etc. When you are healed and are closer to being whole, suddenly, enlightenment starts to creep into your voids. I want to share these lessons with you, because I want to believe my last existence was for something and could have greater meaning and greater impact. I hope you find some solace, truth and love in my words.

I have more to say. I will be back through this channel, because I want to share my experiences in the afterlife. Until then, this is Michael Hutchence, bidding you adieu and telling the world, I am alive. I am well. I am at peace. Love never dies. The soul never dies, and I love my family and friends very, very much. I am home on this side waiting for all of you. We will have a great party when we reunite. I am sorry for the pain I caused, the way I left, and the lack of time I gave some of you in my final years, but keep me alive in your hearts and please know that I am closer than you think. I have gone to what you call the light, and I will guide you to it. Some of you I know and love will see me the day you cross over, and I will lead you home. You will find me whole, healed and full of love for you and all there is. Do not forget me, think of the Michael I am now, not the broken man who was out of his mind at the end. I am not the man who at the end of his days was ruled by fear. I am now guided by love.

My soul is simply shining through. I hope my true legacy is not only the 20 years of music I left behind but more than that, my beautiful daughter, Tiger Lily, who I love more than the stars in the sky. Let these words also be my legacy, please let them fill your hearts and minds. Just because I am not sitting there in my human body saying them, does it make them untrue? Do the words of my soul or your soul not count? I am thankful someone can hear me and took the time to write this down.

Without Further Adieu

The tide is now receding
Too many bridges burned
But you hold me in your heart
Because you can't seem to let go

The sea never changes
yet it's different every day
I want you to know
The embers of my life

will remain inside your memory
But without further adieu
it's time for me to go

Jim Morrison & Michael Hutchence

I am home now, no longer
Wandering the globe
I search no more
because my truth is alongside me now

You can't hold onto me the way you once did
You can't hold on to me the way you would like
Ashes to ashes, dust to dust
I must go on this journey
and you must go back to yours

I wave goodbye and take my final bow
Please don't cry or my life was all for nothing

—*channeled from Michael Hutchence*

A TALE OF TWO BROTHERS

My Brother Michael and I...
My brother Michael plays Mendelssohn,
And I read the book of Nicolas Flamel

My brother and I were both murdered,
He was taken out by lies and debauchery
I was murdered before I was even dead

You murder us over and over again
With your strychnine pen
You just have to speculate on things
You know nothing of

My brother Michael and I lived in a zoo,
We were caged by our circumstances,
The captivity bled us dry

A TALE OF TWO BROTHERS

We were tranquilized predators,
The beautiful creatures many
From far and wide came to observe

Some saw our beastly nature,
Some clinically examined us,
They contained us for too long,
They depleted our stamina to go
Through their horn of plenty

Rest now brother, your life was
Exhausting, here is a little secret,
We dream here too

They can't touch you now man,
You're safe, you're free
And I, your true brother,
Will not dessert you

Michael, why won't they let us go?

—*channeled from Jim Morrison*

My Brother James and I...
I'd thought there'd be a party
When I arrived at my final destination
But it was more of a magical gathering
In the most exotic garden beyond my imagination

I can see clearly now
And breathe like I never did before
No asthma here, no depression, no HIV to speak of
Only deep abiding love, nothing less, nothing more

I met my brother at a banquet
I was once a king you know
I had gold, wives and various assorted concubines
They loved me and I loved them too

Jim Morrison & Michael Hutchence

However it's my brother James
who knows me through and through
But all good kingdoms come to an end
And you end up the loneliest person you've ever known
Nothing can comfort your weariness

No matter how many surround you, in the end you are left
alone I was in Paris when they tried to invoke
my brothers' mystical spirit
He is buried not far from Chopin
James would not wake-up for his hordes of creatures coming to
claim him and ravage him for wisdom

He had the power to move them in his hands
My brother waited to see me at the banquet
He was waiting and waiting for me to return
We had our words, some harsh and unkind

We had our bond that no one shall break apart, it's the kind of
closeness only true brothers find
To my brother, I am still a King
To me, my brother James is a Shaman, magician of everything
He paces and waits for his true love to wake-up, to know he is
here and to return to their haven

He is her slave in this paradise of sorts
He cares nothing of his former cohorts
I watch his impatience and grief, he's so in love,

I'm almost in disbelief
I've never seen him so attached, obsessed and addicted to anyone,
it's too bad we can't share in the same feeling

I am alone here, working toward healing James and I form an
unholy alliance, so they would say back
in the kingdom I use to oversee
Our bond goes back centuries
We have fought, loved and hated each other forever but we shall
never be apart
We were slated together as brothers from the very start

A TALE OF TWO BROTHERS

We eat at our banquet as lunatics in the night try to wake
us, to hear us speak to them and yet, they need to buy a
recording, we shall sing to them into the morning
We will not return, you had us both before, I am so deeply
sorry, if you yearn for more
You have gotten all there is, we are on another plane

We don't want to be the same, we are moving on, growing into
something more
Don't forget you had us before
Time goes on
Time goes by
What's done is done
No more time for all the lies

Our words have more implications than what you first believed
Everything has multiple meanings, it all transmits on the
cosmic airwaves of Jacobs' ladder, climb and you will
find at first you were deceived
That's not all it means

We shall sing to you in the night but not speak again
We shall not haunt your dreams, our life is here now, in the garden
At the banquet and in the depths of wisdom and knowledge
You can't buy it in a book
You can't study it in college

We are learning the truth of the soul
The mystery schools of old and we have a new life and new goals,
for we are free, isn't that what you want us to be?
You cannot wake the dead but we are not dead here, only on earth
You cannot worship a hollow idol in the sham of a temple
you think you hear the voices of the prophets in
You have been indoctrinated since birth with lies and deceptions
All to take you in the wrong direction

We are here to say Adieu
I am sorry I couldn't see you
I am sorry we didn't spend more time and play fewer games
Hear my song, don't forget our names

Jim Morrison & Michael Hutchence

But please don't disturb us, we have gone to a brighter day
Let us go in peace, let us go our way
My brother James wishes to sleep now
He wishes to have tranquility and not incite the riots he
used to when he was younger and experimenting with his
power trips of those so young, with minds so ripe

I wish to sleep now, to put the kingdom under the earth
forevermore
I am no longer a ruler
I do not command a stage
I no longer go on tour
I am no longer in a rage

I no longer put the women in a state of existential ecstasy
I am thankful to be out of a detrimental society
The ecstasy is in me
The riot is my brother
We've gone home now, don't forget us
We are not like any other

—*channeled from Michael Hutchence*

A TALE OF TWO BROTHERS

Jim Morrison & Michael Hutchence

Made in the USA
Lexington, KY
08 May 2015